Diesel & E LOC REGISTER

FIFTH EDITION

Andy Chard

Published by Platform 5 Publishing Ltd,
52 Broadfield Road, Sheffield, S8 0XJ, England.

Printed in England by The Lavenham Press Ltd, Lavenham, Suffolk.

ISBN 978 1 909431 78 2

▲ High Speed Train power car 43206 sits on the blocks and under the canopy of London King's Cross on 20 June 2019. 43313 is on the front of the train which will form the 13.06 to York. **Andy Chard**

CONTENTS

Preface 4

Introduction...5

Layout of Information 5

Abbreviations..13

1. Experimental Locomotives...14
   1.1. Experimental Shunting Locomotives..14
   1.2. Experimental Main Line Diesel Locomotives 15
   1.3. Experimental Gas Turbine Locomotives 19
   1.4. Experimental Main Line Electric Locomotives 20

2. Diesel Locomotives...21
   2.1. Purpose-Built Departmental Locomotives.....................................21
   2.2. Unclassified Diesel Shunting Locomotives 23
   2.3. Diesel Shunting Locomotives with Pre-TOPS Classification 27
   2.4. Diesel Locomotives with TOPS Classification 36

3. Electric Locomotives...183
   3.1. Electric Locomotives with Pre-TOPS Classification 183
   3.2. Electric Locomotives with TOPS Classification 185

Appendix I. Locomotive Summary and Classification Index 209

Appendix II. Multiple TOPS Numbers..212

Appendix III. 1948 BR Number & 1957 BR Number Series Index...............216

Appendix IV. Departmental Numbers...230

Appendix V. Locomotive Names...232

Appendix VI. Locomotives With Unconfirmed Scrapping Details...............253

Front Cover Photograph (top): 37403 has carried three different names since it was refurbished and became a Class 37/4 in the mid-1980s. On 11 July 1999, when it was adorned with BR Green livery and the name "Ben Cruachan", it passes Conwy Castle with the 08.49 Holyhead–Crewe. It remains operational and is now preserved at the Bo'ness & Kinneil Railway. **Gordon Edgar**

Front Cover Photograph (bottom): 91128 passes Frinkley Lane, between Grantham and Newark, with the 16.33 London King's Cross–Leeds on 28 June 2019. **Brad Joyce**

Back Cover Photograph: This fine portrait could be from the 1960s were it not for the locomotive's modern headlight. Once again carrying its original D1944 identity, 47501 "Craftsman" has just left Hellifield and heads for Skipton with a crew training run on 24 June 2020. **Liam Barnes**

PREFACE TO THE FIFTH REVISED EDITION

Two major changes have been made to this new edition of Diesel & Electric Loco Register. Firstly, in a return to the format of the first three editions of this book, the scrapping details have been included for the approaching 5 000 locomotives that are no longer with us, showing where and when they were disposed of. Secondly, all the entries have been fully updated, with more than 1000 changes having been made to the listings. Since the last edition, members of classes 08, 20, 31, 37, 47, 58 and 86 have been scrapped and 60006 became the first Class 60 to be disposed of when it was cut up at Toton depot in 2020. Countering this, the number of locomotives in Britain has been bolstered by the repatriation of Class 03 D2289 from Italy in 2018, Class 66s imported from Sweden and Germany, and converted for use by GBRf and a new class has been created; the Class 69s, which are new locomotives using the body of former Class 56s.

Large numbers of some classes have been retired from service since the last edition, with a quarter of the 194-strong Class 43 high-speed train (HST) fleet and a third of the Class 91s now being in storage. Transfers of locomotives between commercial operators and the interchange of diesels between commercial operators and the well-developed heritage railway movement continues. Since the last edition, members of Classes 08, 31, 37 and 43 (HST) have been given new homes in preservation and the first two Class 60s joined these when 60050 and 60086 arrived at the Wensleydale Railway in 2020. Other locomotives have moved in the opposite direction and returned to the main line, such as 37240, 50007 and 50049, which have all been enjoying higher speed runs again. The charter operator Locomotive Services has also added to its fleet and now has members of 12 locomotive classes within its custody, although some of these have yet to return to the main line.

The locomotive owners and operators continue to be varied and disparate. Freight operators account for the greatest numbers, followed by those in preservation, and passenger and charter operators are responsible for an even smaller proportion. Network Rail and the many spot hire and support companies complete the picture. The owners of the many preserved locomotives include heritage railways, preservation groups and individuals that work tirelessly to restore and maintain hundreds of locomotives across dozens of classes. Some of these are on long-term hire to commercial operators and where this is this case, it is indicated in the listing Notes column.

The appendices at the end of the book have been updated. More than a hundred newly named main line locomotives have been added to Appendix I and the sixth appendix summarises the small proportion of scrappings that are not confirmed.

This book lists all diesel and electric locomotives that have operated on Britain's rail network, as operated by British Rail, its predecessors and its successors. The current status of each locomotive is shown, giving a complete and up to date list of all extant and scrapped locomotives. It is a comprehensive reference work and has been written with the rail enthusiast in mind, who along with many locomotives, now travels between the national network and heritage railways.

Andy Chard
Manchester, March 2021

INTRODUCTION

This book lists every standard gauge (4' 8½") diesel and electric locomotive that is, or has been capable of working on the main line railway network. Locomotives used solely in workshops are excluded, as are those solely built for export. Industrial locomotives are excluded, as they are mainly smaller locomotives whose working lives have generally been spent on private localised sites. Most of the small number of purpose built departmental locomotives are also excluded, as they too are small, low power locomotives akin to their industrial relatives, generally unsuitable for the main line and many of these were scrapped before the TOPS era. A small number of purpose-built departmental locomotives are included, as they did see limited use on the main line.

The information in this book comes from a multitude of different sources, including the traditional reference tools of railway books and magazines, as well as many on-line sources, such as the websites and social media outlets of heritage railways, preservation groups and enthusiasts' and my own observations and records. Of particular use in clarifying some details are the multitude of dated railway photographs that can be found on the website Flickr.com.

Everything has been cross-referenced across many different sources, so that the content is as accurate as possible. The information is updated to 1 March 2021 and has been thoroughly checked but the author would be pleased to hear from any reader with information about any inaccuracies or suggestions for enhancements in future editions. Please send any comments to the publisher's address on the title page of this book, or by email to: updates@platform5.com.

LAYOUT OF INFORMATION

Locomotives are listed in three sections, Experimental Locomotives that were purpose built as prototypes, followed by Diesel Locomotives and then Electric Locomotives. These three sections are sub-divided into locomotive types, which are listed alpha-numerically for experimental locomotives and in class number order for BR pre-TOPS classes and TOPS classes. Classes are further sub-divided by sub-class order where there are sub-classes. Finally, each class or sub-class lists individual locomotives numerically, with the latest number carried shown first. The latest number is one of a TOPS number, a BR 1957 scheme number or a BR 1948 scheme number.

Most locomotives listed have a TOPS class number, which is derived from the classification system first introduced by BR in 1968 and has been used by BR and its successors since. A number of locomotive types were not given TOPS classification or numbers as they no longer existed by the time TOPS was introduced. These are listed by their BR 1955 classification, which is the most commonly used of a number of previous classification systems which BR and its predecessors had prior to the introduction of TOPS.

For some classes, not all the individual locomotives survived until the class was renumbered when a new numbering system was introduced (either the BR 1957 or TOPS numbers). For clarity and to give the most logical listings, some locomotives are listed in the position they would have occupied had they survived long enough to be allocated a 1957 or TOPS number. For example, the first four members of Class 03 did not survive long enough to be given a TOPS number and are therefore listed under their latest carried numbers D2000/01/02/03, whereas the fifth and sixth members of the class were given a TOPS number and D2004 and D2005 are shown in the Previous Number 1 column. Similarly, the Class 47s that did not survive long enough to receive a TOPS number are listed in the position they would be found had they received a TOPS number, e.g. D1671 is listed after 47085 which has the previously carried 1957 number D1670.

As TOPS classes and numbers have been in use for more than 50 years and an increasing number of classes never had a 1957 number or pre-TOPS classification, locomotive classes and individual numbers are listed in TOPS order. The vast majority of diesel and electric locomotives have a TOPS class and of the nearly 7,000 locos listed in this book, less than 300 do not have a TOPS class and most of these have a 1955 BR pre-TOPS class, which leaves a very small number of unclassified and experimental locomotives.

NUMBERING AND CLASSIFICATION SYSTEMS

Under the first universal diesel and electric locomotive numbering scheme adopted by British Railways in 1948, numbers consisted of five digits, with locomotives assigned to one of the five bands below according to their type. Note that locomotives were not numbered consecutively in these bands and fewer than 800 locos in total were given a BR 1948 number, which is considerably less than the number ranges allow for.

10000–10999	Main Line Diesel Locomotives
11000–17999	Shunting and Trip Diesel Locomotives
18000–19999	Gas Turbine Locomotives
20000–25999	Electric DC Third Rail Locomotives
26000–29999	Electric DC Overhead Locomotives

In 1955 a new classification system was introduced with locomotive classes allocated in the Dx/yy format, consisting of a letter (D in most cases), followed by two sets of numbers.

In 1957 British Railways introduced a new numbering system which applied to all diesel locomotives except those built to pre-nationalisation designs. Each locomotive was allocated a number of up to four digits prefixed with a "D" for diesel locomotives or "E" for electric locomotives. Diesel electric shunters already built numbered in the 13xxx series had the "1" replaced by a "D". Diesel mechanical shunters already built numbered in the 11xxx series were allocated numbers in the D2xxx series.

When all steam locomotives had been withdrawn, the prefix letter was officially eliminated from the number of diesel locomotives, although it continued to be carried on many of them. For this reason, no attempt is made to distinguish between those locomotives which did or did not have the "D" prefix removed. Similarly, in preservation, no distinction is made between locomotives which do or do not carry a "D" prefix at present.

British Railways also introduced a new classification system for diesel & electric locomotives. Each main line diesel locomotive class was designated a "Type", based on engine horsepower. This broadly took the following form:

Type	Engine Horsepower (hp)	Number Range	TOPS Classification
1	800–1000	D 8000–D 8999	15–20
2	1001–1499	D 5000–D 6499/D7500–D7999	21–31
3	1500–1999	D 6500–D 7499	33–37
4	2000–2999	D 1 –D 1999	40–53
5	3000+	D 9000–D 9499	55–70
Shunting	150/300	D 2000–D 2999	01–07
Shunting	350/400	D 3000–D 4999	08–13
Shunting/trip	650	D 9500–D 9999	14
AC Electric		E 1000–E 4999	81–92
DC Electric		E 5000–E 6999	71–77

In 1968 British Railways introduced a new classification scheme with two-digit numerical class codes for diesel and electric locomotives (01, 02 etc). Sub-classifications were used to identify variants within classes (27/0, 27/1 etc). The numbering of locomotives remained unaltered until the advent of computerised (TOPS) communications in 1971 when a new numbering scheme was introduced. Each locomotive was allocated a new five-digit number comprising the two-digit class number followed by a three-digit serial number. The first locomotive to carry a TOPS number was 76050, which was renumbered in November 1971 and TOPS numbers have now been in use for approaching 50 years.

LOCOMOTIVE CLASS HEADINGS

Each locomotive class heading has technical details.

WHEEL ARRANGEMENT

This is shown on the right hand side of the title. For smaller shunting locomotives, the Whyte Notation is used, where the number of leading (non-driving) wheels is given first, followed by the number of driving wheels and then the number of trailing (non-driving) wheels.

For main line locomotives, the number of driven axles is given by a letter (A = 1, B = 2, C = 3), followed by a number which states the number of non-powered axles. When a letter o is used, this indicates that each axle is individually powered.

BUILT

The year(s) that locomotives in the class were built and details of the builder and location.

ENGINE

Details of the engine installed and the power rating. Any programmes where locos were re-engined within the class are also given.

TRANSMISSION TYPE

Details of the transmission type for locomotives in the class.

MAXIMUM SPEED

Maximum design speed for locomotives in the class as built.

TRAIN HEATING/SUPPLY

Details of train heating fitted to locomotives when built. There was a general evolution from steam heating to electric train supply (for heating and air-conditioning) and by the late 1980s steam heating was no longer used. Changes to train heating/supply are not given for individual locomotives, such as when steam heating generators were isolated or removed. Where batch changes to heating type were subsequently made as part of a conversion programme, details are listed in the newly created sub-class heading if applicable, such as for Class 37/4s when this batch were fitted with electric train supply.

TRAIN BRAKES

Details of train brakes fitted to locomotives when built. As with train heating, there was a general evolution from vacuum braking to air braking during the lives of many locomotives, resulting in many examples being fitted with dual-brakes. Details of the many changes to individual locomotive braking arrangements made since they were built are not listed.

LOCOMOTIVE SUB-CLASS HEADINGS

Where locomotive classes have been divided into sub-classes, often as a result of a batch of locomotive modifications and renumbering to reflect this, the listings for the class are split into corresponding batches, in numerical sub-class order. For example, Class 37 listings start with the 37/0 sub-class, listing these in numerical order (starting with 37003, being the lowest numbered 37/0 not renumbered), followed by the 37/3 sub-class, then 37/4 sub-class etc. Listing locos this way reflects the long standing situation where locos are listed in their TOPS number order, rather than the order in which they were built, as sub-classes such as 31/4 and 37/4 were renumbered well over three decades ago.

Sub-classes are only listed where they currently exist, or did so at the end of the life of locomotives. Historic sub-classes such as 50/1, 86/3 etc. are not listed as the locomotives within these sub-classes were later renumbered, rendering the sub-class defunct. Details of the numbers carried in these historic sub-classes are shown in the previous numbers carried columns and Appendix II.

Each sub-class heading lists the differences that distinguish the locomotives in the sub-class and any other relevant information. For locomotives that were converted by way of a major change, such as a new engine and new classification, these are given the status of "converted" and details of the newly created locomotive are given in the class heading for the new locomotive.

Where locomotives have carried more than one number and the reader wishes to establish which class particular locomotives are listed under (e.g. it's not obvious that 12052 is a Class 11, or D9500 is a class 14), the appendices can be used to identify the other numbers carried and where each locomotive can be found in this book.

INDIVIDUAL LOCOMOTIVE LISTINGS

Column headings for the locomotive listings are arranged in seven sections.

NUMBERS CARRIED

All official numbers carried while in service are listed, starting with the most recent TOPS number, followed by previous numbers carried in reverse chronological order. The three main series' of numbering cover the vast majority of numbers listed and these are TOPS numbers, the preceding BR 1957 Series numbers and prior BR 1948 Series numbers. For the very small number of diesel and electric locos that existed before the creation of BR in 1948, the pre-BR numbers carried are also listed.

There are a very small number of numbers that were carried by more than one locomotive, although not simultaneously (such as D2956, 20301–20307, 27103, 37271–37274 and 5 x class 76s). To distinguish these, in each case the second locomotive to carry the particular number has been given a suffix of [2].

Unofficial numbers or those carried during periods of industrial service are not included, unless they are still currently carried.

Some TOPS numbers were designated for particular locomotives but were never carried. Such numbers are therefore not included in the listings. For example, when it was renumbered as a Class 27 in 1974, D5393 was initially given the number 27121 and after carrying this for a few months, it was renumbered 27203 later that year. It subsequently had the number 27057 assigned, but never carried this, therefore this number is not listed, whereas the numbers 27121 and 27203 are. Similarly, 27207, 27208 and 27206 had the numbers 27061, 27062 and 27060 assigned respectively, but these were never applied and they were all withdrawn carrying their 27/2 identities.

Departmental locomotive numbers are listed as a renumbering, as there are more instances where the departmental renumbering is a reflection of a change in the locomotive's use, rather than a conversion. Where the departmental number is the latest number carried, this is the first number listed, followed by previously carried numbers, consistent with all locomotive listings.

Where locomotives have been de-registered from TOPS and subsequently re-registered and given a new TOPS number in the 89xxx series, such as preserved locomotives that have been restored, the 89xxx number is not listed, as these are administrative numbers and not carried or visible externally on locomotives.

The appendices can be used to find other numbers carried, including departmental numbers.

YEAR ENTERED SERVICE

This is the year the locomotive first entered service, from the North Eastern Railway electric locomotives that began their lives over a century ago, through to the Class 66s that entered service for GB Railfreight recently after being imported from the continent. Where a locomotive has been converted, such as in the case of Class 57s and 73/9s, the date given is the year the subsequently converted locomotive entered service, irrespective of when the previous incarnation entered service. There are a small number of entries marked as not applicable (n/a) for Year Entered Service, being Class 23 D5910 and the Class 69s, which at the time of writing in 2020 are incomplete conversions, and 70012 which never entered service, as it was returned to USA in 2011 due to damage in transit.

YEAR WITHDRAWN

The year the locomotive was withdrawn from active service from British Rail, or one of its predecessor or successor companies. Where locomotives were reinstated and subsequently withdrawn again, the last known withdrawal date is given. In many cases locomotives are put into storage as the first stage of their demise, especially in the post-BR era and this may lead to withdrawal, or reinstatement in some cases. When a locomotive enters storage in one year and is formally withdrawn in a subsequent year (it's not uncommon for this to be many years later), the year that the locomotive entered the episode of storage which led to its withdrawal is given, rather than the year it was formally withdrawn or de-registered from TOPS, which is years after it has been scrapped in some cases. This is a particularly difficult area to quantify and verify, however multiple sources have been checked to give the most accurate information possible.

For locomotives that currently remain in active service, or are in long term storage under the ownership of commercial operators, no withdrawal date is given, as withdrawal has not taken place.

In some cases locomotives have been purchased directly from a commercial operator and entered preservation in operational condition, as 37688 did for example when it changed hands in 2017. In such instances, the withdrawal date has been left blank, as withdrawal did not take place.

CURRENT STATUS/SCRAPPING DETAILS

Every diesel and electric locomotive is listed under one of the following seven status categories. For those commercially operated or owned, the name of the commercial firm is given. No distinction is made between operational or stored locos, as they can move in and out of storage, both in preservation and commercial service. This includes locomotives being used as a spare parts donor, which are not expected to be restored or run again.

Scrapped
Locomotives that have been scrapped and no longer exist. These are shaded in grey to easily distinguish locomotives that exist from those that don't. The year in which the locomotive was scrapped is listed first. The month is not given, as it usually takes a number of days to dispose of a locomotive and this often straddles two months. When the scrapping began in one year and was completed in a subsequent year, the year in which the scrapping was completed is given.

The location where the locomotive was scrapped follows the year. For the vast majority of listings the locomotive was cut up at either a commercial scrapyard or a British Rail (BR) site. For the former, the company's name and location are given and for BR locations, the name of the depot or Works site is shown. In some cases, slightly more information is given in the Scrapping Location or Notes column, such as for 45147 and 66734 which were scrapped by the lineside after accidents, or 27043 which instead of having the asbestos it contained removed, was disposed of by being buried in a landfill site. For some locomotives one or both cabs remain and this is indicated in the notes column. Most of the scrapping locations are listed in full, however, abbreviations have been used in a handful of cases and these are:

Scrapping Location	Abbreviation used in the listings
Bowater's Paper Mill, Sittingbourne	Bowater's Paper, Sittingbourne
British Industrial Sand, Oakmoor	British Ind. Sand, Oakmoor
British Oak Disposal Point, Crigglestone	British Oak DP, Crigglestone
British Steel, Appleby Frodingham	Br. Steel, Appleby Frodingham
Castle Donnington Power Station	Castle Donington PS
Celsa Group, Vilafranca, Barcelona	Celsa Group, Barcelona
English, Welsh & Scottish Railways, Wigan	EWS Railway, Wigan
Etterby Road Industrial Estate, Carlisle	Etterby Road Ind Est, Carlisle
Hunslet Engine Company, Leeds	Hunslet Engine Co., Leeds
Immingham Railfreight Terminal	Immingham Railfreight Term.
L H Group, Barton under Needwood	LH Group, Barton-u-Needwood
Lucchini Steelworks, Servola, Italy	Lucchini Steel, Servola, Italy
Middlesbrough & Hartlepool Dock Authority	Middlesbrough/Hartlepool DA
Ministry of Defence, Shoeburyness	MoD, Shoeburyness
Newton Stewart, Dumfries & Galloway	Newton Stewart, Dumf & Gall
Pontypool & Blaenavon Railway	Pontypool & Blaenavon Rlwy
Robert Stephenson & Hawthorns, Darlington	Rob. Stephenson & Hawthorns
Robinson & Hannon, Blaydon Sidings	Robinson & Hannon, Blaydon
Sandbach Car & Commercial Dismantlers	Sandbach Car & Commercial
Shipbreaking Industries, Faslane	Shipbreak'g Industries, Faslane
Slag Reduction, Barrow-in-Furness	Slag Reduction, Barrow-in-Fur
South Yorkshire Railway, Meadowhall	SY Railway, Meadowhall
St Leonards Railway Engineering	St Leonards Railway Eng.
Steelbreaking & Dismantling, Chesterfield	Steelbreak & Dism., Chesterf'd
Vias Y Construcciones, Madrid, Spain	Vias Y Construcciones, Madrid
Vulcan Foundry, Newton-le-Willows	Vulcan Foundry, Newton-le-W.
Wanstrow Playground, Somerset	Wanstrow Playground, Som'set
Wolsingham, Weardale Railway	Wolsingham, Weardale Rlwy

Of the 4733 scrapped locomotives listed, there is a degree of uncertainty on the accuracy of where or when (or whether in a few cases) 239 of these were scrapped. Whilst this is only a small fraction, representing just half of one percent of all scrapped locomotives, to ensure this book is as accurate as possible, there is a note in the right-hand column clarifying what is uncertain for each of these. In addition, the unconfirmed scrapping information for these 239 locomotives is summarised in Appendix VI.

Exported
Locomotives that have been exported to another country. Diesel locomotives were exported as long ago as the 1940s and others have been exported for a variety of uses abroad through to recent years. For exported locomotives, a date when the locomotive was withdrawn from service in the UK has been given, with the exception of Class 66s and 92s, as these were exported relatively recently, directly into service abroad, not being withdrawn from service in the UK as most other locomotives were. Also, as the remainder of these two classes are still operational in the UK, the exported examples could potentially return to UK service, unlike locomotives from other classes that have been exported.

Awaiting Disposal
Locomotives that have already been moved to the site of a scrapping firm and their disposal is likely to be soon. Locomotives that are in poor condition, or are being stripped of parts and are expected to be scrapped have not been given this status, as their scrapping may not be inevitable.

Converted
Locomotives that no longer exist in their original condition, having been converted to a new locomotive, as reflected by their new classification and number. For these locomotives, the withdrawal date is given and there is a brief explanation to the right. As the locomotives no longer exist in this form, they are shaded grey in the same way as scrapped locomotives are.

Preserved
Locomotives owned by a heritage railway, preservation group or privately, which are no longer in commercial ownership or operation. This excludes locomotives in industrial use and those operated by a Train Operating Company (TOC), including preserved locos on hire to a TOC. Preserved locomotives can be permanently based at a particular heritage railway, or on short or long-term loan from one heritage railway or base to another. Preserved locomotives can be operational, under restoration or a spare parts donor.

Commercial Owners and Operators
Locomotives in this category are listed by current commercial owner or operating company. This includes passenger and freight train operators which own, lease or hire locomotives, as well as those that aren't train operators but own or operate locomotives at a variety of sites across the UK. Some locomotives are based in a location for long term industrial use and are not approved for operation on the national rail network, such as at quarries, cement and steel works. Others may be owned by spot hire firms which send locomotives to a variety of locations, usually for shorter periods, such as Railway Support Services, RMS Locotec and HNRC. Where a locomotive is on hire to a TOC, it is listed by the current hiring operating company, irrespective of whether it is being hired from a preservation group, or another commercial operator. There have been a variety of changes to the list of commercial owners and operators since the last edition of this book, reflecting defunct and new franchise holders, operators that have commenced locomotive-hauled passenger trains and some commercial takeovers. Locomotives in this category are given the status of one of the following companies:

Alstom	Europhoenix
Arlington Fleet Services	Eurostar International
Arriva Traincare	Freightliner
AV Dawson	GB Railfreight
Bardon Aggregates	Great Western Railway
Boden Rail Engineering	Hanson UK
Class 20189	Harry Needle Railroad Company (HNRC)
Colas Rail	Hunslet Engine Company
Cross Country	Locomotive Services
Data Acquisition & Testing Services (DATS)	London North Eastern Railway (LNER)
DB Cargo	London Overground
DC Rail	Loram UK
Direct Rail Services	Mendip Rail
Eastern Rail Services	Meteor Power Ltd
East Midlands Railway	Nemesis Rail

Network Rail
Rail Operations Group
Railway Support Services
Riviera Trains
RMS Locotec
Russell Logistics
Scotrail
SembCorp Utilities UK
South Western Railway
Southern

Transmart Trains
TransPennine Express
Transport for Wales
UK Rail Leasing
Victoria Group
Vintage Trains
Wabtec
West Coast Railway Company
West Midlands Trains

Stored

From 2018 the operator GWR began to end the lease agreements on some of its Class 43 HST power cars, as did LNER soon after this. The latter has also done this for some of the Class 91s that had been in use on East Coast Main Line services for the previous three decades. Consequently, a quarter of the nearly-200 strong HST fleet and a similar proportion of the Class 91s are now in storage, without an operating company and now face an uncertain future. These locomotives have been given the status of Stored. This category has not been used for locomotives that remain in the custody of a passenger or freight operator that has placed them in short or long-term storage.

NOTES

This section gives details of anything unusual, of interest or exceptions to the definitions described above. The general codes used through the book are given beneath the technical details for each locomotive class and any specific details indicated by a single letter code are explained at the end of the data listings for that class. Items noted in this section include:

- Locomotives that have undergone, or are currently part way through a conversion to another locomotive.
- Instances when two locomotives carried the same numbers, the note stating whether it was the first or second locomotive to carry the number. The second locomotive to carry a duplicate number has a superscript 2 after the duplicate locomotive number to distinguish it from the first locomotive that carried the number.
- Locomotives of one status that are temporarily listed as a different status, due to their current use.
- Anything unusual, such as locomotives that have sustained damage after an accident, had a cab removed, or were not completely disposed of when scrapped.

APPENDICES

At the end of the book, there are six Appendices, with reference information and tables, primarily for locomotives where it may not be obvious where they are listed in this book.

APPENDIX I: LOCOMOTIVE CLASSES

A summary of all locomotives by classification, in the order that they are listed in this book, showing the total number produced and the number ranges for each locomotive classification.

APPENDIX II: MULTIPLE TOPS NUMBERS

Of the more than 5,200 locomotives which have carried a TOPS number, over 800 have carried more than one TOPS number, due to being renumbered. This Appendix lists all previously carried TOPS numbers and shows the locomotive class and latest TOPS number under which the locomotive is listed in this book. Where a locomotive has two or more previously carried TOPS numbers, there are multiple entries for such locomotives. For example 47780 has previously carried three different TOPS numbers (47030, 47618 and 47836), therefore each of these three previously carried numbers are listed, each entry referring to 47780 where the locomotive is found in this book. Locomotives that have only carried one TOPS number are not included in Appendix II.

APPENDIX III: BR 1948 AND 1957 NUMBERS

This lists locomotives that carried a 1948 BR Number or 1957 BR Number and were subsequently given a different number, under which they are listed in this book. The 1948 numbers are listed numerically, showing the corresponding 1957 number (where the locomotive was not given a TOPS number) or TOPS number, under which it can be found in this book. Locomotives that only carried one 1948 or one 1957 number throughout their lives are not listed in this Appendix, as they are listed under that one number.

There are a small number of locomotives where the "Number Loco is listed by" is not the latest number carried, but a previously carried number, to which it is more logical to refer, such as for some industrial or departmental renumberings. For example, for D5061 the table refers to 24061 to find the locomotive, rather than its last carried departmental number RDB968007 and for D8066, it refers to 20066 rather than the last carried number 82.

APPENDIX IV: DEPARTMENTAL NUMBERS

This lists all locomotives that were renumbered for Departmental use. It therefore does not include locomotives that were assigned a Departmental number which was not actually carried, or Departmental locomotives that were not given a separate Departmental number, such as D5901 or the Network Rail HSTs (43013, 43014 and 43062). In each case, the Departmental number is shown, along with the corresponding locomotive class and the number by which it is listed in this book.

APPENDIX V: LOCOMOTIVE NAMES

A list of all official locomotive names carried during main line service with BR or its successors. Names given during preservation are not included. The name listings are case sensitive as carried on locos and where a locomotive has carried more than one name, they are listed chronologically, in the order they were carried.

Names are listed adjacent to the locomotive number carried in the period when the name was also carried. In the case of subsequently renumbered locomotives, this is not the number under which the locomotive's entry can be found in this book. Please refer to Appendices II and III as necessary to locate where the locomotive's details can be found in this book.
Unofficial names are not included and in cases where it is not clear whether a name is official, names on cast nameplates are included and names painted on to the sides of locos have been excluded. Where a crest or plaque is mounted separately and this also includes text, this is not listed. For example, 31602 had a separate "19B" plaque under the "DRIVER DAVE GREEN" nameplate and only the text on the nameplate is included.

APPENDIX VI: UNCONFIRMED SCRAPPING DETAILS

A list of the locomotives for which it has not been possible to confirm some or all the scrapping details. In many cases the details are thought to be, or are likely to be correct, as stated in the Notes column in the locomotive listings and in this appendix.

ABBREVIATIONS

The following general abbreviations are used in this book:

AC	Alternating Current
BR	British Railways, later British Rail
BREL	British Rail Engineering Limited
DA	Dock Authority
DC	Direct Current
DP	Disposal Point
EWS	English, Welsh & Scottish Railway Co
GWR	Great Western Railway
hp	Horsepower
kW	Kilowatts
LMS	London Midland & Scottish Railway
LNER	London & North Eastern Railway
mph	Miles per hour
MoD	Ministry of Defence
NCB	National Coal Board
PS	Power Station
SR	Southern Railway
TOPS	Total Operations Processing System
V	Volts

▲ Four Class 37s were fitted with European Railway Traffic Management System (ERTMS) signalling equipment for use on the Cambrian lines between Shrewsbury, Aberystwyth and Pwllheli; these were renumbered 97301–97304. On 26 May 2020, 97303 and 97302 pass through Wrenbury with the 18.10 Crewe Basford Hall–Llandrindod Wells engineers' service. **Ken Davies**

1. EXPERIMENTAL LOCOMOTIVES

1.1. EXPERIMENTAL SHUNTING LOCOMOTIVES

EXPERIMENTAL ENGLISH ELECTRIC SHUNTER   0-6-0

Built: 1957 by English Electric, Vulcan Foundry, Newton-le-Willows.
Engine: English Electric 6RKT of 373 kW (500 hp) at 750 rpm.
Transmission: D0226 Electric and D0227 Hydraulic.
Maximum Speed: 35 mph.

Latest Number Carried	Previous Number 1	Year Entered Service	Year Withdrawn	Current Status/Scrapping Details	Notes
D226	D0226	1957	1960	Preserved	
D227	D0227	1957	1959	1964: Rob. Stephenson & Hawthorns	

EXPERIMENTAL BRUSH SHUNTER   0-4-0

Built: 1961 by Brush Electrical Engineering Company Ltd, Loughborough.
Engine: Petter McLaren of 200 hp.
Transmission: Electric.
Maximum Speed: 18 mph.

Latest Number Carried	Previous Number 1	Year Entered Service	Year Withdrawn	Current Status/Scrapping Details	Notes
D9998		1961	1962	Exported to Yugoslavia in 1964	

EXPERIMENTAL YORKSHIRE ENGINE CO. SHUNTER   0-6-0

Built: 1956 (JANUS) and 1961 (TAURUS) by Yorkshire Engine Company, Sheffield.
Engine: Two Rolls Royce C6 of 300 kW (400 hp) for JANUS and two Rolls Royce C8 of 450 kW (600 hp) for TAURUS.
Transmission: Electric (JANUS) and Hydraulic (TAURUS).
Maximum Speed: 23 mph (JANUS) and 36 mph (TAURUS).

UL   Scrapping details unconfirmed, but likely to be correct

Latest Number Carried	Previous Number 1	Year Entered Service	Year Withdrawn	Current Status/Scrapping Details	Notes
JANUS		1956	1956	1988: British Steel, Scunthorpe	UL
TAURUS		1961	1964	1965: Yorkshire Engine Company	

EXPERIMENTAL NORTH BRITISH SHUNTER   0-4-0

Built: 1954 by North British Locomotive Company, Glasgow.
Engine: Paxman 6 VRPHXL of 160 kW (225 hp) at 1250 rpm.
Transmission: Hydraulic.
Maximum Speed: 12 mph.

Latest Number Carried	Previous Number 1	Year Entered Service	Year Withdrawn	Current Status/Scrapping Details	Notes
TOM	27414	1954		Preserved	
TIGER		1954		Preserved	

1.2. EXPERIMENTAL MAIN LINE DIESEL LOCOMOTIVES

EXPERIMENTAL ENGLISH ELECTRIC TYPE 3   Co-Co

Built: 1947 (10000) and 1948 (10001) by English Electric, Vulcan Foundry, Newton-le-Willows.
Engine: English Electric 16SVT of 1200 kW (1600 hp) at 750 rpm.
Transmission: Electric.
Maximum Speed: 93 mph.
Train Heating/Supply: Steam.
Train Brakes: Vacuum.

Latest Number Carried	Previous Number 1	Year Entered Service	Year Withdrawn	Current Status/Scrapping Details	Notes
10000		1947	1963	1968: J Cashmore, Great Bridge	
10001		1948	1966	1968: Cox & Danks, North Acton	

EXPERIMENTAL BRITISH RAILWAYS TYPE 4   2-D-2

Built: 1950 by British Railways, Derby Works.
Engine: Four Paxman 12RPH of 1500 kW (2040 hp) at 750 rpm.
Transmission: Mechanical.
Maximum Speed: 84 mph.
Train Heating/Supply: Steam.
Train Brakes: Vacuum.

Latest Number Carried	Previous Number 1	Year Entered Service	Year Withdrawn	Current Status/Scrapping Details	Notes
10100		1950	1958	1960: Derby Works	

EXPERIMENTAL ENGLISH ELECTRIC TYPE 3/TYPE 4   1Co-Co1

Built: 1950–54 by British Railways, Ashford Works and Brighton Works.
Engine: English Electric 16SVT of 1300 kW (1750 hp) for 10201 & 10202 and 1500 kW (2000 hp) for 10203.
Transmission: Electric.
Maximum Speed: 90 mph.
Train Heating/Supply: Steam.
Train Brakes: Vacuum.

Latest Number Carried	Previous Number 1	Year Entered Service	Year Withdrawn	Current Status/Scrapping Details	Notes
10201		1950	1963	1968: J Cashmore, Great Bridge	
10202		1951	1963	1968: J Cashmore, Great Bridge	
10203		1954	1963	1968: J Cashmore, Great Bridge	

EXPERIMENTAL NORTH BRITISH TYPE 1   Bo-Bo

Built: 1950 by North British Locomotive Company, Glasgow.
Engine: Paxman 16PHXL of 617 kW (827 hp), later re-engined with Maybach MD655 of 1000 kW (1400 hp).
Transmission: Electric.
Maximum Speed: 70 mph.
Train Heating/Supply: Steam.
Train Brakes: Vacuum.

Latest Number Carried	Previous Number 1	Year Entered Service	Year Withdrawn	Current Status/Scrapping Details	Notes
10800		1950	1959	1972: Brush, Loughborough	

▲ The two experimental English Electric Type 3s 10000 and 10001 were Britain's first main line diesel locomotives, entering service in 1947 and 1948 respectively. On 1 September 1958, the latter stops at Bletchley with a southbound service formed of non-corridor coaching stock. **Gordon Edgar**

▼ This unusual looking 16-wheeled machine is one of the earliest experimental main line diesel locomotives; 10100 "Fell" was built at BR's Derby Works and entered service in late 1950. It is seen outside Derby Works on 20 April 1952. **Gavin Morrison**

EXPERIMENTAL BRCW/SULZER TYPE 4   Co-Co

Built: 1962 by Birmingham Railway Carriage and Wagon Company.
Engine: Sulzer 12LDA 28C of 2050 kW (2750 hp).
Transmission: Electric.
Maximum Speed: 100 mph.
Train Heating/Supply: Steam.
Train Brakes: Vacuum.

Latest Number Carried	Previous Number 1	Year Entered Service	Year Withdrawn	Current Status/Scrapping Details	Notes
D0260		1962	1963	1965: T W Ward, Attercliffe	

EXPERIMENTAL ARMSTRONG WHITWORTH TYPE 1   1-Co-1

Built: 1933 by Armstrong Whitworth, Newcastle-upon-Tyne.
Engine: Armstrong Sulzer 8LD28 (800 hp) at 700 rpm.
Transmission: Electric.
Maximum Speed: 70mph.
Train Brakes: Vacuum.

Latest Number Carried	Previous Number 1	Year Entered Service	Year Withdrawn	Current Status/Scrapping Details	Notes
D9		1933	1934	1937: Scrapping location unknown	

CLASS 53   Co-Co

Built: 1961 by Brush Electrical Engineering Company Ltd, Loughborough.
Engine: Two Bristol Siddeley Maybach MD655 of 1075 kW (1400 hp) at 1500 rpm.
Transmission: Hydraulic.
Maximum Speed: 100mph.
Train Heating/Supply: Steam.
Train Brakes: Vacuum.

Latest Number Carried	Previous Number 1	Year Entered Service	Year Withdrawn	Current Status/Scrapping Details	Notes
D1200	D0280	1961	1975	1976: J Cashmore, Newport	

EXPERIMENTAL ENGLISH ELECTRIC TYPE 5   Co-Co

Built: 1955 by English Electric, Vulcan Foundry, Newton-le-Willows.
Engine: Two Napier Deltic D18-25 of 1230 kW (1650 hp) at 1500 rpm.
Transmission: Electric.
Maximum Speed: 105 mph.
Train Heating/Supply: Steam.

Latest Number Carried	Previous Number 1	Year Entered Service	Year Withdrawn	Current Status/Scrapping Details	Notes
DELTIC		1955	1961	Preserved	

EXPERIMENTAL CLAYTON TYPE 3   Bo-Bo

Built: 1962–63 by Clayton Equipment Company, Derbyshire.
Engine: Four Rolls Royce C8TFL of 1120 kW (1500 hp).
Transmission: Hydraulic.
Maximum Speed: 90 mph.
Train Heating/Supply: Steam.
Train Brakes: Vacuum.

Latest Number Carried	Previous Number 1	Year Entered Service	Year Withdrawn	Current Status/Scrapping Details	Notes
DHP1		1963	1964	1967: Derby Works	

EXPERIMENTAL ENGLISH ELECTRIC TYPE 4   Co-Co

Built: 1962 by English Electric, Vulcan Foundry, Newton-le-Willows.
Engine: English Electric 16CSVT of 2000 kW (2700 hp).
Transmission: Electric.
Maximum Speed: 90 mph.
Train Heating/Supply: Steam.
Train Brakes: Dual braked (vacuum and air).

Latest Number Carried	Previous Number 1	Year Entered Service	Year Withdrawn	Current Status/Scrapping Details	Notes
DP2		1962	1967	1968: Vulcan Foundry, Newton-le-W.	

EXPERIMENTAL BRUSH TYPE 5   Co-Co

Built: 1968 by Brush Electrical Engineering Company Ltd, Loughborough.
Engine: Sulzer 16LVA24 of 2983 kW (4000 hp) at 1100 rpm.
Transmission: Electric.
Maximum Speed: 110 mph.
Train Heating/Supply: Electric.
Train Brakes: Dual braked (vacuum and air).

UM   Scrapping details unconfirmed, but may be correct

Latest Number Carried	Previous Number 1	Year Entered Service	Year Withdrawn	Current Status/Scrapping Details	Notes
HS4000		1968	1971	1993: Kolomna, Moscow	UM

▲ D0280 was built by Brush in Loughborough and began its working life in late 1961. On 5 August 1962, when it was less than a year old, it races through Hadley Wood with 1G61, the 15.15 London King's Cross–Sheffield Victoria. It was renumbered D1200 in 1970 and withdrawn in 1975.
Geoff Plumb

1.3. EXPERIMENTAL GAS TURBINE LOCOMOTIVES

EXPERIMENTAL BROWN BOVERI GAS TURBINE   A1A-A1A

Built: 1950 by Brown Boveri, Switzerland.
Engine: Brown Boveri gas turbine of 1828 kW (2500 hp).
Transmission: Electric.
Maximum Speed: 90 mph.
Train Heating/Supply: Steam.

Latest Number Carried	Previous Number 1	Year Entered Service	Year Withdrawn	Current Status/Scrapping Details	Notes
18000		1950	1960	Preserved	

EXPERIMENTAL METROPOLITAN VICKERS GAS TURBINE   Co-Co

Built: 1951 by Metropolitan Vickers, Manchester.
Engine: Gas turbine of 2240 kW (3000 hp).
Transmission: Electric.
Maximum Speed: 90 mph.
Train Heating/Supply: Steam.
Train Brakes: Vacuum.
In 1958 18100 was converted to experimental electric Class 80 and renumbered E1000 (see below).

Latest Number Carried	Previous Number 1	Year Entered Service	Year Withdrawn	Current Status/Scrapping Details	Notes
18100		1952	1958	Converted to E1000 in 1958	

EXPERIMENTAL ENGLISH ELECTRIC GAS TURBINE   4-6-0

Built: 1958–61 by English Electric, Vulcan Foundry, Newton-le-Willows.
Engine: EM27L of 2050 kW (2750 hp) at 9000 rpm.
Transmission: Mechanical.
Maximum Speed: 90mph.
Train Heating/Supply: Steam.

Latest Number Carried	Previous Number 1	Year Entered Service	Year Withdrawn	Current Status/Scrapping Details	Notes
GT3		1961	1962	1966: T Ward, Salford	

1.4. EXPERIMENTAL MAIN LINE ELECTRIC LOCOMOTIVES

CLASS 80 {A1A-A1A}

Built: 1951 by Metropolitan Vickers, Manchester (see 18100) and converted to E1000 in 1958.
Electric Supply System: 25 kV AC overhead.
Power Output: 2500 kW (625 hp).
Maximum Speed: 90 mph.
Train Heating/Supply: Electric.
Train Brakes: Vacuum.

UL   Scrapping details unconfirmed, but likely to be correct

Latest Number Carried	Previous Number 1	Year Entered Service	Year Withdrawn	Current Status/Scrapping Details	Notes
E2001	E1000	1958	1968	1973: J Cashmore, Great Bridge	UL a)

a)   Converted from 18100

▲ Experimental gas turbine locomotive 18000 was built in Switzerland by Brown Boveri in 1950 and is seen at Old Oak Common depot on 21 April 1954. It is one of the few early prototype locomotives to have survived and is now on display at the Didcot Railway Centre. **Gavin Morrison**

2. DIESEL LOCOMOTIVES

2.1. PURPOSE-BUILT DEPARTMENTAL LOCOMOTIVES

RUSTON & HORNSBY 0-4-0 SHUNTER   0-4-0

Built: 1955 by Ruston & Hornsby, Lincoln.
Engine: Ruston & Hornsby Mark 4V of 88 hp.
Transmission: Mechanical.
Train Brakes: None.

Latest Number Carried	Previous Number 1	Year Entered Service	Year Withdrawn	Current Status/Scrapping Details	Notes
56		1955	1970	1981: T J Thomson, Stockton	

RUSTON & HORNSBY 0-4-0 SHUNTER   0-4-0

Built: 1958–61 by Ruston & Hornsby, Lincoln.
Engine: Ruston & Hornsby of 150 hp.
Transmission: Mechanical.
Train Brakes: None.

UL   Scrapping details unconfirmed, but likely to be correct

Latest Number Carried	Previous Number 1	Year Entered Service	Year Withdrawn	Current Status/Scrapping Details	Notes
82		1958	1970	1981: T J Thomson, Stockton	
83		1959	1970	1970: W Heselwood, Attercliffe	UL
84		1959	1970	1970: Arnott Young, Parkgate	UL
85		1959	1970	1970: Arnott Young, Parkgate	UL
86		1961	1970	1970: Arnott Young, Parkgate	UL
87		1961	1970	1981: T J Thomson, Stockton	

CLASS 97 RUSTON & HORNSBY 0-4-0 SHUNTER   0-4-0

Built: 1957 by Ruston & Hornsby, Lincoln.
Engine: Ruston 4 Cylinder of 66 kW (88 hp).
Transmission: Mechanical.

Latest Number Carried	Previous Number 1	Year Entered Service	Year Withdrawn	Current Status/Scrapping Details	Notes
97020	20	1957	1981	1982: Reading Signal Works	

CLASS 97 RUSTON & HORNSBY 0-6-0 SHUNTER   0-6-0

Built: 1953–59 by Ruston & Hornsby, Lincoln.
Engine: Ruston 6VPH of 123 kW (165 hp).
Transmission: Electric.
Maximum Speed: 20 mph.
Train Heating/Supply: None.
Train Brakes: Vacuum.

Latest Number Carried	Previous Number 1	Year Entered Service	Year Withdrawn	Current Status/Scrapping Details	Notes
97650	PWM650	1953	1987	Preserved	
97651	PWM651	1959	1998	Preserved	

97652	PWM652	1959	1987	1990: Plymouth Laira Depot
97653	PWM653	1959	1992	2012: Hirst & Sons, Hampshire
97654	PWM654	1959	1997	Preserved

RUSTON & HORNSBY 0-4-0 SHUNTER   0-4-0

Built: 1948 by Ruston & Hornsby, Lincoln.
Engine: Ruston of 48 hp.
Transmission: Mechanical.
Train Brakes: None.

Latest Number Carried	Previous Number 1	Year Entered Service	Year Withdrawn	Current Status/Scrapping Details	Notes
DS1169		1948	1972	1973: G Cohen, Kettering	

FOWLER 0-4-0 SHUNTER   0-4-0

Built: 1935 by John Fowler & Co., Leeds.
Engine: Ruston & Hornsby VQ of 88 hp.
Transmission: Mechanical.
Maximum Speed: 15 mph.
Train Brakes: None.

Latest Number Carried	Previous Number 1	Year Entered Service	Year Withdrawn	Current Status/Scrapping Details	Notes
ED1	2	1935	1962	1962: Derby Works	

FOWLER 0-4-0 SHUNTER   0-4-0

Built: 1949 by John Fowler & Co., Leeds.
Engine: Fowler 4C of 88 hp.
Transmission: Mechanical.
Maximum Speed: 15 mph.
Train Brakes: None.

Latest Number Carried	Previous Number 1	Year Entered Service	Year Withdrawn	Current Status/Scrapping Details	Notes
ED2		1949	1965	1967: Derby Works	
ED3		1949	1967	1968: G Cohen, Kettering	
ED4		1949	1964	1967: J Cashmore, Great Bridge	
ED5		1949	1965	1967: J Cashmore, Great Bridge	
ED6		1949	1967	1968: Valley Goods, Holyhead	

FOWLER 0-4-0 SHUNTER   0-4-0

Built: 1940 by John Fowler & Co., Leeds.
Engine: Fowler Type C of 150 hp.
Transmission: Mechanical.
Maximum Speed: 15 mph.
Train Brakes: None.

Latest Number Carried	Previous Number 1	Year Entered Service	Year Withdrawn	Current Status/Scrapping Details	Notes
ED7		1955	1964	1964: Derby Works	

2.2. UNCLASSIFIED DIESEL SHUNTING LOCOMOTIVES

LMS PAXMAN 400HP SHUNTER   0-6-0

Built: 1934 by London Midland and Scottish Railway, Derby Works.
Engine: Paxman 4 Stroke of 298 kW (400 hp) at 750 rpm.
Transmission: Hydraulic.
Maximum Speed: 25 mph.
Train Brakes: Vacuum.

Latest Number Carried	Previous Number 1	Year Entered Service	Year Withdrawn	Current Status/Scrapping Details	Notes
1831		1934	1939	1955: Crewe Works	a)

a)   Scrapped after 1955, exact date not known

LMS ALLAN 160HP SHUNTER   0-4-0

Built: 1934 by English Electric at Preston works for Drewry Car company.
Engine: W H Allan 8RS18 of 119 kW (160 hp) at 1200 rpm, subsequently fitted with Gardner 6L3 of 114 kW (153 hp).
Transmission: Mechanical.
Maximum Speed: 12 mph.

Latest Number Carried	Previous Number 1	Year Entered Service	Year Withdrawn	Current Status/Scrapping Details	Notes
7050	7400	1934	1943	Preserved	

LMS HUNSLET 150HP SHUNTER   0-6-0

Built: 1933 by Hunslet Engine Company, Leeds.
Engine: MAN WV16/22 of 112 kW (150 hp) at 900 rpm. Later McLaren Ricardo MR6 of 98kW (132 hp).
Transmission: Mechanical.
Maximum Speed: 30 mph.
Train Brakes: None.

Latest Number Carried	Previous Number 1	Year Entered Service	Year Withdrawn	Current Status/Scrapping Details	Notes
7051	7401	1933	1945	Preserved	

LMS HUNSLET 150HP SHUNTER   0-6-0

Built: 1934 by Hunslet Engine Company, Leeds.
Engine: McLaren-Benz 8MDB of 112 kW (150 hp) at 1000 rpm.
Transmission: Mechanical.
Maximum Speed: 8 mph.
Train Brakes: None.

Latest Number Carried	Previous Number 1	Year Entered Service	Year Withdrawn	Current Status/Scrapping Details	Notes
7052	7402	1934	1943	1969: Bird Group, Long Marston	

▲ Hunslet 0-6-0 shunter 7051 is the oldest diesel locomotive listed in this book. It entered service for LMS as 7401 in May 1933 and was renumbered 7051 in 1934. It is stabled at Crewe South depot on 7 May 1939, alongside the more powerful Armstrong Whitworth 1936-built shunter 7066.

George C. Lander/Rail Photoprints

▼ Class D2/7 11116, which went on to become D2500 in 1961, awaits acceptance at Derby in late 1955 shortly after it had been completed by Hudswell Clarke. **R. S. Wilkins/Rail Photoprints**

LMS HUNSLET 150HP SHUNTER 0-6-0

Built: 1934 by Hunslet Engine Company, Leeds.
Engine: Brotherhood-Ricardo RZ5 of 112 kW (150 hp) at 1200 rpm.
Transmission: Mechanical.
Maximum Speed: 14 mph.
Train Brakes: None.

Latest Number Carried	Previous Number 1	Year Entered Service	Year Withdrawn	Current Status/Scrapping Details	Notes
7053	7403	1934	1942	1954: Hunslet Engine Co., Leeds	

LMS HUNSLET 180HP SHUNTER 0-6-0

Built: 1934 by Hunslet Engine Company, Leeds.
Engine: Davey Paxman 6VZS of 134 kW (180 hp) at 900 rpm.
Transmission: Mechanical.
Maximum Speed: 13 mph.
Train Brakes: None.

Latest Number Carried	Previous Number 1	Year Entered Service	Year Withdrawn	Current Status/Scrapping Details	Notes
7054		1934	1943	1974: NCB Hickleton Main Colliery	

LMS HUDSWELL CLARKE 150HP SHUNTER 0-6-0

Built: 1934–35 by Hudswell-Clarke & Company, Leeds.
Engine: Mirrlees Ricardo of 112 kW (150 hp).
Transmission: Mechanical.
Maximum Speed: 19 mph.
Train Brakes: None.

Latest Number Carried	Previous Number 1	Year Entered Service	Year Withdrawn	Current Status/Scrapping Details	Notes
7055		1934	1963	1964: Thornaby Depot	
7056		1935	1955	1956: Thornton Junction	

LMS HARLAND & WOLFF 175HP SHUNTER 0-6-0

Built: 1935 by Harland and Wolff.
Engine: Harland & Wolff TR of 1300 kW (175 hp) at 1100 rpm.
Transmission: Mechanical.
Maximum Speed: 10 mph.
Train Brakes: None.

ES   Locomotive exported and subsequently scrapped

Latest Number Carried	Previous Number 1	Year Entered Service	Year Withdrawn	Current Status/Scrapping Details	Notes
7057		1935	1944	1965: Ulster Transport Authority	ES

LMS ARMSTONG WHITWORTH 250HP SHUNTER 0-6-0

Built: 1934 by Armstrong Whitworth.
Engine: Armstrong Whitworth 6LV22 of 186 kW (250 hp) at 775 rpm.
Transmission: Electric.
Maximum Speed: 30 mph.
Train Brakes: None.

Latest Number Carried	Previous Number 1	Year Entered Service	Year Withdrawn	Current Status/Scrapping Details	Notes
7058	7408	1934	1949	1950: Derby Works	

LMS ARMSTONG WHITWORTH 350HP SHUNTER   0-6-0

Built: 1934 by Armstrong Whitworth.
Engine: Armstrong Whitworth 6LV22 of 186 kW (350 hp) at 775 rpm.
Transmission: Electric.
Maximum Speed: 30 mph.
Train Brakes: None.

ES   Locomotive exported and subsequently scrapped
MS   This locomotive may have been scrapped
UM   Scrapping details unconfirmed, but may be correct

Latest Number Carried	Previous Number 1	Year Entered Service	Year Withdrawn	Current Status/Scrapping Details	Notes
7059		1936	1944	1958: Scrapped in Belgium	ES
7060		1936	1942	1952: Suez, Egypt	ES
7061		1936	1944	1965: Scrapped in Belgium	UM
7062		1936	1944	1975: Dortmund, Germany	UM
7063		1936	1944	1967: Hams Hall Power Station	
7064		1936	1944	1961: Scrapped in Belgium	UM
7065		1936	1942	Exported to Egypt in 1941	MS
7066		1936	1942	Exported to Egypt in 1941	MS
7067		1936	1944	1966: Scrapped in Belgium	UM
7068		1936	1942	Exported to Egypt in 1941	MS

BR BULLEID SHUNTER   0-6-0

Built: 1950 by British Railways, Ashford Works.
Engine: Paxman Ricardo of 373 kW (500 hp) at 1250 rpm.
Transmission: Mechanical.
Maximum Speed: 44 mph.
Train Brakes: None.

Latest Number Carried	Previous Number 1	Year Entered Service	Year Withdrawn	Current Status/Scrapping Details	Notes
11001		1950	1959	1959: Ashford Works	

BR HIBBERD 52HP SHUNTER   0-4-0

Built: 1950 by F C Hibberd & Co Ltd.
Engine: English National DA4 of 39 kW (52 hp) at 1250 rpm.
Transmission: Mechanical.
Maximum Speed: 15 mph.
Train Brakes: None.

Latest Number Carried	Previous Number 1	Year Entered Service	Year Withdrawn	Current Status/Scrapping Details	Notes
11104	52	1950	1967	1967: J Cashmore, Newport	

BR PETTER BRUSH 360HP SHUNTER   0-6-0

Built: 1949 by Brush Electrical Engineering Company, Loughborough.
Engine: Petter SS4 of 268 kW (360 hp).
Transmission: Electric.
Maximum Speed: 20 mph.
Train Brakes: None.

Latest Number Carried	Previous Number 1	Year Entered Service	Year Withdrawn	Current Status/Scrapping Details	Notes
15107		1949	1958	1958: Swindon Works	

2.3. DIESEL SHUNTING LOCOMOTIVES WITH PRE-TOPS CLASSIFICATION

CLASS D1/1 HUNSLET SHUNTER   0-4-0

Built: 1954–55 by Hunslet Engine Company, Leeds.
Engine: Gardner 6L3 of 114 kW (153 hp) at 1200 rpm.
Transmission: Mechanical.
Maximum Speed: 14 mph.
Train Brakes: None.

Latest Number Carried	Previous Number 1	Year Entered Service	Year Withdrawn	Current Status/Scrapping Details	Notes
D2950	11500	1954	1967	1983: Thyssen Ltd, Llanelli	
D2951	11501	1954	1967	1968: C F Booth, Rotherham	
D2952	11502	1955	1966	1967: Slag Reduction, Ickles	

CLASS D1/3 RUSTON & HORNSBY SHUNTER   0-4-0

Built: 1956 by Ruston & Hornsby, Lincoln.
Engine: Ruston 6VPHL of 123 kW (165 hp).
Transmission: Mechanical.
Maximum Speed: 15 mph.
Train Brakes: None.

Latest Number Carried	Previous Number 1	Year Entered Service	Year Withdrawn	Current Status/Scrapping Details	Notes
D2957	11507	1956	1967	1967: Slag Reduction, Ickles	
D2958	11508	1956	1968	1984: C F Booth, Rotherham	

▲ The Class D2/10 consisted of 73 0-4-0 shunters built by North British between 1957 and 1961. When this image of D2729 minus its coupling rods was captured at Perth depot in September 1966, it had probably already reached the end of its working life. It was put into storage two months later and was formally withdrawn in March 1967. **Charlie Cross / The Gordon Edgar Collection**

CLASS D2/1 NORTH BRITISH SHUNTER   0-4-0

Built: 1953–56 by North British Locomotive Company, Glasgow.
Engine: Paxman 6PR of 149 kW (200 hp).
Transmission: Hydraulic.
Maximum Speed: 14 mph (D2700–D2702) and 12 mph (D2703–D2707).
Train Brakes: None.

UL   Scrapping details unconfirmed, but likely to be correct

Latest Number Carried	Previous Number 1	Year Entered Service	Year Withdrawn	Current Status/Scrapping Details	Notes
D2700	11700	1953	1963	1964: Darlington Works	
D2701	11701	1953	1967	1967: A Draper, Hull	
D2702	11702	1954	1967	1967: A Draper, Hull	
D2703	11703	1955	1968	1968: Shipbreak'g Industries, Faslane	UL
D2704	11704	1955	1967	1967: Arnott Young, Carmyle	UL
D2705	11705	1955	1967	1967: J N Connel, Coatbridge	UL
D2706	11706	1955	1967	1967: Slag Reduction, Ickles	
D2707	11707	1956	1967	1967: Slag Reduction, Ickles	

CLASS D2/5 ANDREW BARCLAY SHUNTER   0-6-0

Note that Class D2/5 locomotives differ from Class 05; some sources incorrectly classify Class D2/5 locomotives as Class 05.
Built: 1956–57 by Andrew Barclay, Kilmarnock.
Engine: Gardner 8L3 of 152 kW (204 hp).
Transmission: Mechanical.
Maximum Speed: 17.75 mph.
Train Brakes: None.

UL   Scrapping details unconfirmed, but likely to be correct
UM   Scrapping details unconfirmed, but may be correct

Latest Number Carried	Previous Number 1	Year Entered Service	Year Withdrawn	Current Status/Scrapping Details	Notes
D2400	11177	1956	1967	1968: Slag Reduction, Ickles	
D2401	11178	1956	1968	1969: C F Booth, Rotherham	
D2402	11179	1956	1967	1968: C F Booth, Rotherham	
D2403	11180	1956	1969	1969: C F Booth, Rotherham	
D2404	11181	1956	1969	1969: C F Booth, Rotherham	
D2405	11182	1956	1968	1970: C F Booth, Rotherham	UM
D2406	11183	1956	1967	1968: T W Ward, Beighton	
D2407	11184	1957	1969	1970: C F Booth, Rotherham	
D2408	11185	1957	1967	1968: T W Ward, Beighton	
D2409	11186	1957	1968	1970: C F Booth, Rotherham	UL

CLASS D2/7 HUDSWELL CLARKE SHUNTER   0-6-0

Built: 1955–56 by Hudswell-Clarke & Company, Leeds.
Engine: Gardner 8L3 of 152 kW (204 hp).
Transmission: Mechanical.
Maximum Speed: 14 mph.
Train Brakes: None.

Latest Number Carried	Previous Number 1	Year Entered Service	Year Withdrawn	Current Status/Scrapping Details	Notes
D2500	11116	1955	1967	1968: C F Booth, Rotherham	
D2501	11117	1956	1967	1967: Slag Reduction, Ickles	
D2502	11118	1956	1967	1968: C F Booth, Rotherham	
D2503	11119	1956	1967	1968: C F Booth, Rotherham	
D2504	11120	1956	1967	1968: C F Booth, Rotherham	
D2505	11144	1956	1967	1968: C F Booth, Rotherham	

D2506	11145	1956	1967	1970: Steelbreak & Dism., Chesterf'd
D2507	11146	1956	1967	1967: Slag Reduction, Ickles
D2508	11147	1956	1967	1968: C F Booth, Rotherham
D2509	11148	1956	1967	1968: C F Booth, Rotherham

CLASS D2/10 NORTH BRITISH SHUNTER   0-4-0

Built: 1957–61 by North British Locomotive Company, Glasgow.
Engine: MAN W6V of 168 kW (225 hp) at 1100 rpm.
Transmission: Hydraulic.
Maximum Speed: 15 mph.

UL   Scrapping details unconfirmed, but likely to be correct

Latest Number Carried	Previous Number 1	Year Entered Service	Year Withdrawn	Current Status/Scrapping Details	Notes
D2708	11708	1957	1967	1967: Slag Reduction, Ickles	
D2709	11709	1957	1967	1967: Slag Reduction, Ickles	
D2710	11710	1957	1967	1967: Slag Reduction, Ickles	
D2711	11711	1957	1967	1967: Slag Reduction, Ickles	
D2712	11712	1957	1967	1967: Slag Reduction, Ickles	
D2713	11713	1957	1967	1967: Slag Reduction, Ickles	
D2714	11714	1957	1967	1967: Slag Reduction, Ickles	
D2715	11715	1957	1967	1967: Slag Reduction, Ickles	
D2716	11716	1957	1967	1967: Slag Reduction, Ickles	
D2717	11717	1957	1967	1967: Argosy Salvage, Shettleston	UL
D2718	11718	1957	1967	1967: Argosy Salvage, Shettleston	
D2719	11719	1957	1967	1967: Slag Reduction, Ickles	
D2720		1958	1967	1971: J N Connel, Coatbridge	UL
D2721		1958	1967	1967: Argosy Salvage, Shettleston	
D2722		1958	1967	1967: Slag Reduction, Ickles	
D2723		1958	1967	1971: J N Connel, Coatbridge	UL
D2724		1958	1967	1968: Slag Reduction, Ickles	UL
D2725		1958	1967	1967: Machine & Scrap, Motherwell	
D2726		1958	1967	1971: Shipbreaking, Queenborough	
D2727		1958	1967	1967: Slag Reduction, Ickles	
D2728		1958	1967	1967: Argosy Salvage, Shettleston	
D2729		1958	1967	1967: Slag Reduction, Ickles	
D2730		1958	1967	1968: Argosy Salvage, Shettleston	
D2731		1958	1967	1968: Argosy Salvage, Shettleston	
D2732		1958	1967	1967: Slag Reduction, Ickles	
D2733		1958	1967	1967: Slag Reduction, Ickles	
D2734		1958	1967	1967: Argosy Salvage, Shettleston	UL
D2735		1958	1967	1967: Slag Reduction, Ickles	
D2736		1958	1967	1969: Bird Group, Cardiff	UL
D2737		1958	1967	1967: Slag Reduction, Ickles	
D2738		1958	1967	1979: NCB Killoch Colliery	
D2739		1958	1967	1967: Bird Group, Long Marston	
D2740		1958	1967	1967: Slag Reduction, Ickles	
D2741		1959	1967	1967: Slag Reduction, Ickles	
D2742		1959	1967	1967: Slag Reduction, Ickles	
D2743		1959	1967	1967: Slag Reduction, Ickles	
D2744		1959	1967	1968: Argosy Salvage, Shettleston	UL
D2745		1960	1967	1968: Slag Reduction, Ickles	UL
D2746		1960	1967	1967: Slag Reduction, Ickles	
D2747		1960	1967	1967: Argosy Salvage, Shettleston	
D2748		1960	1967	1967: Argosy Salvage, Shettleston	
D2749		1960	1967	1967: Argosy Salvage, Shettleston	
D2750		1960	1967	1967: J N Connel, Coatbridge	UL
D2751		1960	1967	1967: J N Connel, Coatbridge	UL
D2752		1960	1967	1967: Slag Reduction, Ickles	
D2753		1960	1967	1967: Machine & Scrap, Motherwell	
D2754		1960	1967	1969: Barnes & Bell, Coatbridge	

D2755	1960	1967	1967: Argosy Salvage, Shettleston	
D2756	1960	1968	1968: G Campbell, Airdrie	
D2757	1960	1967	1970: Bird Group, Cardiff	
D2758	1960	1968	1968: G Campbell, Airdrie	
D2759	1960	1967	1968: Argosy Salvage, Shettleston	
D2760	1960	1968	1968: G Campbell, Airdrie	
D2761	1960	1967	1968: Argosy Salvage, Shettleston	
D2762	1960	1967	1967: Slag Reduction, Ickles	
D2763	1960	1967	1977: British Steel, Landore	
D2764	1960	1968	1968: Barnes & Bell, Coatbridge	
D2765	1960	1967	1967: Slag Reduction, Ickles	
D2766	1960	1967	1967: Slag Reduction, Ickles	
D2767	1960	1967	Preserved	
D2768	1960	1968	1968: Shipbreak'g Industries, Faslane	UL
D2769	1960	1968	1968: G Campbell, Airdrie	
D2770	1960	1968	1968: G Campbell, Airdrie	
D2771	1960	1967	1967: Slag Reduction, Ickles	
D2772	1960	1967	1967: Slag Reduction, Ickles	
D2773	1960	1968	1968: Barnes & Bell, Coatbridge	
D2774	1960	1967	Preserved	
D2775	1960	1968	1968: G Campbell, Airdrie	
D2776	1960	1967	1968: Argosy Salvage, Shettleston	
D2777	1960	1967	1968: Bird Group, Cardiff	
D2778	1960	1967	1967: Slag Reduction, Ickles	
D2779	1961	1968	1968: G Campbell, Airdrie	
D2780	1961	1968	1968: Barnes & Bell, Coatbridge	

▲ Four 0-6-0 shunters built by LNER between 1944 and 1945 comprised the Class D3/9; as they were all scrapped more than 50 years ago, few colour photographs of them exist. 15001 rests inside the former North Staffordshire Railway roundhouse at Stoke-on-Trent during May 1966.

Charlie Cross / The Gordon Edgar Collection

CLASS D2/11 BEYER PEACOCK/BRUSH SHUNTER 0-4-0

Built: 1960 by Brush Electrical Engineering Company Ltd, Loughborough and Beyer Peacock & Co., Gorton, Manchester
Engine: National M4AAV6 of 149 kW (200 hp).
Transmission: Electric.
Maximum Speed: 18 mph.
Train Brakes: None.

Latest Number Carried	Previous Number 1	Year Entered Service	Year Withdrawn	Current Status/Scrapping Details	Notes
D2999		1960	1967	1970: C F Booth, Rotherham	

CLASS D2/12 HUSWELL CLARKE SHUNTER 0-6-0

Built: 1961 by Hudswell-Clarke & Company, Leeds.
Engine: Gardner 8L3 of 152 kW (204 hp) at 1200 rpm.
Transmission: Mechanical.
Maximum Speed: 25 mph.

Latest Number Carried	Previous Number 1	Year Entered Service	Year Withdrawn	Current Status/Scrapping Details	Notes
D2510		1961	1967	1968: C F Booth, Rotherham	
D2511		1961	1967	Preserved	
D2512		1961	1967	1968: C F Booth, Rotherham	
D2513		1961	1967	1975: NCB Cadeby Main Colliery	
D2514		1961	1967	1968: C F Booth, Rotherham	
D2515		1961	1967	1968: Bolton Depot	
D2516		1961	1967	1968: Bolton Depot	
D2517		1961	1967	1967: Slag Reduction, Ickles	
D2518		1961	1967	1973: NCB Hatfield Main Colliery	
D2519		1961	1967	1985: Marple & Gillot, Attercliffe	

CLASS D3/1 NORTH BRITISH SHUNTER 0-4-0

Built: 1958–59 North British Locomotive Company, Glasgow.
Engine: NBL MAN W6V of 246 kW (330 hp).
Transmission: Hydraulic.
Maximum Speed: 20 mph.

Latest Number Carried	Previous Number 1	Year Entered Service	Year Withdrawn	Current Status/Scrapping Details	Notes
D2900		1958	1967	1967: Slag Reduction, Ickles	
D2901		1958	1967	1967: Slag Reduction, Ickles	
D2902		1958	1967	1967: Slag Reduction, Ickles	
D2903		1958	1967	1967: Slag Reduction, Ickles	
D2904		1958	1967	1967: Slag Reduction, Ickles	
D2905		1958	1967	1967: Slag Reduction, Ickles	
D2906		1958	1967	1967: Slag Reduction, Ickles	
D2907		1958	1967	1967: Slag Reduction, Ickles	
D2908		1958	1967	1967: Slag Reduction, Ickles	
D2909		1958	1967	1967: Slag Reduction, Ickles	
D2910		1958	1967	1967: Slag Reduction, Ickles	
D2911		1959	1967	1967: Slag Reduction, Ickles	
D2912		1959	1967	1967: Slag Reduction, Ickles	
D2913		1959	1967	1967: Slag Reduction, Ickles	

CLASS D3/3 BR SHUNTER   0-6-0

Built: 1955–57 by British Railways, Derby Works.
Engine: Crossley ESNT6 of 261 kW (350 hp).
Transmission: Electric.
Maximum Speed: 20 mph.
Train Brakes: Vacuum.

UL   Scrapping details unconfirmed, but likely to be correct
UM   Scrapping details unconfirmed, but may be correct

Latest Number Carried	Previous Number 1	Year Entered Service	Year Withdrawn	Current Status/Scrapping Details	Notes
D3117	13117	1955	1967	1967: J Cashmore, Great Bridge	UM
D3118	13118	1955	1967	1967: J Cashmore, Great Bridge	
D3119	13119	1955	1967	1967: J Cashmore, Great Bridge	
D3120	13120	1955	1967	1968: G Cohen, Kettering	
D3121	13121	1955	1967	1968: Slag Reduction, Ickles	
D3122	13122	1955	1966	1967: Steelbreak & Dism., Chesterf'd	UL
D3123	13123	1955	1966	1967: J Cashmore, Great Bridge	
D3124	13124	1955	1966	1967: J Cashmore, Great Bridge	
D3125	13125	1957	1967	1968: G Cohen, Kettering	
D3126	13126	1957	1966	1967: J Cashmore, Great Bridge	

CLASS D3/5 BR SHUNTER   0-6-0

Built: 1955 by British Railways, Darlington Works.
Engine: Lister Blackstone ERT6 of 261 kW (350 hp).
Transmission: Electric.
Maximum Speed: 20 mph.
Train Brakes: Vacuum.

UL   Scrapping details unconfirmed, but likely to be correct

Latest Number Carried	Previous Number 1	Year Entered Service	Year Withdrawn	Current Status/Scrapping Details	Notes
D3152	13152	1955	1967	1968: Slag Reduction, Ickles	
D3153	13153	1955	1967	1968: C F Booth, Rotherham	
D3154	13154	1955	1967	1968: C F Booth, Rotherham	
D3155	13155	1955	1967	1968: C F Booth, Rotherham	
D3156	13156	1955	1967	1968: C F Booth, Rotherham	
D3157	13157	1955	1967	1968: Slag Reduction, Ickles	
D3158	13158	1955	1967	1967: Slag Reduction, Ickles	
D3159	13159	1955	1967	1968: C F Booth, Rotherham	
D3160	13160	1955	1967	1968: Slag Reduction, Ickles	
D3161	13161	1955	1967	1968: C F Booth, Rotherham	
D3162	13162	1955	1967	1968: Slag Reduction, Ickles	
D3163	13163	1955	1967	1968: C F Booth, Rotherham	
D3164	13164	1955	1967	1968: Slag Reduction, Ickles	
D3165	13165	1955	1967	1968: C F Booth, Rotherham	UL
D3166	13166	1955	1967	1968: C F Booth, Rotherham	

CLASS D3/6 LMS SHUNTER   0-6-0

Built: 1934–36 by London Midland and Scottish Railway.
Engine: English Electric 6K of 261 kW (350 hp) at 675 rpm.
Transmission: Electric.
Maximum Speed: 12 mph.

MS   This locomotive may have been scrapped
UM   Scrapping details unconfirmed, but may be correct

Latest Number Carried	Previous Number 1	Year Entered Service	Year Withdrawn	Current Status/Scrapping Details	Notes
7069		1936	1940	Preserved	
7070		1936	1940	1940: Scrapped in France	UM
7071		1936	1940	Exported to France in 1940	MS
7072		1936	1940	Exported to France in 1940	MS
7073		1936	1940	1940: Scrapped in France	UM
12000	7074	1936	1961	1962: Derby Works	
7075		1936	1940	1944: Scrapped in France	UM
12001	7076	1936	1962	1962: Horwich Works	
7077		1936	1940	Exported to France in 1940	MS
7078		1936	1940	1940: Scrapped in France	UM
12002	7079	1934	1956	1956: Derby Works	

CLASS D3/7 LMS SHUNTER 0-6-0

Built: 1939–42 by London Midland and Scottish Railway, Derby.
Engine: English Electric 6KT of 261 kW (350 hp) at 680 rpm.
Transmission: Electric.
Maximum Speed: 20 mph.

MS This locomotive may have been scrapped
UM Scrapping details unconfirmed, but may be correct

Latest Number Carried	Previous Number 1	Year Entered Service	Year Withdrawn	Current Status/Scrapping Details	Notes
12003	7080	1939	1967	1968: Slag Reduction, Ickles	
12004	7081	1939	1967	1968: J Cashmore, Great Bridge	
12005	7082	1939	1967	1968: C F Booth, Rotherham	
12006	7083	1939	1967	1968: Slag Reduction, Ickles	
12007	7084	1939	1967	1968: Slag Reduction, Ickles	
12008	7085	1939	1967	1968: C F Booth, Rotherham	
12009	7086	1939	1967	1968: Slag Reduction, Ickles	
12010	7087	1939	1967	1968: Slag Reduction, Ickles	
12011	7088	1939	1966	1966: Derby Works	UM
12012	7089	1939	1967	1968: Bolton Depot	
12013	7090	1940	1967	1968: Slag Reduction, Ickles	
12014	7091	1940	1967	1968: Slag Reduction, Ickles	
12015	7092	1940	1967	1968: Slag Reduction, Ickles	
12016	7093	1940	1967	1968: Slag Reduction, Ickles	
12017	7094	1940	1967	1968: Slag Reduction, Ickles	
12018	7095	1940	1967	1968: Slag Reduction, Ickles	
12019	7096	1940	1967	1968: Slag Reduction, Ickles	
12020	7097	1940	1967	1968: Slag Reduction, Ickles	
12021	7098	1940	1967	1968: Slag Reduction, Ickles	
12022	7099	1940	1966	1967: J Cashmore, Great Bridge	
7100		1940	1942	Exported to Egypt c1945	MS
7101		1941	1942	Exported to Egypt in 1942	MS
7102		1941	1942	Exported to Egypt in 1943	MS
7103		1941	1942	Exported to Italy in 1943	a)
7104		1941	1942	Exported to Egypt in 1943	MS
7105		1941	1942	1990: Scrivia Works, Italy	UM
7106		1941	1942	Exported to North Africa in 1943	b)
7107		1941	1942	Exported to Egypt in 1943	MS
7108		1941	1942	Exported to Egypt in 1943	
7109		1941	1942	1985: Scrivia Works, Italy	UM
12023	7110	1942	1967	1968: Bolton Depot	
12024	7111	1942	1967	1968: J Cashmore, Great Bridge	
12025	7112	1942	1967	1968: Slag Reduction, Ickles	
12026	7113	1942	1967	1968: Slag Reduction, Ickles	
12027	7114	1942	1967	1968: Slag Reduction, Ickles	
12028	7115	1942	1967	1968: C F Booth, Rotherham	
12029	7116	1942	1966	1966: Derby Works	UM

12030	7117	1942	1964	1964: Derby Works	UM
12031	7118	1942	1967	1968: J Cashmore, Great Bridge	
12032	7119	1942	1967	1968: J Cashmore, Great Bridge	

a) 7103 is now on static display in Italy
b) 7106 was transferred to Italy in 1944

CLASS D3/9 LNER SHUNTER   0-6-0

Built: 1944–45 by London and North Eastern Railway, Doncaster Works.
Engine: English Electric 6KT of 261 kW (350 hp).
Transmission: Electric.
Maximum Speed: 20 mph.
Train Brakes: Vacuum.

Latest Number Carried	Previous Number 1	Year Entered Service	Year Withdrawn	Current Status/Scrapping Details	Notes
15000	8000	1944	1967	1968: A King, Norwich	
15001	8001	1944	1967	1967: J Cashmore, Great Bridge	
15002	8002	1944	1967	1968: Bescot Depot	
15003	8003	1945	1967	1968: Slag Reduction, Ickles	

CLASS D3/10 GWR SHUNTER

Built: 1936 by English Electric at Hawthorn Leslie.
Engine: English Electric 6K of 261 kW (350 hp).
Transmission: Electric.
Maximum Speed: 19 mph.
Train Brakes: None.

UL Scrapping details unconfirmed, but likely to be correct

Latest Number Carried	Previous Number 1	Year Entered Service	Year Withdrawn	Current Status/Scrapping Details	Notes
15100	2	1936	1965	1966: G Cohen, Swansea	UL

CLASS D3/11 ENGLISH ELECTRIC SHUNTER 0-6-0

Built: 1948 by British Railways, Swindon Works.
Engine: English Electric 6KT of 260 kW (350 hp).
Transmission: Electric.
Maximum Speed: 20 mph.
Train Brakes: None.

UL Scrapping details unconfirmed, but likely to be correct

Latest Number Carried	Previous Number 1	Year Entered Service	Year Withdrawn	Current Status/Scrapping Details	Notes
15101		1948	1967	1970: G Cohen, Kettering	
15102		1948	1967	1968: Steelbreak & Dism., Chesterf'd	
15103		1948	1967	1968: Steelbreak & Dism., Chesterf'd	
15104		1948	1967	1968: Steelbreak & Dism., Chesterf'd	
15105		1948	1967	1970: G Cohen, Kettering	
15106		1948	1967	1969: G Cohen, Kettering	UL

CLASS D3/12 SR SHUNTER   0-6-0

Built: 1937 by Southern Railway, Ashford Works.
Engine: English Electric 6K of 260 kW (350 hp).
Transmission: Electric.
Maximum Speed: 30 mph.
Train Brakes: None.

Latest Number Carried	Previous Number 1	Year Entered Service	Year Withdrawn	Current Status/Scrapping Details	Notes
15201	1	1937	1964	1969: G Cohen, Morriston	
15202	2	1937	1964	1966: J Cashmore, Newport	
15203	3	1937	1964	1966: J Cashmore, Newport	

CLASS D3/14 LNER/BRUSH SHUNTER   0-6-0

Built: 1949 by London and North Eastern Railway, Doncaster Works.
Engine: Brush Petter SS of 270 kW (360 hp).
Transmission: Electric.
Maximum Speed: 22 mph.
Train Brakes: Vacuum.

UL   Scrapping details unconfirmed, but likely to be correct

Latest Number Carried	Previous Number 1	Year Entered Service	Year Withdrawn	Current Status/Scrapping Details	Notes
15004		1949	1962	1963: Doncaster Works	UL

▲ After a brief eight-year career with BR, Class 02 D2862 was sold to the National Coal Board which put it to work at Norton Colliery in Staffordshire, where it is seen on 26 June 1976. The colliery closed in 1977 and the 0-4-0 shunter was cut up on site in 1979. **Roy Burt / The Gordon Edgar Collection**

2.4. DIESEL LOCOMOTIVES WITH TOPS CLASSIFICATION

CLASS 01   0-4-0

Built: 1956/58 by Andrew Barclay, Kilmarnock.
Engine: Gardner 6L3 of 114 kW (153 hp) at 1200 rpm.
Transmission: Mechanical.
Maximum Speed: 14 mph.
Train Brakes: None.

Latest Number Carried	Previous Number 1	Previous Number 2	Year Entered Service	Year Withdrawn	Current Status/Scrapping Details	Notes
D2953	11503		1956	1966	Preserved	
01001	D2954	11504	1956	1979	1982: Holyhead Breakwater	
01002	D2955	11505	1956	1981	1982: Holyhead Breakwater	
D2956[1]	11506		1956	1966	Preserved	a)
D2956[2]	81		1958	1967	1969: British Steel, Briton Ferry	b)

a) First of 2 locomotives to be numbered D2956
b) Second of 2 locomotives to be numbered D2956. Numbered D2956 in 1967 after the first D2956 was withdrawn.

CLASS 02   0-4-0

Built: 1960/61 by Yorkshire Engine Company, Sheffield.
Engine: Rolls Royce C6NFL of 127 kW (170 hp) at 1800 rpm.
Transmission: Hydraulic.
Maximum Speed: 19.5 mph.
Train Brakes: Vacuum.

UL   Scrapping details unconfirmed, but likely to be correct

Latest Number Carried	Previous Number 1	Year Entered Service	Year Withdrawn	Current Status/Scrapping Details	Notes
D2850		1960	1970	1971: W Heselwood, Attercliffe	UL
02001	D2851	1960	1975	1976: Allerton Depot	
D2852		1960	1973	1976: Allerton Depot	
02003	D2853	1960	1975	Preserved	
D2854		1960	1970	Preserved	
D2855		1960	1970	1971: W Heselwood, Attercliffe	UL
02004	D2856	1960	1975	1986: Redland, Mountsorrel	
D2857		1960	1971	1992: Bird Group, Long Marston	
D2858		1960	1970	Preserved	
D2859		1960	1970	1971: Bird Group, Long Marston	
D2860		1961	1970	Preserved	
D2861		1961	1969	1971: C F Booth, Rotherham	UL
D2862		1961	1969	1979: NCB Norton Colliery	
D2863		1961	1969	1971: T W Ward, Beighton	
D2864		1961	1970	1971: W Heselwood, Sheffield	
D2865		1961	1970	1985: Vic Berry, Leicester	
D2866		1961	1970	Preserved	
D2867		1961	1970	Preserved	
D2868		1961	1969	Preserved	
D2869		1961	1969	1971: T W Ward, Beighton	UL

CLASS 03

0-6-0

Built: 1957–62 by British Railways, Doncaster & Swindon.
Engine: Gardner 8L3 of 152 kW (204 hp) at 1200 rpm.
Transmission: Mechanical.
Maximum Speed: 28 mph.
Train Brakes: Vacuum. Some were later dual-braked (air & vacuum).

ES   Locomotive exported and subsequently scrapped
UL   Scrapping details unconfirmed, but likely to be correct
UM   Scrapping details unconfirmed, but may be correct

Latest Number Carried	Previous Number 1	Previous Number 2	Previous Number 3	Year Entered Service	Year Withdrawn	Current Status/Scrapping Details	Notes
D2000	11187			1957	1969	1969: Steelbreak & Dism., Chesterf'd	
D2001	11188			1957	1969	1970: C F Booth, Rotherham	
D2002	11189			1957	1969	1969: Ingot Metals, Kentish Town	UL
D2003	11190			1957	1969	1969: Ingot Metals, Kentish Town	UL
03004	D2004	11191		1958	1976	1976: G Cohen, Kettering	
03005	D2005	11192		1958	1976	1977: Doncaster Works	
D2006	11193			1958	1972	1973: Swindon Works	
03007	D2007	11194		1958	1976	1976: G Cohen, Kettering	
03008	D2008	11195		1958	1978	1979: Swindon Works	
03009	D2009	11196		1958	1976	1977: G Cohen, Kettering	
03010	D2010	11197		1958	1974	1986: Lucchini Steel, Servola, Italy	ES UM
D2011	11198			1958	1972	1973: Swindon Works	
03012	D2012	11199		1958	1975	1991: Mayer Parry, Snailwell	
03013	D2013	11200		1958	1976	1977: Doncaster Works	
03014	D2014	11201		1958	1974	1976: Doncaster Works	
D2015	11202			1958	1971	1972: G Cohen, Kettering	
03016	D2016	11203		1958	1978	1979: Swindon Works	
03017	D2017	11204		1958	1982	1982: Swindon Works	
03018	D2018	11205		1958	1975	Preserved	
D2019	11206			1958	1971	Exported to Italy in 1972	a)
03020	D2020	11207		1958	1975	Preserved	
03021	D2021	11208		1958	1982	1983: Swindon Works	
03022	D2022	11209		1958	1982	Preserved	
D2023	11210			1958	1971	Preserved	
D2024	11211			1958	1971	Preserved	
03025	D2025			1958	1977	1978: Swindon Works	
03026	D2026			1958	1983	1984: C F Booth, Rotherham	
03027	D2027			1958	1976	Preserved	
D2028				1958	1969	1972: Doncaster Works	
03029	D2029			1958	1979	1979: Doncaster Works	
D2030				1958	1969	1970: C F Booth, Rotherham	
D2031				1958	1969	1969: Ingot Metals, Kentish Town	UL
D2032				1958	1971	Exported to Italy in 1972	b)
D2033				1958	1971	Exported to Italy in 1972	c)
03034	D2034			1959	1983	1983: C F Booth, Rotherham	
03035	D2035			1959	1976	1977: G Cohen, Kettering	
D2036				1959	1971	Exported to Italy in 1972	d)
03037	D2037			1959	1976	Preserved	
D2038				1959	1972	1972: T W Ward, Beighton	
D2039				1959	1972	1977: T W Ward, Beighton	
D2040				1959	1969	1970: C F Booth, Rotherham	
D2041				1959	1970	Preserved	
D2042				1959	1969	1969: Ingot Metals, Kentish Town	UL
D2043				1959	1971	1973: Shipbreaking, Queenborough	
03044	D2044			1958	1976	1976: G Cohen, Kettering	
03045	D2045			1958	1979	1979: Doncaster Works	
D2046				1958	1971	Preserved	
03047	D2047			1958	1979	1979: Doncaster Works	
D2048				1958	1972	1973: Swindon Works	
D2049				1958	1971	1985: Wath Skip Hire	

03050	D2050	1959	1978	1979: C F Booth, Rotherham	
D2051		1959	1972	Preserved	
D2052		1959	1972	1973: A Draper, Hull	
D2053		1959	1972	1973: A Draper, Hull	
D2054		1959	1972	1982: C F Booth, Rotherham	
03055	D2055	1959	1974	1974: Doncaster Works	
03056	D2056	1959	1980	1981: Doncaster Works	
D2057		1959	1971	1986: C F Booth, Rotherham	
03058	D2058	1959	1975	1977: Doncaster Works	
03059	D2059	1959	1987	Preserved	
03060	D2060	1959	1982	1983: Doncaster Works	
03061	D2061	1959	1980	1982: Swindon Works	
03062	D2062	1959	1980	Preserved	
03063	D2063	1959	1987	Preserved	
03064	D2064	1959	1981	1981: Doncaster Works	
D2065		1959	1972	1973: C F Booth, Rotherham	
03066	D2066	1959	1988	Preserved	
03067	D2067	1959	1981	1982: Doncaster Works	
03068	D2068	1959	1976	1976: G Cohen, Kettering	
03069	D2069	1959	1983	Preserved	
D2070		1959	1971	2001: Cotswold Rail, Quedgeley	
D2071		1959	1972	1973: A Draper, Hull	
03072	D2072	1959	1981	Preserved	
03073	D2073	1959	1989	Preserved	
D2074		1959	1972	1973: A Draper, Hull	
03075	D2075	1959	1976	1979: Doncaster Works	
03076	D2076	1959	1976	1976: G Cohen, Kettering	
D2077		1959	1972	1973: Swindon Works	
03078	D2078	1959	1988	Preserved	
03079	D2079	1960	1996	Preserved	
03080	D2080	1960	1980	1981: Swindon Works	
03081	D2081	1960	1980	Preserved	
D2082		1959	1969	1971: Doncaster Works	
D2083		1959	1969	1969: Pollock & Brown, Southampton	UM
03084	D2084	1959	1987	Preserved	
D2085		1959	1969	1972: Doncaster Works	
03086	D2086	1959	1983	1984: Doncaster Works	
D2087		1959	1971	1973: Pounds Ltd, Fratton	
D2088		1959	1972	1973: C F Booth, Rotherham	
03089	D2089	1960	1987	Preserved	
03090	D2090	1960	1976	Preserved	
03091	D2091	1960	1974	1977: Doncaster Works	
03092	D2092	1960	1977	1978: Doncaster Works	
D2093		1960	1971	1986: C F Booth, Rotherham	
03094	D2094	1960	1988	Preserved	
03095	D2095	1960	1975	1976: G Cohen, Kettering	
03096	D2096	1960	1976	1977: Doncaster Works	
03097	D2097	1960	1976	1979: Doncaster Works	
03098	D2098	1960	1975	Unknown: Scrapped in Italy	e)
03099	D2099	1960	1976	Preserved	
D2100		1960	1971	1972: G Cohen, Kettering	
D2101		1960	1971	1972: T W Ward, Beighton	UM
03102	D2102	1960	1976	1976: G Cohen, Kettering	
03103	D2103	1960	1979	1979: Doncaster Works	
03104	D2104	1960	1975	1976: Doncaster Works	
03105	D2105	1960	1976	1976: G Cohen, Kettering	
03106	D2106	1960	1975	1976: W Heselwood, Sheffield	
03107	D2107	1960	1981	1982: Doncaster Works	
03108	D2108	1960	1976	1977: Doncaster Works	
03109	D2109	1960	1975	1976: Doncaster Works	
03110	D2110	1960	1976	1976: G Cohen, Kettering	
03111	D2111	1960	1980	1981: Swindon Works	
03112	D2112	1960	1987	Preserved	
03113	D2113	1960	1975	Preserved	

D2114				1959	1968	1975: Bird Group, Long Marston	
D2115				1959	1968	1968: G Cohen, Kingsbury	UM
D2116				1959	1971	1973: Marple & Gillot, Attercliffe	
D2117				1959	1971	Preserved	
03118	D2118			1959	1972	Preserved	
03119	D2119			1959	1986	Preserved	
03120	D2120			1959	1986	Preserved	
03121	D2121			1959	1981	1985: Swindon Works	
D2122				1959	1972	1975: J Cashmore, Newport	UL
D2123				1959	1968	1978: Bird Group, Bristol	
D2124				1959	1970	1970: Slag Reduction, Barrow-in-Fur	
D2125				1959	1968	1976: Bird Group, Cardiff	
D2126				1959	1971	1973: Shipbreaking, Queenborough	
D2127				1959	1968	1968: G Cohen, Kingsbury	UL
03901	03128	03901	D2128	1960	1976	Preserved	
03129	D2129			1960	1981	1983: C F Booth, Rotherham	
D2130				1960	1972	1973: C F Booth, Rotherham	
D2131				1960	1968	1968: G Cohen, Kettering	
D2132				1960	1969	1984: C F Booth, Rotherham	
D2133				1960	1969	Preserved	
03134	D2134			1960	1976	Preserved	
03135	D2135			1960	1976	1976: Shipbreaking, Queenborough	
D2136				1960	1972	1972: Robinson & Hannon, Blaydon	UM
03137	D2137			1960	1976	1977: Doncaster Works	
D2138				1960	1969	Preserved	
D2139				1960	1968	Preserved	
D2140				1960	1970	1972: Swindon Works	
03141	D2141			1960	1985		
03142	D2142			1960	1983	1985: Swindon Works	
D2143				1961	1968	1968: J Cashmore, Newport	
03144	D2144			1961	1986	Preserved	
03145	D2145			1961	1985	Preserved	
D2146				1961	1968	1978: Bird Group, Long Marston	
03147	D2147			1960	1975	1976: C F Booth, Doncaster	
D2148				1960	1972	Preserved	
03149	D2149			1960	1982	1983: Doncaster Works	
D2150				1960	1972	2001: Allelys, Studley	
03151	D2151			1960	1985	1985: C F Booth, Rotherham	
03152	D2152			1960	1983	Preserved	
03153	D2153			1960	1975	1986: Scrapped in Italy	ES UM
03154	D2154			1960	1983	1983: Doncaster Works	
03155	D2155			1960	1975	1976: Doncaster Works	
03156	D2156			1960	1975	Exported to Italy in 1976	f)
03157	D2157			1960	1975	1997: Chiari Steelworks, Italy	ES
03158	D2158			1960	1987	Preserved	
03159	D2159			1960	1977	1978: Swindon Works	
03160	D2160			1960	1981	1983: C F Booth, Rotherham	
03161	D2161			1960	1981	1983: C F Booth, Rotherham	
03162	D2162			1960	1989	Preserved	
03163	D2163			1960	1976	1976: G Cohen, Kettering	
03164	D2164			1960	1976	1997: Chiari Steelworks, Italy	ES
03165	D2165			1960	1975	1976: C F Booth, Doncaster	
03166	D2166			1960	1975	1976: C F Booth, Rotherham	
03167	D2167			1960	1975	1976: Doncaster Works	
03168	D2168			1960	1981	1982: Doncaster Works	
03169	D2169			1960	1975	1976: Hull Botanic Gardens Depot	UL
03170	D2170			1960	1989	Preserved	
03171	D2171			1960	1977	1978: G Cohen, Kettering	
03172	D2172			1960	1976	1977: G Cohen, Kettering	
D2173				1960	1973	1977: Doncaster Works	
03174	D2174			1960	1975	1976: C F Booth, Rotherham	
03175	D2175			1961	1983	1983: Doncaster Works	
D2176				1961	1968	1971: G Cohen, Kettering	
D2177				1961	1968	1970: Bird Group, Long Marston	

D2178			1962	1969	Preserved	
03179	D2179		1962		Preserved	
03180	D2180		1962	1984	Preserved	
D2181			1962	1968	1987: Marple & Gillot, Attercliffe	
D2182			1962	1968	Preserved	
D2183			1962	1968	1972: T W Ward, Beighton	UL
D2184			1962	1968	Preserved	
D2185			1962	1968	1977: Bird Group, Cardiff	UM
D2186			1962	1969	1981: A R Adams, Newport	
D2187			1961	1968	1978: Bird Group, Long Marston	
D2188			1961	1968	1978: Bird Group, Long Marston	
03189	D2189		1961	1986	Preserved	
D2190			1961	1968	1970: Bird Group, Long Marston	
D2191			1961	1968	1968: G Cohen, Kingsbury	UL
D2192			1961	1969	Preserved	
D2193			1961	1969	1981: A R Adams, Newport	
D2194			1961	1968	1978: Bird Group, Long Marston	
D2195			1961	1968	1981: Duport Steel, Llanelli	
03196	D2196		1961		West Coast Railway Co	
03197	D2197		1961	1987	Preserved	
D2198			1961	1970	1972: Doncaster Works	
D2199			1961	1972	Preserved	
03370	D2370	91	1958	1982	1983: Doncaster Works	
03371	D2371	92	1958	1987	Preserved	
D2372			1961	1970	1971: G Cohen, Kettering	
D2373			1961	1968	1982: NCB Manvers Main Colliery	
D2374			1961	1968	1968: G Cohen, Kettering	
D2375			1961	1968	1968: G Cohen, Kettering	
D2376			1961	1968	1968: G Cohen, Kettering	
D2377			1961	1968	1969: Swindon Works	UL
D2378			1961	1971	1972: Swindon Works	
D2379			1961	1968	1969: Swindon Works	UL
D2380			1961	1968	1968: G Cohen, Kettering	
D2381			1961		West Coast Railway Co	
03382	D2382		1961	1983	1986: Swindon Works	
D2383			1961	1971	1972: T W Ward, Beighton	UL
D2384			1961	1968	1968: G Cohen, Kettering	
D2385			1961	1970	1970: C F Booth, Rotherham	
03386	D2386		1961	1976	1976: G Cohen, Kettering	
D2387			1961	1972	1973: C F Booth, Rotherham	
D2388			1961	1972	1973: C F Booth, Rotherham	
03389	D2389		1961	1983	1983: C F Booth, Rotherham	
D2390			1961	1968	1968: G Cohen, Kettering	
D2391			1961	1970	1971: G Cohen, Kettering	
D2392			1961	1971	1972: C F Booth, Rotherham	UM
D2393			1961	1969	1971: C F Booth, Rotherham	UM
D2394			1961	1968	1969: C F Booth, Rotherham	
D2395			1961	1968	1968: G Cohen, Kettering	
D2396			1961	1968	1968: G Cohen, Kettering	
03397	D2397		1961	1987	1991: Vic Berry, Leicester	
D2398			1961	1971	1972: Fratton Depot	
03399	D2399		1961	1987	Preserved	

a) D2019 was extant in 2002 and current status is unknown
b) D2032 was extant in 2002 and current status is unknown
c) D2033 was extant in 2004 and current status is unknown
d) D2036 was extant in 2003 and current status is unknown
e) 03098 is thought to have been exported to Italy and scrapped there, but not confirmed.
f) 03156 is now on static display in Italy

▲ 03079 had a lengthy spell on the Isle of Wight between 1984 and 1998. Its cut down cab allowed it to operate through Ryde Tunnel and it was predominantly employed on engineering duties. The locomotive is seen ticking over at Ryde St. Johns on 9 July 1985 and it is now preserved at the Derwent Valley Light Railway in Yorkshire. **Gordon Edgar**

▼ Class 04 D2272 worked for BR from 1958 until 1970, when it was sold into industrial service. It then spent many years working at Blackburn Coal Concentration Depot, where it is seen on 3 September 1988. **Gordon Edgar**

CLASS 04   0-6-0

Built: 1948–62 to Drewry design at Vulcan Foundry, Newton-le-Willows and Robert Stephenson & Hawthorns, Darlington.
Engine: Gardner 8L3 of 152 kW (204 hp) at 1200 rpm.
Transmission: Mechanical.
Maximum Speed: D2200–14/D2341 25 mph; D2215–73/D2296–2340 25.8 mph; D2274–95 27.5 mph.
Train Brakes: Vacuum.

ES   Locomotive exported and subsequently scrapped
UL   Scrapping details unconfirmed, but likely to be correct
UM   Scrapping details unconfirmed, but may be correct

Latest Number Carried	Previous Number 1	Year Entered Service	Year Withdrawn	Current Status/Scrapping Details	Notes
D2200	11100	1952	1968	1968: Barnsley Coking Company	
D2201	11101	1952	1968	1968: Barnsley Coking Company	
D2202	11102	1952	1968	1968: G Cohen, Kettering	
D2203	11103	1952	1967	Preserved	
D2204	11105	1953	1969	1979: Duport Steel, Briton Ferry	
D2205	11106	1953	1969	Preserved	
D2206	11107	1953	1969	1969: Hughes Bolckow, Blyth	UM
D2207	11108	1953	1967	Preserved	
D2208	11109	1953	1968	1979: NCB Silverwood Colliery	
D2209	11110	1953	1968	1985: NCB Kiveton Park Colliery	
D2210	11111	1954	1970	1971: A King, Norwich	
D2211	11112	1954	1970	1980: Rees Industries, Llanelli	
D2212	11113	1954	1970	1972: Norwich Depot	UL
D2213	11114	1954	1968	1978: NCB Manvers Main Colliery	
D2214	11115	1954	1968	1969: C F Booth, Rotherham	
D2215	11121	1955	1969	1970: Bird Group, Long Marston	
D2216	11122	1955	1971	2003: Scrapped in Italy	ES
D2217	11123	1955	1972	1973: C F Booth, Rotherham	
D2218	11124	1955	1968	1970: Steelbreak & Dism., Chesterf'd	
D2219	11125	1955	1968	1977: Barnsley Coking Company	
D2220	11126	1955	1968	1968: G Cohen, Kettering	
D2221	11127	1955	1968	1969: C F Booth, Rotherham	
D2222	11128	1955	1968	1969: C F Booth, Rotherham	
D2223	11129	1955	1971	1971: G Cohen, Kettering	
D2224	11130	1955	1968	1969: A Draper, Hull	
D2225	11131	1955	1969	1985: NCB Wath Colliery	
D2226	11132	1955	1968	1969: A Draper, Hull	
D2227	11133	1955	1968	1969: A Draper, Hull	
D2228	11134	1955	1968	1979: Bowater's Paper, Sittingbourne	
D2229	11135	1955	1969	Preserved	
D2230	11149	1956	1968	1969: Steelbreak & Dism., Chesterf'd	
D2231	11150	1956	1969	1970: Steelbreak & Dism., Chesterf'd	
D2232	11151	1956	1968	1997: Scrapped in Italy	ES UM
D2233	11152	1956	1968	1969: Steelbreak & Dism., Chesterf'd	
D2234	11153	1956	1968	1969: A Draper, Hull	
D2235	11154	1956	1968	1968: Barnsley Coking Company	
D2236	11155	1956	1968	1968: G Cohen, Kettering	
D2237	11156	1956	1969	1970: Hughes Bolckow, Blyth	
D2238	11157	1956	1968	1982: NCB Manvers Main Colliery	
D2239	11158	1956	1971	1986: C F Booth, Rotherham	
D2240	11159	1956	1968	1970: A King, Norwich	
D2241	11160	1956	1971	1976: G Cohen, Kettering	
D2242	11212	1956	1969	1971: C F Booth, Rotherham	
D2243	11213	1956	1969	1973: Middlesbrough/Hartlepool DA	
D2244	11214	1956	1970	1981: A R Adams, Newport	
D2245	11215	1956	1968	Preserved	
D2246	11216	1956	1968	Preserved	
D2247	11217	1956	1969	1979: Duport Steel, Briton Ferry	

D2248	11218	1957	1970	1987: Carol & Good, Rotherham	
D2249	11219	1957	1970	1972: Shipbreaking, Queenborough	
D2250	11220	1957	1968	1969: Pounds Ltd, Fratton	
D2251	11221	1957	1968	1969: Pollock & Brown, Southampton	UL
D2252	11222	1957	1968	1969: Pollock & Brown, Southampton	UL
D2253	11223	1957	1969	1970: G Cohen, Kettering	
D2254	11224	1957	1967	1967: Selhurst Depot	UL
D2255	11225	1957	1968	1968: Pollock & Brown, Southampton	
D2256	11226	1957	1968	1969: Pollock & Brown, Southampton	UL
D2257	11227	1957	1968	1968: Pollock & Brown, Southampton	
D2258	11228	1957	1970	1986: C F Booth, Rotherham	
D2259	11229	1957	1968	1978: Bowater's Paper, Sittingbourne	
D2260		1957	1970	1983: P D Fuels, Coed Bach	
D2261		1957	1970	1970: C F Booth, Rotherham	UL
D2262		1957	1968	1978: Ford Motors, Dagenham	
D2263		1957	1967	1969: Pollock & Brown, Southampton	
D2264		1957	1969	1970: C F Booth, Rotherham	
D2265		1957	1970	1970: C F Booth, Rotherham	UL
D2266		1958	1967	1968: C F Booth, Rotherham	UL
D2267		1958	1969	2003: Mid Norfolk Railway	
D2268		1958	1968	1968: T W Ward, Beighton	UL
D2269		1958	1968	1969: Pounds Ltd, Fratton	
D2270		1958	1968	1979: Duport Steel, Briton Ferry	
D2271		1958	1969	Preserved	
D2272		1958	1970	Preserved	
D2273		1958	1967	1968: C F Booth, Rotherham	
D2274		1959	1969	1980: NCB Maltby Main Colliery	
D2275		1959	1967	1968: Swindon Works	
D2276		1959	1969	1977: A R Adams, Newport	
D2277		1959	1969	1970: H Brahams, Bury St Edmonds	UL
D2278		1959	1970	1971: Stratford Depot	UL
D2279		1960	1971	Preserved	
D2280		1960	1971	Preserved	
D2281		1960	1968	1971: Duport Steel, Briton Ferry	
D2282		1960	1970	1972: Shipbreaking, Queenborough	
D2283		1960	1969	1970: Stratford Depot	UL
D2284		1960	1971	Preserved	
D2285		1960	1969	1970: H Brahams, Bury St Edmonds	UL
D2286		1960	1968	1969: Pounds Ltd, Fratton	
D2287		1960	1968	1969: Pounds Ltd, Fratton	
D2288		1960	1967	1968: Pollock & Brown, Southampton	
D2289		1960	1971	Preserved	a)
D2290		1960	1967	1968: Pollock & Brown, Southampton	
D2291		1960	1967	1968: Pollock & Brown, Southampton	
D2292		1960	1967	1968: Pollock & Brown, Southampton	
D2293		1960	1971	1972: Shipbreaking, Queenborough	
D2294		1960	1971	1985: Shipbreaking, Queenborough	
D2295		1960	1971	1982: Scrapped in Italy	ES UM
D2296		1960	1969	1970: H Brahams, Bury St Edmonds	UL
D2297		1960	1970	1970: H Brahams, Bury St Edmonds	UL
D2298		1960	1968	Preserved	
D2299		1960	1970	1984: C F Booth, Rotherham	
D2300		1960	1969	1985: NCB Manton Colliery	
D2301		1960	1968	1970: Steelbreak & Dism., Chesterf'd	
D2302		1960	1969	Preserved	
D2303		1960	1967	1969: Doncaster Works	
D2304		1960	1968	1977: Duport Steel, Llanelli	
D2305		1960	1968	1981: Duport Steel, Llanelli	
D2306		1960	1968	1981: Duport Steel, Llanelli	
D2307		1960	1968	1979: Duport Steel, Llanelli	
D2308		1960	1968	1980: Duport Steel, Llanelli	
D2309		1960	1968	1969: C F Booth, Rotherham	UL
04110	D2310	1960	1969	Preserved	b)
D2311		1960	1968	1968: Slag Reduction, Ickles	

D2312		1961	1968	1968: Slag Reduction, Ickles	UM
D2313		1961	1968	1968: Slag Reduction, Ickles	
D2314		1961	1968	1968: Slag Reduction, Ickles	
D2315		1961	1968	1968: Hughes Bolckow, Blyth	
D2316		1961	1968	1968: C F Booth, Rotherham	
D2317		1961	1969	1986: NCB Cortonwood Colliery	
D2318		1961	1968	1968: Hughes Bolckow, Blyth	UM
D2319		1961	1968	1968: Arnott Young, Dinsdale	
D2320		1961	1968	1969: C F Booth, Rotherham	UM
D2321		1961	1968	1968: G Cohen, Middlesbrough	
D2322		1961	1968	1985: NCB Kiveton Park Colliery	
D2323		1961	1968	1969: C F Booth, Rotherham	UL
D2324		1961	1968	Preserved	
D2325		1961	1968	Preserved	
D2326		1961	1968	1975: NCB Manvers Main Colliery	
D2327		1961	1968	1984: Coopers Metals, Sheffield	
D2328		1961	1968	1986: NCB Cortonwood Colliery	
D2329		1961	1968	1970: Layerthorpe Station, York	
D2330		1961	1969	1970: M Turnbull Ltd, Thornaby	UL
D2331		1961	1968	1968: T W Ward, Beighton	UL
D2332		1961	1969	1986: NCB Dinnington Colliery	
D2333		1961	1969	1990: Ford Motors, Dagenham	
D2334		1961	1968	Preserved	
D2335		1961	1968	1980: NCB Maltby Main Colliery	
D2336		1961	1968	1978: NCB Manvers Main Colliery	
D2337		1961	1968	Preserved	
D2338		1961	1968	1968: T W Ward, Beighton	UM
D2339		1961	1967	1968: Hughes Bolckow, Blyth	UM
D2340		1962	1968	1979: Duport Steel, Briton Ferry	
D2341	DS1173	1948	1968	1969: Pollock & Brown, Southampton	UL

a) D2289 was repatriated from Italy in 2018
b) The number 04110 has only been carried in preservation

▲ Class 05 D2554 was transferred to the Isle of Wight in 1966, where it was assigned departmental duties until its withdrawal in 1983. It was preserved at the Isle of Wight Steam Railway the following year and is seen at the heritage railway's Havenstreet base on 16 November 2010. **Gordon Edgar**

CLASS 05   0-6-0

Built: 1955–61 by Hunslet Engine Company, Leeds.
Engine: Gardner 8L3 of 152 kW (204 hp) at 1200 rpm.
Transmission: Mechanical.
Maximum Speed: 18 mph.
Train Brakes: Vacuum.

UL   Scrapping details unconfirmed, but likely to be correct
UM   Scrapping details unconfirmed, but may be correct

Latest Number Carried	Previous Number 1	Previous Number 2	Previous Number 3	Previous Number 4	Year Entered Service	Year Withdrawn	Current Status/Scrapping Details	Notes
D2550	11136				1955	1966	1966: Doncaster Works	UL
D2551	11137				1955	1968	1968: Hughes Bolckow, Blyth	
D2552	11138				1956	1967	1968: C F Booth, Rotherham	
D2553	11139				1956	1968	1968: C F Booth, Rotherham	
D2554	97803	05001	D2554	11140	1956	1983	Preserved	
D2555	11141				1956	1968	1968: C F Booth, Rotherham	
D2556	11142				1956	1967	1968: G Campbell, Airdrie	
D2557	11143				1956	1967	1968: C F Booth, Rotherham	
D2558	11161				1956	1967	1968: C F Booth, Rotherham	
D2559	11162				1956	1967	1968: G Campbell, Airdrie	
D2560	11163				1957	1967	1968: Slag Reduction, Ickles	UL
D2561	11164				1957	1967	1972: Duport Steel, Llanelli	
D2562	11165				1957	1968	1968: Slag Reduction, Ickles	
D2563	11166				1957	1967	1968: C F Booth, Rotherham	
D2564	11167				1957	1967	1968: C F Booth, Rotherham	
D2565	11168				1957	1967	1968: C F Booth, Rotherham	
D2566	11169				1957	1968	1968: C F Booth, Rotherham	
D2567	11170				1957	1967	1968: Slag Reduction, Ickles	
D2568	11171				1957	1967	1969: Duport Steel, Briton Ferry	
D2569	11172				1957	1967	1970: Duport Steel, Briton Ferry	
D2570	11173				1957	1967	1971: Duport Steel, Briton Ferry	
D2571	11174				1957	1968	1968: G H Campbell, Airdrie	UM
D2572	11175				1957	1967	1967: Slag Reduction, Ickles	
D2573	11176				1958	1968	1969: J McWilliam, Shettleston	UL
D2574					1958	1968	1969: G Campbell, Airdrie	
D2575					1958	1968	1969: G Campbell, Airdrie	
D2576					1958	1968	1968: Machine & Scrap, Motherwell	UL
D2577					1958	1967	1967: Machine & Scrap, Motherwell	UL
D2578					1958	1967	Preserved	
D2579					1958	1968	1969: G H Campbell, Airdrie	UL
D2580					1958	1968	1969: G Campbell, Airdrie	
D2581					1958	1968	1969: G Campbell, Airdrie	
D2582					1959	1968	1969: G H Campbell, Airdrie	UL
D2583					1959	1968	1969: G H Campbell, Airdrie	UL
D2584					1959	1967	1968: Hunslet Engine Co., Leeds	
D2585					1959	1968	1969: G H Campbell, Airdrie	UL
D2586					1959	1967	1967: Slag Reduction, Ickles	
D2587					1959	1967	Preserved	
D2588					1959	1967	1967: Slag Reduction, Ickles	
D2589					1959	1967	1968: G Campbell, Airdrie	
D2590					1959	1968	1969: G Campbell, Airdrie	
D2591					1959	1967	1969: Slag Reduction, Ickles	
D2592					1959	1968	1969: G H Campbell, Airdrie	UL
D2593					1959	1967	1968: Hunslet Engine Co., Leeds	UM
D2594					1960	1967	1967: Slag Reduction, Ickles	
D2595					1960	1968	Preserved	
D2596					1960	1968	1969: G Campbell, Airdrie	
D2597					1960	1967	1969: G Campbell, Airdrie	
D2598					1960	1967	1975: NCB Philadelphia Colliery	
D2599					1960	1967	1981: NCB Askern Colliery	
D2600					1960	1967	1971: Duport Steel, Briton Ferry	

D2601				1960	1967	1979: Duport Steel, Llanelli	
D2602				1960	1967	1968: Slag Reduction, Ickles	UL
D2603				1960	1967	1968: C F Booth, Rotherham	
D2604				1960	1967	1968: G Cohen, Morriston	
D2605				1960	1967	1968: G Cohen, Morriston	
D2606				1960	1967	1967: Slag Reduction, Ickles	
D2607				1960	1967	1984: Coopers Metals, Sheffield	
D2608				1960	1967	1969: G Campbell, Airdrie	
D2609				1960	1967	1968: C F Booth, Rotherham	
D2610				1960	1967	1968: C F Booth, Rotherham	
D2611				1961	1967	1976: NCB Yorkshire Main Colliery	
88	D2612			1961	1967	1967: Argosy Salvage, Shettleston	UL
D2613				1961	1967	1977: NCB Bentley Colliery	
D2614				1961	1967	1967: A Draper, Hull	
89	D2615			1961	1967	1968: C F Booth, Rotherham	
D2616				1961	1967	1973: NCB Hatfield Main Colliery	
D2617				1961	1967	1976: Hunslet Engine Co., Leeds	UM
D2618				1961	1968	1969: G Campbell, Airdrie	

CLASS 06   0-4-0

Built: 1958–60 by Andrew Barclay, Kilmarnock.
Engine: Gardner 8L3 of 152 kW (204 hp) at 1200 rpm.
Transmission: Mechanical.
Maximum Speed: 22.75 mph.
Train Brakes: Vacuum.

ES   Locomotive exported and subsequently scrapped
UL   Scrapping details unconfirmed, but likely to be correct
UM   Scrapping details unconfirmed, but may be correct

Latest Number Carried	Previous Number 1	Previous Number 2	Previous Number 3	Year Entered Service	Year Withdrawn	Current Status/Scrapping Details	Notes
D2410				1958	1969	1969: G H Campbell, Airdrie	UL
D2411				1958	1968	1969: G H Campbell, Airdrie	UL
D2412				1958	1968	1969: G H Campbell, Airdrie	UL
06001	D2413			1958	1976	1978: G Campbell, Airdrie	
06002	D2414			1958	1981	1982: Swindon Works	
D2415				1958	1968	1969: G Campbell, Airdrie	
D2416				1958	1972	1973: Glasgow Works	
D2417				1958	1968	1969: G Campbell, Airdrie	
D2418				1959	1968	1969: G H Campbell, Airdrie	UL
D2419				1959	1969	1969: G H Campbell, Airdrie	UL
06003	97804	06003	D2420	1959	1984	Preserved	
06004	D2421			1959	1979	1980: Glasgow Works	
06005	D2422			1959	1980	1983: Dundee Depot	
06006	D2423			1959	1980	1983: Dundee Depot	
D2424				1959	1972	1974: Glasgow Works	
D2425				1959	1968	1968: G Campbell, Airdrie	
06007	D2426			1959	1977	1978: Glasgow Works	
D2427				1959	1969	1971: J McWilliam, Shettleston	UL
D2428				1959	1968	1968: G H Campbell, Airdrie	
D2429				1960	1969	1971: J McWilliam, Shettleston	UL
D2430				1960	1968	1969: G H Campbell, Airdrie	UL
D2431				1960	1971	1972: Glasgow Works	
D2432				1960	1968	1986: Lucchini Steel, Servola, Italy	ES UM
D2433				1960	1972	1973: Glasgow Works	
D2434				1960	1969	1971: J McWilliam, Shettleston	UL
D2435				1960	1971	1974: G H Campbell, Airdrie	UM
D2436				1960	1971	1973: Glasgow Works	
06008	D2437			1960	1980	1983: Polmadie Depot	
D2438				1960	1972	1974: G H Campbell, Airdrie	UM
D2439				1960	1971	1972: Glasgow Works	

▲ Class 06 D2436 was only seven years old when this photograph was taken at Ayr depot in August 1967, yet it would be withdrawn in 1971 and scrapped in 1973. Just one member of the 35-strong class survives and this can be found at Peak Rail in Derbyshire.

Charlie Cross / The Gordon Edgar Collection

▼ Class 07s 2996 & 2987 are stabled for the weekend at Southampton Western Docks on 12 July 1970. Both remained in service for BR until 1977, after which they were sold to the National Coal Board and British Industrial Sand respectively. 2987 was later scrapped on-site, however, 2996 survives and is now on display at Barrow Hill Roundhouse. **Gordon Edgar**

06009	D2440	1960	1975	1978: G Campbell, Airdrie	
D2441		1960	1967	1967: Slag Reduction, Ickles	
D2442		1960	1972	1974: G H Campbell, Airdrie	UM
D2443		1960	1972	1973: Glasgow Works	
06010	D2444	1960	1975	1979: Glasgow Works	

CLASS 07   0-6-0

Built: 1962 by Ruston & Hornsby, Lincoln.
Engine: Paxman 6RPHL of 205 kW (275 hp) at 1360 rpm.
Transmission: Electric.
Maximum Speed: 20 mph.
Train Brakes: Vacuum. Some were later dual-braked (air & vacuum).

ES   Locomotive exported and subsequently scrapped
UM   Scrapping details unconfirmed, but may be correct

Latest Number Carried	Previous Number 1	Year Entered Service	Year Withdrawn	Current Status/Scrapping Details	Notes
07001	D2985	1962	2013	Preserved	
07002	D2986	1962	1977	1986: P D Fuels, Kidwelly	
07003	D2987	1962	1976	1985: British Ind. Sand, Oakmoor	
D2988		1962	1973	1974: M Claydon Ltd, Battersea	a)
07005	D2989	1962	1977	Preserved	
07006	D2990	1962	1977	1984: P D Fuels, Kidwelly	
07007	D2991	1962		Arlington Fleet Services	
D2992		1962	1973	1976: Eastleigh Works	
07009	D2993	1962	1976	1997: Scrapped in Italy	ES UM
07010	D2994	1962	1976	Preserved	
07011	D2995	1962	1977	Preserved	
07012	D2996	1962	1977	Preserved	
07013	D2997	1962	1977	Preserved	
D2998		1962	1973	1976: Eastleigh Works	

a)   Scrapping of D2988 began at Eastleigh Works

▲ On the morning of 12 April 1985, 08389 passes Tinsley South Junction with 9T36, a trip working which involved moving several mineral wagons loaded with scrap metal from Meadowhall to Tinsley Yard.   **53A Models of Hull Collection (Garry Cartwright)**

CLASS 08 0-6-0

Built: 1952–62 by British Railways, Derby, Darlington, Crewe, Horwich & Doncaster.
Engine: English Electric 6KT of 298 kW (400 hp) at 680 rpm.
Transmission: Electric.
Maximum Speed: 15 mph.
Train Brakes: Vacuum; except D3092–D3101 which did not have train brakes. Some were later dual-braked (air & vacuum).

SP Locomotive was not self-propelled whilst in departmental use
UC Scrapping details unconfirmed
UL Scrapping details unconfirmed, but likely to be correct
UM Scrapping details unconfirmed, but may be correct

Class 08/0

Latest Number Carried	Previous Number 1	Previous Number 2	Previous Number 3	Previous Number 4	Year Entered Service	Year Withdrawn	Current Status/Scrapping Details	Notes
D3000	13000				1952	1972	Preserved	
D3001	13001				1952	1972	1975: Doncaster Works	
D3002	13002				1952	1972	Preserved	
D3003	13003				1952	1972	1991: Wanstrow Playground, Som'set	
08001	D3004	13004			1952	1978	1979: Swindon Works	
08002	D3005	13005			1952	1977	1978: Swindon Works	
ADB966507	D3006	13006			1952	1979	1980: Doncaster Works	SP
08003	D3007	13007			1952	1977	1979: Glasgow Works	
08004	D3008	13008			1952	1983	1986: Swindon Works	
08005	D3009	13009			1952	1978	1979: Doncaster Works	
08006	D3010	13010			1952	1980	1980: Swindon Works	
D3011	13011				1952	1972	1985: Marple & Gillot, Attercliffe	
08007	D3012	13012			1952	1973	1973: Swindon Works	
D3013	13013				1952	1972	1973: J Cashmore, Newport	
D3014	13014				1952	1972	Preserved	
08008	D3015	13015			1953	1983	1986: Swindon Works	
08009	D3016	13016			1953	1975	1976: Swindon Works	
08010	D3017	13017			1953	1977	1978: Eastleigh Works	
08011	D3018	13018			1953	1991	Preserved	
08012	D3019	13019			1953	1973	Preserved	
08013	D3020	13020			1953	1973	1975: Derby Works	UM
08014	D3021	13021			1953	1980	1981: C F Booth, Rotherham	
08015	D3022	13022			1953	1980	Preserved	
08016	D3023	13023			1953	1980	Preserved	
08017	D3024	13024			1953	1973	1974: Doncaster Works	
08018	D3025	13025			1953	1983	1985: Swindon Works	
D3026	13026				1953	1972	1973: Swindon Works	
08019	D3027	13027			1953	1983	1986: Swindon Works	
08020	D3028	13028			1953	1973	1975: Doncaster Works	
08021	D3029	13029			1953	1986	Preserved	
08022	D3030	13030			1953	1985	Preserved	
08023	D3031	13031			1953	1983	1987: Swindon Works	
08024	D3032	13032			1953	1982	1983: Doncaster Works	
08025	D3033	13033			1953	1977	1978: Swindon Works	
D3034	13034				1953	1972	1973: Derby Works	UM
ADB966508	D3035	13035			1953	1979	1979: Doncaster Works	SP
08026	D3036	13036			1953	1982	1986: Swindon Works	
ADB966510	D3037	13037			1953	1978	1979: Doncaster Works	SP
D3038	13038				1953	1972	1980: NCB Bates Colliery	
08027	D3039	13039			1953	1980	1982: Swindon Works	
08028	D3040	13040			1954	1981	1982: Swindon Works	
08029	D3041	13041			1954	1978	1978: Swindon Works	
08030	D3042	13042			1954	1982	1984: Swindon Works	
08031	D3043	13043			1954	1982	1988: Immingham Depot	
08032	D3044	13044			1954	1974	Preserved	
D3045	13045				1954	1972	1976: Glasgow Works	

08033	D3046	13046	1954	1985	1986: Swindon Works	
08034	D3047	13047	1954	1973	Exported to Liberia in 1975	
08035	D3048	13048	1954	1979	1980: Swindon Works	
08036	D3049	13049	1954	1981	1983: Swindon Works	
08037	D3050	13050	1954	1980	1980: Swindon Works	
08038	D3051	13051	1954	1973	1973: Derby Works	UM
08039	D3052	13052	1954	1973	1974: J Cashmore, Newport	
08040	D3053	13053	1954	1973	1975: Doncaster Works	
08041	D3054	13054	1954	1978	1979: Swindon Works	
08042	D3055	13055	1954	1979	1979: Doncaster Works	
08043	D3056	13056	1954	1977	1978: Swindon Works	
08044	D3057	13057	1954	1978	1979: Doncaster Works	
08045	D3058	13058	1954	1982	1984: Swindon Works	
08046	D3059	13059	1954	1980	Preserved	
08047	D3060	13060	1953	1979	1980: Swindon Works	
08048	D3061	13061	1953	1977	1978: Doncaster Works	
08049	D3062	13062	1953	1981	1983: Swindon Works	
08050	D3063	13063	1953	1981	1983: Swindon Works	
08051	D3064	13064	1953	1982	1986: Swindon Works	
08052	D3065	13065	1953	1981	1982: March Depot	
08053	D3066	13066	1953	1981	1981: Swindon Works	
08054	D3067	13067	1953	1980	Preserved	
08055	D3068	13068	1953	1980	1983: Swindon Works	
ADB966509	D3069	13069	1953	1979	1980: Thornaby Depot	SP
08056	D3070	13070	1953	1986	1989: Vic Berry, Leicester	
08057	D3071	13071	1953	1976	1977: Doncaster Works	
08058	D3072	13072	1953	1982	1983: Doncaster Works	
08059	D3073	13073	1953	1980	1985: Swindon Works	
08060	D3074	13074	1953	1984	Preserved	
08061	D3075	13075	1953	1984	1985: Doncaster Works	
08062	D3076	13076	1954	1984	1985: Doncaster Works	
08063	D3077	13077	1954	1984	1985: Doncaster Works	
ADB966506	D3078	13078	1954	1978	1979: Doncaster Works	SP
08064	D3079	13079	1954	1984	Preserved	
08065	D3080	13080	1954	1977	1978: Doncaster Works	
08066	D3081	13081	1954	1977	1978: Doncaster Works	
08067	D3082	13082	1954	1983	1986: Swindon Works	
08068	D3083	13083	1954	1983	1986: Swindon Works	
08069	D3084	13084	1954	1983	1984: Doncaster Works	
08070	D3085	13085	1954	1977	1980: Glasgow Works	
08071	D3086	13086	1954	1978	1978: Doncaster Works	
08072	D3087	13087	1954	1973	1983: T W Ward, Birchills PS	
08073	D3088	13088	1954	1973	1985: NCB Bates Colliery	
08074	D3089	13089	1954	1973	1977: Derby Works	
08075	D3090	13090	1954	1981	1982: Swindon Works	
08076	D3091	13091	1954	1980	1982: Swindon Works	
D3092	13092		1954	1972	Exported to Liberia in 1974	
D3093	13093		1954	1972	1972: J Cashmore, Newport	UC
D3094	13094		1954	1972	Exported to Liberia in 1974	
D3095	13095		1954	1972	1973: Swindon Works	
D3096	13096		1954	1972	1972: J Cashmore, Newport	UL
D3097	13097		1955	1972	1973: Swindon Works	
D3098	13098		1955	1972	Exported to Liberia in 1974	
D3099	13099		1955	1972	1980: Shipbreaking, Queenborough	
D3100	13100		1955	1972	Exported to Liberia in 1975	
D3101	13101		1955	1972	Preserved	
08077	D3102	13102	1955	1977	2014: LH Group, Barton-u-Needwood	
08078	D3103	13103	1955	1983	1987: Swindon Works	
08079	D3104	13104	1955	1983	1986: Swindon Works	
08080	D3105	13105	1955	1980	1981: Swindon Works	
08081	D3106	13106	1955	1980	1980: Swindon Works	
08082	D3107	13107	1955	1980	1982: Swindon Works	
08083	D3108	13108	1955	1984	1985: Doncaster Works	
08084	D3109	13109	1955	1980	1982: Swindon Works	

					Built	Wdn	Fate	
08085	D3110	13110			1955	1986	1993: C F Booth, Rotherham	
08086	D3111	13111			1955	1980	1981: Swindon Works	
08087	D3112	13112			1955	1979	1980: Swindon Works	
08088	D3113	13113			1955	1983	1986: Swindon Works	
08089	D3114	13114			1955	1980	1980: Swindon Works	
08090	D3115	13115			1955	1977	1978: Swindon Works	
08091	D3116	13116			1955	1982	1984: Doncaster Works	
08092	D3127	13127			1954	1978	1979: Doncaster Works	
08093	D3128	13128			1954	1981	1982: Swindon Works	
08094	D3129	13129			1954	1983	1985: Doncaster Works	
08095	D3130	13130			1954	1983	1986: Swindon Works	
08096	D3131	13131			1954	1984	1985: Doncaster Works	
08097	D3132	13132			1954	1981	1981: Swindon Works	
08098	D3133	13133			1954	1980	1981: Swindon Works	
08099	D3134	13134			1954	1982	1983: Doncaster Works	
08100	D3135	13135			1954	1982	1985: Doncaster Works	
08101	D3136	13136			1954	1983	1984: Doncaster Works	
08102	D3167	13167			1955	1988	Preserved	
08103	D3168	13168			1955	1983	1986: Swindon Works	
08104	D3169	13169			1955	1982	1984: Doncaster Works	
08105	D3170	13170			1955	1983	1984: Doncaster Works	
08106	D3171	13171			1955	1982	1983: Swindon Works	
D3172	13172				1955	1972	1972: Derby Works	UL
08107	D3173	13173			1955	1982	1984: Doncaster Works	
08108	D3174	13174			1955	1984	Preserved	
08109	D3175	13175			1955	1981	1981: Swindon Works	
08110	D3176	13176			1955	1979	1980: Swindon Works	
ADB968012	ADB966512	08111	D3177	13177	1955	1979	1979: Doncaster Works	SP
08112	D3178	13178			1955	1982	1984: Swindon Works	
08113	D3179	13179			1955	1984	2007: Morley Waste Traders, Leeds	
08114	D3180	13180			1955	1983	Preserved	
08115	D3181	13181			1955	1984	1985: Doncaster Works	
08116	D3182	13182			1955	1982	1983: Doncaster Works	
D3183	13183				1955	1972	1989: NCB Merthyr Vale Colliery	UL
ADB968010	ADB968013	ADB966513	08117		1955	1979	1979: Doncaster Works	
08118	D3185	13185			1955	1980	1980: Swindon Works	
ADB968011	ADB966511	08119	D3186	13186	1955	1979	1980: Doncaster Works	SP
08120	D3187	13187			1955	1981	1982: Swindon Works	
08121	D3188	13188			1955	1984	1985: Swindon Works	
08122	D3189	13189			1955	1977	1977: Doncaster Works	
08123	D3190	13190			1955	1984	Preserved	
08124	D3191	13191			1955	1981	1982: Swindon Works	
08125	D3192	13192			1955	1981	1984: Swindon Works	
D3193	13193				1955	1967	1967: Derby Works	UL
08126	D3194	13194			1955	1980	1981: Swindon Works	
08127	D3195	13195			1955	1980	1980: Swindon Works	
08128	D3196	13196			1955	1980	1984: Swindon Works	
08129	D3197	13197			1955	1983	1984: Doncaster Works	
08130	D3198	13198			1955	1982	1985: Swindon Works	
08131	D3199	13199			1955	1981	1981: Swindon Works	
08132	D3200	13200			1955	1986	1988: Bird Group, Long Marston	
13201	08133	D3201	13201		1955	1980	Preserved	a)
08134	D3202	13202			1955	1981	1986: Swindon Works	
08135	D3203	13203			1955	1977	1977: Swindon Works	
08136	D3204	13204			1955	1983	1984: Doncaster Works	
08137	D3205	13205			1955	1982	1985: Doncaster Works	
08138	D3206	13206			1955	1978	1978: Swindon Works	
08139	D3207	13207			1956	1980	1982: Swindon Works	
08140	D3208	13208			1956	1977	1977: Swindon Works	
08141	D3209	13209			1956	1988	1994: C F Booth, Rotherham	
08142	D3210	13210			1956	1983	1987: Swindon Works	
08143	D3211	13211			1956	1976	1977: Swindon Works	
08144	D3212	13212			1956	1977	1979: Glasgow Works	
08145	D3213	13213			1956	1977	1978: Glasgow Works	

08146	D3214	13214		1956	1980	1981: Swindon Works	
08147	D3215	13215		1956	1983	1984: Doncaster Works	
08148	D3216	13216		1956	1984	1984: Doncaster Works	
08149	D3217	13217		1955	1981	1984: Swindon Works	
08150	D3218	13218		1955	1984	1986: Swindon Works	
08151	D3219	13219		1955	1979	1980: Eastleigh Works	
08152	D3220	13220		1955	1980	1980: Swindon Works	
08153	D3221	13221		1955	1982	1986: Swindon Works	
08154	D3222	13222		1955	1979	1980: Swindon Works	
08155	D3223	13223		1955	1979	1980: Swindon Works	
08156	D3224	13224		1955	1979	1980: Swindon Works	
08157	D3225	13225		1955	1977	1996: EMR, Attercliffe	
08158	D3226	13226		1955	1979	1979: Swindon Works	
08159	D3227	13227		1955	1985	1986: Doncaster Works	
08160	D3228	13228		1955	1985	1986: Doncaster Works	
08161	D3229	13229		1955	1985	1986: Doncaster Works	
08162	D3230	13230		1955	1980	1981: Swindon Works	
08163	D3231	13231		1955	1982	1984: Doncaster Works	
08164	D3232	13232		1956	1986	Preserved	
08165	D3233	13233		1956	1980	1980: Swindon Works	
08166	D3234	13234		1956	1982	1983: Doncaster Works	
08167	D3235	13235		1956	1977	1979: Glasgow Works	
08168	D3236	13236		1956		Nemesis Rail	
08169	D3237	13237		1956	1981	1981: Swindon Works	
08170	D3238	13238		1956	1986	1991: C F Booth, Rotherham	
08171	D3239	13239		1956	1983	1983: Doncaster Works	
08172	D3240	13240		1956	1985	1985: Doncaster Works	
PO1[2]	08173	D3241	13241	1956	1978	1987: Thornton Junction	b)
08174	D3242	13242		1956	1981	1982: Swindon Works	
08175	D3243	13243		1956	1978	1986: J R Adams, Glasgow	

▲ 08921 passes Sutton Bridge Junction, Shrewsbury during July 1985 with a mixed trip working consisting of oil tanks and coal wagons. **Brian Robbins/Rail Photoprints**

08176	D3244	13244	1956	1985	1986: Doncaster Works
08177	D3245	13245	1956	1988	1996: Crewe Works
08178	D3246	13246	1956	1982	1984: Swindon Works
08179	D3247	13247	1956	1975	1976: Swindon Works
08180	D3248	13248	1956	1981	1981: Swindon Works
08181	D3249	13249	1956	1982	1984: Swindon Works
08182	D3250	13250	1956	1981	1982: Swindon Works
08183	D3251	13251	1956	1984	1984: Doncaster Works
08184	D3252	13252	1956	1981	1982: Swindon Works
08185	D3253	13253	1956	1982	1982: Swindon Works
08186	D3254	13254	1956	1985	1986: Swindon Works
D3255	13255		1956	1972	Preserved
08187	D3256	13256	1956	1983	1986: Swindon Works
08188	D3257	13257	1956	1983	1986: Swindon Works
08189	D3258	13258	1956	1981	1984: Swindon Works
08190	D3259	13259	1956	1980	1980: Swindon Works
08191	D3260	13260	1956	1988	1989: Vic Berry, Leicester
D3261	13261		1956	1972	Preserved
08192	D3262	13262	1956	1982	1985: Swindon Works
08193	D3263	13263	1956	1983	1986: Swindon Works
08194	D3264	13264	1956	1980	1983: Swindon Works
08195	D3265	13265	1956	1983	Preserved
08196	D3266	13266	1956	1983	1986: J R Adams, Glasgow
08197	D3267	13267	1956	1982	1984: Doncaster Works
08198	D3268	13268	1956	1980	1981: Swindon Works
08199	D3269	13269	1956	1983	1984: Doncaster Works
08200	D3270	13270	1956	1986	1992: C F Booth, Rotherham
08201	D3271	13271	1956	1982	1984: Doncaster Works
08202	D3272	13272	1956	1989	Preserved
08204	D3274	13274	1956	1983	1984: Swindon Works
08205	D3275	13275	1956	1983	1984: Doncaster Works
08206	D3276	13276	1956	1988	1989: Vic Berry, Leicester
08207	D3277	13277	1956	1980	1983: Swindon Works
08208	D3278	13278	1956	1984	1985: Doncaster Works
08209	D3279	13279	1956	1983	1983: Doncaster Works
08210	D3280	13280	1956	1988	1989: C F Booth, Rotherham
08211	D3281	13281	1956	1985	1986: Doncaster Works
08212	D3282	13282	1956	1981	1982: Swindon Works
08213	D3283	13283	1956	1980	1981: Swindon Works
08214	D3284	13284	1956	1984	1986: Doncaster Works
08215	D3285	13285	1956	1982	1983: Doncaster Works
08216	D3286	13286	1956	1980	2001: Barrow Hill Depot
08217	D3287	13287	1956	1982	1983: Doncaster Works
08218	D3288	13288	1956	1980	1981: Swindon Works
08219	D3289	13289	1956	1983	1983: Doncaster Works
08220	D3290	13290	1956	1986	Preserved
08221	D3291	13291	1956	1981	1981: Swindon Works
08222	D3292	13292	1956	1984	1997: Old Oak Common Depot
08223	D3293	13293	1956	1979	1980: Swindon Works
08224	D3294	13294	1956	1988	1993: Gwent Demolition, Margam
08225	D3295	13295	1957	1985	1986: Doncaster Works
08226	D3296	13296	1957	1985	1986: Doncaster Works
08227	D3297	13297	1957	1983	1986: J R Adams, Glasgow
08228	D3298	13298	1956	1985	1986: Doncaster Works
08229	D3299	13299	1956	1977	1978: Doncaster Works
08230	D3300	13300	1956	1980	1983: Swindon Works
08231	D3301	13301	1956	1981	1981: Swindon Works
08232	D3302	13302	1956	1982	1983: Doncaster Works
08233	D3303	13303	1956	1981	1982: Stratford Depot
08234	D3304	13304	1956	1982	1982: Swindon Works
08235	D3305	13305	1956	1983	1984: Doncaster Works
08236	D3306	13306	1956	1975	1976: Swindon Works
08237	D3307	13307	1956	1984	1986: Doncaster Works
08238	D3308	13308	1956	1984	Preserved

08239	D3309	13309			1956	1984	2005: EMR, Kingsbury	
08240	D3310	13310			1956	1982	1985: Swindon Works	
08241	D3311	13311			1956	1981	1982: Swindon Works	
08242	D3312	13312			1956	1986	1990: Lincoln Depot	
08243	D3313	13313			1956	1985	1992: Bird Group, Long Marston	
08244	D3314	13314			1956	1986	1990: C F Booth, Rotherham	
08245	D3315	13315			1956	1984	1986: Doncaster Works	
08246	D3316	13316			1956	1982	1987: D Christie, Camlackie	
PO1[1]	08247	D3317	13317		1956	1981	1981: Swindon Works	c)
08248	D3318	13318			1956	1984	1985: Doncaster Works	
08249	D3319	13319			1956	1985	1987: Swindon Works	
08250	D3320	13320			1956	1988	1991: MC Metals, Glasgow	
08251	D3321	13321			1956	1980	1981: Swindon Works	
08252	D3322	13322			1956	1981	1982: Swindon Works	
08253	D3323	13323			1956	1987	1988: Vic Berry, Leicester	
08254	D3324	13324			1956	1986	1994: C F Booth, Rotherham	
08255	D3325	13325			1956	1984	1986: Doncaster Works	
08256	D3326	13326			1956	1984	1984: Doncaster Works	
08257	D3327	13327			1956	1985	1989: Bury St Edmonds	
08258	D3328	13328			1956	1988	1989: Vic Berry, Leicester	
08260	D3330	13330			1956	1983	1983: Doncaster Works	
08261	D3331	13331			1956	1983	1984: Doncaster Works	
08262	D3332	13332			1957	1984	1984: Swindon Works	
08263	D3333	13333			1957	1984	1984: Doncaster Works	
08264	D3334	13334			1957	1984	1984: Doncaster Works	
08265	D3335	13335			1957	1981	1987: Swindon Works	
08266	D3336	13336			1957	1985	Preserved	
97801	RDB968020	08267	D3337	13337	1957	1981	1985: Vic Berry, Leicester	
08268	D3338	13338			1957	1985	1986: Doncaster Works	
08269	D3339	13339			1957	1984	1985: Doncaster Works	
08270	D3340	13340			1957	1982	1984: Doncaster Works	
08271	D3341	13341			1957	1981	1983: Swindon Works	
08272	D3342	13342			1957	1987	1991: RFS Doncaster	
08273	D3343	13343			1957	1982	1984: Doncaster Works	
08274	D3344	13344			1957	1984	1985: Doncaster Works	
08275	D3345	13345			1957	1983	1984: Doncaster Works	
08276	D3346	13346			1957	1977	1977: Doncaster Works	
08277	D3347	13347			1957	1981	1983: Doncaster Works	
08278	D3348	13348			1957	1977	1977: Glasgow Works	
08279	D3349	13349			1957	1981	1983: Swindon Works	
08280	D3350	13350			1957	1980	1982: Swindon Works	
08281	D3351	13351			1957	1980	1985: Swindon Works	
08282	D3352	13352			1957	1980	1981: Swindon Works	
08283	D3353	13353			1957	1986	1987: C F Booth, Rotherham	
08284	D3354	13354			1957	1985	1987: C F Booth, Rotherham	
08285	D3355	13355			1957	1988	1993: Gwent Demolition, Margam	
08286	D3356	13356			1957	1982	1986: Polmadie Depot	
08287	D3357	13357			1957	1983	1983: Doncaster Works	
08288	D3358				1957	1983	Preserved	
08289	D3359				1957	1985	1992: Bird Group, Long Marston	
08290	D3360				1957	1982	1984: Swindon Works	
08291	D3361				1957	1983	1983: Doncaster Works	
08292	D3362				1957	1984	1994: Deanside Transit	
08293	D3363	13363			1957	1985	1987: C F Booth, Rotherham	
08294	D3364	13364			1957	1980	1981: Swindon Works	
08295	D3365	13365			1957	1988	1993: Gwent Demolition, Margam	
08787[2]	08296[1]	D3366	13366		1957	1991	1994: C F Booth, Rotherham	d)
08297	D3367				1957	1988	1990: Vic Berry, Leicester	
08298	D3368				1957	1981	1981: Swindon Works	
08299	D3369				1957	1981	1982: Swindon Works	
08300	D3370				1957	1983	1984: Doncaster Works	
08301	D3371				1957	1985	1985: Swindon Works	
08302	D3372				1957	1981	1982: Swindon Works	
08303	D3373				1957	1981	1987: Swindon Works	

08304	D3374	1957	1985	1986: Swindon Works
08305	D3375	1957	1988	1995: Gwent Demolition, Margam
08306	D3376	1957	1977	1978: Swindon Works
08307	D3377	1957	1977	1978: Swindon Works
08308	D3378	1957		RMS Locotec
08309	D3379	1957	1992	1995: Gwent Demolition, Margam
08310	D3380	1957	1977	1978: Doncaster Works
08311	D3381	1957	1982	1984: Doncaster Works
08312	D3382	1957	1983	1986: J R Adams, Glasgow
08313	D3383	1957	1982	1983: Doncaster Works
08314	D3384	1957	1981	1981: Glasgow Works
08315	D3385	1957	1979	1980: Doncaster Works
08316	D3386	1957	1976	1977: Swindon Works
08317	D3387	1957	1982	1983: Doncaster Works
08318	D3388	1957	1976	1977: Eastleigh Works
08319	D3389	1957	1983	1986: J R Adams, Glasgow
08320	D3390	1957	1982	2010: EMR, Kingsbury
08321	D3391	1957	1984	1986: J R Adams, Glasgow
08322	D3392	1957	1983	1986: Swindon Works
08323	D3393	1957	1981	1982: Swindon Works
08324	D3394	1957	1984	1985: Doncaster Works
08325	D3395	1957	1984	1985: Swindon Works
08326	D3396	1957	1983	1986: J R Adams, Glasgow
08327	D3397	1957	1983	1987: Swindon Works
08328	D3398	1957	1981	1987: Swindon Works
08329	D3399	1957	1984	1986: Swindon Works
08330	D3400	1957	1984	1985: Doncaster Works
08331	D3401	1957		Class 20189
08332	D3402	1957	1984	1985: Doncaster Works
08333	D3403	1957	1982	1986: Swindon Works
08334	D3404	1957	1986	1994: C F Booth, Rotherham
08335	D3405	1957	1987	1989: Thomas Hill, Kilnhurst
08336	D3406	1957	1981	1982: Swindon Works
08337	D3407	1957	1987	1989: RFS Doncaster
08338	D3408	1958	1985	1989: Swansea, Maliphant
08339	D3409	1958	1984	1985: Doncaster Works
08340	D3410	1958	1981	1982: Swindon Works
08341	D3411	1958	1983	1986: J R Adams, Glasgow
08342	D3412	1958	1982	1983: Swindon Works
08343	D3413	1958	1983	1986: Eastfield Depot
08344	D3414	1958	1984	1986: J R Adams, Glasgow
08345	D3415	1958	1983	2009: C F Booth, Rotherham
08346	D3416	1958	1984	1986: J R Adams, Glasgow
08347	D3417	1958	1983	1986: J R Adams, Glasgow
08348	D3418	1958	1982	1986: Eastfield Depot
08349	D3419	1957	1983	1986: Swindon Works
08350	D3420	1957	1984	2010: Ron Hull Jr, Rotherham
08351	D3421	1957	1984	1986: Swindon Works
08352	D3422	1957	1983	1986: Swindon Works
08353	D3423	1958	1981	1982: Swindon Works
08354	D3424	1958	1986	1991: MC Metals, Glasgow
08355	D3425	1958	1983	1984: Doncaster Works
08356	D3426	1958	1982	1983: Swindon Works
08357	D3427	1958	1977	1979: Swindon Works
08358	D3428	1958	1977	1977: Doncaster Works
08359	D3429	1958	1984	Preserved
08360	D3430	1958	1983	1987: Swindon Works
08361	D3431	1958	1988	1991: MC Metals, Glasgow
08362	D3432	1958	1982	1983: Swindon Works
08363	D3433	1958	1982	1983: Swindon Works
08364	D3434	1958	1983	1983: Swindon Works
08365	D3435	1958	1980	1981: Swindon Works
08366	D3436	1958	1980	1982: Swindon Works
08367	D3437	1958	1988	1994: Gwent Demolition, Margam

08368	D3438		1958	1980	1984: Swindon Works
08369	D3454		1957	1985	1985: Doncaster Works
08370	D3455		1957	1984	1986: Doncaster Works
08371	D3456		1957	1983	1985: Doncaster Works
08372	D3457		1957	1984	1985: Doncaster Works
08373	D3458		1957	1985	1986: Doncaster Works
08374	D3459		1957	1982	1984: Doncaster Works
21	08375	D3460	1957		Victoria Group
08376	D3461		1957	1983	1984: Doncaster Works
08377	D3462		1957	1983	Preserved
08378	D3463		1957	1981	1982: Swindon Works
08379	D3464		1957	1980	1981: Swindon Works
08380	D3465		1957	1982	1983: Swindon Works
08381	D3466		1957	1982	1984: Doncaster Works
08382	D3467		1957	1985	1986: Doncaster Works
08383	D3468		1957	1985	1986: Doncaster Works
08384	D3469		1957	1986	1986: Doncaster Works
08385	D3470		1957	1988	1993: Gwent Demolition, Margam
08386	D3471		1957	1987	1990: Lincoln Depot
08387	D3472		1957	1982	1986: Swindon Works
08388	D3503		1958	1996	2010: EMR, Kingsbury
08389	Celsa 1	D3504	1958		Harry Needle Railroad Co
08390	D3505		1958	1993	2004: Barrow Hill Depot
08391	D3506		1958	1985	1986: Doncaster Works
08392	D3507		1958	1984	1985: Doncaster Works
08393	D3508		1958	2011	2016: LH Group, Barton-u-Needwood
08394	D3509		1958	1987	1989: Vic Berry, Leicester
08395	D3510		1958	1988	1989: C F Booth, Rotherham
08396	D3511		1958	1986	1987: C F Booth, Rotherham
08397	D3512		1958	2004	2010: Ron Hull Jr, Rotherham
08398	D3513		1958	1985	2011: EMR, Kingsbury
08399	D3514		1958	1992	1993: MC Metals, Glasgow
08400	D3515		1958	1987	1989: Vic Berry, Leicester
08401	D3516		1958		Hunslet Engine Co
08402	D3517		1958	2004	2010: T J Thomson, Stockton
08403	D3518		1958	1981	1986: Swindon Works
08404	D3519		1958	1978	1979: Doncaster Works
08405	D3520		1958		East Midlands Railway e)
08406	D3521		1958	1988	1992: C F Booth, Rotherham
08407	D3522		1958	1993	1993: Gwent Demolition, Margam
08408	D3523		1958	1988	1991: MC Metals, Glasgow
08409	D3524		1958	1986	1986: Doncaster Works
08410	D3525		1958		AV Dawson
08411	D3526		1958		Railway Support Services
08412	D3527		1958	1985	1992: C F Booth, Rotherham
08413	D3528		1958	1999	2007: Morley Waste Traders, Leeds
08414	D3529		1958	1999	2007: EMR, Kingsbury
08415	D3530		1958	1996	1997: EMR, Sheffield
08416	D3531		1958	1992	1993: RFS Kilnhurst
08417	D3532		1958		Network Rail
08418	D3533		1958		West Coast Railway Co
08419	D3534		1958	1993	2004: C F Booth, Rotherham
08420	D3535		1958	1988	1995: Gwent Demolition, Margam
08421	D3536		1958	1992	Converted to 09201 in 1992
08422	D3537		1958	1985	1991: Bird Group, Long Marston
14	08423	D3538	1958		RMS Locotec
08424	D3539		1958	1985	1986: J R Adams, Glasgow
08425	D3540		1958	1985	1986: Swindon Works
08426	D3541		1958	1976	1977: Doncaster Works
08427	D3542		1958	1986	1994: Gwent Demolition, Margam
08428	D3543		1958		Harry Needle Railroad Co
08429	D3544		1958	1983	1983: Doncaster Works
08430	D3545		1958	1985	1986: J McWilliam, Shettleston
08431	D3546		1958	1985	1987: Allerton Depot

08432	D3547	1958	1983	1984: Doncaster Works
08433	D3548	1958	1986	1986: J McWilliam, Shettleston
08434	D3549	1958	1992	1994: Gwent Demolition, Margam
08435	D3550	1958	1980	1983: Swindon Works
08436	D3551	1958	1992	Preserved
08437	D3552	1958	1984	1986: J R Adams, Glasgow
08438	D3553	1958	1986	1992: C F Booth, Rotherham
08439	D3554	1958	1988	1994: Gwent Demolition, Margam
08440	D3555	1958	1990	1991: MC Metals, Glasgow
08441	D3556	1958		Railway Support Services
08442	D3557	1958		Arriva Traincare
08443	D3558	1958	1985	Preserved
08444	D3559	1958	1986	Preserved
08445	D3560	1958		Hunslet Engine Co
08446	D3561	1958	1985	1986: J McWilliam, Shettleston
08447	D3562	1958		Russell Logistics
08448	D3563	1958	1994	2007: EMR, Kingsbury
08449	D3564	1958	1996	2007: EMR, Kingsbury
08450	D3565	1958	1986	1992: Bird Group, Long Marston
08451	D3566	1958		Alstom
08452	D3567	1958	1985	1987: Swindon Works
08453	D3568	1958	1980	1982: Swindon Works
08454	D3569	1958		Alstom
08455	D3570	1958	1981	1987: Swindon Works
08456	D3571	1959	1988	1989: C F Booth, Rotherham
08457	D3572	1959	1981	1986: Swindon Works
08458	D3573	1958	1988	1991: MC Metals, Glasgow
08459	D3574	1958	1988	1989: Vic Berry, Leicester
08460	D3575	1958		Railway Support Services
08461	D3576	1958	1988	1991: MC Metals, Glasgow
08463	D3578	1958	1989	1992: C F Booth, Rotherham
08464	D3579	1958	1981	1987: Swindon Works
08465	D3580	1958	1985	1986: Doncaster Works
08466	D3581	1958	2009	2007: C F Booth, Rotherham
08467	D3582	1958	1981	1982: Swindon Works
08468	D3583	1958	1988	1995: Gwent Demolition, Margam
08469	D3584	1958	1981	1986: Swindon Works
08470	D3585	1958	1986	1996: Crewe Works
08471	D3586	1958	1985	Preserved
08472	D3587	1958		Wabtec
08473	D3588	1958	1986	Preserved (Partially dismantled)
08474	D3589	1958	1986	1988: Vic Berry, Leicester
08475	D3590	1958	1987	1987: C F Booth, Rotherham
08476	D3591	1958	1985	Preserved
08477	D3592	1958	1986	1990: Allerton Depot
08478	D3593	1958	1988	1994: Gwent Demolition, Margam
08479	D3594	1958	1991	Preserved
08480	D3595	1958		Railway Support Services
08481	D3596	1958	2005	2011: EMR, Kingsbury
08482	D3597	1958	2010	2011: C F Booth, Rotherham
08483	D3598	1958		Locomotive Services
08484	D3599	1958		Railway Support Services
08485	D3600	1958		West Coast Railway Co
08486	D3601	1958	1986	1991: MC Metals, Glasgow
08487	D3602	1958	1988	1991: MC Metals, Glasgow
08488	D3603	1958	1986	1991: MC Metals, Glasgow
08489	D3604	1958	2004	2009: T J Thomson, Stockton
08490	D3605	1958	1985	Preserved
08491	D3606	1958	1985	1991: MC Metals, Glasgow
08492	D3607	1958	2000	2012: EMR, Kingsbury
08493	D3608	1958	1999	2008: C F Booth, Rotherham
08494	D3609	1958	1988	1991: MC Metals, Glasgow
08495	D3610	1958		Preserved
08496	D3611	1958	1990	1994: Bird Group, Long Marston

08497	D3652	1958	1985	1986: Doncaster Works
08498	D3653	1958	1994	1994: Stratford Depot
08499	D3654	1958		Colas Rail
08500	D3655	1958		Harry Needle Railroad Co
08501	D3656	1958	1985	1991: MC Metals, Glasgow
08502	D3657	1958		Harry Needle Railroad Co
08503	D3658	1958	1988	Preserved
08504	D3659	1958	1988	1992: C F Booth, Rotherham
08505	D3660	1958	1981	1983: Swindon Works
08506	D3661	1958	2004	2007: T J Thomson, Stockton
08507	D3662	1958		Riviera Trains
08508	D3663	1958	1991	1994: Gwent Demolition, Margam
08509	D3664	1958	1999	2009: C F Booth, Rotherham
08510	D3672	1958	2004	2009: C F Booth, Rotherham
08511	D3673	1958		Railway Support Services
08512	D3674	1958	2008	2011: C F Booth, Rotherham
08513	D3675	1958	1978	1978: Doncaster Works
08514	D3676	1958	2008	2011: EMR, Kingsbury
08515	D3677	1958	1992	2001: Gateshead Depot
08516	D3678	1958		Arriva Traincare
08517	D3679	1958	1999	2011: C F Booth, Rotherham
08518	D3680	1958	1986	1994: Gwent Demolition, Margam
08519	D3681	1958	1999	2000: C F Booth, Rotherham
08520	D3682	1958	1986	1986: Doncaster Works
08521	D3683	1958	1993	1994: Allerton Depot
08522	D3684	1958	1985	1985: Doncaster Works
08523	D3685	1958		RMS Locotec
08524	D3686	1958	1986	1987: C F Booth, Rotherham
08525	D3687	1959		East Midlands Railway
08526	D3688	1959	2006	2008: T J Thomson, Stockton
08527	D3689	1959		Harry Needle Railroad Co
08528	D3690	1959	2005	Preserved
08529	D3691	1959	1999	2008: C F Booth, Rotherham
08530	D3692	1959		Freightliner
08531	D3693	1959		Freightliner
08532	D3694	1959	1993	1994: Allerton Depot
08533	D3695	1959	1992	1994: Gwent Demolition, Margam
08534	D3696	1959	2002	2007: T J Thomson, Stockton
D3697		1959	1965	Converted to D4502 (slave) in 1965
D3698		1959	1965	Converted to D4500 (slave) in 1965
08535	D3699	1959	2000	2009: C F Booth, Rotherham
08536	D3700	1959		Preserved
08537	D3701	1959	1992	1994: Bescot Depot
08538	D3702	1959	2009	2011: EMR, Kingsbury
08539	D3703	1959	1992	1993: MC Metals, Glasgow
08540	D3704	1959	2004	2010: EMR, Kingsbury
08541	D3705	1959	1999	2008: EMR, Kingsbury
08542	D3706	1959	2000	2006: EMR, Kingsbury
08543	D3707	1959	2004	2010: EMR, Kingsbury
08544	D3708	1959	1992	1994: Gwent Demolition, Margam
08545	D3709	1959	1980	1983: Swindon Works
08546	D3710	1959	1985	1986: Doncaster Works
08547	D3711	1959	1981	1982: Swindon Works
08548	D3712	1959	1982	1983: Doncaster Works
08549	D3713	1959	1985	1992: C F Booth, Rotherham
08550	D3714	1959	1983	1986: Swindon Works
08551	D3715	1959	1982	1983: Doncaster Works
08552	D3716	1959	1982	1983: Doncaster Works
08553	D3717	1959	1981	1983: Swindon Works
08554	D3718	1959	1982	1983: Doncaster Works
08555	D3722	1959	1982	1983: Doncaster Works
08556	D3723	1959	1990	Preserved
08557	D3724	1959	1982	1983: Doncaster Works
08558	D3725	1959	1986	1989: Vic Berry, Leicester

			Built	Withdrawn	Disposal	Note
08559	D3726		1959	1981	1983: Swindon Works	
08560	D3727		1959	1981	1982: Swindon Works	
08561	D3728		1959	2005	2011: C F Booth, Rotherham	
08562	D3729		1959	1994	1997: Old Oak Common Depot	
08563	D3730		1959	1982	1987: D Christie, Camlackie	
08564	D3731		1959	1985	1986: J McWilliam, Shettleston	
08565	D3732		1959	1993	1997: Motherwell Depot	
08566	D3733		1959	1975	1977: Glasgow Works	
08567	D3734		1959		Arlington Fleet Services	
08568	D3735		1959		Railway Support Services	
08569	D3736		1959	2004	2011: C F Booth, Rotherham	
08570	D3737		1959	1992	1993: Motherwell Depot	
08571	D3738		1959		Wabtec	
08731²	08572¹	D3739	1959	1995	2009: J W Ransome, Frome	f)
08573	D3740		1959		RMS Locotec	
08574	D3741		1959	1981	1986: Swindon Works	
08575	D3742		1959		Freightliner	
08576	D3743		1959	2006	2007: T J Thomson, Stockton	
08577	D3744		1959	2004	2011: EMR, Kingsbury	
08578	D3745		1959		Harry Needle Railroad Co	
08579	D3746		1959	1988	1995: Gwent Demolition, Margam	
08580	D3747		1959		LNER	g)
08581	D3748		1959	1995	2000: C F Booth, Rotherham	
08582	D3749		1959	2004	2009: C F Booth, Rotherham	
08583	D3750		1959	1993	1996: C F Booth, Rotherham	
08584	D3751		1959	1991	1993: MC Metals, Glasgow	
08585	D3752		1959		Freightliner	
08586	D3753		1959	1999	2000: Ayr Depot	
08587	D3754		1959	2006	2009: T J Thomson, Stockton	
08588	D3755		1959		RMS Locotec	
08589	D3756		1959	1992	1994: Gwent Demolition, Margam	
08590	D3757		1959	1993	Preserved	
08591	D3758		1959	1993	1993: MC Metals, Glasgow	
08593	D3760		1959		Railway Support Services	
08594	D3761		1959	1999	2010: EMR, Kingsbury	
08595	D3762		1959	1993	1995: C F Booth, Rotherham	
08596	D3763		1959		Wabtec	
08597	D3764		1959	2004	2011: C F Booth, Rotherham	
08598	D3765		1959		AV Dawson	
08599	D3766		1959	2004	2008: T J Thomson, Stockton	
08600	97800	D3767	1959		AV Dawson	
08601	D3768		1959	1999	2008: Bryn Engineering, Wigan	
004	08602	D3769	1959		Harry Needle Railroad Co	
08603	D3770		1959	1994	1994: Bird Group, Long Marston	
08604	D3771		1959	1993	Preserved	
08605	D3772		1959		Riviera Trains	
08606	D3773		1959	1988	1989: Vic Berry, Leicester	
08607	D3774		1959	1996	2007: EMR, Kingsbury	
08608	D3775		1959	1988	1994: C F Booth, Rotherham	
08609	D3776		1959	1993	2000: C F Booth, Rotherham	
08610	D3777		1959	1994	2004: C F Booth, Rotherham	
08611	D3778		1959		Alstom	
08612	D3779		1959	1990	1991: MC Metals, Glasgow	
08613	D3780		1959		RMS Locotec	
08614	D3781		1959	1993	1994: Gwent Demolition, Margam	
08615	D3782		1959		Wabtec	
08616	D3783		1959		West Midlands Trains	
08617	D3784		1959		Alstom	
08618	D3785		1959	1990	2001: Gateshead Depot	
08619	D3786		1959	1998	2001: C F Booth, Rotherham	
08620	D3787		1959	1992	Converted to 09205 in 1992	
08621	D3788		1959	1988	1989: Vic Berry, Leicester	
08622	D3789		1959		RMS Locotec	
08623	D3790		1959		Harry Needle Railroad Co	

08624	D3791		1959		Freightliner	
08625	D3792		1959	1997	2004: EMR, Kingsbury	
08626	D3793		1959	1988	1994: Allerton Depot	
08627	D3794		1959	1994	1997: Ipswich Depot	
08628	D3795		1959	1999	2016: EMR, Kingsbury	
08629	D3796		1959		Meteor Power Ltd	
Celsa 3	08630	D3797	1959		Harry Needle Railroad Co	
08631	D3798		1959		Locomotive Services	
08632	D3799		1959		Railway Support Services	
08633	D3800		1959	2014	Preserved	
08634	D3801		1959	1993	2005: Carnforth Depot	
08635	D3802		1959	2004	Preserved	
08636	D3803		1958	1980	1983: Swindon Works	
08637	D3804		1958	1991	1993: MC Metals, Glasgow	
08638	D3805		1958	1992	1994: Gwent Demolition, Margam	
08639	D3806		1958	1988	1989: Vic Berry, Leicester	
08640	D3807		1958	1988	1991: MC Metals, Glasgow	
08641	D3808		1959		Great Western Railway	
08642	D3809		1959	2006	2005: C F Booth, Rotherham	
08643	D3810		1959		Mendip Rail	
08644	D3811		1959		Great Western Railway	
08645	D3812		1959		Great Western Railway	
08646	D3813		1959	2009	2015: EMR, Kingsbury	
08647	D3814		1959	1993	1997: S Yorks Railway, Meadowhall	
08648	D3815		1959		Scotrail	h)
08649	D3816		1959		Meteor Power Ltd	
08650	D3817		1959		Mendip Rail	
08651	D3818		1959	2004	2005: EMR, Kingsbury	
08652	D3819		1959		Railway Support Services	
08653	D3820		1959		Harry Needle Railroad Co	
08654	D3821		1959	1991	1994: C F Booth, Rotherham	
08655	D3822		1959	2004	2007: LH Group, Barton-u-Needwood	
08656	D3823		1959	1993	1994: Gwent Demolition, Margam	
08657	D3824		1959	1991	1994: Gwent Demolition, Margam	
08658	D3825		1959	1993	1994: Gwent Demolition, Margam	
08659	D3826		1959	1991	1995: Gwent Demolition, Margam	
08660	D3827		1959	1991	1994: Gwent Demolition, Margam	
08661	D3828		1959	2003	2005: EWS Railway, Wigan	
08662	D3829		1959	2011	2012: T J Thomson, Stockton	
08663	D3830		1959		Railway Support Services	j)
08664	D3831		1959	2008	2012: EMR, Kingsbury	
08665	D3832		1960	2004	2011: EMR, Kingsbury	
08666	D3833		1960	1994	2006: EMR, Kingsbury	
08667	D3834		1960	1992	1995: Gwent Demolition, Margam	
08668	D3835		1960	1997	2011: EMR, Kingsbury	
08669	D3836		1960		Wabtec	
08670	D3837		1960		Railway Support Services	
08671	D3838		1960	1988	1994: C F Booth, Rotherham	
08672	D3839		1960	1992	1994: Gwent Demolition, Margam	
08673	D3840		1960	1995	2003: S Norton, Liverpool	
08674	D3841		1960	1981	1983: Swindon Works	
08675	D3842		1959	1999	2007: T J Thomson, Stockton	
08676	D3843		1959		Harry Needle Railroad Co	
08677	D3844		1959	1999	2000: C F Booth, Rotherham	
08678	D3845		1959		West Coast Railway Co	
08679	D3846		1959	1976	1986: C F Booth, Rotherham	
08680	D3847		1959	1992	1993: Motherwell Depot	
08681	D3848		1959	1985	1986: Doncaster Works	
08682	D3849		1959		Harry Needle Railroad Co	
08683	D3850		1959		Railway Support Services	
08684	D3851		1959	1986	1995: S M McGregor, Bicester	
08685	D3852		1959		Harry Needle Railroad Co	
08686	D3853		1959	1991	1994: Allerton Depot	
08688	D3855		1959	1991	1994: Allerton Depot	

08689	D3856		1959	2007	2010: EMR, Kingsbury	
08690	D3857		1959		East Midlands Railway	
08691	D3858		1959		Freightliner	
08692	D3859		1959	1994	2005: Carnforth Depot	
08693	D3860		1959	1999	2000: EWS Railway, Wigan	
08694	D3861		1959	2004	Preserved	
08695	D3862		1959	2004	2009: C F Booth, Rotherham	
08696	D3863		1959		Alstom	
08697	D3864		1959	2014	2014: Wards Recycling, Ilkeston	
08698	D3865		1959	2005	2011: C F Booth, Rotherham	
08699	D3866		1960	1993	2018: Wolsingham, Weardale Rlwy	
08700	D3867		1960		Harry Needle Railroad Co	
08701	D3868		1960		Harry Needle Railroad Co	
08702	D3869		1960	1998	2004: C F Booth, Rotherham	
08703	D3870		1960		DB Cargo	
08704	D3871		1960		Riviera Trains	
08705	D3872		1960	1994	1994: Stratford Depot	
08706	D3873		1960		Harry Needle Railroad Co	
08707	D3874		1960	1993	2005: Carnforth Depot	
08708	D3875		1960	1992	1994: Gwent Demolition, Margam	
08709	D3876		1960		Railway Support Services	
08710	D3877		1960	1993	1993: Motherwell Depot	
08711	D3878		1960		Harry Needle Railroad Co	
08712	D3879		1960	1992	1993: Motherwell Depot	
08713	D3880		1960	1998	2009: C F Booth, Rotherham	
08714	D3881		1960		Harry Needle Railroad Co	
08715	D3882		1960	1998	2009: T J Thomson, Stockton	
08716	D3883		1960	1988	1990: Vic Berry, Leicester	
08717	D3884		1960	1992	Converted to 09204 in 1992	
D3885			1960	1972	1972: Glasgow Works	
08718	D3886		1960	1999	2000: Ayr Depot	
08719	D3887		1960	1991	1994: Gwent Demolition, Margam	
08720	D3888		1960	2002	2007: T J Thomson, Stockton	
08721	D3889		1960		Alstom	
08722	D3890		1960	1987	1988: Vic Berry, Leicester	
08723	D3891		1960	1995	2002: EMR, Kingsbury	
08724	D3892		1960		Wabtec	
08725	D3893		1960	1992	1993: Motherwell Depot	
08726	D3894		1960	1987	1987: Thornton Yard	
08727	D3895		1960	1993	1993: Motherwell Depot	
08728	D3896		1960	1987	2009: C F Booth, Rotherham	
08729	D3897		1960	1990	1994: Gwent Demolition, Margam	
08730	D3898		1960		Railway Support Services	
08572²	08731¹	D3899	1960	1981	1983: Swindon Works	k)
08732	D3900		1960	1992	Converted to 09202 in 1992	
08733	D3901		1960	1993	2000: EWS Railway, Wigan	
08734	D3902		1960	1999	2011: Sims Metals, Newport	
08735	D3903		1960		Arriva Traincare	
08736	D3904		1960	1987	2009: C F Booth, Rotherham	
D3905	08737	D3905	1960		Locomotive Services	
08738	D3906		1960		Railway Support Services	
08739	D3907		1960	1997	2005: S Norton, Liverpool	
08740	D3908		1960	1997	2007: LH Group, Barton-u-Needwood	
08741	D3909		1960	1991	1994: C F Booth, Rotherham	
08742	D3910		1960		Harry Needle Railroad Co	
08743	D3911		1960		SembCorp Utilities UK	
08744	D3912		1960	1992	1993: MC Metals, Glasgow	
08745	D3913		1960	2012	2012: C F Booth, Rotherham	
08746	D3914		1960	1999	2004: C F Booth, Rotherham	
08747	D3915		1960	1990	1993: Gwent Demolition, Margam	
08748	D3916		1960	1994	1997: Ipswich Depot	
08749	D3917		1960	1993	Converted to 09104 in 1993	
08750	D3918		1960	1997	2018: Wolsingham, Weardale Rlwy	
08751	D3919		1960	1997	2004: C F Booth, Rotherham	

08752	D3920		1960		Railway Support Services
08753	D3921		1960	1993	1993: Motherwell Depot
08754	D3922		1961		RMS Locotec
08755	D3923		1961	1993	2000: C F Booth, Rotherham
08756	D3924		1961		RMS Locotec
08757	D3925		1961	2012	Preserved
08758	D3926		1961	1997	2005: Ron Hull Jr, Rotherham
08759	D3927		1961	1993	Converted to 09106 in 1993
08760	D3928		1961	1992	1997: Eastleigh Works
08761	D3929		1961	1992	1993: MC Metals, Glasgow
08762	D3930		1961		RMS Locotec
08763	D3931		1961	1989	1990: Eastfield Depot
08764	D3932		1961		Alstom
08765	D3933		1961		Harry Needle Railroad Co
08766	D3934		1961	1992	Converted to 09103 in 1992
08767	D3935		1961	1994	Preserved
08768	D3936		1961	2000	2007: T J Thomson, Stockton
08769	D3937		1960	1989	Preserved
08770	D3938		1960	2008	2011: T J Thomson, Stockton
08771	D3939		1960	1992	1994: Gwent Demolition, Margam
08772	D3940		1960	1994	Preserved
08773	D3941		1960	1999	Preserved
08774	D3942		1960		AV Dawson
08775	D3943		1960	2008	2009: C F Booth, Rotherham
08776	D3944		1960	2008	2011: C F Booth, Rotherham
08777	D3945		1960	1991	1996: C F Booth, Rotherham
08778	D3946		1960	1992	1994: Gwent Demolition, Margam
08779	D3947		1960	1988	1991: MC Metals, Glasgow
D3948	08780	D3948	1960	2005	Preserved
08781	D3949		1960	1992	Converted to 09203 in 1992
08782	D3950		1960		Harry Needle Railroad Co
08783	D3951		1960		Awaiting Disposal m)
08784	D3952		1960	2011	Preserved
08785	D3953		1960		Freightliner
08786	D3954		1960		Harry Needle Railroad Co
08296[2]	08787[1]	D3955	1960		Mendip Rail n)
08788	D3956		1960		RMS Locotec
08789	D3957		1960	1993	1995: S M McGregor, Bicester
08790	D3958		1960		Alstom
08791	D3959		1960	1992	1993: MC Metals, Glasgow
08792	D3960		1960	2004	2007: T J Thomson, Stockton
08793	D3961		1960	1993	2000: C F Booth, Rotherham
08794	D3962		1960	1992	1995: Gwent Demolition, Margam
08795	D3963		1960		Preserved
08796	D3964		1960	1990	1993: MC Metals, Glasgow
08797	D3965		1960	1990	1994: Gwent Demolition, Margam
08798	D3966		1960		Harry Needle Railroad Co
08799	D3967		1960		Harry Needle Railroad Co
08800	D3968		1960	1993	1994: Gwent Demolition, Margam
08801	D3969		1960	2000	2004: C F Booth, Rotherham
08802	D3970		1960		Harry Needle Railroad Co
08803	D3971		1960	1992	1994: Gwent Demolition, Margam
08804	D3972		1960		Harry Needle Railroad Co
08805	D3973		1960		West Midlands Trains
08806	D3974		1960	2001	2007: T J Thomson, Stockton
08807	D3975		1960	2004	2017: C L Prosser, Middlesbrough
08808	D3976		1960	1990	1992: C F Booth, Rotherham
08809	D3977		1960		RMS Locotec
08810	D3978		1960		Arriva Traincare
08811	D3979		1960	1997	1997: Old Oak Common Depot
08812	D3980		1960	1978	1978: Swindon Works
08813	D3981		1960	2005	2011: T J Thomson, Stockton
08814	D3982		1960	1992	1994: Gwent Demolition, Margam
08815	D3983		1960	1996	2005: C F Booth, Rotherham

08816	D3984			1960	1986	1999: Wabtec, Doncaster
08817	D3985			1960	1999	2005: Bryn Engineering, Wigan
08818	D3986			1960		Harry Needle Railroad Co
08819	D3987			1960	1999	2008: C F Booth, Rotherham
08820	D3988			1960	1990	1991: MC Metals, Glasgow
08821	D3989			1960	1992	1993: Gwent Demolition, Margam
08822	D3990			1960		Great Western Railway
08823	D3991			1960		Hunslet Engine Co
IEMD 01	08824	D3992		1960		Harry Needle Railroad Co
08825	D3993			1960	1999	Preserved
08826	D3994			1960	1999	2011: Eastleigh Works
08827	D3995			1960	2000	2011: EMR, Kingsbury
08828	D3996			1960	2004	2011: T J Thomson, Stockton
08829	D3997			1960	1993	2005: Carnforth Depot
08830	D3998			1960	2006	Preserved
08831	D3999			1960	1993	1994: Gwent Demolition, Margam
08832	D4000			1960	1992	Converted to 09102 in 1992
08833	D4001			1960	1992	Converted to 09101 in 1992
08834	D4002			1960		Harry Needle Railroad Co
08835	D4003			1960	1993	Converted to 09105 in 1993
08836	D4004			1960		Great Western Railway
08837	D4005			1960	2000	2005: S Norton, Liverpool
08838	D4006			1960	1990	1994: Gwent Demolition, Margam
08839	D4007			1960	1992	1993: Gwent Demolition, Margam
08840	D4008			1960	1991	1994: Allerton Depot
08841	D4009			1960	1990	1993: MC Metals, Glasgow
08842	D4010			1960	2008	2012: EMR, Kingsbury
08843	D4011			1961	1990	1991: MC Metals, Glasgow
08844	D4012			1961	2009	2012: EMR, Kingsbury
08845	D4013			1961	1993	Converted to 09107 in 1993
08846	003	08846	D4014	1961		Railway Support Services
08847	D4015			1961		RMS Locotec
08848	D4016			1961	1992	1994: Gwent Demolition, Margam
08849	D4017			1961	1993	1997: Crewe Works
08850	D4018			1961	1992	Preserved
08851	D4019			1961	1990	1991: MC Metals, Glasgow
08852	D4020			1961	1988	1989: MC Metals, Glasgow
08853	D4021			1961		Wabtec
08854	D4022			1961	2008	2012: EMR, Kingsbury
08855	D4023			1961	1993	2001: Wabtec, Doncaster
08856	D4024			1961	2004	2011: T J Thomson, Stockton
08857	D4025			1961	1991	1993: MC Metals, Glasgow
08858	D4026			1961	1992	1994: Allerton Depot
08859	D4027			1961	1992	1994: Gwent Demolition, Margam
08860	D4028			1960	1981	1981: Swindon Works
08861	D4029			1960	1981	1982: Swindon Works
08862	D4030			1960	1980	1981: Swindon Works
08863	D4031			1960	1980	1981: Swindon Works
08864	D4032			1960	1981	1982: Swindon Works
08865	D4033			1960		Harry Needle Railroad Co
08866	D4034			1960	2008	2012: EMR, Kingsbury
08867	D4035			1960	1999	2007: T J Thomson, Stockton
08868	D4036			1960		Arriva Traincare
08869	D4037			1960	1997	2011: EMR, Kingsbury
H024	08870	D4038		1960		Eastern Rail Services
08871	H074	D4039		1960		RMS Locotec
08872	D4040			1960		Harry Needle Railroad Co
08873	D4041			1960		Hunslet Engine Co
08874	D4042			1960		RMS Locotec
08875	D4043			1960	1991	1993: RFS Kilnhurst
08876	D4044			1960	1991	1994: RFS Doncaster
08877	D4045			1960		Harry Needle Railroad Co
08878	D4046			1960	1997	1997: Old Oak Common Depot
08879	D4047			1960		Harry Needle Railroad Co

08880	D4048		1960	1996	2005: S Norton, Liverpool
08881	D4095		1961	2004	Preserved
08882	D4096		1961	2001	2005: Ron Hull Jr, Rotherham
08883	D4097		1961	2004	2007: T J Thomson, Stockton
08884	D4098		1961	2004	2010: EMR, Kingsbury
08885	H042	D4115	1962		RMS Locotec
08886	D4116		1962	2012	2016: EMR, Kingsbury
08887	D4117		1962		Alstom
08888	D4118		1962	2016	Preserved
08889	D4119		1962	1992	1994: Gwent Demolition, Margam
08890	D4120		1962	2004	2009: C F Booth, Rotherham
08891	D4121		1962		Freightliner
08892	D4122		1962		Harry Needle Railroad Co
08893	D4123		1962	1994	2005: Ron Hull Jr, Rotherham
08894	D4124		1962	1998	2007: T J Thomson, Stockton
08895	D4125		1962	1993	2000: Margam Depot
08896	D4126		1962	2004	Preserved
08897	D4127		1962	2009	2011: C F Booth, Rotherham
08898	D4128		1962	1988	1998: RFS Doncaster
08899	D4129		1962		East Midlands Railway
08900	D4130		1962	2005	2009: T J Thomson, Stockton
08901	D4131		1962	1993	2005: Ron Hull Jr, Rotherham
08902	D4132		1962	1996	2007: T J Thomson, Stockton
08903	D4133		1962		SembCorp Utilities UK
08904	D4134		1962		Harry Needle Railroad Co
08905	D4135		1962		Harry Needle Railroad Co
08906	D4136		1962	1998	2007: T J Thomson, Stockton
08907	D4137		1962	2014	Preserved
08908	D4138		1962		East Midlands Railway
08909	D4139		1962	2011	2012: C F Booth, Rotherham
08910	D4140		1962	2002	2007: T J Thomson, Stockton
08911	D4141		1962	2004	Preserved
08912	D4142		1962		AV Dawson
08913	D4143		1962		Awaiting Disposal m)
08914	D4144		1962	1997	2005: Ron Hull Jr, Rotherham
08915	D4145		1962	2004	Preserved
08916	D4146		1962	1992	1994: Allerton Depot
08917	D4147		1962	1991	1994: Allerton Depot
08918	D4148		1962		Harry Needle Railroad Co
08919	D4149		1962	2004	2009: C F Booth, Rotherham
08920	D4150		1962	2004	2011: EMR, Kingsbury
08921	D4151		1962		Railway Support Services
08922	D4152		1962	2011	Preserved o)
08923	D4153		1962	1993	1994: Stratford Depot
CELSA2	08924	D4154	1962		Harry Needle Railroad Co
08925	D4155		1962		GB Railfreight
08926	D4156		1962	1996	2007: EMR, Kingsbury
08927	D4157		1962		Railway Support Services
08928	D4158		1962	2001	2010: EMR, Kingsbury
08929	D4159		1962	1991	1994: Gwent Demolition, Margam
08930	D4160		1962	1990	1991: MC Metals, Glasgow
08931	D4161		1962	1995	2005: Ron Hull Jr, Rotherham
08932	D4162		1962	1999	2005: Crewe Diesel Depot
08933	D4163		1962		Mendip Rail
08934	D4164		1962		GB Railfreight
08935	D4165		1962	1993	1994: Gwent Demolition, Margam
08936	D4166		1962		RMS Locotec
08937	D4167		1962		Bardon Aggregates
08938	D4168		1962	1999	2000: EWS Railway, Wigan
08939	D4169		1962		Railway Support Services
08940	D4170		1962	2003	2003: S Norton, Liverpool
08941	D4171		1962	2008	2011: C F Booth, Rotherham
08942	D4172		1962	1998	2007: T J Thomson, Stockton
08943	D4173		1962		Harry Needle Railroad Co

08944	D4174			1962	1999	Preserved	
08945	D4175			1962	1993	1993: Gwent Demolition, Margam	
08946	D4176			1962	2002	2008: Goodman's, Sutton Coldfield	
08947	D4177			1962		Mendip Rail	
08948	D4178			1962		Eurostar International	
08949	D4179			1962	1993	1994: Gwent Demolition, Margam	
08950	D4180			1962		East Midlands Railway	
08951	D4181			1962	2011	2011: C F Booth, Rotherham	
08952	D4182			1962	1999	2000: EWS Railway, Wigan	
08953	D4183			1962	2006	2012: EMR, Attercliffe	
08954	D4184			1962		Alstom	p)
08955	D4185			1962	2000	2009: C F Booth, Rotherham	
08956	D4186			1962		LORAM UK	
D4187				1962	1965	Converted to D4502 (master) in 1965	
D4188				1962	1965	Converted to D4500 (master) in 1965	
D4189				1962	1965	Converted to D4501 (master) in 1965	
D4190				1962	1965	Converted to D4501 (slave) in 1965	
08957	D4191			1962	2001	2004: EMR, Kingsbury	
08958	D4192			1962	2001	2001: EWS Railway, Wigan	

a) Reverted to 13201 in preservation
b) Second of two locomotives to be numbered PO1
c) First of two locomotives to be numbered PO1
d) Second locomotive to carry 08787, renumbered shortly before scrapping
e) RSS locomotive on hire to EMR
f) Second locomotive to carry 08731, renumbered during repairs in 1983
g) RSS locomotive on hire to LNER
h) RMS Locotec loco on hire to Scotrail
j) Preserved locomotive on hire to RSS
k) Second locomotive to carry 08572, renumbered shortly before scrapping
m) At EMR Kingsbury
n) Second locomotive to carry 08296, the body of 08296 was renumbered in 1992
o) Preserved locomotive on hire to Hitachi, Newton Aycliffe
p) HNRC loco on hire to Alstom

Class 08/9
Cabs cut down to reduce height.
Details as Class 08.

Latest Number Carried	Previous Number 1	Previous Number 2	Previous Number 3	Year Entered Service	Year Withdrawn	Current Status/Scrapping Details	Notes
08991	08203	D3273	13273	1956	1987	1989: Vic Berry, Leicester	
08992	08259	D3329	13329	1956	1987	1989: Vic Berry, Leicester	
08993	08592	D3759		1959	2015	Preserved	
08994	08462	D3577		1958		Harry Needle Railroad Co	
08995	08687	D3854		1959	2013	Preserved	

CLASS 09   0-6-0

Built: 1959–62 by British Railways, Darlington & Horwich.
Engine: English Electric 6KT of 298 kW (400 hp) at 680 rpm.
Transmission: Electric.
Maximum Speed: 27 mph.
Train Brakes: Vacuum. All were later dual-braked (air & vacuum)

Class 09/0

Latest Number Carried	Previous Number 1	Previous Number 2	Year Entered Service	Year Withdrawn	Current Status/Scrapping Details	Notes
09001	D3665		1959	2009	Preserved	
09002	D3666		1959		GB Railfreight	
09003	D3667		1959	2008	2011: EMR, Kingsbury	
09004	D3668		1959	1999	Preserved	
09005	D3669		1959	2009	2011: C F Booth, Rotherham	
09006	D3670		1959		Harry Needle Railroad Co	

09007	D3671		1959		London Overground			
09008	D3719		1959	2004	2011: EMR, Kingsbury			
09009	D3720		1959		GB Railfreight			
09010	D3721		1959	2010	Preserved			
09011	D4099		1961	2005	2011: EMR, Kingsbury			
09012	D4100		1961	2004	Preserved			
09013	D4101		1961	2008	2011: C F Booth, Rotherham			
09014	D4102		1961		Harry Needle Railroad Co			
09015	D4103		1961	2007	Preserved			
09016	D4104		1961	2004	2011: EMR, Kingsbury			
09017	97806	D4105	1961	2010	Preserved			
09018	D4106		1961	2013	Preserved			a)
09019	D4107		1961	2013	Preserved			
09020	D4108		1961	2011	2012: EMR, Kingsbury			
09021	D4109		1961	2004	2008: C F Booth, Rotherham			
09022	D4110		1961		Victoria Group			
09023	D4111		1961		Awaiting Disposal			b)
09024	D4112		1961	2008	Preserved			
09025	D4113		1962	2005	Preserved			
09026	D4114		1962	2016	Preserved			

a) HNRC loco on long term loan to Bluebell Railway
b) At EMR Attercliffe

Class 09/1
Converted from Class 08. 110V electrical equipment.
Details as Class 09/0.

Latest Number Carried	Previous Number 1	Previous Number 2	Previous Number 3	Year Entered Service	Year Withdrawn	Current Status/Scrapping Details	Notes
09101	08833	D4001		1992	2008	2011: C F Booth, Rotherham	
09102	08832	D4000		1992	2005	2011: T J Thomson, Stockton	
09103	08766	D3934		1992	2008	2010: Ayr Harbour	
09104	08749	D3917		1993	2002	2011: EMR, Hartlepool	
09105	08835	D4003		1993	2009	2011: C F Booth, Rotherham	
6	09106	08759	D3927	1993		Harry Needle Railroad Co	
09107	08845	D4013		1993	2010	Preserved	

Class 09/2
Converted from Class 08. 90V electrical equipment.
Details as Class 09/0.

Latest Number Carried	Previous Number 1	Previous Number 2	Year Entered Service	Year Withdrawn	Current Status/Scrapping Details	Notes
09201	08421	D3536	1992		Harry Needle Railroad Co	
09202	08732	D3900	1992	2006	2011: C F Booth, Rotherham	
09203	08781	D3949	1992	2005	2012: C F Booth, Rotherham	
09204	08717	D3884	1992		Arriva Traincare	
09205	08620	D3787	1992	2008	2012: T J Thomson, Stockton	

▲ Class 09s are identical to the more numerous Class 08s, except that they are geared differently to allow a higher maximum speed. While it was allocated to the relatively nearby Selhurst depot, 09016 is seen stabled at Clapham Junction during 1979. **Les Peters/Rail Photoprints**

▼ D4076 was one of the 146 Blackstone-engined 0-6-0 shunters that were designated Class 10 under TOPS, although none survived long enough to carry a TOPS number. The locomotive, which was only in service for seven years, is seen stabled at Peterborough during 1963.
John Chalcraft/Rail Photoprints

CLASS 10   0-6-0

Built: 1955–62 by British Railways, Darlington & Doncaster.
Engine: Blackstone ERT6 of 261 kW (350 hp) at 750 rpm.
Transmission: Electric.
Maximum Speed: 20 mph.
Train Brakes: Vacuum.

UL   Scrapping details unconfirmed, but likely to be correct
UM   Scrapping details unconfirmed, but may be correct

Latest Number Carried	Previous Number 1	Year Entered Service	Year Withdrawn	Current Status/Scrapping Details	Notes
D3137	13137	1955	1970	1971: C F Booth, Doncaster	UL
D3138	13138	1955	1972	1973: C F Booth, Rotherham	
D3139	13139	1955	1968	1969: C F Booth, Rotherham	
D3140	13140	1955	1968	1969: C F Booth, Rotherham	UL
D3141	13141	1955	1971	1972: C F Booth, Rotherham	UL
D3142	13142	1955	1968	1969: C F Booth, Rotherham	UL
D3143	13143	1955	1969	1970: G Cohen, Kettering	UL
D3144	13144	1955	1969	1969: Hughes Bolckow, Blyth	UL
D3145	13145	1955	1972	1973: C F Booth, Rotherham	
D3146	13146	1955	1968	1968: Hughes Bolckow, Blyth	UL
D3147	13147	1955	1968	1969: C F Booth, Rotherham	
D3148	13148	1955	1968	1969: C F Booth, Rotherham	
D3149	13149	1955	1970	1970: C F Booth, Rotherham	
D3150	13150	1955	1968	1969: C F Booth, Rotherham	UL
D3151	13151	1955	1967	1968: Hughes Bolckow, Blyth	UL
D3439		1957	1968	1969: Steelbreak & Dism., Chesterf'd	
D3440		1957	1968	1969: G Cohen, Kettering	UL
D3441		1957	1968	1969: G Cohen, Kettering	
D3442		1957	1968	1969: C F Booth, Rotherham	
D3443		1957	1968	1969: C F Booth, Rotherham	UL
D3444		1957	1968	1969: G Cohen, Kettering	
D3445		1957	1968	1969: Cox & Danks, North Acton	UL
D3446		1957	1968	1969: Steelbreak & Dism., Chesterf'd	UL
D3447		1957	1968	1968: C F Booth, Rotherham	
D3448		1957	1968	1969: Steelbreak & Dism., Chesterf'd	UL
D3449		1957	1967	1968: C F Booth, Rotherham	
D3450		1957	1968	1969: C F Booth, Rotherham	
D3451		1957	1968	1969: C F Booth, Rotherham	
D3452		1957	1968	Preserved	
D3453		1957	1968	1969: C F Booth, Rotherham	UL
D3473		1957	1968	1969: C F Booth, Rotherham	
D3474		1957	1968	1969: C F Booth, Rotherham	UL
D3475		1957	1968	1969: C F Booth, Rotherham	
D3476		1957	1968	2009: T J Thomson, Stockton	
D3477		1957	1968	1969: G Cohen, Kettering	
D3478		1958	1968	1969: C F Booth, Rotherham	
D3479		1958	1969	1969: G Cohen, Kettering	UL
D3480		1958	1968	1969: Steelbreak & Dism., Chesterf'd	
D3481		1958	1968	1969: C F Booth, Rotherham	
D3482		1958	1968	1969: C F Booth, Rotherham	
D3483		1958	1969	1969: G Cohen, Kettering	UL
D3484		1958	1968	1969: Steelbreak & Dism., Chesterf'd	UL
D3485		1958	1968	1969: G Cohen, Kettering	UL
D3486		1958	1970	1971: C F Booth, Rotherham	
D3487		1958	1968	1969: C F Booth, Rotherham	UL
D3488		1958	1968	1969: G Cohen, Kettering	
D3489		1958	1968	Preserved	
D3490		1958	1968	1969: C F Booth, Rotherham	
D3491		1958	1968	1969: G Cohen, Kettering	
D3492		1958	1969	1969: G Cohen, Kettering	UL
D3493		1958	1968	1969: C F Booth, Rotherham	

D3494	1958	1968	1969: G Cohen, Kettering	
D3495	1958	1968	1969: C F Booth, Rotherham	
D3496	1958	1967	1968: Doncaster Works	
D3497	1957	1968	1990: ECC Ports Ltd, Fowey	
D3498	1957	1968	1969: C F Booth, Rotherham	
D3499	1957	1968	1968: C F Booth, Rotherham	
D3500	1958	1968	1968: J Cashmore, Great Bridge	
D3501	1958	1968	1969: C F Booth, Rotherham	
D3502	1958	1968	1968: J Cashmore, Great Bridge	
D3612	1958	1969	1969: G Cohen, Kettering	
D3613	1958	1969	1985: NCB Moorgreen Colliery	
D3614	1958	1969	1969: Steelbreak & Dism., Chesterf'd	
D3615	1958	1968	1969: G Cohen, Kettering	
D3616	1958	1969	1969: Steelbreak & Dism., Chesterf'd	
D3617	1958	1969	1969: Steelbreak & Dism., Chesterf'd	UL
D3618	1958	1969	1985: NCB Moorgreen Colliery	
D3619	1958	1969	1985: NCB Moorgreen Colliery	
D3620	1958	1967	1967: Slag Reduction, Ickles	
D3621	1958	1969	1969: C F Booth, Rotherham	UM
D3622	1958	1969	1969: C F Booth, Rotherham	
D3623	1958	1969	1969: C F Booth, Rotherham	
D3624	1958	1968	1969: C F Booth, Rotherham	
D3625	1958	1968	1969: C F Booth, Rotherham	
D3626	1958	1968	1969: C F Booth, Rotherham	
D3627	1958	1968	1969: C F Booth, Rotherham	
D3628	1958	1967	1968: C F Booth, Rotherham	
D3629	1958	1969	1969: G Cohen, Kettering	UL
D3630	1958	1968	1969: Cox & Danks, North Acton	UL
D3631	1958	1967	1967: Stratford Depot	UL
D3632	1958	1968	1969: C F Booth, Rotherham	
D3633	1958	1968	1969: G Cohen, Kettering	UL
D3634	1958	1971	1972: C F Booth, Rotherham	UL
D3635	1958	1968	1969: G Cohen, Kettering	
D3636	1958	1968	1969: Stratford Depot	
D3637	1958	1968	1969: G Cohen, Kettering	
D3638	1958	1970	1975: NCB Ashington Colliery	
D3639	1958	1969	Exported to Guinea in 1970	
D3640	1958	1968	1969: G Cohen, Kettering	UL
D3641	1958	1971	1973: C F Booth, Rotherham	
D3642	1958	1969	1978: Br. Steel, Appleby Frodingham	
D3643	1958	1968	1969: G Cohen, Kettering	UL
D3644	1958	1970	1971: C F Booth, Rotherham	UL
D3645	1958	1969	1969: C F Booth, Rotherham	
D3646	1958	1971	1971: C F Booth, Rotherham	UL
D3647	1958	1970	1970: C F Booth, Rotherham	UL
D3648	1959	1971	1977: NCB Bates Colliery	
D3649	1959	1969	Exported to Guinea in 1970	
D3650	1959	1971	1972: C F Booth, Rotherham	UL
D3651	1959	1971	1972: C F Booth, Rotherham	UL
D4049	1961	1972	1972: G Cohen, Kettering	UL
D4050	1961	1971	1972: C F Booth, Rotherham	
D4051	1961	1971	1972: C F Booth, Rotherham	UL
D4052	1961	1970	1971: C F Booth, Rotherham	
D4053	1961	1971	1972: C F Booth, Rotherham	
D4054	1961	1972	1973: G Cohen, Kettering	UL
D4055	1961	1971	1972: C F Booth, Rotherham	
D4056	1961	1972	1983: NCB Shilbottle Colliery	
D4057	1961	1972	1972: C F Booth, Rotherham	
D4058	1961	1972	1972: G Cohen, Kettering	UL
D4059	1961	1971	1972: G Cohen, Kettering	UL
D4060	1961	1971	1972: C F Booth, Rotherham	UL
D4061	1961	1972	1972: C F Booth, Rotherham	
D4062	1961	1972	1972: C F Booth, Rotherham	
D4063	1961	1972	1973: G Cohen, Kettering	

D4064		1961	1968	1969: C F Booth, Rotherham	UL
D4065		1961	1971	1972: C F Booth, Rotherham	
D4066		1961	1972	1973: G Cohen, Kettering	
10119	D4067	1961	1970	Preserved	a)
D4068		1961	1972	1985: NCB Whittle Colliery	
D4069		1961	1972	1985: NCB Whittle Colliery	
D4070		1961	1972	1985: NCB Whittle Colliery	
D4071		1961	1968	1969: G Cohen, Kettering	
D4072		1961	1972	1985: NCB Philadelphia Colliery	
D4073		1961	1972	1973: G Cohen, Kettering	
D4074		1961	1972	1978: NCB Philadelphia Colliery	
D4075		1961	1972	1973: G Cohen, Kettering	
D4076		1961	1968	1969: C F Booth, Rotherham	
D4077		1961	1970	1971: C F Booth, Rotherham	
D4078		1961	1972	1973: G Cohen, Kettering	
D4079		1961	1972	1973: G Cohen, Kettering	
D4080		1961	1968	1968: C F Booth, Rotherham	
D4081		1962	1968	1969: C F Booth, Rotherham	UL
D4082		1962	1968	1969: C F Booth, Rotherham	UL
D4083		1962	1968	1969: C F Booth, Rotherham	
D4084		1962	1968	1969: C F Booth, Rotherham	UM
D4085		1962	1968	1969: C F Booth, Rotherham	UM
D4086		1962	1968	1969: C F Booth, Rotherham	UL
D4087		1962	1968	1969: G Cohen, Kettering	
D4088		1962	1968	1969: C F Booth, Rotherham	
D4089		1962	1968	1969: C F Booth, Rotherham	
D4090		1962	1968	1969: G Cohen, Kettering	
D4091		1962	1968	1969: C F Booth, Rotherham	UL
D4092		1962	1968	Preserved	
D4093		1962	1968	1969: G Cohen, Kettering	
D4094		1962	1968	1969: G Cohen, Kettering	

a) Number 10119 carried during preservation only

▲ Despite what its number could incorrectly suggest, this is a Class 11 carrying its BR 1957 Series number 12051. The 350hp shunter is seen at Crewe during 1949. **R. A. Whitfield/Rail Photoprints**

CLASS 11 0-6-0

Built: 1945–52 by LMS/British Railways Derby & Darlington.
Engine: English Electric 6KT of 261 kW (350 hp) at 750 rpm.
Transmission: Electric.
Maximum Speed: 20mph.
Train Brakes: None when built.

UL Scrapping details unconfirmed, but likely to be correct
UM Scrapping details unconfirmed, but may be correct

Latest Number Carried	Previous Number 1	Year Entered Service	Year Withdrawn	Current Status/Scrapping Details	Notes
12033	7120	1945	1969	1970: J Cashmore, Great Bridge	
12034	7121	1945	1968	1969: J McWilliam, Shettleston	UL
12035	7122	1945	1968	1969: J McWilliam, Shettleston	UL
12036	7123	1945	1968	1970: J Cashmore, Great Bridge	
12037	7124	1945	1968	1970: J Cashmore, Great Bridge	
12038	7125	1945	1969	1971: G Cohen, Kettering	
12039	7126	1947	1968	1970: J Cashmore, Great Bridge	
12040	7127	1947	1968	1970: J Cashmore, Great Bridge	
12041	7128	1947	1968	1969: Swindon Works	
12042	7129	1947	1968	1969: J Cashmore, Newport	
12043	7130	1948	1968	1969: J Cashmore, Great Bridge	
12044	7131	1948	1968	1969: J Cashmore, Great Bridge	
12045		1948	1969	1969: J Cashmore, Great Bridge	
12046		1948	1969	1969: Bletchley Depot	UL
12047		1948	1969	1970: J Cashmore, Great Bridge	
12048		1948	1969	1970: J Cashmore, Great Bridge	
12049[1]		1949	1971	2011: EMR, Kingsbury	a)
12050		1949	1970	1972: NCB Philadelphia Colliery	
12051		1949	1971	1973: J Cashmore, Great Bridge	
12052		1949	1971	Preserved	
12053		1949	1971	1969: Bird Group, Long Marston	UL
12054		1949	1970	1984: A R Adams, Newport	
12055		1949	1971	1972: C F Booth, Rotherham	UL
12056		1949	1971	1973: G Cohen, Kettering	
12057		1949	1969	1970: J Cashmore, Great Bridge	
12058		1949	1971	1973: J Cashmore, Newport	
12059		1949	1969	1969: J Cashmore, Great Bridge	
12060		1949	1971	1985: NCB Philadelphia Colliery	
12061		1949	1971	2013: EMR, Attercliffe	
12062		1949	1970	1971: Derby Works	UM
12063		1949	1972	1987: NCB Nantgarw Coking Plant	
12064		1949	1969	1969: J Cashmore, Great Bridge	
12065		1949	1971	1972: C F Booth, Rotherham	UL
12066		1949	1969	1970: J Cashmore, Great Bridge	
12067		1950	1969	1970: G Cohen, Kettering	
12068		1950	1967	1968: G Cohen, Kettering	
12069		1950	1971	1972: Bird Group, Long Marston	UL
12070		1950	1969	1970: C F Booth, Rotherham	
12071		1950	1971	1995: Coopers Metals, Attercliffe	UL
12072		1950	1968	1969: G Cohen, Kettering	
12073		1950	1971	1972: C F Booth, Rotherham	
12074		1950	1972	2002: EMR, Kingsbury	
12075		1950	1971	1973: G Cohen, Kettering	
12076		1950	1971	1973: G Cohen, Kettering	
12077		1950	1971	Preserved	
12078		1950	1971	1971: G Cohen, Kettering	
12079		1950	1971	1972: C F Booth, Rotherham	UL
12080		1950	1971	1972: Doncaster Works	
12081		1950	1970	1972: C F Booth, Rotherham	
12049[2]	12082	1950	1971	Preserved	b)
12083		1950	1971	Preserved	

12084	1950	1971	1985: NCB Philadelphia Colliery	
12085	1950	1971	1973: T W Ward, Barrow in Furness	
12086	1950	1969	1970: J Cashmore, Great Bridge	
12087	1950	1971	1973: G Cohen, Kettering	
12088	1951	1971	Preserved	
12089	1951	1970	1971: Derby Works	UM
12090	1951	1971	1972: C F Booth, Rotherham	
12091	1951	1970	1971: Derby Works	UM
12092	1951	1969	1970: J Cashmore, Great Bridge	
12093	1951	1971	Preserved	
12094	1951	1971	1972: C F Booth, Rotherham	
12095	1951	1969	1970: J Cashmore, Great Bridge	
12096	1951	1969	1970: G Cohen, Kettering	
12097	1951	1971	1972: Doncaster Works	
12098	1952	1971	2006: EMR, Kingsbury	
12099	1952	1971	Preserved	
12100	1952	1969	1969: J Cashmore, Great Bridge	
12101	1952	1970	1971: G Cohen, Kettering	
12102	1952	1971	1971: G Cohen, Kettering	
12103	1952	1971	1973: J Cashmore, Newport	
12104	1952	1967	1967: Stratford Depot	
12105	1952	1971	1972: Stratford Depot	
12106	1952	1970	1971: C F Booth, Rotherham	
12107	1952	1967	1968: J McWilliam, Shettleston	
12108	1952	1971	1977: T W Ward, Beighton	
12109	1952	1972	1973: Marple & Gillot, Attercliffe	
12110	1952	1972	1973: Marple & Gillot, Attercliffe	
12111	1952	1971	1972: Stratford Depot	
12112	1952	1969	1970: C F Booth, Rotherham	UL
12113	1952	1971	1971: G Cohen, Kettering	
12114	1952	1970	1972: Stratford Depot	
12115	1952	1970	1972: Stratford Depot	
12116	1952	1969	1970: G Cohen, Kettering	UL
12117	1952	1969	1969: Arnott Young, Parkgate	UL
12118	1952	1971	1971: G Cohen, Kettering	
12119	1952	1968	1985: NCB Philadelphia Colliery	
12120	1952	1969	1980: NCB Philadelphia Colliery	
12121	1952	1971	1972: C F Booth, Rotherham	UL
12122	1952	1971	1985: British Oak DP, Crigglestone	
12123	1952	1967	1967: T W Ward, Beighton	
12124	1952	1968	1969: G Cohen, Kettering	
12125	1952	1969	1969: J McWilliam, Shettleston	UL
12126	1952	1968	1969: Arnott Young, Parkgate	
12127	1952	1972	1975: Doncaster Works	
12128	1952	1970	1971: C F Booth, Rotherham	
12129	1952	1967	1968: Steelbreak & Dism., Chesterf'd	
12130	1952	1972	1973: J Cashmore, Newport	
12131	1952	1969	Preserved	
12132	1952	1972	1973: J Cashmore, Newport	
12133	1952	1969	1985: NCB Philadelphia Colliery	
12134	1952	1972	1973: G Cohen, Kettering	
12135	1952	1969	1969: J McWilliam, Shettleston	UL
12136	1952	1971	1977: T W Ward, Beighton	
12137	1952	1968	1969: Stratford Depot	
12138	1952	1968	1969: G Cohen, Kettering	

a) First of 2 locomotives to be numbered 12049
b) Second of 2 locomotives to be numbered 12049 (only in Preservation)

CLASS 12   0-6-0

Built: 1949–52 by British Railways, Ashford Works.
Engine: English Electric 6KT of 261 kW (350hp) at 750 rpm.
Transmission: Electric.
Maximum Speed: 27.5 mph.
Train Brakes: None when built.

UL   Scrapping details unconfirmed, but likely to be correct

Latest Number Carried	Previous Number 1	Year Entered Service	Year Withdrawn	Current Status/Scrapping Details	Notes
15211		1949	1971	1973: J Cashmore, Newport	
15212		1949	1971	1972: J Cashmore, Newport	
15213		1949	1968	1970: Hither Green Depot	UL
15214		1949	1971	1972: J Cashmore, Newport	
15215		1949	1968	1968: Swindon Works	
15216		1949	1969	1969: Swindon Works	UL
15217		1949	1970	1971: Selhurst Depot	UL
15218		1949	1970	1970: C F Booth, Rotherham	
15219		1949	1971	1972: J Cashmore, Newport	
15220		1949	1971	1973: J Cashmore, Newport	
15221		1949	1971	1972: J Cashmore, Newport	
15222		1949	1971	1978: J Williams, Kidwelly	
15223		1949	1969	1970: C F Booth, Rotherham	
15224		1949	1971	Preserved	
15225		1949	1971	1972: J Cashmore, Newport	
15226		1950	1969	1969: J Cashmore, Newport	
15227		1951	1970	1970: Eastleigh Works	
15228		1951	1969	1969: Swindon Works	
15229		1951	1971	1972: J Cashmore, Newport	
15230		1951	1971	1972: J Cashmore, Newport	
15231		1951	1971	1984: Tilcon Grassington	
15232		1951	1971	1972: Swindon Works	
15233		1951	1969	1969: J Cashmore, Newport	
15234		1951	1968	1969: Swindon Works	
15235		1951	1971	1973: J Cashmore, Newport	
15236		1952	1968	1972: Swindon Works	

CLASS 13   0-6-0 + 0-6-0

Each shunting locomotive was formed from two former Class 08s, one master and one slave for hump shunting in Tinsley Yard, Sheffield.

Conversions Completed: 1965
Engine: Two English Electric 6KT.
Horsepower: 700hp.
Transmission: Electric.
Maximum Speed: 20 mph.
Train Brakes: Vacuum.

Latest Number Carried	Previous Number 1	Year Entered Service	Year Withdrawn	Current Status/Scrapping Details	Notes
13001	D4501	1965	1985	1985: Swindon Works	
13002	D4502	1965	1981	1982: Swindon Works	
13003	D4500	1965	1985	1986: Doncaster Works	

▲ The Class 12 was a slightly lighter and faster development of the Southern Railway's 1937-built Class D3/12 experimental shunter. The 26 locomotives entered service between 1949–1952 and had all been withdrawn by 1971. Consequently, none survived long enough to be given a TOPS number. During their latter days, 15221 and 15212 are seen between duties at Hither Green depot on 7 June 1970. **Gordon Edgar**

▼ The Class 13 was created in 1965, when three pairs of 08s were permanently coupled together to form three more powerful units for operation within Tinsley Yard. In each case, one of the shunters had its cab removed. On 12 May 1985, shortly after it had been withdrawn, 13003 awaits scrapping at Doncaster Works. **Gordon Edgar**

CLASS 14

0-6-0

Built: 1964–65 by British Railways, Swindon Works.
Engine: Paxman Ventura 6YJXL of 485 kW (650 hp) at 680 rpm.
Transmission: Hydraulic.
Maximum Speed: 40 mph.
Train Heating/Supply: None.
Train Brakes: Vacuum.

ES   Locomotive exported and subsequently scrapped
UL   Scrapping details unconfirmed, but likely to be correct
UM   Scrapping details unconfirmed, but may be correct

Latest Number Carried	Previous Number 1	Year Entered Service	Year Withdrawn	Current Status/Scrapping Details	Notes
D9500		1964	1969	Preserved	
D9501		1964	1968	1968: C F Booth, Rotherham	UL
D9502		1964	1969	Preserved	
D9503		1964	1968	1980: British Steel, Corby	
D9504		1964	1968	Preserved	
D9505		1964	1968	1999: Ghent, Belguim	ES
D9506		1964	1968	1968: Arnott Young, Parkgate	
D9507		1964	1968	1982: British Steel, Corby	
D9508		1964	1968	1984: NCB Ashington Colliery	
D9509		1964	1968	1971: G Cohen, Kettering	
D9510		1964	1968	1982: British Steel, Corby	
D9511		1964	1968	1979: NCB Ashington Colliery	
D9512		1964	1968	1982: British Steel, Corby	
38	D9513	1964	1968	Preserved	
D9514		1964	1969	1985: NCB Ashington Colliery	
D9515		1964	1968	2002: Madrid, Spain	ES
D9516		1964	1968	Preserved	
D9517		1964	1968	1984: NCB Ashington Colliery	
D9518		1964	1969	Preserved	
D9519		1964	1968	1971: G Cohen, Kettering	
D9520		1964	1968	Preserved	
D9521		1964	1969	Preserved	
D9522		1964	1967	1968: Arnott Young, Parkgate	
D9523		1964	1968	Preserved	
14901	D9524	1964	1969	Preserved	
D9525		1965	1968	Preserved	
D9526		1965	1968	Preserved	
D9527		1965	1969	1984: NCB Ashington Colliery	
D9528		1965	1969	1981: NCB Ashington Colliery	
D9529		1965	1968	Preserved	
D9530		1965	1968	1982: NCB Mardy Colliery	
D9531		1965	1967	Preserved	
D9532		1965	1968	1982: British Steel, Corby	
D9533		1965	1968	1982: British Steel, Corby	
D9534		1965	1968	2005: Brescia, Italy	ES UM
D9535		1965	1968	1984: NCB Ashington Colliery	
D9536		1965	1969	1985: NCB Ashington Colliery	
D9537		1965	1968	Preserved	
D9538		1965	1969	1982: British Steel, Corby	
D9539		1965	1968	Preserved	
D9540		1965	1968	1984: NCB Ashington Colliery	
D9541		1965	1968	1982: British Steel, Corby	
D9542		1965	1968	1982: British Steel, Corby	
D9543		1965	1968	1968: C F Booth, Rotherham	
D9544		1965	1968	1980: British Steel, Corby	
D9545		1965	1968	1979: NCB Ashington Colliery	
D9546		1965	1968	1968: C F Booth, Rotherham	
D9547		1965	1968	1982: British Steel, Corby	
D9548		1965	1968	2002: Barcelona, Spain	ES UM

D9549	1965	1968	2003: Zaragoza, Spain	ES
D9550	1965	1968	1968: C F Booth, Rotherham	
D9551	1965	1968	Preserved	
D9552	1965	1968	1980: British Steel, Corby	
D9553	1965	1968	Preserved	
D9554	1965	1968	1982: British Steel, Corby	
D9555	1965	1969	Preserved	

CLASS 15   Bo-Bo

Built: 1957–61 by Yorkshire Engine Company, Sheffield and BTH/Clayton Equipment Company, Derbyshire.
Engine: Paxman 16YHXL of 485 kW (800 hp) at 1500 rpm.
Transmission: Electric.
Maximum Speed: 60 mph.
Train Heating/Supply: None.
Train Brakes: Vacuum.

SP   Locomotive was not self-propelled whilst in departmental use

Latest Number Carried	Previous Number 1	Year Entered Service	Year Withdrawn	Current Status/Scrapping Details	Notes
D8200		1957	1971	1972: Crewe Works	
D8201		1958	1971	1972: Crewe Works	
D8202		1958	1968	1969: G Cohen, Kettering	
ADB968003	D8203	1958	1981	1981: Colchester Depot	SP
D8204		1958	1971	1972: Crewe Works	
D8205		1958	1968	1969: G Cohen, Kettering	
D8206		1958	1968	1970: D Woodham, Barry	
D8207		1958	1971	1972: Crewe Works	
D8208		1958	1968	1969: G Cohen, Kettering	
D8209		1958	1971	1972: Crewe Works	
D8210		1959	1971	1972: Crewe Works	
D8211		1959	1971	1971: Crewe Works	
D8212		1959	1968	1969: G Cohen, Kettering	
D8213		1959	1968	1969: G Cohen, Kettering	
D8214		1959	1970	1971: Crewe Works	
D8215		1959	1970	1971: Crewe Works	
D8216		1959	1971	1972: Crewe Works	
D8217		1960	1968	1969: G Cohen, Kettering	
D8218		1960	1971	1971: Crewe Works	
D8219		1960	1968	1969: G Cohen, Kettering	
D8220		1960	1971	1971: Crewe Works	
D8221		1960	1971	1971: Crewe Works	
D8222		1960	1971	1971: Crewe Works	
D8223		1960	1968	1969: G Cohen, Kettering	
D8224		1960	1971	1971: Crewe Works	
D8225		1960	1971	1971: Crewe Works	
D8226		1960	1971	1971: Crewe Works	
D8227		1960	1968	1969: G Cohen, Kettering	
D8228		1960	1971	1971: Crewe Works	
D8229		1960	1971	1972: Crewe Works	
D8230		1960	1971	1971: Crewe Works	
D8231		1960	1971	1972: Crewe Works	
D8232		1960	1971	1971: Crewe Works	
ADB968001	D8233	1960	1982	Preserved	SP
D8234		1960	1971	1971: Crewe Works	
D8235		1960	1968	1969: G Cohen, Kettering	
D8236		1960	1968	1969: G Cohen, Kettering	
ADB968002	D8237	1960	1982	1985: Marple & Gillot, Attercliffe	SP
D8238		1960	1968	1969: G Cohen, Kettering	
D8239		1961	1971	1972: Crewe Works	
D8240		1961	1968	1969: G Cohen, Kettering	

▲ The diesel-hydraulic Class 14 was designed for short-distance freight workings, but a lack of such duties caused BR to dispose of the entire class by the end of 1970. Some were scrapped as little as three years after they were built, but most were sold to industrial operators, for whom they gave many years of reliable service. 19 have been preserved, including D9551, which on 17 May 2019 was stabled at Bridgnorth on the Severn Valley Railway. **Andy Chard**

▼ Of the 44 British Thomson-Houston Type 1s introduced between 1957 and 1961, none survived long enough to be given TOPS numbers. These unusual looking engines were assigned to BR's Eastern Region, but were forfeit in favour of the English Electric Type 1 (Class 20). D8210 is seen stabled at Colchester on either the 5 or 6 June 1970. **53A Models of Hull Collection (John Senior)**

D8241		1961	1968	1968: J Cashmore, Great Bridge	
D8242		1961	1971	1971: Crewe Works	
ADB968000	D8243	1961	1987	1991: Vic Berry, Leicester	SP

CLASS 16 Bo-Bo

Built: 1958 by North British Locomotive Company, Glasgow.
Engine: Paxman 16YHXL of 597 kW (800 hp) at 1250 rpm.
Transmission: Electric.
Maximum Speed: 60 mph.
Train Heating/Supply: None.
Train Brakes: Vacuum.

Latest Number Carried	Previous Number 1	Year Entered Service	Year Withdrawn	Current Status/Scrapping Details	Notes
D8400		1958	1968	1969: G Cohen, Kettering	
D8401		1958	1968	1969: G Cohen, Kettering	
D8402		1958	1968	1969: G Cohen, Kettering	
D8403		1958	1968	1969: G Cohen, Kettering	
D8404		1958	1968	1968: Cox & Danks, North Acton	
D8405		1958	1968	1969: G Cohen, Kettering	
D8406		1958	1968	1969: Bird Group, Long Marston	
D8407		1958	1968	1969: G Cohen, Kettering	
D8408		1958	1968	1969: G Cohen, Kettering	
D8409		1958	1968	1969: G Cohen, Kettering	

CLASS 17 Bo-Bo

Built: 1962–65 by Clayton Equipment Company, Derbyshire and Beyer Peacock & Co, Manchester.
Engine: Paxman 2 x 6ZHXL of 336 kW (450 hp) at 1500 rpm (except D8586 & D8587 which had 2 x Rolls Royce D Series engines).
Transmission: Electric.
Maximum Speed: 60mph.
Train Heating/Supply: None.
Train Brakes: Vacuum.

SP Locomotive was not self-propelled whilst in departmental use
UL Scrapping details unconfirmed, but likely to be correct

Latest Number Carried	Previous Number 1	Year Entered Service	Year Withdrawn	Current Status/Scrapping Details	Notes
D8500		1962	1971	1971: Glasgow Works	
D8501		1962	1968	1971: Glasgow Works	
D8502		1962	1971	1973: Glasgow Works	
D8503		1962	1971	1972: Glasgow Works	
D8504		1962	1971	1975: J Cashmore, Great Bridge	
D8505		1962	1971	1974: Glasgow Works	
D8506		1962	1971	1971: Glasgow Works	
D8507		1962	1971	1975: A King, Norwich	
D8508		1962	1971	1975: A King, Norwich	
D8509		1962	1968	1972: Glasgow Works	
D8510		1962	1971	1971: Glasgow Works	
D8511		1962	1968	1970: J McWilliam, Shettleston	
D8512		1962	1972	1973: Glasgow Works	a)
D8513		1962	1971	1971: Glasgow Works	
D8514		1963	1968	1971: Glasgow Works	
D8515		1963	1971	1972: Glasgow Works	
D8516		1963	1971	1975: A King, Norwich	
D8517		1963	1968	1970: J McWilliam, Shettleston	
D8518		1963	1968	1972: Glasgow Works	
D8519		1963	1968	1972: Glasgow Works	
D8520		1963	1968	1972: Glasgow Works	

▲ This early colour image of the first-built North British Type 1 (TOPS Class 16) D8400 shows it at Temple Mills Yard in East London circa 1959. Only ten were built; the entire class was withdrawn in 1968 and they had all been scrapped by 1969. **53A Models of Hull Collection**

▼ The cabs of the 117 Class 17s were located centrally in an attempt to improve driver visibility, but this arrangement did not catch on. With the exception of the three locomotives retained for departmental duties, the entire class had been withdrawn by 1971. D8599, which had a career lasting only seven years, is stabled at Tyne Yard with a classmate during July 1969. **53A Models of Hull Collection (D R Vickers)**

S18521	D8521	1963	1978	1979: Glasgow Works	SP
D8522		1963	1968	1972: Glasgow Works	
D8523		1963	1968	1972: Glasgow Works	
D8524		1963	1968	1970: J McWilliam, Shettleston	
D8525		1963	1971	1976: A King, Norwich	
D8526		1963	1968	1972: Glasgow Works	
D8527		1963	1968	1972: Glasgow Works	
D8528		1963	1971	1973: Glasgow Works	
D8529		1963	1971	1976: A King, Norwich	
D8530		1963	1971	1971: Glasgow Works	
D8531		1963	1971	1975: A King, Norwich	
D8532		1963	1968	1972: Glasgow Works	
D8533		1963	1968	1972: Glasgow Works	
D8534		1963	1968	1973: Glasgow Works	
D8535		1963	1971	1971: Glasgow Works	
D8536		1963	1971	1975: A King, Norwich	
D8537		1963	1968	1969: J McWilliam, Shettleston	
D8538		1963	1971	1972: Glasgow Works	
D8539		1963	1971	1976: A King, Norwich	
D8540		1963	1971	1973: Glasgow Works	
D8541		1963	1971	1973: Glasgow Works	
D8542		1963	1971	1975: J Cashmore, Great Bridge	
D8543		1963	1971	1972: Glasgow Works	
D8544		1963	1969	1971: J McWilliam, Shettleston	
D8545		1963	1971	1973: Glasgow Works	
D8546		1963	1971	1975: J Cashmore, Great Bridge	
D8547		1963	1969	1970: Bird Group, Cardiff	UL
D8548		1963	1971	1975: J Cashmore, Great Bridge	
D8549		1963	1971	1972: Glasgow Works	
D8550		1963	1971	1975: J Cashmore, Great Bridge	
D8551		1963	1971	1975: J Cashmore, Great Bridge	
D8552		1963	1971	1975: R A King, Norwich	
D8553		1963	1968	1969: J McWilliam, Shettleston	
D8554		1963	1969	1971: J McWilliam, Shettleston	UL
D8555		1963	1971	1972: Glasgow Works	
D8556		1963	1969	1970: Bird Group, Long Marston	
D8557		1963	1971	1975: J McWilliam, Shettleston	
D8558		1963	1971	1973: Glasgow Works	
D8559		1963	1971	1974: Glasgow Works	
D8560		1963	1969	1969: Bird Group, Long Marston	
D8561		1963	1971	1973: Glasgow Works	
D8562		1963	1971	1973: Glasgow Works	
D8563		1963	1971	1975: J Cashmore, Great Bridge	
D8564		1963	1969	1970: Bird Group, Long Marston	
D8565		1963	1971	1973: Glasgow Works	
D8566		1963	1968	1969: J McWilliam, Shettleston	
D8567		1964	1971	1973: Glasgow Works	
D8568		1964	1971	Preserved	
D8569		1964	1968	1969: J McWilliam, Shettleston	
D8570		1964	1968	1969: Bird Group, Long Marston	
D8571		1964	1969	1971: J McWilliam, Shettleston	
D8572		1964	1969	1970: J Cashmore, Great Bridge	
D8573		1964	1971	1975: J McWilliam, Shettleston	
D8574		1964	1971	1975: A King, Norwich	
D8575		1964	1968	1969: J McWilliam, Shettleston	
D8576		1964	1969	1970: Bird Group, Long Marston	UL
D8577		1964	1969	1970: Bird Group, Long Marston	
D8578		1964	1969	1971: J McWilliam, Shettleston	UL
D8579		1964	1971	1973: Glasgow Works	
D8580		1964	1971	1975: A King, Norwich	
D8581		1964	1971	1974: Glasgow Works	
D8582		1964	1969	1969: J McWilliam, Shettleston	
D8583		1964	1971	1973: Glasgow Works	
D8584		1964	1968	1969: J McWilliam, Shettleston	

D8585	1964	1968	1969: J McWilliam, Shettleston	
D8586	1964	1971	1973: Glasgow Works	
D8587	1965	1971	1974: Glasgow Works	
D8588	1964	1971	1973: Glasgow Works	
D8589	1964	1970	1971: Gateshead Depot	UL
D8590	1964	1971	1971: Glasgow Works	
D8591	1964	1968	1969: J McWilliam, Shettleston	UL
D8592	1964	1971	1972: Glasgow Works	
D8593	1964	1971	1973: Glasgow Works	
D8594	1964	1971	1972: Glasgow Works	
D8595	1964	1968	1969: J McWilliam, Shettleston	
D8596	1964	1968	1969: J McWilliam, Shettleston	
D8597	1964	1971	1973: Glasgow Works	
D8598	1964	1978	1979: Glasgow Works	b)
D8599	1964	1971	1971: Glasgow Works	
D8600	1964	1971	1973: Glasgow Works	
D8601	1964	1971	1974: Glasgow Works	
D8602	1964	1971	1972: Glasgow Works	
D8603	1964	1971	1972: Glasgow Works	
D8604	1964	1971	1972: Glasgow Works	
D8605	1964	1968	1970: A Draper, Hull	
D8606	1964	1971	1972: Glasgow Works	
D8607	1964	1971	1975: J McWilliam, Shettleston	
D8608	1964	1971	1975: J McWilliam, Shettleston	
D8609	1964	1968	1969: J McWilliam, Shettleston	UL
D8610	1964	1971	1973: Glasgow Works	
D8611	1964	1968	1969: J McWilliam, Shettleston	UL
D8612	1965	1971	1975: J McWilliam, Shettleston	
D8613	1965	1971	1975: J McWilliam, Shettleston	
D8614	1965	1971	1972: Glasgow Works	
D8615	1965	1971	1973: Glasgow Works	
D8616	1965	1971	1975: J McWilliam, Shettleston	

a) D8512 was a departmental loco between 1969 and 1972
b) D8598 was a departmental loco between 1972 and 1978

CLASS 20 Bo-Bo

Built: 1957–68 by English Electric, Vulcan Foundry, Newton-le-Willows and Robert Stephenson & Hawthorns, Darlington.
Engine: English Electric 8SVT of 746 kW (1000 hp) at 850 rpm.
Transmission: Electric.
Maximum Speed: 75 mph.
Train Heating/Supply: None.
Train Brakes: Built vacuum, most later dual braked (air & vacuum).
CR   The cab remains

Class 20/0

Latest Number Carried	Previous Number 1	Previous Number 2	Previous Number 3	Year Entered Service	Year Withdrawn	Current Status/Scrapping Details	Notes
20001	D8001			1957	1988	Preserved	
20002	D8002			1957	1988	1990: MC Metals, Glasgow	
20003	D8003			1957	1982	1984: Crewe Works	
20004	D8004			1957	1990	1991: MC Metals, Glasgow	
20005	D8005			1957	1989	1990: MC Metals, Glasgow	
20006	D8006			1957	1990	1991: MC Metals, Glasgow	
20007	D8007			1957		Class 20189	
20008	D8008			1957	1989	1993: MC Metals, Glasgow	
20009	D8009			1957	1989	1993: MC Metals, Glasgow	
20010	D8010			1957	1991	1993: MC Metals, Glasgow	
20011	D8011			1957	1987	1994: MC Metals, Glasgow	
20012	D8012			1957	1976	1977: Glasgow Works	
20013	D8013			1957	1991	1993: MC Metals, Glasgow	

20014	D8014			1957	1976	1977: Glasgow Works	
20015	D8015			1957	1987	1988: Vic Berry, Leicester	
20016	D8016			1958	1993	Preserved	
20017	D8017			1958	1982	1985: Crewe Works	
20018	D8018			1958	1976	1978: Glasgow Works	
20019	D8019			1958	1991	1994: MC Metals, Glasgow	
20020	D8020			1959	1990	Preserved	
20021	D8021			1959	1991	1992: MC Metals, Glasgow	
20022	D8022			1959	1988	1990: Vic Berry, Leicester	
20023	20301[1]	20023	D8023	1959	1991	1992: MC Metals, Glasgow	a)
20024	D8024			1959	1977	1978: Glasgow Works	
20025	D8025			1959	1991	1995: MC Metals, Glasgow	
20026	D8026			1959	1990	1991: MC Metals, Glasgow	
20027	D8027			1959	1982	1986: Glasgow Works	
20028	D8028			1959	1992	1995: MC Metals, Glasgow	
20029	D8029			1959	1991	1993: MC Metals, Glasgow	
20030	D8030			1959	1990	1991: MC Metals, Glasgow	
20031	D8031			1960	1990	Preserved	
20032	D8032			1960	1993	2012: EMR, Kingsbury	
20033	D8033			1960	1977	1980: Crewe Works	
20034	D8034			1960	1990	1991: MC Metals, Glasgow	
2001	20035	D8035		1959	1991	2019: EMR Kingsbury	
20036	D8036			1959	1984	1986: Glasgow Works	
20037	D8037			1959	1987	1988: Vic Berry, Leicester	
20038	D8038			1959	1976	1977: Glasgow Works	
20039	D8039			1959	1986	1988: Vic Berry, Leicester	
20040	D8040			1959	1991	1992: MC Metals, Glasgow	
20043	D8043			1959	1991	1995: MC Metals, Glasgow	
20044	D8044			1959	1989	1991: MC Metals, Glasgow	
20045	D8045			1959	1990	1991: MC Metals, Glasgow	
20046	D8046			1959	1993	1993: MC Metals, Glasgow	
20048	D8048			1959	1990	Class 20189	
20049	D8049			1959	1987	1988: Vic Berry, Leicester	
20050	D8000			1957	1980	Preserved	
20051	D8051			1961	1991	1993: RFS Kilnhurst	
20052	D8052			1961	1990	1991: MC Metals, Glasgow	
20053	D8053			1961	1990	1991: MC Metals, Glasgow	
20054	D8054			1961	1989	1991: MC Metals, Glasgow	
20055	D8055			1961	1993	1995: MC Metals, Glasgow	
81	20056	D8056		1961		Harry Needle Railroad Co	
20057	D8057			1961	1994	Preserved	
20058	D8058			1961	1992	1994: MC Metals, Glasgow	
20059	20302[1]	20059	D8059	1961	1993	Preserved	b)
20061	D8061			1961	1991	1994: MC Metals, Glasgow	
20062	D8062			1961	1976	1979: Derby Works	
2002	20063	D8063		1961	1991	Preserved	
20064	D8064			1961	1990	1991: MC Metals, Glasgow	
20065	D8065			1961	1991	1991: MC Metals, Glasgow	
82	20066	D8066		1961		Harry Needle Railroad Co	
20067	D8067			1961	1987	1988: Vic Berry, Leicester	
20068	D8068			1961	1987	1993: MC Metals, Glasgow	
20069	D8069			1961	1991	Harry Needle Railroad Co	
20070	D8070			1961	1991	1992: MC Metals, Glasgow	
20071	D8071			1961	1993	1995: MC Metals, Glasgow	
20072	D8072			1961	1992	2012: EMR, Kingsbury	
20073	D8073			1961	1992	2006: C F Booth, Rotherham	
20074	D8074			1961	1976	1976: Glasgow Works	
20076	D8076			1961	1988	1988: Vic Berry, Leicester	
20077	D8077			1961	1988	1990: Vic Berry, Leicester	
20078	D8078			1961	1992	1993: MC Metals, Glasgow	
20079	D8079			1961	1977	1978: Derby Works	
20080	D8080			1961	1990	1993: MC Metals, Glasgow	
20081	D8081			1961	1993	Preserved	
20082	D8082			1961	1993	1995: MC Metals, Glasgow	

20085	D8085			1961	1991	1994: Castle Donington PS	
20086	D8086			1961	1988	1991: MC Metals, Glasgow	
20087	D8087			1961	1995	Harry Needle Railroad Co	
20088	D8088			1961	1991	Preserved	
20089	D8089			1961	1987	1993: MC Metals, Glasgow	
20090	D8090			1961	1993	1995: MC Metals, Glasgow	
20091	D8091			1961	1978	1978: Glasgow Works	
20092	D8092			1961	1994	2016: EMR, Kingsbury	
20093	D8093			1961	1991	1992: MC Metals, Glasgow	
20094	D8094			1961	1993	2004: Cymru Metals, Llanelli	
D8096	20096	D8096		1961		Locomotive Services	c)
20097	D8097			1961	1989	1991: MC Metals, Glasgow	
20098	D8098			1961	1991	Preserved	
20099	D8099			1961	1991	1993: MC Metals, Glasgow	
20100	D8100			1961	1989	1991: MC Metals, Glasgow	
20103	D8103			1961	1991	1992: MC Metals, Glasgow	
20105	D8105			1961	1991	2010: T J Thomson, Stockton	
20106	D8106			1961	1993	1994: MC Metals, Glasgow	
20107	D8107			1961		Locomotive Services	c)
20108	D8108			1961	1991	2005: EMR, Kingsbury	
20109	D8109			1961	1982	1983: Glasgow Works	
20110	D8110			1962	1990	Harry Needle Railroad Co	
20111	D8111			1962	1987	1988: Vic Berry, Leicester	
20112	D8112			1962	1991	1993: MC Metals, Glasgow	
20113	D8113			1962	1991	2003: Etterby Road Ind Est, Carlisle	
20114	D8114			1962	1990	1991: MC Metals, Glasgow	
20115	D8115			1962	1987	1988: Vic Berry, Leicester	
20116	D8116			1962	1987	1988: Vic Berry, Leicester	
20118	D8118			1962		Harry Needle Railroad Co	
20119	D8119			1962	1992	2009: C F Booth, Rotherham	
20121	D8121			1962		Harry Needle Railroad Co	
20122	D8122			1962	1991	1993: MC Metals, Glasgow	
20123	D8123			1962	1987	1988: Vic Berry, Leicester	
20124	D8124			1962	1991	1993: MC Metals, Glasgow	
20125	D8125			1962	1986	1988: Vic Berry, Leicester	
20126	D8126			1962	1989	1992: MC Metals, Glasgow	
20129	D8129			1966	1990	1991: MC Metals, Glasgow	
20130	D8130			1966	1990	1991: MC Metals, Glasgow	
20132	D8132			1966		Harry Needle Railroad Co	
20133	D8133			1966	1991	2003: C F Booth, Rotherham	
20134	20303[1]	20134	D8134	1966	1989	1991: MC Metals, Glasgow	d)
20135	D8135			1966	1993	2004: Cymru Metals, Llanelli	
20136	D8136			1966	1990	1991: MC Metals, Glasgow	
20137	D8137			1966	1992	Preserved	
20138	D8138			1966	1995	2010: C F Booth, Rotherham	
20139	D8139			1966	1991	2010: EMR, Kingsbury	
20140	D8140			1966	1993	1994: MC Metals, Glasgow	
20141	D8141			1966	1991	1993: MC Metals, Glasgow	
20142	D8142			1966		Class 20189	
20143	D8143			1966	1992	1993: MC Metals, Glasgow	
20144	D8144			1966	1990	1993: MC Metals, Glasgow	
20145	D8145			1966	1991	2009: EMR, Kingsbury	
20146	D8146			1966	1988	1989: MC Metals, Glasgow	
20147	D8147			1966	1989	1991: MC Metals, Glasgow	
20148	D8148			1966	1991	1994: MC Metals, Glasgow	
20149	D8149			1966	1987	1988: Vic Berry, Leicester	
20150	D8150			1966	1987	1990: Vic Berry, Leicester	
20151	D8151			1966	1993	1995: MC Metals, Glasgow	
20152	D8152			1966	1988	1988: MC Metals, Glasgow	
20153	D8153			1966	1987	1988: Vic Berry, Leicester	
20154	D8154			1966	1993	Preserved	
20155	D8155			1966	1987	1987: Vic Berry, Leicester	
20156	D8156			1966	1991	1993: MC Metals, Glasgow	
20157	D8157			1966	1990	1992: MC Metals, Glasgow	

				Built	Withdrawn	Note	
20158	D8158			1966	1989	1991: MC Metals, Glasgow	
20159	D8159			1966	1991	2005: EMR, Kingsbury	
20160	D8160			1966	1990	1994: MC Metals, Glasgow	
20161	D8161			1966	1988	1990: Vic Berry, Leicester	
20162	D8162			1966	1987	1987: Vic Berry, Leicester	
20163	D8163			1966	1992	1994: MC Metals, Glasgow	
20164	D8164			1966	1987	1988: Vic Berry, Leicester	
20165	D8165			1966	1995	2001: Michael Douglas Ltd, Carlisle	
20166	D8166			1966		Harry Needle Railroad Co	e)
20167	D8167			1966	1987	1988: Vic Berry, Leicester	
2	20168	20304[1]	20168	1966		Harry Needle Railroad Co	f)
20169	D8169			1966	2001	Preserved	
20170	D8170			1966	1991	1993: MC Metals, Glasgow	
20171	D8171			1966	1989	1991: MC Metals, Glasgow	
20172	20305[1]	20172	D8172	1966	1990	1995: MC Metals, Glasgow	g)
20173	20306[1]	20173	D8173	1966	1991	1992: MC Metals, Glasgow	h)
20174	D8174			1966	1988	1993: MC Metals, Glasgow	
20175	D8175			1966	1991	2003: Etterby Road Ind Est, Carlisle	
20176	D8176			1966	1991	1993: MC Metals, Glasgow	
20177	D8177			1966	1993	2017: C F Booth, Rotherham	CR
20178	D8178			1966	1989	1992: MC Metals, Glasgow	
20179	D8179			1966	1989	1991: MC Metals, Glasgow	
20180	D8180			1966	1988	1990: Vic Berry, Leicester	
20181	D8181			1966	1987	1994: MC Metals, Glasgow	
20182	D8182			1966	1991	1993: MC Metals, Glasgow	
20183	D8183			1966	1990	1990: Vic Berry, Leicester	
20184	D8184			1966	1986	1988: Vic Berry, Leicester	
20185	D8185			1967	1992	1994: MC Metals, Glasgow	
20186	D8186			1967	1993	1995: MC Metals, Glasgow	
20188	D8188			1967	1990	Preserved	
20189	D8189			1967		Class 20189	
20191	D8191			1967	1987	1987: Vic Berry, Leicester	
20192	D8192			1967	1989	1991: MC Metals, Glasgow	
20193	D8193			1967	1989	1991: MC Metals, Glasgow	
20195	D8195			1967	1993	1995: MC Metals, Glasgow	
20196	20308[1]	20196	D8196	1967	1993	1993: MC Metals, Glasgow	j)
20197	D8197			1967	1991	2011: EMR, Kingsbury	
20198	D8198			1967	1991	1993: MC Metals, Glasgow	
20199	D8199			1967	1990	1993: MC Metals, Glasgow	
20200	D8300			1967	1979	1979: Glasgow Works	
20201	D8301			1967	1988	1990: Vic Berry, Leicester	
20202	D8302			1967	1989	1993: MC Metals, Glasgow	
20203	D8303			1967	1988	1992: MC Metals, Glasgow	
20204	D8304			1967	1989	1989: MC Metals, Glasgow	
20205	D8305			1967		Preserved	
20206	D8306			1967	1991	2004: C F Booth, Rotherham	
20207	D8307			1967	1983	1986: Glasgow Works	
20208	D8308			1967	1991	1994: Castle Donington PS	
20209	D8309			1967	1989	2001: Michael Douglas Ltd, Carlisle	
20210	D8310			1967	1993	1993: MC Metals, Glasgow	
20211	D8311			1967	1991	1993: MC Metals, Glasgow	
20212	D8312			1967	1991	1993: MC Metals, Glasgow	
20213	D8313			1967	1991	1992: MC Metals, Glasgow	
20214	D8314			1967	1993	Preserved	
20215	D8315			1967	1991	2009: C F Booth, Rotherham	
20216	D8316			1967	1987	1988: Vic Berry, Leicester	
20217	D8317			1967	1989	1991: MC Metals, Glasgow	
20218	D8318			1967	1989	1993: MC Metals, Glasgow	
20220	D8320			1967	1987	1994: MC Metals, Glasgow	
20221	D8321			1967	1987	1994: MC Metals, Glasgow	
20222	D8322			1967	1987	1988: MC Metals, Glasgow	
20223	D8323			1967	1987	1993: MC Metals, Glasgow	
20224	D8324			1967	1990	1991: MC Metals, Glasgow	
20226	D8326			1968	1988	1992: MC Metals, Glasgow	

20227	D8327		1968		Preserved
2004	20228	D8128	1966	1991	Preserved

a) First of 2 locomotives to be numbered 20301
b) First of 2 locomotives to be numbered 20302
c) HNRC locomotive on hire to Locomotive Services
d) First of 2 locomotives to be numbered 20303
e) HNRC locomotive on long term loan to Wensleydale Railway
f) First of 2 locomotives to be numbered 20304. Also carried previous number D8168
g) First of 2 locomotives to be numbered 20305
h) First of 2 locomotives to be numbered 20306
j) First of 2 locomotives to be numbered 20308

Class 20/3 First Batch
In 1986 eight Class 20s were fitted with Slow Speed Control for Peak Forest aggregate workings and renumbered 20301–20308. All locos reverted to their original Class 20/0 numberings before the end of 1986 and are therefore listed with Class 20/0s.

Class 20/3 Second Batch
Refurbished locos with extra fuel tanks and air brakes.
Details as Class 20/0 except:
Maximum Speed: 60 mph (some locos 75 mph).

Latest Number Carried	Previous Number 1	Previous Number 2	Previous Number 3	Year Entered Service	Year Withdrawn	Current Status/Scrapping Details	Notes
20301²	20047	D8047		1959		Direct Rail Services	a)
20302²	20084	D8084		1961		Direct Rail Services	b)
20303²	20127	D8127		1962		Direct Rail Services	c)
20304²	20120	D8120		1962		Direct Rail Services	d)
20305²	20095	D8095		1961		Direct Rail Services	e)
20306²	20131	D8131		1966	2009	2013: C F Booth, Rotherham	f)
20307²	20128	D8050		1961	2013	2013: C F Booth, Rotherham	g)
20308²	20187	D8187		1967		Direct Rail Services	h)
20309	20075	D8075		1961		Direct Rail Services	
20310	20190	D8190		1967	2008	2013: C F Booth, Rotherham	
20311	20102	D8102		1961		Harry Needle Railroad Co	
20312	20042	D8042		1959		Direct Rail Services	
20313	20194	20307¹	D8194	1967	2008	2013: C F Booth, Rotherham	j)
20314	20117	D8117		1962		Harry Needle Railroad Co	
20315	20104	D8104		1961	2008	2013: C F Booth, Rotherham	

a) Second of 2 locomotives to be numbered 20301
b) Second of 2 locomotives to be numbered 20302
c) Second of 2 locomotives to be numbered 20303
d) Second of 2 locomotives to be numbered 20304
e) Second of 2 locomotives to be numbered 20305
f) Second of 2 locomotives to be numbered 20306
g) Second of 2 locomotives to be numbered 20307
h) Second of 2 locomotives to be numbered 20308
j) First of 2 locomotives to be numbered 20307

Class 20/9
Refurbished locos with air brakes.

Latest Number Carried	Previous Number 1	Previous Number 2	Previous Number 3	Year Entered Service	Year Withdrawn	Current Status/Scrapping Details	Notes
20901	20101	D8101		1961		GB Railfreight	
20902	20060	D8060		1961	2003	2011: EMR, Kingsbury	
20903	20083	D8083		1961		Harry Needle Railroad Co	
20904	20041	D8041		1959		Harry Needle Railroad Co	
20905	20225	D8325		1967		GB Railfreight	
3	20906	20219	D8319	1968		Harry Needle Railroad Co	

▲ On 4 July 2013, 20305 (front) and 20309 pass St. Bees on the Cumbrian Coast route with three containers containing low-level radioactive waste which are being transferred from Workington Port to Sellafield. **Gordon Edgar**

▼ The pioneer North British Type 2 (TOPS Class 21) D6100 was only three months old when this photograph was taken to the south-west of Royston on 13 March 1959. Its pristine appearance suggests it has done little work to date. This locomotive was one of a batch of 20 that were re-engined and converted to Class 29s during the 1960s. **53A Models of Hull Collection**

CLASS 21

Bo-Bo

Built: 1958–60 by North British Locomotive Company, Glasgow.
Engine D6100–D6109: MAN L12V18 of 746 kW (1000 hp) at 1445 rpm.
D6110–D6157: MAN L12V21 of 820 kW (1100 hp) at 1530 rpm.
Transmission: Electric.
Maximum Speed: 75 mph.
Train Heating/Supply: Steam heating.
Train Brakes: Vacuum.

UL   Scrapping details unconfirmed, but likely to be correct

Latest Number Carried	Previous Number 1	Year Entered Service	Year Withdrawn	Current Status/Scrapping Details	Notes
D6100		1958	1967	Re-engined 1967 with Paxman Ventura engine and reclassified as Class 29	
D6101		1958	1965	Re-engined 1965 with Paxman Ventura engine and reclassified as Class 29	
D6102		1958	1965	Re-engined 1965 with Paxman Ventura engine and reclassified as Class 29	
D6103		1959	1965	Re-engined 1965 with Paxman Ventura engine and reclassified as Class 29	
D6104		1959	1967	1968: Barnes & Bell, Coatbridge	UL
D6105		1959	1968	1968: J McWilliam, Shettleston	UL
D6106		1959	1965	Re-engined 1965 with Paxman Ventura engine and reclassified as Class 29	
D6107		1959	1967	Re-engined 1967 with Paxman Ventura engine and reclassified as Class 29	
D6108		1959	1967	Re-engined 1967 with Paxman Ventura engine and reclassified as Class 29	
D6109		1959	1968	1969: J McWilliam, Shettleston	
D6110		1959	1968	1969: J McWilliam, Shettleston	
D6111		1959	1968	1969: J McWilliam, Shettleston	UL
D6112		1959	1966	Re-engined 1966 with Paxman Ventura engine and reclassified as Class 29	
D6113		1959	1966	Re-engined 1966 with Paxman Ventura engine and reclassified as Class 29	
D6114		1959	1966	Re-engined 1966 with Paxman Ventura engine and reclassified as Class 29	
D6115		1959	1968	1968: J McWilliam, Shettleston	
D6116		1959	1966	Re-engined 1966 with Paxman Ventura engine and reclassified as Class 29	
D6117		1959	1968	1968: J McWilliam, Shettleston	UL
D6118		1959	1967	1968: J McWilliam, Shettleston	
D6119		1959	1967	Re-engined 1967 with Paxman Ventura engine and reclassified as Class 29	
D6120		1959	1967	1968: J McWilliam, Shettleston	a)
D6121		1959	1966	1980: D Woodham, Barry	a)
D6122		1959	1967	Re-engined 1966 with Paxman Ventura engine and reclassified as Class 29	
D6123		1959	1963	Re-engined 1963 with Paxman Ventura engine and reclassified as Class 29	
D6124		1959	1967	Re-engined 1967 with Paxman Ventura engine and reclassified as Class 29	
D6125		1959	1967	1968: Barnes & Bell, Coatbridge	UL
D6126		1959	1968	1969: J McWilliam, Shettleston	
D6127		1959	1967	1968: Barnes & Bell, Coatbridge	UL
D6128		1959	1967	1968: J McWilliam, Shettleston	
D6129		1959	1967	Re-engined 1967 with Paxman Ventura engine and reclassified as Class 29	
D6130		1959	1966	Re-engined 1966 with Paxman Ventura engine and reclassified as Class 29	
D6131		1959	1967	1968: J McWilliam, Shettleston	
D6132		1959	1966	Re-engined 1966 with Paxman Ventura engine and reclassified as Class 29	
D6133		1959	1966	Re-engined 1966 with Paxman Ventura engine and reclassified as Class 29	
D6134		1959	1967	1968: Barnes & Bell, Coatbridge	UL
D6135		1959	1967	1968: J McWilliam, Shettleston	
D6136		1959	1967	1968: Barnes & Bell, Coatbridge	UL
D6137		1959	1967	Re-engined 1967 with Paxman Ventura engine and reclassified as Class 29	
D6138		1960	1967	1968: J McWilliam, Shettleston	
D6139		1960	1967	1968: J McWilliam, Shettleston	
D6140		1960	1967	1968: J McWilliam, Shettleston	
D6141		1960	1967	1968: J McWilliam, Shettleston	
D6142		1960	1967	1968: J McWilliam, Shettleston	
D6143		1960	1967	1968: Barnes & Bell, Coatbridge	UL
D6144		1960	1967	1968: J McWilliam, Shettleston	
D6145		1960	1967	1968: J McWilliam, Shettleston	
D6146		1960	1967	1968: Inverurie Works	
D6147		1960	1967	1968: J McWilliam, Shettleston	
D6148		1960	1967	1968: J McWilliam, Shettleston	
D6149		1960	1967	1968: J McWilliam, Shettleston	

D6150	1960 1967	1968: J McWilliam, Shettleston	
D6151	1960 1967	1968: J McWilliam, Shettleston	
D6152	1960 1968	1968: J McWilliam, Shettleston	
D6153	1960 1967	1968: J McWilliam, Shettleston	UL
D6154	1960 1967	1968: J McWilliam, Shettleston	
D6155	1960 1967	1968: J McWilliam, Shettleston	
D6156	1960 1967	1968: J McWilliam, Shettleston	
D6157	1960 1967	1968: J McWilliam, Shettleston	

a)   D6121 and D6122 are believed to have swapped identities in 1964. D6121, the former D6122, was re-engined in 1966 with a Paxman Ventura engine and reclassified as Class 29.

CLASS 22
B-B

Built: 1959–62 by North British Locomotive Company, Glasgow.
Engine D6300–D6305: MAN L12V18 of 750 kW (1000 hp) at 1445 rpm.
D6306–D6357: MAN L12V21 of 820 kW (1100 hp) at 1530 rpm.
Transmission: Hydraulic.
Maximum Speed: 75 mph.
Train Heating/Supply: Steam heating.
Train Brakes: Vacuum.

Latest Number Carried	Previous Number 1	Year Entered Service	Year Withdrawn	Current Status/Scrapping Details	Notes
D6300		1959	1968	1968: J Cashmore, Newport	
D6301		1959	1967	1968: G Cohen, Morriston	
D6302		1959	1968	1968: J Cashmore, Newport	
D6303		1959	1968	1968: J Cashmore, Newport	
D6304		1959	1968	1968: J Cashmore, Newport	
D6305		1960	1968	1968: J Cashmore, Newport	
D6306		1959	1968	1969: J Cashmore, Newport	
D6307		1959	1971	1971: Swindon Works	
D6308		1960	1971	1972: Swindon Works	
D6309		1960	1971	1971: Swindon Works	
D6310		1960	1971	1972: Swindon Works	
D6311		1960	1968	1969: J Cashmore, Newport	
D6312		1960	1971	1972: Swindon Works	
D6313		1960	1968	1968: J Cashmore, Newport	
D6314		1960	1969	1969: J Cashmore, Newport	
D6315		1960	1971	1972: Swindon Works	
D6316		1960	1968	1968: J Cashmore, Newport	
D6317		1960	1968	1969: J Cashmore, Newport	
D6318		1960	1971	1972: Swindon Works	
D6319		1960	1971	1972: Swindon Works	
D6320		1960	1971	1972: Swindon Works	
D6321		1960	1968	1969: J Cashmore, Newport	
D6322		1960	1971	1972: Swindon Works	
D6323		1960	1971	1972: Swindon Works	
D6324		1960	1968	1969: J Cashmore, Newport	
D6325		1960	1968	1969: J Cashmore, Newport	
D6326		1960	1971	1972: Swindon Works	
D6327		1960	1971	1972: Swindon Works	
D6328		1960	1971	1972: Swindon Works	
D6329		1960	1968	1969: J Cashmore, Newport	
D6330		1960	1971	1972: Swindon Works	
D6331		1960	1971	1972: Swindon Works	
D6332		1960	1971	1971: Swindon Works	
D6333		1960	1972	1972: Swindon Works	
D6334		1960	1971	1972: Swindon Works	
D6335		1961	1968	1969: J Cashmore, Newport	
D6336		1961	1972	1972: Swindon Works	
D6337		1962	1971	1972: Swindon Works	
D6338		1962	1972	1972: Swindon Works	

D6339	1962	1972	1972: Swindon Works
D6340	1962	1971	1972: Swindon Works
D6341	1962	1968	1969: J Cashmore, Newport
D6342	1962	1968	1969: J Cashmore, Newport
D6343	1962	1971	1972: Swindon Works
D6344	1962	1968	1969: J Cashmore, Newport
D6345	1962	1968	1969: J Cashmore, Newport
D6346	1962	1969	1969: J Cashmore, Newport
D6347	1962	1968	1968: J Cashmore, Newport
D6348	1962	1971	1972: Swindon Works
D6349	1962	1968	1971: Swindon Works
D6350	1962	1968	1969: J Cashmore, Newport
D6351	1962	1968	1969: J Cashmore, Newport
D6352	1962	1971	1971: Swindon Works
D6353	1962	1968	1969: J Cashmore, Newport
D6354	1962	1971	1972: Swindon Works
D6355	1962	1968	1969: J Cashmore, Newport
D6356	1962	1971	1972: Swindon Works
D6357	1962	1968	1969: J Cashmore, Newport

▲ The North British diesel-hydraulic Type 2 was assigned TOPS Class 22, but none of the 58 locomotives remained in service long enough to be given a TOPS number and the entire class had been scrapped by 1972. D6308, one of the later survivors, is seen within the confines of Plymouth Laira depot on 30 May 1971. **Gordon Edgar**

CLASS 23
Bo-Bo

Built: 1959 by English Electric, Vulcan Foundry, Newton-le-Willows.
Engine: Deltic T9-29 of 820 kW (1100 hp) at 1600 rpm.
Transmission: Electric.
Maximum Speed: 75 mph.
Train Heating/Supply: Steam heating.
Train Brakes: Vacuum.

Latest Number Carried	Previous Number 1	Year Entered Service	Year Withdrawn	Current Status/Scrapping Details	Notes
D5900		1959	1968	1969: G Cohen, Kettering	
D5901		1959	1975	1977: Doncaster Works	a)
D5902		1959	1969	1970: G Cohen, Kettering	
D5903		1959	1968	1969: G Cohen, Kettering	
D5904		1959	1969	1969: G Cohen, Kettering	
D5905		1959	1971	1973: G Cohen, Kettering	
D5906		1959	1968	1969: G Cohen, Kettering	
D5907		1959	1968	1969: G Cohen, Kettering	
D5908		1959	1969	1970: J Cashmore, Great Bridge	
D5909		1959	1971	1973: G Cohen, Kettering	
D5910	N/A			Preserved	b)

a) D5901 was a departmental loco between 1969 and 1975
b) Created from body of 37372 on Class 20 bogies

CLASS 24
Bo-Bo

Class 24 locomotives were divided into two sub classes, 24/0 (24001–24049) and 24/1 (24050–24150) which had small differences in electrical equipment, weight and fuel capacity.

Built: 1958–61 by British Rail Derby, Crewe and Darlington.
Engine: Sulzer 6LDA28 of 870 kW (1160 hp) at 750 rpm.
Transmission: Electric.
Maximum Speed: 75mph.
Train Heating/Supply: Steam heating.
Train Brakes: Vacuum.

SP   Locomotive was not self-propelled whilst in departmental use

Class 24/0

Latest Number Carried	Previous Number 1	Year Entered Service	Year Withdrawn	Current Status/Scrapping Details	Notes
24001	D5001	1958	1975	1977: Doncaster Works	
24002	D5002	1958	1975	1977: Glasgow Works	
24003	D5003	1958	1975	1976: Doncaster Works	
24004	D5004	1958	1975	1977: Glasgow Works	
D5005		1959	1969	1977: Swindon Works	
24005	D5000	1958	1976	1977: Swindon Works	a)
24006	D5006	1959	1975	1980: Glasgow Works	
24007	D5007	1959	1975	1978: Doncaster Works	
24008	D5008	1959	1975	1976: Doncaster Works	
24009	D5009	1959	1976	1977: Doncaster Works	
24010	D5010	1959	1975	1977: Doncaster Works	
24011	D5011	1959	1975	1977: Glasgow Works	
24012	D5012	1959	1975	1976: Doncaster Works	
24013	D5013	1959	1975	1978: Doncaster Works	
24014	D5014	1959	1975	1978: Doncaster Works	
24015	D5015	1959	1975	1977: Doncaster Works	
24016	D5016	1959	1975	1977: Doncaster Works	
24017	D5017	1959	1975	1977: Doncaster Works	
24018	D5018	1959	1975	1976: Doncaster Works	
24019	D5019	1959	1975	1978: Doncaster Works	
24020	D5020	1959	1975	1977: Swindon Works	

▲ As the ten Class 23s had a smaller version of the Deltic engine fitted to the Class 55s and they shared some visual similarities with their larger English Electric cousins, they were known as the "Baby Deltics". D5909 and D5905 are stabled at Hitchin diesel depot during June 1969; these were the last two members of the class to be withdrawn, remaining in service until 1971.
The Geoff Plumb Collection

▼ Of the 151 Class 24s built, just four survive today. One of these is the East Lancashire Railway's long-term resident D5054, which is seen on the rear of the 09.45 Heywood–Rawtenstall on 21 September 2019. The train has just departed from Irwell Vale and is being hauled by Class 25 D7629. **Ken Davies**

Latest Number Carried	Previous Number 1	Year Entered Service	Year Withdrawn	Current Status/Scrapping Details	Notes
24021	D5021	1959	1975	1977: Swindon Works	
24022	D5022	1959	1976	1978: Doncaster Works	
24023	D5023	1959	1978	1978: Doncaster Works	
24024	D5024	1959	1975	1977: Swindon Works	
24025	D5025	1959	1976	1969: Derby Works	b)
24026	D5026	1959	1975	1977: Swindon Works	
24027	D5027	1959	1976	1977: Swindon Works	
D5028		1959	1972	1972: Crewe Works	
24029	D5029	1959	1975	1977: Swindon Works	
24030	D5030	1959	1976	1977: Swindon Works	
24031	D5031	1959	1975	1976: Swindon Works	
24032	D5032	1959	1976	Preserved	
24033	D5033	1959	1975	1977: Swindon Works	
24034	D5034	1959	1976	1977: Swindon Works	
24035	D5035	1959	1978	1979: Doncaster Works	
24036	D5036	1959	1977	1978: Doncaster Works	
24037	D5037	1959	1976	1977: Swindon Works	
24038	D5038	1959	1976	1977: Swindon Works	
24039	D5039	1959	1976	1978: Swindon Works	
24040	D5040	1959	1976	1977: Swindon Works	
24041	D5041	1959	1976	1978: Swindon Works	
24042	D5042	1959	1975	1976: Swindon Works	
D5043		1959	1969	1970: J Cashmore, Great Bridge	c)
24044	D5044	1959	1976	1977: Swindon Works	
24045	D5045	1959	1975	1976: Swindon Works	
24046	D5046	1959	1976	1977: Swindon Works	
24047	D5047	1959	1978	1979: Doncaster Works	
24048	D5048	1959	1975	1976: Swindon Works	
24049	D5049	1959	1976	1976: Swindon Works	

a) Body shell transferred to D5025 in 1969
b) Received body shell of D5005 during repairs in 1969
c) Scrapping began at Chester Depot and was completed at Great Bridge

Class 24/1

Latest Number Carried	Previous Number 1	Previous Number 2	Previous Number 3	Previous Number 4	Year Entered Service	Year Withdrawn	Current Status/Scrapping Details	Notes
24050	D5050				1959	1975	1976: Swindon Works	
D5051					1959	1967	1968: Inverurie Works	
24052	D5052				1959	1976	1978: Swindon Works	
24053	D5053				1959	1976	1976: Swindon Works	
D5054	ADB968008	24054	D5054		1959	1982	Preserved	SP
24055	D5055				1959	1975	1976: Swindon Works	
24056	D5056				1959	1975	1976: Swindon Works	
24057	D5057				1959	1978	1978: Doncaster Works	
24058	D5058				1960	1975	1976: Swindon Works	
24059	D5059				1959	1975	1977: Swindon Works	
24060	D5060				1960	1975	1977: Swindon Works	
D5061	97201	RDB968007	24061	D5061	1988	1988	Preserved	
24062	D5062				1960	1975	1976: Swindon Works	
24063	D5063				1960	1979	1979: Doncaster Works	
24064	D5064				1960	1976	1976: Swindon Works	
24065	D5065				1960	1976	1977: Swindon Works	
24066	D5066				1959	1976	1978: Doncaster Works	
D5067					1959	1972	1973: Glasgow Works	
D5068					1959	1972	1973: Glasgow Works	
24069	D5069				1960	1976	1977: Doncaster Works	
24070	D5070				1960	1976	1976: Doncaster Works	
24071	D5071				1960	1975	1977: Doncaster Works	
24072	D5072				1960	1975	1977: Doncaster Works	
24073	D5073				1960	1978	1978: Doncaster Works	
24074	D5074				1960	1975	1976: J Cashmore, Great Bridge	
24075	D5075				1960	1976	1976: Swindon Works	
24076	D5076				1960	1975	1977: Swindon Works	

24077	D5077	1960	1976	1978: Swindon Works	
24078	D5078	1960	1976	1978: Swindon Works	
24079	D5079	1960	1976	1978: Swindon Works	
24080	D5080	1960	1976	1978: Doncaster Works	
24081	D5081	1960	1980	Preserved	
24082	D5082	1960	1979	1979: Doncaster Works	
24083	D5083	1960	1976	1977: Swindon Works	
24084	D5084	1960	1976	1978: Swindon Works	
24085	D5085	1960	1976	1978: Swindon Works	
24086	D5086	1960	1976	1977: Doncaster Works	
24087	D5087	1960	1978	1978: Doncaster Works	
D5088		1960	1970	1972: G Cohen, Kettering	
24089	D5089	1960	1976	1977: Swindon Works	
24090	D5090	1960	1976	1978: Doncaster Works	
24091	D5091	1960	1977	1978: Doncaster Works	
24092	D5092	1960	1975	1976: Swindon Works	
D5093		1960	1969	1970: J Cashmore, Great Bridge	d)
24094	D5094	1960	1976	1977: Doncaster Works	
24095	D5095	1960	1975	1976: Doncaster Works	
24096	D5096	1960	1975	1976: Doncaster Works	
24097	D5097	1960	1976	1977: Doncaster Works	
24098	D5098	1960	1975	1976: Doncaster Works	
24099	D5099	1960	1976	1977: Doncaster Works	
24100	D5100	1960	1976	1976: Doncaster Works	
24101	D5101	1960	1976	1976: Doncaster Works	
24102	D5102	1960	1976	1978: Doncaster Works	
24103	D5103	1960	1976	1977: Doncaster Works	
24104	D5104	1960	1976	1977: Doncaster Works	
24105	D5105	1960	1975	1978: Doncaster Works	
24106	D5106	1960	1976	1977: Doncaster Works	
24107	D5107	1960	1976	1977: Swindon Works	
24108	D5108	1960	1976	1978: Doncaster Works	
24109	D5109	1960	1976	1978: Doncaster Works	
24110	D5110	1960	1976	1977: Doncaster Works	
24111	D5111	1960	1976	1978: Doncaster Works	
24112	D5112	1960	1976	1977: Doncaster Works	
24113	D5113	1961	1976	1977: Doncaster Works	
D5114		1960	1972	1973: Glasgow Works	
24115	D5115	1960	1976	1977: Swindon Works	
24116	D5116	1960	1976	1977: Doncaster Works	
24117	D5117	1960	1976	1977: Doncaster Works	
24118	D5118	1960	1976	1977: Doncaster Works	
24119	D5119	1960	1976	1977: Doncaster Works	
24120	D5120	1960	1976	1977: Doncaster Works	
24121	D5121	1960	1976	1978: Doncaster Works	
D5122		1960	1968	1971: Glasgow Works	
24123	D5123	1960	1976	1977: Doncaster Works	
24124	D5124	1960	1976	1977: Swindon Works	
24125	D5125	1960	1976	1977: Doncaster Works	
24126	D5126	1960	1976	1977: Doncaster Works	
24127	D5127	1960	1976	1977: Doncaster Works	
24128	D5128	1960	1976	1977: Doncaster Works	
24129	D5129	1960	1976	1977: Doncaster Works	
24130	D5130	1960	1976	1977: Doncaster Works	
D5131		1960	1971	1972: Glasgow Works	
24132	D5132	1960	1976	1976: Doncaster Works	
24133	D5133	1960	1978	1978: Doncaster Works	
24134	D5134	1960	1976	1978: Swindon Works	
24135	D5135	1960	1976	1977: Swindon Works	
24136	D5136	1960	1975	1977: Swindon Works	
24137	D5137	1960	1976	1978: Doncaster Works	
D5138		1960	1969	1970: J Cashmore, Great Bridge	d)
D5139		1960	1969	1970: J Cashmore, Great Bridge	d)
24140	D5140	1960	1976	1976: Swindon Works	

▲ 24119 was one of a batch of Class 24s that were allocated to Inverness when new in 1960, working hard on the highland gradients until they were transferred south in late 1975. At the end of this era, 24119 runs round at Thurso on 20 August 1975. Note the recess in the cab for the tablet catcher.

Stephen C Marshall

▼ 25132 rounds the curve to the west of March and heads for Whitemoor Yard on 8 May 1980. It is hauling a mixed freight which consists of revenue earning coal and cement traffic, plus a selection of loaded engineer's wagons.

Gordon Edgar

24141	D5141		1960	1976	1978: Swindon Works	
ADB968009	24142	D5142	1960	1982	1984: Coopers Metals, Sheffield	SP
24143	D5143		1960	1976	1976: Swindon Works	
24144	D5144		1960	1976	1976: Swindon Works	
24145	D5145		1960	1976	1976: Swindon Works	
24146	D5146		1960	1976	1976: Swindon Works	
24147	D5147		1960	1976	1977: Doncaster Works	
24148	D5148		1960	1975	1977: Doncaster Works	
D5149			1961	1972	1973: Glasgow Works	
24150	D5150		1961	1976	1977: Doncaster Works	

d) Scrapping began at Chester Depot and was completed at Great Bridge

CLASS 25 — Bo-Bo

Class 25 locomotives were initially divided into four sub-classes, 25/0 (25001–25025), 25/1 (25026–25082), 25/2 (25083–25247) and 25/3 (25248–25327), mainly due to differences in electrical equipment. 25/9 sub-class was created when a number of locomotives were renumbered.

Built: 1961–67 by British Railways Darlington, Derby and Beyer Peacock & Co, Manchester.
Engine: Sulzer 6LDA28B of 930 kW (1250 hp) at 750 rpm.
Transmission: Electric.
Maximum Speed: 90 mph.
Train Heating/Supply: D5176–78, D5183–5237 and D7568–97 were built with steam heating generators.
Train Brakes: 25308–25319 were built with dual brakes (air & vacuum); other locomotives were built with vacuum brakes only and from 1968 air brakes were fitted so that many of the class were dual braked.

SP Locomotive was not self-propelled whilst in departmental use

Class 25/0

Latest Number Carried	Previous Number 1	Year Entered Service	Year Withdrawn	Current Status/Scrapping Details	Notes
25001	D5151	1961	1980	1980: Swindon Works	
25002	D5152	1961	1980	1981: Swindon Works	
25003	D5153	1961	1976	1978: Glasgow Works	
25004	D5154	1961	1976	1977: Glasgow Works	
25005	D5155	1961	1980	1981: Swindon Works	
25006	D5156	1961	1980	1983: Swindon Works	
25007	D5157	1961	1980	1982: Swindon Works	
25008	D5158	1961	1980	1980: Glasgow Works	
25009	D5159	1961	1980	1980: Glasgow Works	
25010	D5160	1961	1980	1981: Swindon Works	
25011	D5161	1961	1980	1981: Swindon Works	
25012	D5162	1961	1977	1977: Glasgow Works	
25013	D5163	1961	1980	1983: Swindon Works	
25014	D5164	1961	1977	1977: Glasgow Works	
25015	D5165	1961	1975	1977: Doncaster Works	
25016	D5166	1961	1976	1976: Swindon Works	
25017	D5167	1961	1976	1976: Swindon Works	
25018	D5168	1961	1976	1978: Glasgow Works	
25019	D5169	1961	1980	1981: Swindon Works	
25020	D5170	1961	1976	1976: Swindon Works	
25021	D5171	1962	1980	1980: Swindon Works	
25022	D5172	1962	1976	1978: Glasgow Works	
25023	D5173	1962	1980	1983: Swindon Works	
25024	D5174	1962	1976	1976: Glasgow Works	
25025	D5175	1962	1977	1978: Glasgow Works	

Class 25/1

Latest Number Carried	Previous Number 1	Year Entered Service	Year Withdrawn	Current Status/Scrapping Details	Notes
25026	D5176	1963	1980	1981: Swindon Works	
25027	D5177	1963	1983	1987: Vic Berry, Leicester	
25028	D5178	1963	1980	1987: Vic Berry, Leicester	
25029	D5179	1963	1977	1978: Glasgow Works	
25030	D5180	1963	1976	1980: Derby Works	
25031	D5181	1963	1977	1978: Glasgow Works	
25032	D5182	1963	1986	1988: Vic Berry, Leicester	
25033	D5183	1963	1983	1986: Derby Etches Park Depot	
25034	D5184	1963	1986	1988: Vic Berry, Leicester	
25035	D5185	1963	1987	Preserved	
25036	D5186	1963	1982	1985: Swindon Works	
25037	D5187	1963	1987	1987: Vic Berry, Leicester	
25038	D5188	1963	1981	1982: Derby Works	
25039	D5189	1963	1981	1981: Swindon Works	
25040	D5190	1963	1980	1982: Swindon Works	
25041	D5191	1963	1981	1983: Swindon Works	
25042	D5192	1963	1986	1987: Vic Berry, Leicester	
25043	D5193	1963	1981	1981: Derby Works	
25044	D5194	1963	1985	1986: Doncaster Works	
25045	D5195	1963	1975	1979: Derby Works	
25046	D5196	1963	1981	1987: Vic Berry, Leicester	
25047	D5197	1963	1980	1981: Swindon Works	
25048	D5198	1963	1986	1987: Vic Berry, Leicester	
25049	D5199	1963	1984	1985: Swindon Works	
25050	D5200	1963	1983	1985: Swindon Works	
25051	D5201	1963	1985	1987: Vic Berry, Leicester	
25052	D5202	1963	1980	1980: Swindon Works	
25053	D5203	1963	1980	1981: Swindon Works	

▲ Several years before they received their Class 25 identities, D7599 & D7632 are seen stabled at Wath depot in March 1966. The near locomotive, D7599, had only entered service the previous month, whereas D7632 was comparatively old at the time, having reached an age of six months.

Charlie Cross / The Gordon Edgar Collection

25054	D5204	1963	1985	1986: Doncaster Works
25055	D5205	1963	1980	1981: Swindon Works
25056	D5206	1963	1982	1985: Swindon Works
25057	D5207	1963	1987	Harry Needle Railroad Co
25058	D5208	1963	1987	1989: Vic Berry, Leicester
25059	D5209	1963	1987	Preserved
25060	D5210	1963	1985	1987: Vic Berry, Leicester
25061	D5211	1963	1980	1983: Swindon Works
25062	D5212	1963	1982	1985: Swindon Works
25063	D5213	1963	1980	1983: Swindon Works
25064	D5214	1963	1985	1987: Vic Berry, Leicester
25065	D5215	1963	1981	1982: Swindon Works
25066	D5216	1963	1981	1983: Derby Works
25067	D5217	1963	1982	Preserved
25068	D5218	1963	1980	1981: Glasgow Works
25069	D5219	1963	1983	1986: Swindon Works
25070	D5220	1963	1980	1983: Swindon Works
25071	D5221	1963	1981	1983: Swindon Works
25072	D5222	1963	1985	Preserved
25073	D5223	1963	1981	1982: Swindon Works
25074	D5224	1963	1980	1982: Swindon Works
25075	D5225	1963	1983	1987: Vic Berry, Leicester
25076	D5226	1963	1984	1986: Swindon Works
25077	D5227	1963	1978	1978: Glasgow Works
25078	D5228	1963	1985	1987: Vic Berry, Leicester
25079	D5229	1963	1983	1983: Swindon Works
25080	D5230	1963	1985	1993: MC Metals, Glasgow
25081	D5231	1963	1982	1982: Swindon Works
25082	D5232	1963	1981	1983: Swindon Works

Class 25/2

Latest Number Carried	Previous Number 1	Previous Number 2	Year Entered Service	Year Withdrawn	Current Status/Scrapping Details	Notes
25083	D5233		1963	1984	Preserved	
25084	D5234		1963	1983	1986: Swindon Works	
25085	D5235		1963	1982	1983: Derby Works	
25086	D5236		1963	1983	1986: Swindon Works	
25087	D5237		1963	1980	1981: Swindon Works	
25088	D5238		1963	1981	1986: Derby Etches Park Depot	
25089	D5239		1963	1986	1987: Vic Berry, Leicester	
25090	D5240		1964	1983	1985: Swindon Works	
25091	D5241		1964	1978	1979: Glasgow Works	
25092	D5242		1964	1980	1982: Derby Works	
25093	D5243		1964	1982	1988: Vic Berry, Leicester	
25094	D5244		1964	1981	1982: Derby Works	
25095	D5245		1964	1986	1989: Vic Berry, Leicester	
25096	D5246		1964	1977	1978: Glasgow Works	
25097	D5247		1964	1983	1985: Swindon Works	
25098	D5248		1964	1978	1979: Glasgow Works	
25099	D5249		1964	1980	1981: Swindon Works	
25100	D5250		1964	1981	1983: Swindon Works	
25101	D5251		1964	1983	1985: Swindon Works	
25102	D5252		1964	1980	1980: Swindon Works	
25103	D5253		1964	1980	1983: Swindon Works	
25104	D5254		1964	1982	1986: Swindon Works	
25105	D5255		1964	1982	1985: Swindon Works	
25106	D5256		1964	1983	1984: Swindon Works	
25107	D5257		1964	1981	1981: Swindon Works	
25108	D5258		1964	1980	1980: Glasgow Works	
25109	D5259		1964	1987	1987: Vic Berry, Leicester	
25110	D5260		1964	1980	1982: Swindon Works	
25111	D5261		1964	1980	1980: Swindon Works	
25112	D5262		1964	1980	1982: Swindon Works	

25113	D5263		1964	1983	1983: Swindon Works
25114	D5264		1964	1981	1981: Swindon Works
25115	D5265		1964	1983	1985: Swindon Works
25116	D5266		1964	1980	1982: Swindon Works
25117	D5267		1964	1984	1984: Swindon Works
25118	D5268		1964	1981	1983: Swindon Works
25119	D5269		1964	1985	1986: Doncaster Works
25120	D5270		1964	1983	1984: Swindon Works
25121	D5271		1964	1980	1982: Swindon Works
25122	D5272		1964	1980	1983: Swindon Works
25123	D5273		1964	1983	1987: Vic Berry, Leicester
25124	D5274		1964	1983	1986: Swindon Works
25125	D5275		1964	1981	1983: Swindon Works
25126	D5276		1964	1982	1987: Vic Berry, Leicester
25127	D5277		1964	1980	1983: Swindon Works
D5278			1964	1971	1971: Peak Forest
25129	D5279		1964	1982	1985: Swindon Works
25130	D5280		1964	1982	1987: Swindon Works
97202	25131	D5281	1964	1984	1987: Vic Berry, Leicester
25132	D5282		1964	1982	1984: Swindon Works
25133	D5283		1964	1983	1987: Vic Berry, Leicester
25134	D5284		1964	1982	1988: Vic Berry, Leicester
25135	D5285		1964	1983	1986: Swindon Works
25136	D5286		1964	1983	1986: Swindon Works
25137	D5287		1964	1980	1983: Swindon Works
25138	D5288		1964	1983	1986: Swindon Works
25139	D5289		1964	1982	1986: Swindon Works
25140	D5290		1964	1983	1986: Swindon Works
25141	D5291		1964	1982	1987: Swindon Works
25142	D5292		1964	1981	1982: Swindon Works
25143	D5293		1964	1982	1984: Swindon Works
25144	D5294		1964	1983	1987: Vic Berry, Leicester
25145	D5295		1964	1986	1987: Vic Berry, Leicester
25146	D5296		1964	1983	1985: Swindon Works
25147	D5297		1964	1980	1980: Swindon Works
25148	D5298		1964	1981	1982: Swindon Works
25149	D5299		1965	1982	1983: Swindon Works
25150	D7500		1964	1982	1985: Swindon Works
25151	D7501		1964	1982	1988: Toton Depot
25152	D7502		1964	1984	1985: Swindon Works
25153	D7503		1964	1983	1987: Swindon Works
25154	D7504		1964	1985	1987: Vic Berry, Leicester
25155	D7505		1964	1980	1981: Swindon Works
25156	D7506		1964	1981	1982: Swindon Works
25157	D7507		1964	1982	1987: Swindon Works
25158	D7508		1964	1983	1987: Vic Berry, Leicester
25159	D7509		1964	1980	1981: Swindon Works
25160	D7510		1964	1982	1987: Vic Berry, Leicester
25161	D7511		1964	1984	1988: Vic Berry, Leicester
25162	D7512		1964	1981	1982: Swindon Works
25163	D7513		1964	1980	1983: Swindon Works
25164	D7514		1964	1983	1987: Vic Berry, Leicester
25165	D7515		1964	1978	1979: Derby Works
25166	D7516		1964	1980	1981: Swindon Works
25167	D7517		1964	1983	1984: Swindon Works
25168	D7518		1964	1983	1984: Swindon Works
25169	D7519		1965	1981	1982: Swindon Works
25170	D7520		1964	1982	1983: Derby Works
25171	D7521		1965	1978	1979: Arbroath Goods Yard
25172	D7522		1965	1981	1983: Swindon Works
25173	D7523		1965	1987	Preserved
25174	D7524		1965	1976	1978: Derby Works
25175	D7525		1965	1985	1987: Vic Berry, Leicester
25176	D7526		1965	1987	1988: Vic Berry, Leicester

25177	D7527	1965	1982	1986: Swindon Works
25178	D7528	1965	1985	1989: Vic Berry, Leicester
25179	D7529	1965	1982	1987: Swindon Works
25180	D7530	1965	1982	1988: Vic Berry, Leicester
25181	D7531	1965	1986	1988: Eastleigh Depot
25182	D7532	1965	1985	1985: Swindon Works
25183	D7533	1965	1980	1981: Swindon Works
25184	D7534	1965	1983	1984: Swindon Works
25185	D7535	1965	1984	Preserved
25186	D7536	1965	1982	1987: Swindon Works
25187	D7537	1965	1982	1987: Swindon Works
25188	D7538	1965	1982	1987: Swindon Works
25189	D7539	1965	1985	1986: Doncaster Works
25190	D7540	1965	1987	1987: Vic Berry, Leicester
25191	D7541	1965	1987	Preserved
25192	D7542	1965	1986	1987: Vic Berry, Leicester
25193	D7543	1965	1984	1987: Vic Berry, Leicester
25194	D7544	1965	1985	1994: MC Metals, Glasgow
25195	D7545	1965	1985	1986: Vic Berry, Leicester
25196	D7546	1965	1986	1987: Vic Berry, Leicester
25197	D7547	1965	1980	1983: Swindon Works
25198	D7548	1965	1986	1987: Vic Berry, Leicester
25199	D7549	1965	1987	1989: Vic Berry, Leicester
25200	D7550	1965	1986	1987: Vic Berry, Leicester
25201	D7551	1965	1987	1988: Vic Berry, Leicester
25202	D7552	1965	1986	1989: Vic Berry, Leicester
25203	D7553	1965	1980	1982: Swindon Works
25204	D7554	1965	1980	1980: Swindon Works
25205	D7555	1965	1986	1995: MC Metals, Glasgow
25206	D7556	1965	1986	1995: MC Metals, Glasgow
25207	D7557	1965	1984	1988: Vic Berry, Leicester
25208	D7558	1965	1984	1987: Vic Berry, Leicester
25209	D7559	1965	1985	1992: MC Metals, Glasgow
25210	D7560	1965	1985	1986: Doncaster Works
25211	D7561	1965	1986	1995: MC Metals, Glasgow
25212	D7562	1965	1985	1987: Vic Berry, Leicester
25213	D7563	1965	1987	1990: Vic Berry, Leicester
25214	D7564	1965	1982	1986: Swindon Works
25215	D7565	1965	1983	1983: Swindon Works
25216	D7566	1966	1980	1983: Derby Works
25217	D7567	1966	1981	1982: Derby Works
25218	D7568	1963	1985	1985: Swindon Works
25219	D7569	1963	1983	1987: Swindon Works
25220	D7570	1963	1982	1985: Swindon Works
25221	D7571	1963	1984	1986: Swindon Works
25222	D7572	1963	1980	1981: Swindon Works
25223	D7573	1963	1980	1980: Swindon Works
25224	D7574	1963	1986	1987: Vic Berry, Leicester
25225	D7575	1963	1980	1980: Swindon Works
25226	D7576	1963	1985	1986: Doncaster Works
25227	D7577	1963	1983	1983: Swindon Works
25228	D7578	1963	1984	1987: Vic Berry, Leicester
25229	D7579	1963	1985	1986: Swindon Works
25230	D7580	1963	1986	1987: Vic Berry, Leicester
25231	D7581	1963	1985	1987: Vic Berry, Leicester
25232	D7582	1964	1980	1983: Swindon Works
25233	D7583	1964	1983	1985: Swindon Works
25234	D7584	1964	1985	1987: Vic Berry, Leicester
25235	D7585	1964	1985	Preserved
25236	D7586	1964	1984	1986: Swindon Works
25237	D7587	1964	1985	1986: Doncaster Works
25238	D7588	1964	1980	1983: Swindon Works
25239	D7589	1964	1984	1986: Swindon Works
25240	D7590	1964	1983	1983: Swindon Works

25241	D7591		1964	1981	1981: Swindon Works
25242	D7592		1964	1984	1984: Swindon Works
25243	D7593		1964	1983	1984: Swindon Works
25244	D7594		1964	1986	Preserved
25245	D7595		1964	1985	1986: Doncaster Works
25246	D7596		1964	1981	1983: Swindon Works
25247	D7597		1964	1983	1983: Swindon Works

Class 25/3

Latest Number Carried	Previous Number 1	Previous Number 2	Year Entered Service	Year Withdrawn	Current Status/Scrapping Details	Notes
25248	D7598		1966	1982	1986: Swindon Works	
25249	D7599		1966	1987	1989: Vic Berry, Leicester	
25250	D7600		1966	1984	1985: Swindon Works	
25251	D7601		1966	1985	1986: Swindon Works	
25252	D7602		1966	1980	1980: Swindon Works	
25253	D7603		1966	1983	1985: Swindon Works	
25254	D7604		1966	1986	1989: Vic Berry, Leicester	
D7605			1966	1972	1972: Derby Works	
25256	D7606		1966	1985	1986: Swindon Works	
25257	D7607		1966	1985	1987: Vic Berry, Leicester	
25258	D7608		1966	1984	1986: Swindon Works	
25259	D7609		1966	1986	1995: MC Metals, Glasgow	
25260	D7610		1966	1982	1987: Vic Berry, Leicester	
25261	D7611		1966	1981	1985: Derby Works	
25263	D7613		1966	1980	1983: Swindon Works	
25264	D7614		1966	1980	1983: Swindon Works	
25265	D7615		1966	1987	Preserved	
25266	D7616		1966	1986	1989: Vic Berry, Leicester	
25267	D7617		1966	1981	1982: Derby Works	
25269	D7619		1966	1986	1987: Vic Berry, Leicester	
25270	D7620		1966	1982	1986: Swindon Works	
25271	D7621		1966	1981	1982: Derby Works	
25272	D7622		1966	1981	1982: Derby Works	
25273	D7623		1966	1981	1982: Swindon Works	
25274	D7624		1965	1982	1985: Swindon Works	
25275	D7625		1965	1982	1985: Swindon Works	
25277	D7627		1965	1984	1985: Swindon Works	
25278	D7628		1965	1987	Preserved	
25279	D7629		1965	1987	Preserved	
25280	D7630		1965	1981	1983: Swindon Works	
25281	D7631		1965	1981	1981: Swindon Works	
25282	D7632		1965	1986	1989: Vic Berry, Leicester	
25284	D7634		1965	1985	1986: Swindon Works	
25285	D7635		1965	1986	1987: Vic Berry, Leicester	
25287	D7637		1965	1985	1986: Vic Berry, Leicester	
25288	D7638		1965	1987	1988: Vic Berry, Leicester	
25289	D7639		1965	1984	1984: Swindon Works	
25290	D7640		1965	1981	1983: Derby Works	
25291	D7641		1966	1981	1982: Swindon Works	
25292	D7642		1966	1981	1983: Swindon Works	
25293	D7643		1966	1981	1981: Swindon Works	
25294	D7644		1966	1982	1985: Swindon Works	
25295	D7645		1966	1978	1981: Derby Works	
25298	D7648		1966	1985	1986: Doncaster Works	
25299	D7649		1966	1981	1982: Derby Works	
25300	D7650		1966	1985	1986: Doncaster Works	
25301	D7651		1966	1983	1984: Swindon Works	
25302	D7652		1966	1985	1986: Doncaster Works	
25303	D7653		1966	1986	1987: Vic Berry, Leicester	
25304	D7654		1966	1982	1985: Swindon Works	
97251	25305	D7655	1966	1993	1994: MC Metals, Glasgow	SP
25306	D7656		1966	1985	1988: Vic Berry, Leicester	

25308	D7658		1966	1983	1984: Swindon Works	SP
97250	25310	D7660	1966	1993	1994: MC Metals, Glasgow	
25311	D7661		1966	1986	1989: Vic Berry, Leicester	
25312	D7662		1966	1982	1985: Swindon Works	
25313	D7663		1966	1987	Preserved	
97252	25314	D7664	1966	1993	1994: MC Metals, Glasgow	SP
25317	D7667		1967	1983	1986: Swindon Works	
25318	D7668		1967	1982	1987: Vic Berry, Leicester	
25319	D7669		1967	1983	1985: Swindon Works	
25320	D7670		1967	1983	1985: Swindon Works	
25321	D7671		1967	1986	Preserved	
25323	D7673		1967	1987	1987: Vic Berry, Leicester	
25324	D7674		1967	1985	1987: Vic Berry, Leicester	
25325	D7675		1967	1985	1990: MC Metals, Glasgow	
25326	D7676		1967	1985	1986: Swindon Works	
25327	D7677		1967	1984	1988: Vic Berry, Leicester	

Class 25/9

Class 25s assigned to industrial mineral railfreight in the North West in 1985.
Details as Class 25/0:

Latest Number Carried	Previous Number 1	Previous Number 2	Year Entered Service	Year Withdrawn	Current Status/Scrapping Details	Notes
25901	25262	D7612	1966	1987	Preserved	
25902	25268	D7618	1966	1987	1987: Vic Berry, Leicester	
25903	25276	D7626	1965	1987	1989: Vic Berry, Leicester	
25904	25283	D7633	1965	1987	Harry Needle Railroad Co	
25905	25286	D7636	1965	1986	1990: MC Metals, Glasgow	
25906	25296	D7646	1966	1986	1987: Vic Berry, Leicester	
25907	25297	D7647	1966	1986	1989: Vic Berry, Leicester	
25908	25307	D7657	1966	1986	1989: Vic Berry, Leicester	
25909	25309	D7659	1966	1986	Preserved	
25910	25315	D7665	1966	1987	1987: Vic Berry, Leicester	
25911	25316	D7666	1966	1986	1989: Vic Berry, Leicester	
25912	25322	D7672	1967	1991	Preserved	

CLASS 26   Bo-Bo

Built: 1958–59 by Birmingham Railway Carriage and Wagon Company.
Engine: Sulzer 6LDA28A of 870 kW (1160 hp) at 750 rpm.
Transmission: Electric.
Maximum Speed: 75 mph.
Train Heating/Supply: Steam heating.
Train Brakes: Built with vacuum brakes; most were later dual-braked (air & vacuum).

Class 26/0

Latest Number Carried	Previous Number 1	Year Entered Service	Year Withdrawn	Current Status/Scrapping Details	Notes
26001	D5301	1958	1993	Preserved	
26002	D5302	1958	1992	Preserved	
26003	D5303	1958	1993	1995: MC Metals, Glasgow	
26004	D5304	1958	1992	Preserved	
26005	D5305	1958	1993	1995: MC Metals, Glasgow	
26006	D5306	1958	1993	1995: MC Metals, Glasgow	
26007	D5300	1958	1993	Preserved	
26008	D5308	1958	1993	1994: MC Metals, Glasgow	
26009	D5309	1958	1977	1978: Glasgow Works	
26010	D5310	1959	1992	Preserved	
26011	D5311	1959	1992	Preserved	
26012	D5312	1959	1982	1982: Glasgow Works	
26013	D5313	1959	1985	1987: Vic Berry, Leicester	
26014	D5314	1959	1992	Preserved	
26015	D5315	1959	1991	1994: MC Metals, Glasgow	

26016	D5316	1959	1975	1976: Glasgow Works	
26017	D5317	1959	1977	1978: Glasgow Works	
26018	D5318	1959	1982	1982: Glasgow Works	
26019	D5319	1959	1985	1987: Thornton Yard	
26020	D5307	1958	1977	1978: Glasgow Works	

Class 26/1

Latest Number Carried	Previous Number 1	Year Entered Service	Year Withdrawn	Current Status/Scrapping Details	Notes
26021	D5321	1959	1991	1994: MC Metals, Glasgow	
26022	D5322	1959	1981	1981: Glasgow Works	
26023	D5323	1959	1990	1991: MC Metals, Glasgow	
26024	D5324	1959	1992	Preserved	
26025	D5325	1959	1993	Preserved	
26026	D5326	1959	1992	1995: MC Metals, Glasgow	
26027	D5327	1959	1991	1995: MC Metals, Glasgow	
26028	D5320	1959	1991	1992: MC Metals, Glasgow	
D5328		1959	1972	1972: Glasgow Works	
26029	D5329	1959	1988	1989: MC Metals, Glasgow	
26030	D5330	1959	1985	1987: Thornton Yard	
26031	D5331	1959	1989	1990: MC Metals, Glasgow	
26032	D5332	1959	1993	1995: MC Metals, Glasgow	
26033	D5333	1959	1985	1987: Thornton Yard	
26034	D5334	1959	1989	1990: MC Metals, Glasgow	
26035	D5335	1959	1992	Preserved	
26036	D5336	1959	1993	1995: MC Metals, Glasgow	
26037	D5337	1959	1993	1995: MC Metals, Glasgow	
26038	D5338	1959	1992	Preserved	
26039	D5339	1959	1990	1993: MC Metals, Glasgow	
26040	D5340	1959	1992	Preserved	
26041	D5341	1959	1992	1995: MC Metals, Glasgow	
26042	D5342	1959	1992	1995: MC Metals, Glasgow	
26043	D5343	1959	1993	Preserved	
26044	D5344	1959	1984	1987: Thornton Yard	
26045	D5345	1959	1983	1987: Vic Berry, Leicester	
26046	D5346	1959	1991	1993: MC Metals, Glasgow	

CLASS 27   Bo-Bo

Built: 1961–62 by Birmingham Railway Carriage and Wagon Company.
Engine: Sulzer 6LDA28B of 930 kW (1250 hp) at 750 rpm.
Transmission: Electric.
Maximum Speed: 90 mph.
Train Heating/Supply: D5347–69 and D5379–5415 were built with steam heating generators. D5374 subsequently fitted.
Train Brakes: Built with vacuum brakes; some were later dual-braked (air & vacuum).

UL   Scrapping details unconfirmed, but likely to be correct

Class 27/0

Latest Number Carried	Previous Number 1	Previous Number 2	Previous Number 3	Year Entered Service	Year Withdrawn	Current Status/Scrapping Details	Notes
27001	D5347			1961	1987	Preserved	
27002	D5348			1961	1986	1988: Vic Berry, Leicester	
27003	D5349			1961	1987	1987: MC Metals, Glasgow	
27004	D5350			1961	1986	1987: Vic Berry, Leicester	
27005	D5351			1961	1987	Preserved	
27006	D5352			1961	1976	1977: Glasgow Works	
27007	D5353			1961	1985	Preserved	a)
27008	D5354			1961	1987	1987: MC Metals, Glasgow	
27009	D5355			1961	1980	1982: Glasgow Works	

▲ On 17 July 1989, 26025 climbs away from Montrose with a southbound train consisting of fertiliser wagons that are bound for Dundee. **Geoff Plumb**

▼ D5350 had been working alongside steam locomotives for five years when it was captured outside Glasgow's Eastfield depot in the company of "Black Five" 45467 and D8079 (later 20079) in August 1966. It became 27004 in 1974, was withdrawn in 1986 and was scrapped in 1987.
Charlie Cross / The Gordon Edgar Collection

27010	D5356			1961	1986	1987: Vic Berry, Leicester	
27011	D5357			1961	1981	1982: Derby Works	
27012	D5358			1961	1986	1987: Vic Berry, Leicester	
27013	D5359			1961	1976	1977: Glasgow Works	
27014	D5360			1961	1986	1987: Vic Berry, Leicester	
27015	D5361			1961	1977	1977: Glasgow Works	
27016	D5362			1961	1984	1987: Vic Berry, Leicester	
27017	D5363			1961	1986	1988: Vic Berry, Leicester	
27018	D5364			1961	1986	1989: MC Metals, Glasgow	
27019	D5365			1961	1984	1985: Swindon Works	
27020	D5366			1962	1986	1987: Thornton Yard	
27021	D5367			1962	1985	1987: Thornton Yard	
27022	D5368			1962	1985	1987: Vic Berry, Leicester	
27023	D5369			1962	1986	1989: Vic Berry, Leicester	
ADB968028	27024	D5370		1962	1989	Preserved	
27025	D5371			1962	1987	1989: Vic Berry, Leicester	
27026	D5372			1962	1987	1988: Vic Berry, Leicester	
27027	D5373			1962	1983	1987: Thornton Yard	
27028	D5375			1962	1984	1985: Swindon Works	
27029	D5376			1962	1986	1987: Thornton Yard	
27030	D5377			1962	1986	1987: Vic Berry, Leicester	
27031	D5378			1962	1978	1978: Glasgow Works	
27032	D5379			1962	1985	1987: Thornton Yard	
27033	D5381			1962	1986	1987: Thornton Yard	
27034	D5382			1962	1984	1985: Swindon Works	
D5383				1962	1966	1967: J Cashmore, Great Bridge	UL
27035	D5384			1962	1976	1977: Glasgow Works	
27036	D5385			1962	1986	1987: Thornton Yard	
27037	D5389			1962	1986	1989: Vic Berry, Leicester	
27038	D5390			1962	1987	1987: Vic Berry, Leicester	
27039	D5398			1962	1975	1977: Glasgow Works	
27040	D5402			1962	1986	1987: Thornton Yard	
27041	D5405			1962	1986	1989: Vic Berry, Leicester	
27042	D5406			1962	1987	1987: Vic Berry, Leicester	
27043	D5414			1962	1980	1985: Patterson's Tip, Mount Vernon	b)
27044	D5415			1962	1980	1982: Glasgow Works	
27045	27101	D5374		1962	1986	1989: Vic Berry, Leicester	
27046	27102	D5380		1962	1987	1988: MC Metals, Glasgow	
27047	27103²	27118	D5413	1962	1986	1987: Vic Berry, Leicester	c)
27048	27104	D5387		1962	1986	1987: Vic Berry, Leicester	
27049	27105	D5388		1962	1987	1988: Vic Berry, Leicester	
27050	27106	D5394		1962	1987	Preserved	
27051	27107	D5395		1962	1987	1987: Vic Berry, Leicester	
27052	27108	D5396		1962	1987	1987: Vic Berry, Leicester	
27053	27109	D5397		1962	1987	1989: Vic Berry, Leicester	
27054	27110	D5399		1962	1987	1988: MC Metals, Glasgow	
27055	27111	D5400		1962	1987	1988: Vic Berry, Leicester	
27056	27112	D5401		1962	1987	Preserved	
27058	27204	27122	D5403	1962	1986	1987: Vic Berry, Leicester	
27059	27205	27123	D5410	1962	1987	Preserved	
27063	27209	27115	D5408	1962	1987	1989: Vic Berry, Leicester	
27064	27210	27116	D5409	1962	1986	1987: Vic Berry, Leicester	
27065	27211	27117	D5411	1962	1986	1987: Vic Berry, Leicester	
27066	27212	27103¹	D5386	1962	1987	Preserved	d)

a) 27007 has been assigned for conversion to a Class 21
b) Disposed of in landfill site
c) Second of 2 locomotives to be numbered 27103
d) First of 2 locomotives to be numbered 27103

Class 27/1
24 Class 27s were converted for push-pull operation between Glasgow and Edinburgh. Locomotives 27101-118 were steam heat only and 27119–124 were electric supply only. All Class 27/1 were subsequently renumbered back to Class 27/0 after removal of push-pull equipment or converted to Class 27/2.

Class 27/2

Modified for push-pull operation between Glasgow and Edinburgh; locomotives were fitted with electric train supply and some reverted back to Class 27/0 numbers after removal of push-pull equipment.

Details as Class 27/0 except:
Train Heating/Supply: Electric.

Latest Number Carried	Previous Number 1	Previous Number 2	Previous Number 3	Year Entered Service	Year Withdrawn	Current Status/Scrapping Details	Notes
27201	27119	D5391		1962	1979	1979: Glasgow Works	
27202	27120	D5392		1962	1980	1982: Glasgow Works	
27203	27121	D5393		1962	1983	1986: Derby Etches Park Depot	
27206	27124	D5412		1962	1986	1987: Vic Berry, Leicester	
ADB968025	27207	27113	D5404	1962	1987	1988: MC Metals, Glasgow	
27208	27114	D5407		1962	1986	1989: Vic Berry, Leicester	

▲ The Metropolitan-Vickers Type 2 (TOPS Class 28) is unique among British locomotives in that it has one six-wheeled bogie and one four-wheeled bogie, an arrangement denoted as Co-Bo. D5712 is stabled outside Reddish depot on 26 May 1968, less than four months before it would be withdrawn, ending a brief nine-year career. **Gordon Edgar**

CLASS 28 Co-Bo

Built: 1958–59 by Metropolitan Vickers, Manchester and Bowesfield Works, Stockton.
Engine: Crossley HST V8 of 896 kW (1200 hp) at 625 rpm.
Transmission: Electric.
Maximum Speed: 75 mph.
Train Heating/Supply: Steam heating.
Train Brakes: Vacuum.

SP   Locomotive was not self-propelled whilst in departmental use

Latest Number Carried	Previous Number 1	Previous Number 2	Previous Number 3	Year Entered Service	Year Withdrawn	Current Status/Scrapping Details	Notes
D5700				1958	1967	1968: J McWilliam, Shettleston	
D5701				1958	1968	1969: J Cashmore, Great Bridge	
D5702				1958	1968	1969: J Cashmore, Great Bridge	
D5703				1958	1967	1968: J McWilliam, Shettleston	
D5704				1958	1967	1968: J McWilliam, Shettleston	
D5705	TDB968006	S15705	D5705	1958	1977	Preserved	SP
D5706				1958	1968	1969: J Cashmore, Great Bridge	
D5707				1958	1968	1969: J Cashmore, Great Bridge	
D5708				1959	1968	1969: J Cashmore, Great Bridge	
D5709				1959	1967	1968: J McWilliam, Shettleston	
D5710				1959	1967	1968: J McWilliam, Shettleston	
D5711				1959	1968	1969: J Cashmore, Great Bridge	
D5712				1959	1968	1969: J Cashmore, Great Bridge	
D5713				1959	1967	1968: J McWilliam, Shettleston	
D5714				1959	1968	1969: J Cashmore, Great Bridge	
D5715				1959	1968	1968: J McWilliam, Shettleston	
D5716				1959	1968	1969: J Cashmore, Great Bridge	
D5717				1959	1968	1969: J Cashmore, Great Bridge	
D5718				1959	1968	1968: J McWilliam, Shettleston	
D5719				1959	1968	1969: J Cashmore, Great Bridge	

CLASS 29 Bo-Bo

20 Locomotives were converted from Class 21 Locomotives. No change in number when reclassified as Class 29. Technical details were the same as Class 21, with the following differences:

Conversions Completed: 1963–67.
Engine: Paxman Ventura 12YJXL of 1010 kW (1350 hp).
Maximum Speed: 80 mph.

Latest Number Carried	Previous Number 1	Year Entered Service	Year Withdrawn	Current Status/Scrapping Details	Notes
D6100		1967	1971	1972: Glasgow Works	
D6101		1965	1971	1972: Glasgow Works	
D6102		1965	1971	1972: Glasgow Works	
D6103		1965	1971	1972: Glasgow Works	
D6106		1965	1971	1972: Glasgow Works	
D6107		1967	1971	1972: Glasgow Works	
D6108		1967	1969	1971: J McWilliam, Shettleston	
D6112		1966	1971	1972: Glasgow Works	
D6113		1966	1971	1972: Glasgow Works	
D6114		1966	1971	1972: Glasgow Works	
D6116		1966	1971	1972: Glasgow Works	
D6119		1967	1971	1972: Glasgow Works	
D6121		1966	1971	1972: Glasgow Works	a)

D6123	1963	1971	1972: Glasgow Works
D6124	1967	1971	1972: Glasgow Works
D6129	1967	1971	1972: Glasgow Works
D6130	1966	1971	1972: Glasgow Works
D6132	1966	1971	1972: Glasgow Works
D6133	1966	1971	1972: Glasgow Works
D6137	1967	1971	1972: Glasgow Works

a) D6121 and D6122 are believed to have swapped identities in 1964. D6121, the former D6122, was re-engined in 1966 with a Paxman Ventura engine and reclassified as Class 29.

CLASS 30 AND CLASS 31   A1A-A1A

Classes 30 and 31 are the same locomotives. They were all introduced between 1957 and 1968 with a Mirrlees JVS12T engine but between 1965 and 1969 all were re-engined with English Electric 12SVT engines. Under the 1968 classification system, Mirrlees-engined locomotives were designated Class 30 and re-engined locomotives Class 31. By the time TOPS numbers came to be applied, the re-engining programme was complete and all locomotives thus received numbers as Class 31. The class was sub-divided, with 19 of the 20 pilot scheme locomotives (31001–31019) fitted with electro-magnetic control) being Class 31/0 and standard locomotives (with electro-pneumatic control) Class 31/1. The twentieth pilot scheme locomotive was substantially rebuilt with electro-pneumatic control following accident damage and thus became Class 31/1. Locomotives with electric train supply were Class 31/4. Sub-classes 31/5 and 31/6 were created later after further modifications.

Built: 1957–62 by Brush Traction, Loughborough.
Engine: Re-engined with English Electric 12SVT of 1100 kW (1170 hp) at 850 rpm.
Transmission: Electric.
Maximum Speed: 75 mph.
Train Heating/Supply: Steam Heating.
Train Brakes: Built vacuum.

C1 One cab remains
SP Locomotive was not self-propelled whilst in departmental use

Class 31/0

Latest Number Carried	Previous Number 1	Previous Number 2	Year Entered Service	Year Withdrawn	Current Status/Scrapping Details	Notes
31001	D5501		1957	1976	1977: Doncaster Works	
ADB968014	31002	D5502	1957	1982	1984: Crewe Works	SP
31003	D5503		1958	1980	1980: Doncaster Works	
31004	D5504		1958	1980	1981: Swindon Works	
31005	D5505		1958	1980	1980: Doncaster Works	
31006	D5506		1958	1980	1980: Doncaster Works	
31007	D5507		1958	1976	1978: Doncaster Works	
ADB968016	31008	D5508	1958	1982	1985: Crewe Works	SP
31009	D5509		1958	1976	1977: Doncaster Works	
31010	D5510		1958	1976	1977: Doncaster Works	
31011	D5511		1958	1976	1977: Doncaster Works	
31012	D5512		1958	1976	1978: Doncaster Works	
ADB968013	31013	D5513	1958	1983	1983: Doncaster Works	SP
ADB968015	31014	D5514	1958	1982	1983: Doncaster Works	SP
31015	D5515		1958	1980	1980: Doncaster Works	
31016	D5516		1958	1976	1976: Doncaster Works	
31017	D5517		1958	1980	1983: Swindon Works	
31018	D5500		1957	1976	Preserved	
31019	D5519		1958	1980	1981: Swindon Works	

Class 31/1
Details as per Class 31/0 except:
Maximum Speed: 75–90 mph.
Train Heating/Supply: Steam heating, boilers subsequently isolated.
Train Brakes: Vacuum, most were later dual braked (air & vacuum).

Latest Number Carried	Previous Number 1	Previous Number 2	Previous Number 3	Year Entered Service	Year Withdrawn	Current Status/Scrapping Details	Notes
31101	D5518			1958	1993	Preserved	
31102	D5520			1959	1996	2007: EMR, Kingsbury	
31103	D5521			1959	1980	1983: Swindon Works	
31105	D5523			1959		Preserved	
31106	D5524			1959		Preserved	
31107	D5525			1959	1995	2009: Ron Hull Jr, Rotherham	
31108	D5526			1959	1991	Preserved	
31109	D5527			1959	1988	1989: C F Booth, Rotherham	
31110	D5528			1959	2001	2007: T J Thomson, Stockton	
31111	D5529			1959	1983	1986: Swindon Works	
31112	D5530			1959	1997	2003: T J Thomson, Stockton	
31113	D5531			1959	1999	2008: EMR, Kingsbury	
31116	D5534			1959	1995	2003: T J Thomson, Stockton	
31117	D5535			1959	1987	1988: Doncaster Works	
31118	D5536			1959	1989	1990: MC Metals, Glasgow	
31119	D5537			1959	1995	Preserved	
31120	D5538			1959	1991	1994: C F Booth, Rotherham	
31121	D5539			1959	1988	1990: MC Metals, Glasgow	
31122	D5540			1959	1988	1987: Stratford Depot	
31123	D5541			1959	1992	2006: C F Booth, Rotherham	
31124	D5542			1959	1990	1991: MC Metals, Glasgow	
31125	D5543			1959	1994	2001: EMR, Kingsbury	
31126	D5544			1959	1999	1999: EWS Railway, Wigan	
31127	D5545			1959	1989	1990: Vic Berry, Leicester	
31128	D5546			1959		Nemesis Rail	
31130	D5548			1959	1997	Preserved	
31131	D5549			1959	1989	1990: Vic Berry, Leicester	
31132	D5550			1959	1995	2003: T J Thomson, Stockton	
31134	D5552			1959	1996	1999: EWS Railway, Wigan	
31135	D5553			1959	1994	2000: T J Thomson, Stockton	
31136	D5554			1959	1980	1980: Swindon Works	
31138	D5556			1959	1989	1990: MC Metals, Glasgow	
31141	D5559			1959	1989	1989: MC Metals, Glasgow	
31142	D5560			1959	1999	2003: T J Thomson, Stockton	
31143	D5561			1959	1988	1989: C F Booth, Rotherham	
31144	D5562			1959	1996	2014: Wolsingham, Weardale Rlwy	C1
31145	D5563			1959	1997	1999: EWS Railway, Wigan	
31146	D5564			1959	1998	2004: C F Booth, Rotherham	
31147	D5565			1959	1996	2001: Barrow Hill Depot	
31149	D5567			1959	1996	2004: T J Thomson, Stockton	
31150	D5568			1959	1975	1976: Doncaster Works	
31152	D5570			1959	1989	1990: Vic Berry, Leicester	
31154	D5572			1959	1999	2006: Ron Hull Jr, Rotherham	
31155	D5573			1959	1995	2004: T J Thomson, Stockton	
31156	D5574			1959	1992	1995: MC Metals, Glasgow	
31158	D5576			1959	1994	2003: T J Thomson, Stockton	
31159	D5577			1959	1996	1996: MC Metals, Glasgow	
31160	D5578			1960	1996	1999: EWS Railway, Wigan	
31162	D5580			1960	1992	Preserved	
97205	31163	D5581		1960	1999	Preserved	a)
31164	D5582			1960	1995	2000: T J Thomson, Stockton	
31165	D5583			1960	1996	1998: Crewe Works	
31166	D5584			1960	1999	2009: T J Thomson, Stockton	
31167	D5585			1960	1988	1989: Vic Berry, Leicester	
31168	D5586			1960	1991	2001: EMR, Kingsbury	
31170	D5588			1960	1990	1991: MC Metals, Glasgow	

31171	D5590	1960	1993	2003: T J Thomson, Stockton
31173	D5593	1960	1989	1991: MC Metals, Glasgow
31174	D5594	1960	1994	2001: EMR, Kingsbury
31175	D5595	1960	1987	1988: Carlisle Kingmoor Depot
31176	D5597	1960	1987	1988: Vic Berry, Leicester
31178	D5599	1960	1995	2003: T J Thomson, Stockton
31180	D5601	1960	1995	2003: T J Thomson, Stockton
31181	D5602	1960	1995	2003: T J Thomson, Stockton
31183	D5604	1960	1988	1989: C F Booth, Rotherham
31184	D5607	1960	1994	2003: T J Thomson, Stockton
31185	D5608	1960	1996	2001: T J Thomson, Stockton
31187	D5610	1960	1995	2003: T J Thomson, Stockton
31188	D5611	1960	1999	2008: T J Thomson, Stockton
31189	D5612	1960	1989	1989: Vic Berry, Leicester
31190	D5613	1960		RMS Locotec
31192	D5615	1960	1982	1983: Doncaster Works
31195	D5619	1960	1988	1988: Doncaster Works
31196	D5620	1960	1993	2001: Stratford Depot
31198	D5622	1960	1990	1991: MC Metals, Glasgow
31199	D5623	1960	1996	2003: T J Thomson, Stockton
31200	D5624	1960	1996	2007: C F Booth, Rotherham
31201	D5625	1960	1999	2004: C F Booth, Rotherham
31202	D5626	1960	1988	1988: Cricklewood Depot
31203	D5627	1960	2000	Preserved
31205	D5629	1960	1995	2002: T J Thomson, Stockton
31206	D5630	1960	1999	Preserved
31207	D5631	1960	2001	Preserved

▲ After a 58-year main line career, **31233** entered preservation in operational condition when it was sold by Network Rail in 2018. It is therefore one of a handful of locomotives where no withdrawal date is listed. On 15 April 2014, it passes Irthlingborough, with a Network Rail infrastructure monitoring train from Hither Green to Derby which has 37610 on the rear. **Brad Joyce**

31208	D5632	1960	1990	1992: MC Metals, Glasgow
31209	D5633	1960	1995	2003: T J Thomson, Stockton
31210	D5634	1960	1992	Preserved
31212	D5636	1960	1991	1995: MC Metals, Glasgow
31214	D5638	1960	1983	1983: Doncaster Works
31215	D5639	1960	1993	1995: MC Metals, Glasgow
31217	D5642	1960	1993	1999: Vic Berry, Leicester
31218	D5643	1960	1988	1989: C F Booth, Rotherham
31219	D5644	1960	1995	2003: T J Thomson, Stockton
31221	D5647	1960	1991	1995: MC Metals, Glasgow
31222	D5648	1960	1988	1990: Vic Berry, Leicester
31223	D5649	1960	1991	1995: MC Metals, Glasgow
31224	D5650	1960	1995	2002: T J Thomson, Stockton
31225	D5651	1960	1989	1991: MC Metals, Glasgow
31226	D5652	1960	1989	1991: MC Metals, Glasgow
31227	D5653	1960	1988	1989: Vic Berry, Leicester
31229	D5655	1960	1998	2001: EMR, Kingsbury
31230	D5657	1960	1994	2000: T J Thomson, Stockton
31231	D5658	1960	1990	1991: MC Metals, Glasgow
31232	D5659	1960	1995	2003: T J Thomson, Stockton
31233	D5660	1960		Preserved
31234	D5661	1960	1993	1994: MC Metals, Glasgow
31235	D5662	1960		Preserved
31237	D5664	1960	1995	2004: T J Thomson, Stockton
31238	D5665	1960	1996	1999: EWS Railway, Wigan
31240	D5667	1960	1990	1994: Stratford Depot
31241	D5668	1960	1982	1982: Swindon Works
31242	D5670	1961	1998	1999: EWS Railway, Wigan
31243	D5671	1961	1991	1994: Stratford Depot
31244	D5672	1961	1983	1983: Doncaster Works
31245	D5673	1961	1987	1988: Stratford Depot
31247	D5675	1961	1995	2003: T J Thomson, Stockton
31248	D5676	1961	1993	2000: T J Thomson, Stockton
31249	D5677	1961	1991	1995: MC Metals, Glasgow
31250	D5678	1961	2000	2000: T J Thomson, Stockton
31252	D5680	1961	1995	2000: Peterborough LIP
31254	D5682	1961	1979	1980: Old Oak Common Depot
31255	D5683	1961	1999	Preserved
31257	D5685	1961	1990	1992: C F Booth, Rotherham
31259	D5687	1961	1989	1990: Vic Berry, Leicester
31260	D5688	1961	1990	1991: MC Metals, Glasgow
31261	D5689	1961	1987	1988: Stratford Depot
31262	D5690	1961	1983	1983: Doncaster Works
31263	D5693	1961	1994	2001: EMR, Kingsbury
31264	D5694	1961	1991	1995: MC Metals, Glasgow
31268	D5698	1961	1995	2000: T J Thomson, Stockton
31270	D5800	1961	1995	Preserved
31271	D5801	1961	1997	Preserved
31272	D5802	1961	1995	1995: MC Metals, Glasgow
31273	D5803	1961	1998	2004: C F Booth, Rotherham
31275	D5805	1961	1997	2005: Carnforth Depot
31276	D5806	1961	1995	2000: T J Thomson, Stockton
31278	D5808	1961	1989	1989: MC Metals, Glasgow
31280	D5810	1961	1988	1991: C F Booth, Rotherham
31281	D5811	1961	1989	1990: Vic Berry, Leicester
31282	D5813	1961	1994	2001: EMR, Kingsbury
31283	D5815	1961	1989	2001: Stratford Depot
31284	D5816	1961	1989	1991: MC Metals, Glasgow
31285	D5817	1961		Preserved
31286	D5818	1961	1991	2001: EMR, Kingsbury
31287	D5819	1961	1987	1989: MC Metals, Glasgow
31288	D5820	1961	1991	1992: C F Booth, Rotherham
31289	D5821	1961	1992	Preserved
31290	D5822	1961	1995	2003: T J Thomson, Stockton

Latest Number Carried	Previous Number 1	Previous Number 2	Previous Number 3	Year Entered Service	Year Withdrawn	Current Status/Scrapping Details
31292	D5825			1961	1990	1990: MC Metals, Glasgow
31293	D5826			1961	1990	1994: Stratford Depot
31294	D5827			1961	1995	2003: T J Thomson, Stockton
31296	D5829			1962	1993	2004: Crewe LNWR Depot
97203	31298	D5831		1962	1987	1989: C F Booth, Rotherham
31299	D5832			1962	1990	2001: Stratford Depot
31301	D5834			1962	1999	2011: C F Booth, Rotherham
31302	D5835			1962	1999	1999: EWS Railway, Wigan
31304	D5837			1962	1996	1999: EWS Railway, Wigan
31305	D5838			1962	1991	1994: MC Metals, Glasgow
31306	D5839			1962	1999	2006: Old Oak Common Depot
31308	D5841			1962	1999	2006: Old Oak Common Depot
31309	D5843			1962	1991	1992: C F Booth, Rotherham
31311	D5845			1962	1989	1989: MC Metals, Glasgow
31312	D5846			1962	1996	1999: EWS Railway, Wigan
31313	D5847			1962	1983	1983: Doncaster Works
31314	D5848			1962	1982	1983: Doncaster Works
31317	D5851			1962	1995	2000: T J Thomson, Stockton
31319	D5853			1962	1997	2007: C F Booth, Rotherham
31320	D5854			1962	1990	2001: Stratford Depot
31322	D5857			1962	1989	1989: Vic Berry, Leicester
31323	D5858			1962	1989	1991: MC Metals, Glasgow
31324	D5859			1962	1993	1994: C F Booth, Rotherham
31970	97204	31326	D5861	1962	1991	1997: Crewe Works
31327	D5862			1962	1995	Preserved

a) 97205 is a fictional departmental number only carried in preservation

Class 31/4
Details as Class 31/1 except:
Maximum Speed: 90 mph.
Train Heating/Supply: Electric Train Supply. Some retained steam heating.

Latest Number Carried	Previous Number 1	Previous Number 2	Previous Number 3	Previous Number 4	Year Entered Service	Year Withdrawn	Current Status/Scrapping Details	Notes
31400	31161	D5579			1960	1991	1993: C F Booth, Rotherham	
31401	D5589				1960	1988	1988: Doncaster Works	
31402	D5592				1960	1992	2002: T J Thomson, Stockton	
31403	D5596				1960	1995	2003: T J Thomson, Stockton	
31404	D5605				1960	1991	1994: C F Booth, Rotherham	
31405	D5606				1960	1999	2000: Doncaster Carr Depot	
31406	D5616				1960	1991	1991: MC Metals, Glasgow	
31407	31507	31407	D5640		1960	1998	2006: Ron Hull Jr, Rotherham	
31408	D5646				1960	1994	2001: EWS Railway, Wigan	
31409	D5656				1960	1991	1992: MC Metals, Glasgow	
31410	D5669				1960	1997	2014: C F Booth, Rotherham	
31411	31511	31411	D5691		1961	1995	2005: Ron Hull Jr, Rotherham	
31412	31512	31412	D5692		1961	1998	2006: Ron Hull Jr, Rotherham	
31413	D5812				1961	1997	1998: C F Booth, Rotherham	
31415	D5824				1961	1995	2009: C F Booth, Rotherham	
31417	D5856				1962	1995	2006: Ron Hull Jr, Rotherham	
31418	D5522				1959	1995	Preserved	
31420	31172	D5591			1960	2001	2007: C F Booth, Rotherham	
31421	31140	D5558			1959	1997	2007: EMR, Kingsbury	
31422	31522	31422	31310	D5844	1962	1999	2014: C F Booth, Rotherham	
31423	31197	D5621			1960	1996	2009: T J Thomson, Stockton	
31425	31274	D5804			1961	1991	1994: C F Booth, Rotherham	
31426	31526	31426	31193	D5617	1960	1995	2006: Ron Hull Jr, Rotherham	
31427	31194	D5618			1960	1999	2007: C F Booth, Rotherham	
31428	31211	D5635			1960	1991	2001: EMR, Kingsbury	
31429	31269	D5599			1961	1991	1993: C F Booth, Rotherham	
31432	31153	D5571			1959	1996	2001: EWS Railway, Wigan	
31433	31533	31433	31236	D5663	1960	1995	2006: Ron Hull Jr, Rotherham	
31434	31258	D5686			1961	1998	2003: C F Booth, Rotherham	
31435	31179	D5600			1960	1995	Preserved	

31436	31151	D5569			1959	1986	1988: Doncaster Works	
31437	31537	31437	31182	D5603	1960	1999	2011: C F Booth, Rotherham	
31439	31239	D5666			1960	1999	2011: C F Booth, Rotherham	
31440	31204	D5628			1960	1987	1988: Vic Berry, Leicester	
31442	31251	D5679			1960	1993	2004: C F Booth, Rotherham	
31443	31177	D5598			1960	1989	1990: Vic Berry, Leicester	
31444	31544	31444	31137	D5555	1959	1995	2001: EWS Railway, Wigan	
31450	31133	D5551			1959	1998	1999: EWS Railway, Wigan	
31452	31552	31452	31279	D5809	1961		RMS Locotec	
31454	31554	31454	31228	D5654	1960		Preserved	
31455	31555	31455	31246	D5674	1960	1996	2000: EWS Railway, Wigan	
31457	31169	D5587			1960	1994	1994: C F Booth, Rotherham	
31459	31256	D5684			1961		Harry Needle Railroad Co	b)
31460	31266	D5696			1961	1992	2007: T J Thomson, Stockton	
31461	31129	D5547			1959		Nemesis Rail	
31462	31315	D5849			1962	1998	2006: Ron Hull Jr, Rotherham	
31464	31325	D5860			1962	1991	1991: MC Metals, Glasgow	
31465	31565	31465	31213	D5637	1960		Preserved	
31466	31115	D5533			1959	2001	Preserved	
31467	31216	D5641			1960	1998	2008: EMR, Kingsbury	
31468	31568	31468	31321	D5855	1962	2007	2018: Wolsingham, Weardale Rlwy	

b)   HNRC locomotive on loan to Weardale Railway

Class 31/5
Details as Class 31/4 except:
Train Heating/Supply: Electric Train Supply isolated.

Latest Number Carried	Previous Number 1	Previous Number 2	Previous Number 3	Previous Number 4	Previous Number 5	Year Entered Service	Year Withdrawn	Current Status/Scrapping Details	Notes
31514	31414	D5814				1961	1999	Preserved	
31516	31416	D5842				1962	1995	2001: EMR, Kingsbury	
31519	31419	D5697				1961	1995	2001: EWS Railway, Wigan	
31524	31424	31157	D5575			1959	1996	2006: Ron Hull Jr, Rotherham	
31530	31430	31265	D5695			1961	1999	Preserved	c)
31531	31431	31253	D5681			1961	1995	2003: T J Thomson, Stockton	
31538	31438	31139	D5557			1959	1995	Preserved	
31541	31441	31220	D5645			1960	1996	2002: Old Oak Common Depot	
31545	31445	31300	D5833			1962	1997	2002: C F Booth, Rotherham	
31546	31446	31316	D5850			1962	1995	2003: T J Thomson, Stockton	
31547	31447	31295	D5828			1961	1996	2002: T J Thomson, Stockton	
31548	31448	31148	D5566			1959	1995	2001: EMR, Kingsbury	
31549	31449	31307	D5840			1962	1996	2005: Ron Hull Jr, Rotherham	
31551	31451	31318	D5852			1962	1996	1998: Crewe Works	
31553	31453	31114	D5532			1959	1995	2001: T J Thomson, Stockton	
31556	31456	31556	31456	31291	D5823	1961	1995	2010: C F Booth, Rotherham	
31558	31458	31303	D5836			1962	1996	2005: Ron Hull Jr, Rotherham	
31563	31463	31297	D5830			1962	1998	Preserved	
31569	31469	31277	D5807			1961	1995	2003: T J Thomson, Stockton	

c)   Carries number 31430 in preservation

Class 31/6
Details as Class 31/4 except:
Train Heating/Supply: None. Through-wired for electric train supply.

Latest Number Carried	Previous Number 1	Previous Number 2	Year Entered Service	Year Withdrawn	Current Status/Scrapping Details	Notes
31601	31186	D5609	1960		Preserved	
31602	31191	D5614	1960	2013	2018: Wolsingham, Weardale Rlwy	

▲ On 8 November 2012, Devon & Cornwall Railways' 31601 heads east at Wantage Road with a Chiltern Mark 3 coach that it is moving from Bristol Barton Hill depot to Wembley depot. The locomotive was sold into preservation in 2018 and can now be found at the Ecclesbourne Valley Railway. **Geoff Plumb**

▼ 33207 is part of the West Coast Railway Company's varied diesel fleet. On 16 July 2019, it approaches Putney with the 12.43 Windsor & Eton Riverside–London Waterloo empty coaching stock working in preparation for that afternoon's "Royal Windsor Steam Express" charter. **Gordon Edgar**

CLASS 33   Bo-Bo

Built: 1960–62 by Birmingham Railway Carriage and Wagon Company.
Engine: Sulzer 8LDA28A of 1160 kW (1550 hp) at 750 rpm.
Transmission: Electric.
Maximum Speed: 85 mph.
Train Heating/Supply: Electric.
Train Brakes: Dual braked (air & vacuum).

Class 33/0

Latest Number Carried	Previous Number 1	Previous Number 2	Previous Number 3	Year Entered Service	Year Withdrawn	Current Status/Scrapping Details	Notes
33001	D6500			1960	1988	1989: Eastleigh Depot	
33002	D6501			1960	1996	Preserved	
D6502				1960	1964	1964: Itchingfield Junction	
33003	D6503			1960	1987	1990: Eastleigh Depot	
33004	D6504			1960	1991	1992: Eastleigh Works	
33005	D6505			1960	1987	1990: Vic Berry, Leicester	
33006	D6506			1960	1991	1994: C F Booth, Rotherham	
33007	D6507			1960	1986	1987: Eastleigh Works	
33008	D6508			1960	1996	Preserved	
33009	D6509			1960	1992	1997: Eastleigh Works	
33010	D6510			1960	1988	1989: Eastleigh Depot	
33011	D6512			1960	1989	1990: Vic Berry, Leicester	
33012	D6515			1960	1997	Preserved	
33013	D6518			1960	1989	1991: MC Metals, Glasgow	
33014	D6522			1960	1986	1986: Eastleigh Depot	
33015	D6523			1960	1989	1990: Vic Berry, Leicester	
33016	D6524			1960	1989	1991: MC Metals, Glasgow	
33017	D6526			1960	1988	1990: Vic Berry, Leicester	
33018	TDB968030	33018	D6530	1960	2000	Preserved	
33019	D6534			1960		Nemesis Rail	
33020	D6537			1960	1993	1997: Stewarts Lane Depot	
33021	D6539			1961	2003	Preserved	
33022	D6540			1961	1989	1991: MC Metals, Glasgow	
33023	D6541			1961	1997	2005: EMR, Kingsbury	
33024	D6542			1961	1986	1986: Eastleigh Depot	
33025	D6543			1961		West Coast Railway Co	
33026	D6544			1961	1998	2003: Eastleigh Depot	
33027	D6545			1961	1991	1992: Eastleigh Depot	
33028	D6546			1961	1988	1989: Eastleigh Works	
33029	D6547			1961		West Coast Railway Co	
33030	D6548			1961		West Coast Railway Co	
33031	D6549			1961	1989	1991: MC Metals, Glasgow	
33032	D6550			1961	1987	1987: Eastleigh Works	
33033	D6551			1961	1993	1997: Stewarts Lane Depot	
33034	D6552			1961	1988	2013: Swanage Railway	
33035	D6553			1961	1996	Preserved	
33036	D6554			1961	1979	1979: Slade Green Depot	
33037	D6555			1961	1987	1991: MC Metals, Glasgow	
33038	D6556			1961	1988	2001: EMR, Kingsbury	
33039	D6557			1961	1989	1991: MC Metals, Glasgow	
33040	D6558			1961	1993	1997: Stewarts Lane Depot	
33041	D6559			1961	1975	1976: Selhurst Depot	
33042	D6560			1961	1996	1997: Stewarts Lane Depot	
33043	D6561			1961	1987	1991: MC Metals, Glasgow	
33044	D6562			1961	1987	1990: Vic Berry, Leicester	
33045	D6563			1961	1987	1990: Vic Berry, Leicester	
33046	D6564			1961	1998	Preserved	
33047	D6565			1961	1997	1997: Eastleigh Depot	
33048	D6566			1961	1997	Preserved	
33049	D6567			1961	1988	1989: Eastleigh Works	
33050	D6568			1961	1993	1997: Stewarts Lane Depot	

33051	D6569	1961	1998	2003: Eastleigh Depot
33052	D6570	1961	1997	Preserved
33053	D6571	1961	1997	Preserved
33054	D6572	1961	1986	1987: Eastleigh Works
33055	D6573	1961	1989	1991: MC Metals, Glasgow
33056	D6574	1961	1991	2006: C F Booth, Rotherham
33057	D6575	1961	1997	Preserved
D6576		1961	1968	1969: Eastleigh Works
33058	D6577	1961	1991	1994: C F Booth, Rotherham
33059	D6578	1961	1988	1991: MC Metals, Glasgow
33060	D6579	1961	1990	1992: Eastleigh Depot
33061	D6581	1961	1987	1987: Eastleigh Works
33062	D6582	1961	1987	1990: Vic Berry, Leicester
33063	D6583	1962	1997	Preserved
33064	D6584	1962	1994	1997: Old Oak Common Depot
33065	D6585	1962	1997	Preserved

Class 33/1
Fitted with push-pull control system. Triple-braked (air, vacuum & electro-pneumatic).
Details as Class 33/0.

Latest Number Carried	Previous Number 1	Year Entered Service	Year Withdrawn	Current Status/Scrapping Details	Notes
33101	D6511	1960	1993	1997: Eastleigh Depot	
33102	D6513	1960	1992	Preserved	
33103	D6514	1960	1997	Preserved	
33104	D6516	1960	1985	1985: Slade Green Depot	
33105	D6517	1960	1987	1990: Vic Berry, Leicester	
33106	D6519	1960	1990	1992: Eastleigh Depot	
33107	D6520	1960	1989	1991: MC Metals, Glasgow	
33108	D6521	1960	2003	Preserved	
33109	D6525	1960	1997	Preserved	
33110	D6527	1960	1992	Preserved	
33111	D6528	1960	1991	Preserved	
33112	D6529	1960	1988	1992: Eastleigh Depot	
33113	D6531	1960	1992	1997: Stewarts Lane Depot	
33114	D6532	1960	1993	1996: Eastleigh Yard	
33115	D6533	1960	1989	1996: St Leonards Railway Eng.	
33116	D6535	1960	1998	Preserved	
33117	D6536	1960	1997	Preserved	
33118	D6538	1961	1993	1997: Eastleigh Depot	
33119	D6580	1961	1989	1992: MC Metals, Glasgow	

Class 33/2
Built to the former loading gauge of the Tonbridge–Battle line.
Details as Class 33/0.

Latest Number Carried	Previous Number 1	Previous Number 2	Previous Number 3	Year Entered Service	Year Withdrawn	Current Status/Scrapping Details	Notes
33201	D6586			1962	1993	Preserved	
33202	D6587			1962	2007	Preserved	
33203	D6588			1962	1991	2006: Newton Stewart, Dumf & Gall	
33204	D6589			1962	1997	2002: Mid Hants Railway	
33205	33302	33205	D6590	1962	1992	2003: Barrow Hill Depot	
33206	D6591			1962	1996	1997: Eastleigh Depot	
33207	D6592			1962		West Coast Railway Co	
33208	D6593			1962	1997	Preserved	
33209	D6594			1962	1988	1989: Eastleigh Works	
33210	D6595			1962	1987	1990: Vic Berry, Leicester	
33211	D6596			1962	1993	1997: Stewarts Lane Depot	
33212	D6597			1962	1987	1991: MC Metals, Glasgow	

▲ Two preserved Class 33s are based at the Churnet Valley Railway in Staffordshire; 33102 "Sophie" and 33021 "Eastleigh" bask in the sun at the railway's Cheddleton traction maintenance depot on 21 September 2019. **Andy Chard**

▼ Class 35 "Hymek" D7076 has been preserved at the East Lancashire Railway since the 1980s, enjoying far greater longevity there than it did during its ten-year career with BR. On 21 August 2020, it was operating on home turf and accelerates away from Irwell Vale with a southbound Ramsbottom to Heywood service. **Liam Barnes**

CLASS 35 B-B

Built: 1961–64 by Beyer Peacock & Co., Manchester.
Engine: Bristol Siddeley Maybach MD 870 of 1269 kW (1700 hp) at 1500 rpm.
Transmission: Hydraulic.
Maximum Speed: 90 mph.
Train Heating/Supply: Steam heating.
Train Brakes: Vacuum.

Latest Number Carried	Previous Number 1	Year Entered Service	Year Withdrawn	Current Status/Scrapping Details	Notes
D7000		1961	1973	1975: Swindon Works	
D7001		1961	1974	1975: G Cohen, Kettering	
D7002		1961	1971	1972: Swindon Works	
D7003		1961	1972	1972: Swindon Works	
D7004		1961	1972	1972: Swindon Works	
D7005		1961	1972	1972: Swindon Works	
D7006		1961	1971	1972: Swindon Works	
D7007		1961	1972	1972: Swindon Works	
D7008		1961	1972	1972: Swindon Works	
D7009		1961	1973	1974: Swindon Works	
D7010		1961	1972	1972: Swindon Works	
D7011		1961	1975	1977: Marple & Gillot, Attercliffe	
D7012		1961	1972	1972: Swindon Works	
D7013		1961	1972	1972: Swindon Works	
D7014		1961	1972	1972: Swindon Works	
D7015		1961	1972	1972: Swindon Works	
D7016		1962	1974	1975: Swindon Works	
D7017		1962	1975	Preserved	
D7018		1962	1975	Preserved	
D7019		1962	1972	1972: Swindon Works	
D7020		1962	1972	1972: Swindon Works	
D7021		1962	1972	1972: Swindon Works	
D7022		1962	1975	1977: G Cohen, Kettering	
D7023		1962	1973	1975: Swindon Works	
D7024		1962	1972	1972: Swindon Works	
D7025		1962	1972	1972: Swindon Works	
D7026		1962	1974	1977: G Cohen, Kettering	
D7027		1962	1971	1972: Swindon Works	
D7028		1962	1975	1977: G Cohen, Kettering	
D7029		1962	1975	Preserved	
D7030		1962	1973	1974: Bird Group, Long Marston	
D7031		1962	1973	1975: Swindon Works	
D7032		1962	1973	1975: Swindon Works	
D7033		1962	1972	1972: Swindon Works	
D7034		1962	1972	1972: Swindon Works	
D7035		1962	1972	1972: Swindon Works	
D7036		1962	1972	1972: Swindon Works	
D7037		1962	1972	1972: Swindon Works	
D7038		1962	1972	1973: Swindon Works	
D7039		1962	1972	1972: Swindon Works	
D7040		1962	1972	1972: Swindon Works	
D7041		1962	1972	1972: Swindon Works	
D7042		1962	1972	1972: Swindon Works	
D7043		1962	1972	1972: Swindon Works	
D7044		1962	1973	1974: Bird Group, Long Marston	
D7045		1962	1972	1973: Swindon Works	
D7046		1962	1972	1972: Swindon Works	
D7047		1962	1972	1972: Swindon Works	
D7048		1962	1972	1972: Swindon Works	
D7049		1962	1972	1972: Swindon Works	
D7050		1962	1972	1973: Swindon Works	
D7051		1962	1972	1972: Swindon Works	

D7052	1962	1972	1973: Swindon Works
D7053	1962	1972	1972: Swindon Works
D7054	1962	1972	1975: Swindon Works
D7055	1962	1973	1975: Swindon Works
D7056	1962	1972	1972: Swindon Works
D7057	1962	1972	1972: Swindon Works
D7058	1962	1971	1972: Swindon Works
D7059	1962	1971	1972: Swindon Works
D7060	1962	1971	1972: Swindon Works
D7061	1962	1972	1972: Swindon Works
D7062	1963	1971	1972: Swindon Works
D7063	1962	1971	1972: Swindon Works
D7064	1963	1971	1972: Swindon Works
D7065	1963	1972	1972: Swindon Works
D7066	1963	1971	1972: Swindon Works
D7067	1963	1971	1972: Swindon Works
D7068	1963	1972	1975: Swindon Works
D7069	1963	1971	1972: Swindon Works
D7070	1963	1972	1972: Swindon Works
D7071	1963	1972	1972: Swindon Works
D7072	1963	1971	1972: Swindon Works
D7073	1963	1971	1972: Swindon Works
D7074	1963	1972	1975: Swindon Works
D7075	1963	1973	1974: Bird Group, Long Marston
D7076	1963	1973	Preserved
D7077	1963	1972	1972: Swindon Works
D7078	1963	1971	1972: Swindon Works
D7079	1963	1971	1972: Swindon Works

▲ Direct Rail Services is one of several operators with the versatile veteran Class 37s on their books. On 29 June 2016, 37259 & 37069 cross the River Esk courtesy of the 302-metre long Eskmeals Viaduct, with the 17.18 Sellafield–Crewe nuclear flasks service. **Gordon Edgar**

D7080	1963	1972	1973: Swindon Works
D7081	1963	1971	1972: Swindon Works
D7082	1963	1972	1972: Swindon Works
D7083	1963	1971	1972: Swindon Works
D7084	1963	1972	1972: Swindon Works
D7085	1963	1972	1972: Swindon Works
D7086	1963	1972	1972: Swindon Works
D7087	1963	1972	1973: Swindon Works
D7088	1963	1972	1972: Swindon Works
D7089	1963	1973	1976: T J Thomson, Stockton
D7090	1963	1972	1972: Swindon Works
D7091	1963	1972	1972: Swindon Works
D7092	1963	1972	1972: Swindon Works
D7093	1963	1974	1977: G Cohen, Kettering
D7094	1963	1972	1973: Swindon Works
D7095	1963	1972	1972: Swindon Works
D7096	1963	1972	1986: Marple & Gillot, Attercliffe
D7097	1963	1972	1975: Swindon Works
D7098	1964	1972	1975: Swindon Works
D7099	1964	1972	1972: Swindon Works
D7100	1964	1972	1974: Swindon Works

CLASS 37   Co-Co

Built: 1960–65 by English Electric, Vulcan Foundry, Newton-le-Willows and Robert Stephenson & Hawthorns, Darlington.
Engine: English Electric 12CSVT of 1300 kW (1750 hp) at 850 rpm.
Transmission: Electric.
Maximum Speed: 90 mph.
Train Heating/Supply: D6700–D6938 were built with steam heating generators. Subsequently fitted to D6947/D6960–D6968 and later D6948 after preservation. Most were later isolated or removed. The remainder were built with through steam pipes.
Train Brakes: Built vacuum. All except D6983 were later converted to dual braked (air & vacuum).

C1   One cab remains
ES   Locomotive exported and subsequently scrapped

Class 37/0
Includes Class 37/3 First Batch, which were renumbered 37310–37314 and 37320–37326. Previous numbers were 37152, 37156, 37137, 37145, 37190, 37026, 37037, 37049, 37088, 37099, 37108 and 37111 respectively; unrefurbished Class 37/0s selected for exclusive use on Scottish Region air-braked steel traffic.
All reverted to 37/0 numbers in 1988–89 and are therefore listed with Class 37/0s.

Latest Number Carried	Previous Number 1	Previous Number 2	Previous Number 3	Previous Number 4	Year Entered Service	Year Withdrawn	Current Status/Scrapping Details	Notes
37003	D6703				1960	1998	Preserved	
37004	D6704				1961	1996	1996: MC Metals, Glasgow	
37008	37352	37008	D6708		1961	1992	1996: Crewe Works	
37010	D6710				1961	2005	2007: C F Booth, Rotherham	
37011	D6711				1961	1987	1989: J Rollason, Wellington	
37012	D6712				1961	1999	2003: Sims Metals, Beeston	
37013	D6713				1961	1999	2007: EMR, Kingsbury	
37019	D6719				1961	1995	2004: Sims Metals, Beeston	
37023	D6723				1961	1999	Preserved	
37025	D6725				1961		Colas Rail	a)
37026	37320	37026	D6726		1961	1996	2000: EWS Railway, Wigan	
37029	D6729				1961	2006	Preserved	
37031	D6731				1961	1994	1997: Cardiff Canton Depot	
37032	37353	37032	D6732		1962	1994	Preserved	
37035	D6735				1962	1996	2000: C F Booth, Rotherham	
37037	37321	37037	D6737		1962	2003	Preserved	
37038	D6738				1962		Direct Rail Services	
37040	D6740				1962	2000	2006: C F Booth, Rotherham	

37042	D6742				1962	2011	Preserved	
37043	37354	37043	D6743		1962	2000	2003: Sims Metals, Beeston	
37046	D6746				1962	2000	2009: C F Booth, Rotherham	
37047	D6747				1962	2007	2008: EMR, Kingsbury	
37048	D6748				1962	1996	2003: Toton Training Compound	
37051	D6751				1962	2005	2008: Sims Metals, Beeston	
37054	D6754				1962	1999	2003: Motherwell Depot	
37055	D6755				1962	2002	2008: EMR, Kingsbury	
37057	D6757				1962		Colas Rail	
37058	D6758				1962	2000	2009: C F Booth, Rotherham	
37059	D6759				1962		Direct Rail Services	
37062	D6762				1962	1989	1990: Vic Berry, Leicester	
37063	D6763				1962	1994	2001: EMR, Kingsbury	
37065	D6765				1962	2007	2007: EMR, Kingsbury	
37066	D6766				1962	1997	1997: Crewe Works	
37068	37356	37068	D6768		1962	1995	2005: C F Booth, Rotherham	
37069	D6769				1962		Direct Rail Services	
37070	D6770				1962	1996	2004: Toton Training Compound	
37071	D6771				1962	2000	2005: C F Booth, Rotherham	
37072	D6772				1962	1997	2004: EMR, Kingsbury	
37073	D6773				1962	2000	2003: East Lancashire Railway	
37074	D6774				1962	2000	2005: C F Booth, Rotherham	
37075	D6775				1962	1999	Preserved	
37077	D6777				1962	2000	2010: C F Booth, Rotherham	
37078	D6778				1962	1993	2004: EMR, Kingsbury	
37079	37357	37079	D6779		1962	1998	2008: EMR, Kingsbury	
37080	D6780				1962	1996	1997: Cardiff Canton Depot	
37083	D6783				1962	1994	2000: Immingham Depot	
37087	D6787				1962	2012	2013: C F Booth, Rotherham	
37088	37323	37088	D6788		1963	1996	2002: C F Booth, Rotherham	
37092	D6792				1963	1996	2001: T J Thomson, Stockton	
37095	D6795				1963	1999	2005: Carnforth Depot	
37096	D6796				1962	1991	1991: MC Metals, Glasgow	
37097	D6797				1962	1998	Preserved	
37098	D6798				1962	1998	2002: Old Oak Common Depot	
37099	37324	37099	D6799		1962		Colas Rail	
37104	D6804				1963	1997	2000: Immingham Depot	
37106	D6806				1963	1999	2000: EWS Railway, Wigan	
37107	D6807				1963	1999	2001: EWS Railway, Wigan	
37108	37325	37108	D6808		1963	1996	Preserved	
37109	D6809				1963	2007	Preserved	
37110	D6810				1963	1995	2000: Immingham Depot	
37111	37326	37111	D6811		1963	1996	2003: EMR, Kingsbury	
37113	D6813				1963	1995	1995: Portobello Yard, Edinburgh	
37114	D6814				1963	2007	2008: EMR, Kingsbury	
37116	D6816				1963		Colas Rail	
37131	D6831				1963	1999	2007: C F Booth, Rotherham	
37133	D6833				1963	2000	2004: Carnforth Depot	
37137	37312	37137	D6837		1963	2006	2006: T J Thomson, Stockton	
37138	D6838				1963	1996	2004: Toton Training Compound	
37139	D6839				1963	1994	2004: T J Thomson, Stockton	
37140	D6840				1963	1999	2001: EWS Railway, Wigan	
37141	D6841				1963	1997	2005: Carnforth Depot	
37142	D6842				1963	1997	Preserved	
37144	D6844				1963	1994	2003: Sims Metals, Beeston	
37146	D6846				1963		Europhoenix	
37310	37152	37310	37152	D6852	1963	1999	Preserved	b)
37153	D6853				1963	1999	2001: C F Booth, Rotherham	
37154	D6854				1963	1999	2000: EWS Railway, Wigan	
37156	37311	37156	D6856		1963	1999	2000: EWS Railway, Wigan	
37158	D6858				1963	1999	2008: Carnforth Depot	
37162	D6862				1963	2000	2005: C F Booth, Rotherham	
37165	37374	37165	D6865		1963		West Coast Railway Co	
37174	D6874				1963	2005	2008: EMR, Kingsbury	

				Built	Withdrawn	Status	Note
37175	D6875			1963		Colas Rail	
37184	D6884			1963	1996	2001: T J Thomson, Stockton	
37185	D6885			1963	1999	2006: C F Booth, Rotherham	
37188	D6888			1964	1996	2019: UKRL Leicester	
37190	37314	37190	D6890	1964	1993	Locomotive Services	
37191	D6891			1964	1999	2001: EWS Railway, Wigan	
37194	D6894			1964	2015	2017: C F Booth, Rotherham	
37196	D6896			1964	2000	2009: C F Booth, Rotherham	
37197	D6897			1964	2007	2012: EMR, Kingsbury	
37198	D6898			1964		Network Rail	
37201	D6901			1963	1996	2009: C F Booth, Rotherham	
37203	D6903			1963	2009	2010: Ron Hull Jr, Rotherham	
37207	D6907			1963		Europhoenix	
37209	D6909			1963	1992	2002: Doncaster Carr Depot	
37211	D6911			1963	1999	2007: EMR, Kingsbury	
37212	D6912			1964	1999	2004: Eastleigh Depot	
37213	D6913			1964	1996	2003: T J Thomson, Stockton	
37214	D6914			1964	1997	Preserved	
37215	D6915			1964	1993	Preserved	
37216	D6916			1964	2004	Preserved	
37218	D6918			1964		Direct Rail Services	
37219	D6919			1964		Colas Rail	
37220	D6920			1964	2000	2007: EMR, Kingsbury	
37221	D6921			1964	2000	2009: C F Booth, Rotherham	
37222	D6922			1964	1997	2008: T J Thomson, Stockton	
37223	D6923			1964	1995	2003: Sims Metals, Beeston	
37225	D6925			1964	1999	2004: C F Booth, Rotherham	
37227	D6927			1964	1997	Preserved	
37229	D6929			1964	2012	2013: C F Booth, Rotherham	
37230	D6930			1964	2000	2006: C F Booth, Rotherham	
37232	D6932			1964	1996	2000: EWS Railway, Wigan	
37235	D6935			1964	1995	2008: Carnforth Depot	
37238	D6938			1964	2000	2009: C F Booth, Rotherham	
37240	D6940			1964	1997	Boden Rail Engineering	
37241	D6941			1964	1996	2001: T J Thomson, Stockton	
37242	D6942			1964	1999	2006: C F Booth, Rotherham	
37244	D6944			1964	1999	2000: EWS Railway, Wigan	
37245	D6945			1964	1999	2000: EWS Railway, Wigan	
37248	D6948			1964		Preserved	
37250	D6950			1964	2000	Preserved	
37251	D6951			1964	1996	2001: C F Booth, Rotherham	
37252	D6952			1965	1995	2002: Doncaster Carr Depot	
37254	D6954			1965		Colas Rail	
37255	D6955			1965	1999	Nemesis Rail	
37259	37380	37259	D6959	1965		Direct Rail Services	
37260	D6960			1965	1989	1991: MC Metals, Glasgow	
37261	D6961			1965	2014	Preserved	
37262	D6962			1965	1999	2004: Sims Metals, Beeston	
37263	D6963			1965	1999	Preserved	
37264	D6964			1965	2001	Preserved	
37273²	37306	D6606		1965	1991	1993: Cardiff Canton Depot	c)
37275	D6975			1965	1999	Preserved	
37278	D6978			1965	1994	2003: T J Thomson, Stockton	
37280	D6980			1965	1994	1997: Old Oak Common Depot	
D6983				1965	1966	1966: R S Hayes, Bridgend	
37293	D6993			1965	2000	2009: C F Booth, Rotherham	
37294	D6994			1965	2004	Preserved	
37298	D6998			1965	2000	2006: C F Booth, Rotherham	
37308	37274²	37308	D6608	1965	2007	Preserved	d)

a)   Preserved locomotive on hire to Colas Rail
b)   Reverted to 37310 in preservation
c)   Second of 2 locomotives to be numbered 37273
d)   Second of 2 locomotives to be numbered 37274

Class 37/3 Second Batch

Fitted with regeared CP7 Bogies. Locos 37352, 37353, 37354, 37355, 37356, 37357, 37374 & 37380 later reverted to their Class 37/0 numbers.
Details as Class 37/0 except:
Maximum Speed: 80 mph.

Latest Number Carried	Previous Number 1	Previous Number 2	Previous Number 3	Previous Number 4	Year Entered Service	Year Withdrawn	Current Status/Scrapping Details	Notes
37330	37128	D6828			1963	1997	2001: T J Thomson, Stockton	
37331	37202	D6902			1963	1995	2003: Barrow Hill Depot	
37332	37239	D6939			1964	1998	2000: Old Oak Common Depot	
37333	37271[2]	37303	D6603		1965	1997	1997: Crewe Works	e)
37334	37272[2]	37304	D6604		1965	2005	2005: C F Booth, Rotherham	f)
37335	37285	D6985			1965	1994	2000: Immingham Depot	
37340	37009	D6709			1961	1995	Preserved	
37341	37015	D6715			1961	1994	2003: C F Booth, Rotherham	
37343	37049	37322	37049	D6749	1962	1995	2003: Toton Training Compound	
37344	37053	D6753			1962	1996	2006: C F Booth, Rotherham	
37345	37101	D6801			1962	1994	2003: Immingham Depot	
37350	37119	D6700			1960	1999	Preserved	
37351	37002	D6702			1960	1999	2007: T J Thomson, Stockton	
37355	37045	D6745			1962	1998	2003: Toton Training Compound	
37358	37091	D6791			1963	2006	2007: T J Thomson, Stockton	
37359	37118	D6818			1963	1994	2005: Carnforth Depot	
37370	37127	D6827			1963	2000	2005: C F Booth, Rotherham	
37371	37147	D6847			1963	1999	2001: EWS Railway, Wigan	
37372	37159	D6859			1963	2004	Being converted to D5910 (Class 23)	
37373	37160	D6860			1963	1993	1997: Old Oak Common Depot	
37375	37193	D6893			1964	2007	2008: EMR, Kingsbury	
37376	37199	D6899			1963	2000	2006: C F Booth, Rotherham	
37377	37200	D6900			1963	2001	2009: C F Booth, Rotherham	C1
37378	37204	D6904			1963	1996	1996: C F Booth, Rotherham	
37379	37226	D6926			1964	2001	2008: C F Booth, Rotherham	
37381	37284	D6984			1965	1993	2000: Froddingham Depot	
37382	37145	37313	37145	D6845	1963	1994	2000: Immingham Depot	
37383	37167	D6867			1963	1999	2008: Crewe LNWR Depot	
37384	37258	D6958			1965	1999	2005: EMR, Kingsbury	

e) Second of 2 locomotives to be numbered 37271
f) Second of 2 locomotives to be numbered 37272

Class 37/4

Fitted with regeared CP7 Bogies.
Details as Class 37/0 except:
Maximum Speed: 80 mph.
Train Heating/Supply: Electric.

Latest Number Carried	Previous Number 1	Previous Number 2	Year Entered Service	Year Withdrawn	Current Status/Scrapping Details	Notes
37401	37268	D6968	1965		Direct Rail Services	
37402	37274[1]	D6974	1965		Direct Rail Services	g)
37403	37307	D6607	1965		Preserved	
37404	37286	D6986	1965	1999	2002: C F Booth, Rotherham	
37405	37282	D6982	1965		Direct Rail Services	
37406	37295	D6995	1965	2009	2013: C F Booth, Rotherham	
37407	37305	D6605	1965		Direct Rail Services	
37408	37289	D6989	1965	2005	2008: EMR, Kingsbury	
37409	37270	D6970	1965		Direct Rail Services	
37410	37273[1]	D6973	1965	2007	2013: C F Booth, Rotherham	h)
37411	37290	D6990	1965	2008	2013: C F Booth, Rotherham	C1
37412	37301	D6601	1965	2004	2012: EMR, Kingsbury	
37413	37276	D6976	1965	2000	2017: C F Booth, Rotherham	
37414	37287	D6987	1965	2000	2009: T J Thomson, Stockton	
37415	37277	D6977	1965	2003	2013: C F Booth, Rotherham	
37416	37302	D6602	1965	2006	2013: C F Booth, Rotherham	

37417	37269	D6969	1965	2008	2013: C F Booth, Rotherham	
37418	37271[1]	D6971	1965		Colas Rail	j)
37419	37291	D6991	1965		Direct Rail Services	
37420	37297	D6997	1965	2000	2008: Ron Hull Jr, Rotherham	
37421	37267	D6967	1965		Colas Rail	
37422	37266	D6966	1965		Direct Rail Services	
37423	37296	D6996	1965		Direct Rail Services	
37424	37279	D6979	1965		Direct Rail Services	k)
37425	37292	D6992	1965		Direct Rail Services	
37426	37299	D6999	1965	2003	2013: C F Booth, Rotherham	
37427	37288	D6988	1965	2006	2013: C F Booth, Rotherham	
37428	37281	D6981	1965	2004	2013: C F Booth, Rotherham	
37429	37300	D6600	1965	2002	2008: EMR, Kingsbury	
37430	37265	D6965	1965	2000	2008: EMR, Kingsbury	
37431	37272[1]	D6972	1965	1999	2000: EWS Railway, Wigan	m)

g) First of 2 locomotives to be numbered 37274
h) First of 2 locomotives to be numbered 37273
j) First of 2 locomotives to be numbered 37271. Preserved locomotive on hire to Colas Rail
k) Temporarily carries number 37558
m) First of 2 locomotives to be numbered 37272

▲ Less than a year after it was refurbished and renumbered at Crewe Works, Class 37/5 37695 heads east through Hungerford with a rake of empty MGR wagons on 6 May 1987. **Geoff Plumb**

Class 37/5
Refurbished locomotives fitted with regeared CP7 Bogies.
Details as Class 37/0 except:
Maximum Speed: 80 mph.
Train Heating/Supply: None.

Latest Number Carried	Previous Number 1	Previous Number 2	Previous Number 3	Year Entered Service	Year Withdrawn	Current Status/Scrapping Details	Notes
37503	37017	D6717		1961		Preserved	
37505	37028	D6728		1961	2000	2008: EMR, Kingsbury	
37509	37093	D6793		1963	2001	2005: Cardiff Canton Depot	
37510	37112	D6812		1963		Rail Operations Group	n)
37513	37056	D6756		1962	2000	2008: C F Booth, Rotherham	
37515	37064	D6764		1962	2008	2010: T J Thomson, Stockton	
37516	37086	D6786		1962		West Coast Railway Co	
37517	37018	D6718		1961		West Coast Railway Co	
37518	37076	D6776		1962		West Coast Railway Co	
37519	37027	D6727		1961	1999	2008: C F Booth, Rotherham	
37520	37041	D6741		1962	2002	2007: T J Thomson, Stockton	
D6817	37521	37117	D6817	1963		Locomotive Services	

n)   Europhoenix locomotive on hire to ROG

Class 37/6
No train supply, but electric through-wired. All formerly Class 37/5.
Details as Class 37/0 except:
Maximum Speed: 90 mph.
Train Brakes: Air.

Latest Number Carried	Previous Number 1	Previous Number 2	Previous Number 3	Year Entered Service	Year Withdrawn	Current Status/Scrapping Details	Notes
37601	37501	37005	D6705	1961		Rail Operations Group	n)
37602	37502	37082	D6782	1962		Direct Rail Services	
37603	37504	37039	D6739	1962		Direct Rail Services	
37604	37506	37007	D6707	1961		Direct Rail Services	
37605	37507	37036	D6736	1962		Direct Rail Services	
37606	37508	37090	D6790	1963		Direct Rail Services	
37607	37511	37103	D6803	1963		Colas Rail	o)
37608	37512	37022	D6722	1961		Rail Operations Group	n)
37609	37514	37115	D6815	1963		Direct Rail Services	
37610	37687	37181	D6881	1963		Colas Rail	o)
37611	37690	37171	D6871	1963		Rail Operations Group	n)
37612	37691	37179	D6879	1963		Colas Rail	o)

n)   Europhoenix locomotive on hire to ROG
o)   HNRC locomotive on hire to Colas Rail

Class 37/5 (continued)

Latest Number Carried	Previous Number 1	Previous Number 2	Previous Number 3	Year Entered Service	Year Withdrawn	Current Status/Scrapping Details	Notes
D6851	37667	37151	D6851	1963		Locomotive Services	
37668	37257	D6957		1965		West Coast Railway Co	
37669	37129	D6829		1963		West Coast Railway Co	
37670	37182	D6882		1963	2009	2018: NAP Construction, Leicester	
37671	37247	D6947		1964	2000	2011: EMR, Attercliffe	
37672	37189	D6889		1964	2000	2010: T J Thomson, Stockton	
37673	37132	D6832		1963	2000	2008: EMR, Kingsbury	
37674	37169	D6869		1963	2005	Preserved	
37675	37164	D6864		1963	2004	2010: EMR, Kingsbury	
37676	37126	D6826		1963		West Coast Railway Co	
37677	37121	D6821		1963	2002	2008: C F Booth, Rotherham	
37678	37256	D6956		1965	2000	2007: EMR, Kingsbury	
37679	37123	D6823		1963		Preserved	
37680	37224	D6924		1964	2001	2010: T J Thomson, Stockton	
37681	37130	D6830		1963	1992	1995: Crewe Works	

37682	37236	D6936	1964	2014	2016: C F Booth, Rotherham	
37683	37187	D6887	1964	2000	2013: C F Booth, Rotherham	
37684	37134	D6834	1963	2004	2010: C F Booth, Rotherham	
37685	37234	D6934	1964		West Coast Railway Co	
37686	37172	D6872	1963	2000	2006: C F Booth, Rotherham	
37688	37205	D6905	1963		Locomotive Services	p)
37689	37195	D6895	1964	2005	2011: EMR, Attercliffe	
37692	37122	D6822	1963	2004	2009: C F Booth, Rotherham	
37693	37210	D6910	1963	2000	2011: EMR, Attercliffe	
37694	37192	D6892	1964	2007	2008: EMR, Kingsbury	
37695	37157	D6857	1963	2004	2008: Ron Hull Jr, Rotherham	
37696	37228	D6928	1964	2000	2014: C F Booth, Rotherham	
37697	37243	D6943	1964	1999	2006: C F Booth, Rotherham	
37698	37246	D6946	1964	2009	2010: C F Booth, Rotherham	
37699	37253	D6953	1965	1997	1997: Crewe Works	

p)   Preserved locomotive on hire to Locomotive Services

Class 37/7
Refurbished locomotives fitted with regeared CP7 Bogies and ballast weight added.
Details as Class 37/0 except:
Maximum Speed: 80 mph.
Train Heating/Supply: None.

Latest Number Carried	Previous Number 1	Previous Number 2	Year Entered Service	Year Withdrawn	Current Status/Scrapping Details	Notes
37701	37030	D6730	1961	1999	2008: EMR, Kingsbury	
37702	37020	D6720	1961	2007	2007: Puig Vert, Spain	ES
37703	37067	D6767	1962		Direct Rail Services	q)
37704	37034	D6734	1962	2003	2009: T J Thomson, Stockton	
37705	37060	D6760	1962	1999	2007: T J Thomson, Stockton	
37706	37016	D6716	1961		West Coast Railway Co	
37707	37001	D6701	1960	2007	2011: EMR, Kingsbury	
37708	37089	D6789	1963	2002	2008: C F Booth, Rotherham	
37709	37014	D6714	1961	2007	2011: EMR, Kingsbury	
37710	37044	D6744	1962		West Coast Railway Co	
37711	37085	D6785	1962	1999	2006: EMR, Kingsbury	
37712	37102	D6802	1963		West Coast Railway Co	
37713	37052	D6752	1962	2000	2007: Crewe Diesel Depot	
37714	37024	D6724	1961		Preserved	
37715	37021	D6721	1961	1999	2005: EMR, Kingsbury	
37716	37094	D6794	1963		Direct Rail Services	
37717	37050	D6750	1962	2004	2009: C F Booth, Rotherham	
37718	37084	D6784	1962	2012	2015: C F Booth, Rotherham	
37719	37033	D6733	1962	1999	2008: EMR, Kingsbury	
37796	37105	D6805	1963	2000	2009: C F Booth, Rotherham	
37797	37081	D6781	1962	2005	2006: C F Booth, Rotherham	
37798	37006	D6706	1961	2005	2009: C F Booth, Rotherham	
37799	37061	D6761	1962	2008	2011: Celsa Group, Barcelona	ES
37800	37143	D6843	1963		Rail Operations Group	n)
37801	37173	D6873	1963	2008	2011: Celsa Group, Barcelona	ES
37802	37163	D6863	1963	2003	2003: Calatayud, Spain	ES
37803	37208	D6908	1963	2000	2007: EMR, Kingsbury	
37883	37176	D6876	1963	2011	2011: Celsa Group, Barcelona	ES
37884	37183	D6883	1963		Rail Operations Group	n)
37885	37177	D6877	1963	2002	2003: Vias Y Construcciones, Madrid	ES
37886	37180	D6880	1963	2005	2011: EMR, Kingsbury	
37887	37120	D6820	1963	1999	2008: C F Booth, Rotherham	
37888	37135	D6835	1963	2007	2007: Puig Vert, Spain	ES
37889	37233	D6933	1964	1999	2007: Crewe Diesel Depot	
37890	37168	D6868	1963	2009	2010: Ron Hull Jr, Rotherham	
37891	37166	D6866	1963	2000	2011: EMR, Attercliffe	
37892	37149	D6849	1963	2000	2008: EMR, Kingsbury	
37893	37237	D6937	1964	2009	2012: Ron Hull Jr, Rotherham	

37894	37124	D6824	1963	2000	2008: EMR, Kingsbury	
37895	37283	D6819	1963	2005	2011: EMR, Kingsbury	
37896	37231	D6931	1964	2009	2010: Ron Hull Jr, Rotherham	
37897	37155	D6855	1963	2000	2008: EMR, Kingsbury	
37898	37186	D6886	1963	1999	2011: EMR, Kingsbury	
37899	37161	D6861	1963	2002	2003: Vias Y Construcciones, Madrid	ES

n)   Europhoenix locomotive on hire to ROG
q)   DRS locomotive on loan to Bo'ness & Kinneil Railway

Class 37/9
Locomotives fitted with regeared CP7 Bogies and ballast weight added.
Details as Class 37/0 except:
Engine: Mirrlees MB275T (37901–904); Ruston RK270T (37905/906).
Maximum Speed: 80 mph.

Latest Number Carried	Previous Number 1	Previous Number 2	Year Entered Service	Year Withdrawn	Current Status/Scrapping Details	Notes
37901	37150	D6850	1963		Europhoenix	
37902	37148	D6848	1963	1998	2005: Sims Metals, Beeston	
37903	37249	D6949	1964	1998	2005: Crewe Diesel Depot	
37904	37125	D6825	1963	1996	2004: C F Booth, Rotherham	
37905	37136	D6836	1963		UK Rail Leasing	
37906	37206	D6906	1963		UK Rail Leasing	r)

r)   On loan to preserved railway

Class 97 (Class 37)
Refurbished for Network Rail for use on Cambrian lines, fitted with ERTMS.
Details as Class 37/0.

Latest Number Carried	Previous Number 1	Previous Number 2	Year Entered Service	Year Withdrawn	Current Status/Scrapping Details	Notes
97301	37100	D6800	1962		Network Rail	
97302	37170	D6870	1963		Network Rail	
97303	37178	D6878	1963		Network Rail	
97304	37217	D6917	1964		Network Rail	

▲ On 23 September 2016, four of the surviving seven Class 40s were gathered outside Bury Baron Street depot to form this imposing view. From left to right the line-up consists of D213 "ANDANIA", 40135, 40106 and 40145. Note the variety of nose ends, which include disc, split and central headcode examples. **Liam Barnes**

CLASS 40   1Co-Co1

Built: 1958–62 by English Electric, Vulcan Foundry, Newton-le-Willows and Robert Stephenson & Hawthorns, Darlington.
Engine: English Electric 16SVT MkII of 1492 kW (2000 hp) at 850 rpm.
Transmission: Electric.
Maximum Speed: 90 mph.
Train Heating/Supply: Steam heating, later removed or isolated on many locomotives.
Train Brakes: Built vacuum, many were later dual braked (air & vacuum).

Latest Number Carried	Previous Number 1	Previous Number 2	Previous Number 3	Year Entered Service	Year Withdrawn	Current Status/Scrapping Details	Notes
40001	D201			1958	1984	1987: Swindon Works	
40002	D202			1958	1984	1985: Doncaster Works	
40003	D203			1958	1982	1984: Doncaster Works	
40004	D204			1958	1984	1986: Crewe Works	
40005	D205			1958	1976	1977: Crewe Works	
40006	D206			1958	1983	1984: Crewe Works	
40007	D207			1958	1983	1984: Doncaster Works	
40008	D208			1958	1982	1988: Crewe Works	
40009	D209			1958	1984	1985: Doncaster Works	
40010	D210			1959	1981	1983: Swindon Works	
40011	D211			1959	1980	1980: Swindon Works	
40012	97407	40012	D212	1959	1986	Preserved	
40013	D213			1959		Locomotive Services	a)
40014	D214			1959	1981	1983: Swindon Works	
40015	D215			1959	1984	1986: Swindon Works	
40016	D216			1959	1981	1983: Swindon Works	
40017	D217			1959	1981	1981: Swindon Works	
40018	D218			1959	1981	1983: Crewe Works	
40019	D219			1959	1981	1984: Doncaster Works	
40020	D220			1959	1982	1987: Crewe Works	
40021	D221			1959	1976	1977: Crewe Works	
40022	D222			1959	1984	1984: Doncaster Works	
40023	D223			1959	1981	1984: Crewe Works	
40024	D224			1959	1984	1985: Crewe Works	
40025	D225			1959	1982	1985: Doncaster Works	
40026	D226			1959	1980	1983: Swindon Works	
40027	D227			1959	1983	1984: Crewe Works	
40028	D228			1959	1984	1988: Crewe Works	
40029	D229			1959	1984	1984: Doncaster Works	
40030	D230			1959	1983	1984: Crewe Works	
40031	D231			1959	1981	1983: Crewe Works	
40032	D232			1959	1981	1983: Swindon Works	
40033	D233			1959	1984	1985: Doncaster Works	
40034	D234			1959	1984	1984: Doncaster Works	
40035	D235			1959	1984	1985: Crewe Works	
40036	D236			1959	1982	1982: Swindon Works	
40037	D237			1959	1981	1983: Swindon Works	
40038	D238			1959	1980	1982: Swindon Works	
40039	D239			1959	1976	1976: Crewe Works	
40040	D240			1959	1980	1980: Doncaster Works	
40041	D241			1959	1976	1978: Crewe Works	
40042	D242			1959	1980	1981: Derby Works	
40043	D243			1959	1976	1977: Crewe Works	
40044	D244			1959	1985	1988: Crewe Works	
40045	D245			1959	1976	1977: Derby Works	
40046	D246			1959	1983	1987: Vic Berry, Leicester	
40047	D247			1959	1984	1986: Doncaster Works	
40048	D248			1959	1977	1980: Doncaster Works	
40049	D249			1959	1983	1985: Crewe Works	
40050	D250			1959	1983	1983: Doncaster Works	
40051	D251			1959	1978	1978: Doncaster Works	

40052	D252		1959	1983	1983: Crewe Works
40053	D253		1960	1976	1976: Crewe Works
40054	D254		1959	1977	1978: Crewe Works
40055	D255		1960	1982	1983: Doncaster Works
40056	D256		1960	1984	1985: Doncaster Works
40057	D257		1960	1984	1988: Crewe Works
40058	D258		1960	1984	1987: Crewe Works
40059	D259		1960	1977	1978: Doncaster Works
97405	40060	D260	1960	1987	1988: Vic Berry, Leicester
40061	D261		1960	1983	1984: Crewe Works
40062	D262		1960	1981	1983: Swindon Works
40063	D263		1960	1984	1987: Vic Berry, Leicester
40064	D264		1960	1982	1983: Crewe Works
40065	D265		1960	1981	1985: Crewe Works
40066	D266		1960	1981	1981: Swindon Works
40067	D267		1960	1981	1982: Doncaster Works
40068	D268		1960	1983	1983: Doncaster Works
40069	D269		1960	1983	1984: Doncaster Works
40070	D270		1960	1981	1982: Doncaster Works
40071	D271		1960	1980	1981: Swindon Works
40072	D272		1960	1977	1978: Glasgow Works
40073	D273		1960	1983	1984: Crewe Works
40074	D274		1960	1984	1984: Doncaster Works
40075	D275		1960	1981	1987: Vic Berry, Leicester
40076	D276		1960	1983	1983: Doncaster Works
40077	D277		1960	1983	1984: Doncaster Works
40078	D278		1960	1981	1983: Swindon Works
40079	D279		1960	1985	1985: Doncaster Works
40080	D280		1960	1983	1984: Doncaster Works
40081	D281		1960	1983	1983: Doncaster Works
40082	D282		1960	1984	1986: Crewe Works
40083	D283		1960	1981	1985: Swindon Works
40084	D284		1960	1983	1984: Crewe Works
40085	D285		1960	1984	1985: Doncaster Works
40086	D286		1960	1985	1985: Doncaster Works
40087	D287		1960	1982	1985: Doncaster Works
40088	D288		1960	1982	1988: Crewe Works b)
40089	D289		1960	1976	1978: Crewe Works
40090	D290		1960	1983	1984: Doncaster Works
40091	D291		1960	1984	1988: Crewe Works
40092	D292		1960	1982	1986: Swindon Works
40093	D293		1960	1983	1984: Doncaster Works
40094	D294		1960	1982	1985: Doncaster Works
40095	D295		1960	1981	1983: Swindon Works
40096	D296		1960	1983	1984: Doncaster Works
40097	D297		1960	1983	1984: Doncaster Works
40098	D298		1960	1981	1983: Swindon Works
40099	D299		1960	1984	1985: Doncaster Works
40100	D300		1960	1980	1981: Swindon Works
40101	D301		1960	1982	1984: Crewe Works
40102	D302		1960	1976	1977: Crewe Works
40103	D303		1960	1982	1983: Crewe Works
40104	D304		1960	1985	1988: Crewe Works
40105	D305		1960	1980	1981: Swindon Works
40106	D306		1960	1983	Preserved
40107	D307		1960	1981	1984: Crewe Works
40108	D308		1960	1980	1980: Swindon Works
40109	D309		1960	1980	1984: Swindon Works
40110	D310		1960	1980	1983: Swindon Works
40111	D311		1960	1981	1982: Swindon Works
40112	D312		1960	1980	1985: Swindon Works
40113	D313		1960	1981	1984: Swindon Works
40114	D314		1960	1980	1982: Swindon Works
40115	D315		1961	1982	1988: Crewe Works

40116	D316			1961	1981	1981: Swindon Works	
40117	D317			1961	1981	1983: Swindon Works	
40118	97408	40118	D318	1961	1986	Preserved	
40119	D319			1961	1980	1982: Swindon Works	
40120	D320			1961	1981	1983: Swindon Works	
40121	D321			1961	1983	1983: Crewe Works	
D322				1961	1967	1967: Crewe Works	
40122	D200			1958	1988	Preserved	
40123	D323			1961	1980	1983: Crewe Works	
40124	D324			1961	1984	1984: Doncaster Works	
40125	D325			1960	1981	1983: Swindon Works	
40126	D326			1960	1984	1984: Doncaster Works	
40127	D327			1960	1982	1983: Swindon Works	
40128	D328			1961	1982	1983: Doncaster Works	
40129	D329			1961	1984	1984: Doncaster Works	
40130	D330			1961	1982	1983: Swindon Works	
40131	D331			1961	1983	1984: Crewe Works	
40132	D332			1961	1982	1987: Vic Berry, Leicester	
40133	D333			1961	1984	1984: Doncaster Works	
40134	D334			1961	1981	1983: Swindon Works	
40135	97406	40135	D335	1961	1986	Preserved	
40136	D336			1961	1982	1983: Crewe Works	
40137	D337			1961	1981	1981: Swindon Works	
40138	D338			1961	1982	1984: Crewe Works	
40139	D339			1961	1982	1988: Crewe Works	
40140	D340			1961	1982	1983: Crewe Works	
40141	D341			1961	1983	1984: Doncaster Works	
40142	D342			1961	1980	1983: Crewe Works	
40143	D343			1961	1985	1986: Crewe Works	
40144	D344			1961	1981	1983: Swindon Works	
40145	D345			1961	1983	Locomotive Services	a)
40146	D346			1961	1980	1983: Swindon Works	
40147	D347			1961	1980	1983: Swindon Works	
40148	D348			1961	1982	1985: Doncaster Works	
40149	D349			1961	1981	1986: Swindon Works	
40150	D350			1961	1985	1987: Crewe Works	
40151	D351			1961	1981	1982: Swindon Works	
40152	D352			1961	1985	1985: Doncaster Works	
40153	D353			1961	1983	1984: Crewe Works	
40154	D354			1961	1982	1985: Crewe Works	
40155	D355			1961	1985	1988: Crewe Works	
40156	D356			1961	1980	1980: Swindon Works	
40157	D357			1961	1983	1983: Doncaster Works	
40158	D358			1961	1983	1984: Doncaster Works	
40159	D359			1961	1982	1984: Swindon Works	
40160	D360			1961	1984	1987: Crewe Works	
40161	D361			1961	1980	1981: Swindon Works	
40162	D362			1961	1982	1986: Millerhill Yard	
40163	D363			1961	1982	1987: Vic Berry, Leicester	
40164	D364			1961	1983	1983: Doncaster Works	
40165	D365			1961	1981	1983: Doncaster Works	
40166	D366			1961	1982	1983: Crewe Works	
40167	D367			1961	1984	1984: Doncaster Works	
40168	D368			1961	1984	1986: Crewe Works	
40169	D369			1961	1983	1984: Doncaster Works	
40170	D370			1961	1983	1984: Doncaster Works	
40171	D371			1961	1981	1982: Swindon Works	
40172	D372			1962	1983	1984: Doncaster Works	
40173	D373			1962	1981	1985: James A White, Inverkeithing	
40174	D374			1962	1984	1984: Doncaster Works	
40175	D375			1962	1981	1983: Swindon Works	
40176	D376			1962	1981	1985: Swindon Works	
40177	D377			1962	1984	1986: Crewe Works	
40178	D378			1962	1981	1983: Swindon Works	

40179	D379	1962	1981	1982: Swindon Works
40180	D380	1962	1983	1984: Crewe Works
40181	D381	1962	1985	1986: Crewe Works
40182	D382	1962	1982	1984: Crewe Works
40183	D383	1962	1983	1986: Crewe Works
40184	D384	1962	1982	1983: Doncaster Works
40185	D385	1962	1983	1983: Doncaster Works
40186	D386	1962	1982	1983: Doncaster Works
40187	D387	1962	1982	1985: Doncaster Works
40188	D388	1962	1983	1984: Crewe Works
40189	D389	1962	1976	1976: Crewe Works
40190	D390	1962	1976	1976: Crewe Works
40191	D391	1962	1983	1984: Crewe Works
40192	D392	1962	1985	1985: Doncaster Works
40193	D393	1962	1981	1986: Swindon Works
40194	D394	1962	1985	1985: Doncaster Works
40195	D395	1962	1984	1988: Crewe Works
40196	D396	1962	1984	1985: Doncaster Works
40197	D397	1962	1983	1984: Doncaster Works
40198	D398	1962	1983	1984: Doncaster Works
40199	D399	1962	1982	1983: Doncaster Works

a)   Preserved locomotive on hire to Locomotive Services
b)   Cab remains owned by Class 40 Preservation Society

CLASS 41   A1A-A1A

This class was designated Class 41 by BR at the end of 1967, however none carried TOPS numbers.

Built: 1958–59 by North British Locomotive Company, Glasgow.
Engine: Two NBL L12V18/21A of 746 kW (1000 hp) at 1445 rpm.
Transmission: Hydraulic.
Maximum Speed: 90 mph.
Train Heating/Supply: Steam heating.
Train Brakes: Vacuum.

Latest Number Carried	Previous Number 1	Year Entered Service	Year Withdrawn	Current Status/Scrapping Details	Notes
D600		1958	1967	1970: D Woodham, Barry	
D601		1958	1967	1980: D Woodham, Barry	
D602		1958	1967	1968: J Cashmore, Newport	
D603		1958	1967	1968: J Cashmore, Newport	
D604		1959	1967	1968: J Cashmore, Newport	

CLASS 41   HST POWER CAR   Bo-Bo

Built: 1972 by BREL, Crewe.
Engine: Paxman Valenta 12RP200L of 1680 kW (2250 hp) at 1500 rpm.
Transmission: Electric.
Maximum Speed: 125 mph.
Train Heating/Supply: Electric.
Train Brakes: Air.

Latest Number Carried	Previous Number 1	Previous Number 2	Previous Number 3	Year Entered Service	Year Withdrawn	Current Status/Scrapping Details	Notes
41001	ADB975812	43000	41001	1972	1982	Preserved	
ADB975813	43001	41002		1972	1988	1990: C F Booth, Rotherham	

CLASS 42 B-B

Built: 1958–61 by British Railways, Swindon
Engine: D800–D802: Two Bristol Siddeley Maybach MD650 of 796 kW (1000 hp) at 1400 rpm.
D830: Two Paxman 12YJXL 895 kW of (1200 hp) at 1500 rpm.
D803–D829, D831–D832 & D866–D870: Two Bristol Siddeley Maybach MD650 of 821 kW (1100 hp) at 1530 rpm.
Transmission: Hydraulic.
Maximum Speed: 90 mph.
Train Heating/Supply: Steam heating.
Train Brakes: Vacuum.

Latest Number Carried	Previous Number 1	Year Entered Service	Year Withdrawn	Current Status/Scrapping Details	Notes
D800		1958	1968	1969: J Cashmore, Newport	
D801		1958	1968	1970: Swindon Works	
D802		1958	1968	1970: Swindon Works	
D803		1959	1972	1972: Swindon Works	
D804		1959	1971	1972: Swindon Works	
D805		1959	1972	1973: Swindon Works	
D806		1959	1972	1975: Swindon Works	
D807		1959	1972	1972: Swindon Works	
D808		1959	1971	1972: Swindon Works	
D809		1959	1971	1972: Swindon Works	
D810		1959	1972	1973: Swindon Works	
D811		1959	1972	1972: Swindon Works	
D812		1959	1972	1973: Swindon Works	
D813		1959	1972	1972: Swindon Works	
D814		1960	1972	1974: Swindon Works	
D815		1960	1971	1972: Swindon Works	
D816		1960	1972	1972: Swindon Works	
D817		1960	1971	1972: Swindon Works	
D818		1960	1972	1985: Swindon Works	
D819		1960	1972	1972: Swindon Works	

▲ The five prototype "Warships" were designated Class 41 under TOPS. As they were much heavier than the production locomotives and were considered non-standard, they were all withdrawn in 1967. D603 "CONQUEST" is seen at Truro on 24 July 1966. **Richard Lewis/Rail Photoprints**

D820	1960	1972	1973: Swindon Works
D821	1960	1972	Preserved
D822	1960	1971	1972: Swindon Works
D823	1960	1971	1972: Swindon Works
D824	1960	1972	1975: Swindon Works
D825	1960	1972	1972: Swindon Works
D826	1960	1971	1972: Swindon Works
D827	1960	1972	1972: Swindon Works
D828	1960	1971	1972: Swindon Works
D829	1960	1972	1974: Swindon Works
D830	1961	1969	1971: Swindon Works
D831	1961	1972	1972: Swindon Works
D832	1961	1972	Preserved
D866	1961	1972	1972: Swindon Works
D867	1961	1971	1972: Swindon Works
D868	1961	1971	1972: Swindon Works
D869	1961	1971	1972: Swindon Works
D870	1961	1971	1972: Swindon Works

CLASS 43   NORTH BRITISH TYPE 4   B-B

Built: 1960–62 by North British Locomotive Company, Glasgow.
Engine: Two MAN L12V18/21 of 820 kW (1100 hp) at 1530 rpm.
Transmission: Hydraulic.
Maximum Speed: 90 mph.
Train Heating/Supply: Steam heating.
Train Brakes: Vacuum.

Latest Number Carried	Previous Number 1	Year Entered Service	Year Withdrawn	Current Status/Scrapping Details	Notes
D833		1960	1971	1972: Swindon Works	
D834		1960	1971	1972: Swindon Works	
D835		1960	1971	1971: Swindon Works	
D836		1960	1971	1972: Swindon Works	
D837		1960	1971	1972: Swindon Works	
D838		1960	1971	1972: Swindon Works	
D839		1960	1971	1972: Swindon Works	
D840		1961	1969	1970: Swindon Works	
D841		1960	1971	1972: Swindon Works	
D842		1960	1971	1972: Swindon Works	
D843		1961	1971	1972: Swindon Works	
D844		1961	1971	1972: Swindon Works	
D845		1961	1971	1972: Swindon Works	
D846		1961	1971	1971: Swindon Works	
D847		1961	1971	1972: Swindon Works	
D848		1961	1969	1970: Swindon Works	
D849		1961	1971	1972: Swindon Works	
D850		1961	1971	1972: Swindon Works	
D851		1961	1971	1972: Swindon Works	
D852		1961	1971	1972: Swindon Works	
D853		1961	1971	1972: Swindon Works	
D854		1961	1971	1972: Swindon Works	
D855		1961	1971	1972: Swindon Works	
D856		1961	1971	1972: Swindon Works	
D857		1961	1971	1972: Swindon Works	
D858		1961	1971	1972: Swindon Works	
D859		1962	1971	1972: Swindon Works	
D860		1962	1971	1971: Swindon Works	
D861		1962	1971	1972: Swindon Works	
D862		1962	1971	1972: Swindon Works	
D863		1962	1969	1969: J Cashmore, Newport	
D864		1962	1971	1971: Swindon Works	
D865		1962	1971	1972: Swindon Works	

▲ BR diesel-hydraulic Class 42 "Warship" D806 passes St. Erth with an eastbound light engine movement on 12 September 1972. **Rail Photoprints**

▼ The 33 North British Class 43 "Warships" were similar to the earlier BR-built Class 42 variant and had slightly more powerful engines. On 10 July 1971, D853 "THRUSTER" passes Southall with an Acton to St. Erth empty milk tank working. **Dave Moulden/Rail Photoprints**

CLASS 43   HST POWER CAR   Bo-Bo

Built: 1975–82 by BREL, Crewe.
Engine as Built: Paxman Valenta 12RP200L of 1680 kW (2250 hp) at 1500 rpm.
Subsequent Engines: Mirlees MB190 of 1680 kW (2250 hp) fitted to 43167–43170 between 1987 and 1996; Paxman Valenta engines were then reinstalled.
Paxman 12VP185 of 1565 kW (2100 hp) at 1500 rpm fitted to 43043–050, 052, 054–055, 058–061, 064, 066, 072–076, 081–083, 089, 165, 167–170, 173, 175, 177, 179 & 191.
MTU 16V4000 R41R of 1680 kW (2250 hp) at 1500rpm were fitted to the remaining power cars with original Paxman Valenta engines from 2005.
Transmission: Electric.
Maximum Speed: 125 mph.
Train Heating/Supply: Electric.
Train Brakes: Air.

Latest Number Carried	Previous Number 1	Previous Number 2	Year Entered Service	Year Withdrawn	Current Status/Scrapping Details	Notes
43002			1976		Preserved	
43003			1976		Scotrail	
43004			1976		Great Western Railway	
43005			1976		Great Western Railway	
43009			1976		Great Western Railway	
43010			1976		Great Western Railway	
43011			1976	1999	2002: Crewe Works	
43012			1976		Scotrail	
43013			1976		Network Rail	
43014			1976		Network Rail	
43015			1976		Scotrail	
43016			1976		Great Western Railway	
43017			1976		Stored	
43018			1976		Preserved	
43019			1976	2004	2005: Sims Metals, Beeston	
43020			1976		Stored	
43021			1976		Scotrail	
43022			1976		Great Western Railway	
43023			1976		Stored	
43024			1976		Stored	
43025			1976		Stored	
43026			1976		Scotrail	
43027			1976		Great Western Railway	
43028			1976		Scotrail	
43029			1976		Great Western Railway	
43030			1976		Scotrail	
43031			1976		Scotrail	
43032			1976		Scotrail	
43033			1976		Scotrail	
43034			1976		Scotrail	
43035			1976		Scotrail	
43036			1976		Scotrail	
43037			1976		Scotrail	
43040			1976		Great Western Railway	
43041			1976		Great Western Railway	
43042			1977		Great Western Railway	
43043			1977		Stored	
43044			1977		Stored	
43045			1977		Colas Rail	
43046			1977		Locomotive Services	
43047			1977		Stored	
43048			1977		Preserved	
43049			1977		Stored	
43050			1977		Colas Rail	
43052			1977		Data Acquisition & Testing Services	
43053			1977		Stored	

43054			1977	Data Acquisition & Testing Services
43055			1977	Locomotive Services
43056			1977	Stored
43058			1977	Locomotive Services
43059			1977	Locomotive Services
43060			1977	Colas Rail
43061			1977	Stored
43062			1977	Network Rail
43063			1977	Stored
43064			1977	Stored
43066			1977	Data Acquisition & Testing Services
43069			1977	Stored
43070			1977	Stored
43071			1977	Stored
43073			1977	Stored
43075			1977	Stored
43076			1977	Data Acquisition & Testing Services
43078			1978	Stored
43079			1978	Stored
43081			1978	Stored
43082			1978	Stored
43083			1978	Locomotive Services
43086			1978	Stored
43087			1978	Stored
43088			1978	Great Western Railway
43089			1978	Preserved
43091			1978	Stored
43092			1978	Great Western Railway
43093			1978	Great Western Railway
43094			1978	Great Western Railway
43097			1978	Great Western Railway
43098			1978	Great Western Railway
43102	43302	43102	1978	East Midlands Railway
43122			1979	Great Western Railway
43124			1981	Scotrail
43125			1979	Scotrail
43126			1979	Scotrail
43127			1979	Scotrail
43128			1979	Scotrail
43129			1979	Scotrail
43130			1979	Scotrail
43131			1979	Scotrail
43132			1979	Scotrail
43133			1979	Scotrail
43134			1979	Scotrail
43135			1979	Scotrail
43136			1979	Scotrail
43137			1979	Scotrail
43138			1979	Scotrail
43139			1980	Scotrail
43140			1980	Scotrail
43141			1980	Scotrail
43142			1980	Scotrail
43143			1981	Scotrail
43144			1981	Scotrail
43145			1981	Scotrail
43146			1981	Scotrail
43147			1981	Scotrail
43148			1981	Scotrail
43149			1981	Scotrail
43150			1981	Scotrail
43151			1981	Scotrail
43152			1981	Scotrail
43153			1981	Great Western Railway

43154		1981		Great Western Railway
43155		1981		Great Western Railway
43156		1981		Great Western Railway
43158		1981		Great Western Railway
43159		1981		Stored
43160		1981		Great Western Railway
43161		1981		Stored
43162		1981		Great Western Railway
43163		1981		Scotrail
43164		1981		Scotrail
43165		1981		Stored
43168		1981		Scotrail
43169		1981		Scotrail
43170		1981		Great Western Railway
43171		1981		Great Western Railway
43172		1981		Great Western Railway
43173		1981	1998	2003: MoD, Shoeburyness
43174		1981		Stored
43175		1981		Scotrail
43176		1981		Scotrail
43177		1981		Scotrail
43179		1981		Scotrail
43180		1981		Stored
43181		1981		Scotrail
43182		1981		Scotrail
43183		1982		Scotrail
43185		1982		Stored
43186		1982		Great Western Railway
43187		1982		Great Western Railway
43188		1982		Great Western Railway
43189		1982		Great Western Railway
43190		1982		Stored
43191		1982		Stored
43192		1982		Great Western Railway
43193		1982		Stored
43194		1982		Great Western Railway
43195		1982		Stored
43196		1982		Stored
43197		1982		Stored
43198		1982		Great Western Railway
43206	43006	1976		Stored
43207	43007	1976		Cross Country
43208	43008	1976		Cross Country
43238	43038	1976		East Midlands Railway
43239	43039	1976		Cross Country
43251	43051	1977		East Midlands Railway
43257	43057	1977		East Midlands Railway
43272	43072	1977		East Midlands Railway
43274	43074	1977		East Midlands Railway
43277	43077	1977		Stored
43285	43085	1978		Cross Country
43290	43090	1978		Stored
43295	43095	1978		East Midlands Railway
43296	43096	1978		Stored
43299	43099	1978		Stored
43300	43100	1978		Stored
43301	43101	1978		Cross Country
43303	43103	1978		Cross Country
43304	43104	1978		Cross Country
43305	43105	1978		East Midlands Railway
43306	43106	1978		East Midlands Railway
43307	43107	1978		Stored
43308	43108	1978		Stored
43309	43109	1979		East Midlands Railway

43310	43110	1979	East Midlands Railway
43311	43111	1979	Stored
43312	43112	1979	Stored
43313	43113	1979	Stored
43314	43114	1979	Stored
43315	43115	1979	Stored
43316	43116	1979	East Midlands Railway
43317	43117	1979	Stored
43318	43118	1979	Stored
43319	43119	1979	East Midlands Railway
43320	43120	1977	East Midlands Railway
43321	43121	1977	Cross Country
43357	43157	1981	Cross Country
43366	43166	1981	Cross Country
43367	43167	1981	Stored
43378	43178	1981	Cross Country
43384	43184	1982	Cross Country
43423	43123	1979	Stored
43465	43065	1977	Stored
43467	43067	1977	Stored
43468	43068	1977	Stored
43480	43080	1978	Stored
43484	43084	1978	Stored

▲ 43317 and 43309 (rear) are two of several HST power cars which only had minor cosmetic changes when they were transferred from LNER to EMR recently. They race through Cossington, Leicestershire with the 05.19 Leeds–London St. Pancras on 31 July 2020. **Brad Joyce**

CLASS 44 1Co-Co1

Built: 1959–60 by British Railways, Derby.
Engine: Sulzer 12LDA28A of 1720 kW (2300 hp) at 750 rpm.
Transmission: Electric.
Maximum Speed: 90 mph.
Train Heating/Supply: Built with steam heating, subsequently removed.
Train Brakes: Vacuum.

Latest Number Carried	Previous Number 1	Year Entered Service	Year Withdrawn	Current Status/Scrapping Details	Notes
44001	D1	1959	1976	1977: Derby Works	
44002	D2	1959	1979	1978: Derby Works	
44003	D3	1959	1976	1976: Derby Works	
44004	D4	1959	1980	Preserved	
44005	D5	1959	1978	1978: Derby Works	
44006	D6	1959	1977	1977: Derby Works	
44007	D7	1959	1980	1981: Derby Works	
44008	D8	1959	1980	Preserved	
44009	D9	1959	1979	1980: Derby Works	
44010	D10	1960	1977	1978: Derby Works	

CLASS 45 1Co-Co1

Built: 1960–63 by British Railways, Crewe and Derby.
Engine: Sulzer 12LDA28B of 1860 kW (2500 hp) at 750 rpm.
Transmission: Electric.
Maximum Speed: 90 mph.
Train Heating/Supply: Built with steam heating, subsequently isolated on many.
Train Brakes: Built vacuum braked and later converted to dual braked (air & vacuum).

C1   One cab remains

Class 45/0

Latest Number Carried	Previous Number 1	Previous Number 2	Year Entered Service	Year Withdrawn	Current Status/Scrapping Details	Notes
45001	D13		1960	1986	1988: MC Metals, Glasgow	
45002	D29		1961	1984	1988: MC Metals, Glasgow	
45003	D133		1961	1985	1987: Vic Berry, Leicester	
45004	D77		1960	1985	1988: MC Metals, Glasgow	
45005	D79		1960	1986	1988: Vic Berry, Leicester	
45006	D89		1961	1986	1988: Vic Berry, Leicester	
45007	D119		1961	1988	1992: MC Metals, Glasgow	
45008	D90		1961	1980	1983: Swindon Works	
45009	D37		1961	1986	1988: Vic Berry, Leicester	
45010	D112		1961	1985	1989: MC Metals, Glasgow	
45011	D12		1960	1981	1981: Derby Works	
45012	D108		1961	1988	1992: MC Metals, Glasgow	
45013	D20		1961	1987	1994: MC Metals, Glasgow	
45014	D137		1961	1986	1986: Ashton Road Yard, Manchester	
45015	D14		1960	1986	Preserved	
45016	D16		1960	1985	1986: Vic Berry, Leicester	
ADB968024	45017	D23	1961	1988	1993: MC Metals, Glasgow	
45018	D15		1960	1981	1982: Swindon Works	
45019	D33		1961	1985	1986: Vic Berry, Leicester	
45020	D26		1961	1985	1988: Vic Berry, Leicester	
45021	D25		1961	1980	1983: Swindon Works	
97409	45022	D60	1962	1988	1991: MC Metals, Glasgow	
45023	D54		1962	1984	1986: Vic Berry, Leicester	
45024	D17		1960	1980	1983: Swindon Works	
45025	D19		1960	1981	1981: Derby Works	
45026	D21		1961	1986	1989: MC Metals, Glasgow	
45027	D24		1961	1981	1983: Swindon Works	

▲ 44010 began its life in early 1960 with the 1957 Series number D10 and received its TOPS identity in 1974. Two years later, it was hauling a heavy coal train near Stapleford and Sandiacre on 21 June 1976. **Stephen C Marshall**

▼ In glorious conditions on 18 June 1983, 45131 accelerates through a fine display of semaphore signals at Dawlish Warren with the 17.25 Paignton–York. **Stephen Dance**

45028	D27		1961	1981	1983: Swindon Works	
97410	45029	D30	1961	1988	1991: MC Metals, Glasgow	
45030	D31		1961	1980	1981: Derby Works	
45031	D36		1961	1981	1981: Derby Works	
45032	D38		1961	1980	1983: Swindon Works	
45033	D39		1961	1988	1992: MC Metals, Glasgow	
97411	45034	D42	1961	1988	1992: MC Metals, Glasgow	
45035	D44		1961	1981	1981: Derby Works	
45036	D45		1961	1986	1988: Vic Berry, Leicester	
45037	D46		1961	1988	1992: MC Metals, Glasgow	
45038	D48		1961	1985	1986: Vic Berry, Leicester	
45039	D49		1961	1980	1983: Swindon Works	
97412	45040	D50	1962	1988	1991: MC Metals, Glasgow	
45041	D53		1962	1988	Preserved	
45042	D57		1963	1985	1986: Vic Berry, Leicester	
45043	D58		1962	1984	1987: Vic Berry, Leicester	
45044	D63		1962	1987	1988: MC Metals, Glasgow	
45045	D64		1962	1983	1986: Vic Berry, Leicester	
45046	D68		1960	1988	1992: MC Metals, Glasgow	
45047	D69		1960	1980	1981: Derby Works	
45048	D70		1960	1985	1989: MC Metals, Glasgow	
45049	D71		1960	1987	1989: MC Metals, Glasgow	
45050	D72		1960	1984	1987: Vic Berry, Leicester	
45051	D74		1960	1987	1988: MC Metals, Glasgow	
45052	D75		1960	1988	1991: MC Metals, Glasgow	
45053	D76		1960	1983	1988: Crewe Works	
45054[2]	D95		1960	1985	1985: Toton Depot	a)
45055	D84		1960	1985	1986: Vic Berry, Leicester	
45056	D91		1961	1985	1986: Vic Berry, Leicester	
45057	D93		1961	1985	1987: Vic Berry, Leicester	
45058	D97		1961	1987	1994: MC Metals, Glasgow	
45059	D98		1961	1986	1988: Vic Berry, Leicester	
45060	D100		1961	1985	Preserved	
45061	D101		1961	1981	1982: Swindon Works	
45062	D103		1961	1987	1994: MC Metals, Glasgow	
45063	D104		1961	1986	1988: Vic Berry, Leicester	
45064	D105		1961	1985	1988: Vic Berry, Leicester	
45065	D110		1961	1985	1988: Vic Berry, Leicester	
97413	45066	D114	1961	1988	1992: MC Metals, Glasgow	
45067	D115		1961	1977	1980: Derby Works	
45068	D118		1961	1986	1986: Allerton Depot	
45069	D121		1961	1986	1988: Vic Berry, Leicester	
45070	D122		1961	1987	1989: MC Metals, Glasgow	
45071	D125		1961	1981	1983: Swindon Works	
45072	D127		1961	1985	1986: Vic Berry, Leicester	
45073	D129		1961	1981	1982: Derby Works	
45074	D131		1961	1985	1988: Vic Berry, Leicester	
45075	D132		1961	1985	1987: Vic Berry, Leicester	
45076	D134		1961	1986	1994: MC Metals, Glasgow	
45077	D136		1961	1986	1988: Vic Berry, Leicester	

a)   Second of 2 locomotives to be numbered 45054

Class 45/1
Details as Class 45/0 except:
Train Heating/Supply: Electric.

Latest Number Carried	Previous Number 1	Previous Number 2	Year Entered Service	Year Withdrawn	Current Status/Scrapping Details	Notes
45101	D96		1961	1986	1988: Vic Berry, Leicester	
45102	D51		1962	1986	1988: Vic Berry, Leicester	
45103	D116		1961	1988	1990: MC Metals, Glasgow	
45104	D59		1962	1988	1992: MC Metals, Glasgow	
45105	D86		1961	1987	Preserved	
45106	D106		1961	1989	1992: C F Booth, Rotherham	

45107	D43	1961	1988	1990: MC Metals, Glasgow
45108	D120	1961	1987	Preserved
45109	D85	1961	1986	1986: Vic Berry, Leicester
45110	D73	1960	1988	1990: MC Metals, Glasgow
45111	D65	1962	1987	1992: MC Metals, Glasgow
45112	D61	1962	1987	Preserved
45113	D80	1960	1988	1990: MC Metals, Glasgow
45114	D94	1961	1987	1994: MC Metals, Glasgow
45115	D81	1960	1988	1990: MC Metals, Glasgow
45116	D47	1961	1986	1988: Vic Berry, Leicester
45117	D35	1961	1986	1987: Vic Berry, Leicester
45118	D67	1962		Locomotive Services
45119	D34	1961	1987	1994: MC Metals, Glasgow
45120	D107	1961	1987	1993: MC Metals, Glasgow
45121	D18	1960	1987	1993: Derby Litchurch Lane Works
45122	D11	1960	1987	1994: MC Metals, Glasgow
45123	D52	1962	1986	1988: Vic Berry, Leicester
45124	D28	1961	1988	1992: MC Metals, Glasgow
45125	D123	1961	1987	Preserved
45126	D32	1961	1987	1992: MC Metals, Glasgow
45127	D87	1961	1987	1994: Crewe Gresty Lane Depot
45128	D113	1961	1989	1992: MC Metals, Glasgow
45129	D111	1961	1987	1988: Vic Berry, Leicester
45130	D117	1961	1987	1992: MC Metals, Glasgow
45131	D124	1961	1986	1988: Vic Berry, Leicester
45132	D22	1961	1987	Preserved
45133	D40	1961	1987	Preserved

C1

▲ On 28 November 1978, 46019 was in charge of the 07.38 Leeds–Penzance. The train, which consisted of a parcel van, eight pressure ventilated Mark 2s and a Mark 1 buffet, is seen near Totnes. **Stephen C Marshall**

45134	D126	1961	1987	1994: MC Metals, Glasgow	
45135	D99	1961	1987	Preserved	
45136	D88	1961	1987	1992: MC Metals, Glasgow	
45137	D56	1962	1987	1994: MC Metals, Glasgow	
45138	D92	1961	1986	1994: MC Metals, Glasgow	
45139	D109	1961	1987	1994: MC Metals, Glasgow	
45140	D102	1961	1988	1994: MC Metals, Glasgow	C1
45141	D82	1960	1988	1992: MC Metals, Glasgow	
45142	D83	1960	1987	1994: MC Metals, Glasgow	
45143	D62	1962	1987	1994: MC Metals, Glasgow	
45144	D55	1962	1987	1988: Vic Berry, Leicester	
45145	D128	1961	1988	1992: MC Metals, Glasgow	
45146	D66	1962	1987	1992: MC Metals, Glasgow	
45147	D41	1961	1985	1985: Lineside at Patricroft	
45148	D130	1961	1987	1992: MC Metals, Glasgow	
45149	D135	1961	1987	Preserved	
45150	45054[1]	D78	1960	1988	1991: MC Metals, Glasgow	b)

b)   First of 2 locomotives to be numbered 45054

CLASS 46   1Co-Co1

Built: 1961–63 by British Railways, Derby.
Engine: Sulzer 12LDA28B of 1860 kW (2500 hp) at 750 rpm.
Transmission: Electric.
Maximum Speed: 90 mph.
Train Heating/Supply: Steam Heating.
Train Brakes: Built vacuum braked and later converted to dual braked (air & vacuum).

Latest Number Carried	Previous Number 1	Previous Number 2	Previous Number 3	Year Entered Service	Year Withdrawn	Current Status/Scrapping Details	Notes
46001	D138			1961	1981	1982: Swindon Works	
46002	D139			1961	1981	1984: Swindon Works	
46003	D140			1961	1978	1980: Derby Works	
46004	D141			1961	1983	1985: Swindon Works	
46005	D142			1961	1977	1978: Derby Works	
46006	D143			1961	1982	1985: Swindon Works	
46007	D144			1961	1982	1985: Swindon Works	
46008	D145			1961	1981	1982: Swindon Works	
46009	D146			1961	1983	1984: Old Dalby Test Site	
46010	D147			1961	1984	Preserved	
46011	D148			1961	1984	1986: Swindon Works	
46012	D149			1961	1980	1980: Swindon Works	
46013	D150			1961	1980	1985: Swindon Works	
46014	D151			1962	1984	1986: Swindon Works	
46015	D152			1962	1980	1985: Swindon Works	
46016	D153			1962	1983	1984: Swindon Works	
46017	D154			1962	1984	1986: Swindon Works	
46018	D155			1962	1983	1985: Swindon Works	
46019	D156			1962	1980	1983: Swindon Works	
46020	D157			1962	1980	1984: Swindon Works	
46021	D158			1962	1983	1985: Swindon Works	
46022	D159			1962	1982	1983: Swindon Works	
46023	D160			1962	1983	1994: Crewe Basford Hall Yard	
46024	D161			1962	1978	1978: Derby Works	
46025	D162			1962	1984	1985: Doncaster Works	
46026	D163			1962	1984	1985: Doncaster Works	
46027	D164			1962	1984	1986: Vic Berry, Leicester	
46028	D165			1962	1984	1986: Doncaster Works	
46029	D166			1962	1983	1986: Swindon Works	
46030	D167			1962	1980	1982: Swindon Works	
46031	D168			1962	1983	1983: Swindon Works	
46032	D169			1962	1984	1985: Doncaster Works	

46033	D170			1962	1983	1984: Swindon Works
46034	D171			1962	1980	1982: Swindon Works
D172	97403	46035	D172	1962	1991	Preserved
46036	D173			1962	1982	1983: Swindon Works
46037	D174			1962	1984	1985: Doncaster Works
46038	D175			1962	1982	1985: Swindon Works
46039	D176			1962	1983	1985: Swindon Works
46040	D177			1962	1980	1982: Derby Works
46041	D178			1962	1980	1983: Swindon Works
46042	D179			1962	1980	1982: Swindon Works
46043	D180			1962	1980	1984: Swindon Works
46044	D181			1962	1984	1986: Swindon Works
D182	97404	46045	D182	1962	1990	Preserved
46046	D183			1962	1984	1985: Doncaster Works
46047	D184			1962	1984	1986: Swindon Works
46048	D185			1962	1981	1983: Swindon Works
46049	D186			1962	1982	1985: Swindon Works
46050	D187			1962	1982	1985: Swindon Works
46051	D188			1962	1983	1984: Swindon Works
46052	D189			1963	1984	1986: Doncaster Works
46053	D190			1963	1981	1981: Derby Works
46054	D191			1963	1982	1983: Swindon Works
46055	D192			1963	1982	1984: Swindon Works
46056	D193			1963	1982	1985: Swindon Works

CLASS 47 — Co-Co

Built: 1962–68 by British Railways, Crewe and Brush Electrical Engineering Company, Loughborough.
Engine: Sulzer 12LDA28C of 1920 kW (2580 hp) at 750 rpm. D1702–D1706 were initially fitted with Sulzer 12LVA24 engines and classified as Class 48. They were subsequently fitted with standard 12LDA28C engines between 1969 and 1971 and converted to Class 47.
Transmission: Electric.
Maximum Speed: 95 mph.
Train Heating/Supply: Built with steam heating, except Class 47/3 (built D1782–D1836 & D1875–D1900) which had no heating and 47401–47420 (built D1500–D1519) 47803 (D1960) and 47515 (D1961) which were built with dual heating (electric & steam).
Train Brakes: Built vacuum braked, except D1100–D1111, D1631–D1681 and D1758–D1999 which were built dual braked (air & vacuum). Remaining locos were later converted to dual braked, except early withdrawals D1562 & D1734.

48	1 of 5 experimental Class 48s, converted back to Class 47 before TOPS renumbering
C1	One cab remains
C2	Two cabs remain

Class 47/0
Standard design built with steam heating generators, subsequently isolated or removed on most.

Latest Number Carried	Previous Number 1	Previous Number 2	Previous Number 3	Year Entered Service	Year Withdrawn	Current Status/Scrapping Details	Notes
47001	D1521			1963	1986	1994: C F Booth, Rotherham	
47002	D1522			1963	1991	1994: C F Booth, Rotherham	
47003	D1523			1963	1991	1992: C F Booth, Rotherham	
47004	D1524			1963	1998	Preserved	
47005	D1526			1963	1991	1994: C F Booth, Rotherham	
47006	D1528			1963	1991	1993: C F Booth, Rotherham	
47007	D1529			1963	1991	1994: C F Booth, Rotherham	
47008	D1530			1963	1989	1994: Stratford Depot	
47009	D1532			1963	1991	1992: C F Booth, Rotherham	
47010	D1537			1963	1992	1993: C F Booth, Rotherham	
47011	D1538			1963	1987	1994: C F Booth, Rotherham	
47012	D1539			1963	1989	1992: C F Booth, Rotherham	
47013	D1540			1963	1987	1988: Doncaster Works	
47014	D1543			1963	1991	1992: C F Booth, Rotherham	

47015	D1544			1963	1987	1994: C F Booth, Rotherham	
47016	D1546			1963	1998	2000: EWS Railway, Wigan	
47017	D1570			1964	1991	1992: C F Booth, Rotherham	
47018	D1572			1964	1991	1994: Coopers Metals, Attercliffe	
47019	D1573			1964	1997	1997: Eastleigh Works	
47033	D1613			1964	1999	2008: T J Thomson, Stockton	
47049	D1631			1964	1998	2000: EWS Railway, Wigan	
47050	D1632			1964	1994	1996: Tinsley Depot	
47051	D1633			1964	1998	2000: EWS Railway, Wigan	
47052	D1634			1964	2000	2003: Crewe Basford Hall Yard	
47053	D1635			1964	1998	2007: EMR, Kingsbury	
47054	D1638			1964	1992	1993: C F Booth, Rotherham	
47060	D1644			1965	1999	Converted to 57008 in 1999	
47063	D1647			1965	1995	1996: Crewe Works	
47079	D1664			1965	2000	Converted to 57009 in 2000	
47085	D1670			1965	1998	2000: EWS Railway, Wigan	
D1671				1965	1966	1966: R S Hayes, Bridgend	
47089	D1675			1965	1987	1989: Coopers Metals, Attercliffe	
47093	D1679			1965	1988	1990: MC Metals, Glasgow	
47094	D1680			1965	1992	1994: MC Metals, Glasgow	
47095	D1681			1965	1998	2004: Carnforth Depot	
47096	D1682			1963	1995	2000: C F Booth, Rotherham	
47097	D1684			1963	1990	1992: C F Booth, Rotherham	
47098	D1685			1963	1991	1993: Eastleigh Yard	
47099	D1686			1963	1991	1994: C F Booth, Rotherham	
47100	D1687			1963	1991	1994: C F Booth, Rotherham	C1
47101	D1688			1963	1989	1994: C F Booth, Rotherham	
47102	D1690			1963	1995	1998: C F Booth, Rotherham	
47103	D1691			1963	1987	1989: Vic Berry, Leicester	
47104	D1692			1963	1988	1990: MC Metals, Glasgow	
47105	D1693			1963	1993	Preserved	
47106	D1694			1963	1988	1989: Vic Berry, Leicester	
47107	D1695			1963	1991	1994: Coopers Metals, Attercliffe	
47108	D1696			1963	1994	1997: Old Oak Common Depot	
47109	D1697			1963	1987	1989: MC Metals, Glasgow	
47110	D1698			1964	1989	1993: Thornaby Depot	
47111	D1699			1963	1986	1987: Cardiff Canton Depot	
47112	D1700			1964	1991	1997: Old Oak Common Depot	
47113	D1701			1964	1988	1990: Vic Berry, Leicester	
47114	D1702			1965	2001	2005: C F Booth, Rotherham	48
47115	D1703			1965	1991	1995: Froddingham Depot	48
47116	D1704			1966	1990	1994: C F Booth, Rotherham	48
47117	D1705			1965	1991	Preserved	48
47118	D1706			1965	1991	1995: Doncaster Depot	48
47119	D1708			1964	1992	1995: Froddingham Depot	
47120	D1709			1964	1991	1994: C F Booth, Rotherham	
47121	D1710			1964	1996	1997: Old Oak Common Depot	
47122	D1711			1964	1987	1989: MC Metals, Glasgow	
47123	D1712			1964	1991	1994: Coopers Metals, Attercliffe	
47124	D1714			1964	1989	1990: MC Metals, Glasgow	
47125	D1715			1964	1997	2002: EMR, Kingsbury	
47130	D1721			1964	1988	1990: MC Metals, Glasgow	
47131	D1722			1964	1987	1988: Vic Berry, Leicester	
47137	D1729			1964	1987	1991: MC Metals, Glasgow	
47140	D1732			1964	1988	1989: Vic Berry, Leicester	
D1734				1964	1965	1965: Crewe Works	
47142	D1735			1964	1998	1999: Vic Berry, Leicester	
47143	D1736			1964	1989	1994: Doncaster Depot	
47144	D1737			1964	1998	1998: C F Booth, Rotherham	
47145	D1738			1964	2007	2009: T J Thomson, Stockton	
47146	D1739			1964	1998	2006: C F Booth, Rotherham	
47147	D1740			1964	1998	1999: Vic Berry, Leicester	
47148	D1741			1964	1987	1989: MC Metals, Glasgow	
47150	47399	47150	D1743	1964	2007	2010: T J Thomson, Stockton	

47152	47398	47152	D1745	1964	2001	2003: Southampton Maritime Depot	
47156	D1749			1964	1996	2005: C F Booth, Rotherham	
47157	D1750			1964	2001	2004: C F Booth, Rotherham	
47159	D1752			1964	1988	1993: Thornaby Depot	
47162	D1756			1964	1987	1987: Crewe Works	
47186	D1781			1964	1998	2007: EMR, Kingsbury	
47187	D1837			1965	1999	Converted to 57006 in 1999	
47188	D1838			1965	1998	2005: Crewe Diesel Depot	
47189	D1839			1965	1989	1992: MC Metals, Glasgow	
47190	D1840			1965	1994	1998: C F Booth, Rotherham	
47191	D1841			1965	1987	1993: Wigan Springs Branch Depot	
47192	D1842			1965	1988	Preserved	
47193	D1843			1965	2000	2004: C F Booth, Rotherham	
47194	D1844			1965		West Coast Railway Co	
47195	D1845			1965	1991	1994: Coopers Metals, Attercliffe	
47196	D1846			1965	1994	1994: Coopers Metals, Attercliffe	
47197	D1847			1965	2005	2008: T J Thomson, Stockton	
47198	D1848			1965	1989	1994: Cardiff Canton Depot	
47199	D1849			1965	1987	1993: MC Metals, Glasgow	
47200	D1850			1965	2006	2008: T J Thomson, Stockton	
47201	D1851			1965	1998	2007: EMR, Kingsbury	
47202	D1852			1965	1987	1991: Bristol Bath Road Depot	
47203	D1853			1965	1989	1990: Vic Berry, Leicester	
47204	47388	47204	D1854	1965	2000	Converted to 57012 in 2000	
47205	47395	47205	D1855	1965	2001	Preserved	
47206	D1856			1965	2004	Converted to 57605 in 2004	
47207	D1857			1965	2001	2005: C F Booth, Rotherham	
47208	D1858			1965	1980	1980: Dundee Depot	
47209	47393	47209	D1859	1965	2004	Converted to 57604 in 2004	
47210	D1860			1965	1998	2000: EWS Railway, Wigan	
47211	47394	47211	D1861	1965	1998	2003: Eastleigh Depot	
47212	D1862			1965	2003	2004: Crewe LNWR Depot	
47213	D1863			1965	1999	2005: Crewe Diesel Depot	
47214	D1864			1965	1994	1998: C F Booth, Rotherham	
47215	D1865			1965	1991	1993: Eastleigh Yard	
47217	D1867			1965	1999	2005: C F Booth, Rotherham	
47218	D1868			1965	1999	2002: EMR, Kingsbury	
47219	D1869			1965	1999	2007: EMR, Kingsbury	
47220	D1870			1965	1993	1994: Coopers Metals, Attercliffe	
47221	D1871			1965	1996	2002: EMR, Kingsbury	
47222	D1872			1965	1998	1998: C F Booth, Rotherham	
47223	D1873			1965	1995	2005: C F Booth, Rotherham	
47224	D1874			1965	2003	2007: Crewe LNWR Depot	
47225	D1901			1965	2003	Converted to 57307 in 2003	
47226	47384	47226	D1902	1965	1999	2008: EMR, Kingsbury	
47227	D1903			1965	1993	1994: Coopers Metals, Attercliffe	
47228	D1904			1965	1999	2007: EMR, Kingsbury	
47229	D1905			1965	1998	2007: T J Thomson, Stockton	
47230	D1906			1965	1987	1989: C F Booth, Rotherham	
47231	D1907			1965	2000	Converted to 57010 in 2000	
D1908				1965	1969	1969: Crewe Works	
47233	D1910			1965	1991	1995: Froddingham Depot	
47234	D1911			1965	2004	Converted to 57315 in 2004	
47235	D1912			1965	1988	1990: Vic Berry, Leicester	
47236	D1913			1965	1999	2017: West Coast Railways, Carnforth	C2
47237	D1914			1965		West Coast Railway Co	
47238	D1915			1965	1995	2001: EMR, Kingsbury	
47241	D1918			1965	1999	2006: C F Booth, Rotherham	
47245	D1922			1966		West Coast Railway Co	
47249	D1926			1966	1996	1998: C F Booth, Rotherham	
47256	D1934			1966	1995	2002: Doncaster Carr Depot	
47258	D1938			1966	2001	2005: C F Booth, Rotherham	
47270	D1971			1965		West Coast Railway Co	
47275	D1977			1965	1986	1989: C F Booth, Rotherham	

47276	D1978		1965	1999	2001: EWS Railway, Wigan
47277	D1979		1965	1994	2000: Immingham Depot
47278	D1980		1965	1999	1999: EWS Railway, Wigan
47279	D1981		1965	2003	2007: T J Thomson, Stockton
47280	D1982		1965	2002	2007: EMR, Kingsbury
47281	D1983		1965	1998	2000: EWS Railway, Wigan
47282	D1984		1966	1986	1989: C F Booth, Rotherham
47283	D1985		1966	1999	2004: EMR, Kingsbury
47284	D1986		1966	1999	1999: EWS Railway, Wigan
47285	D1987		1966	1999	2005: Ron Hull Jr, Rotherham
47286	D1988		1966	1999	2000: EWS Railway, Wigan
47287	D1989		1966	2002	2005: C F Booth, Rotherham
47288	D1990		1966	1995	1996: Tinsley Depot
47289	D1991		1966	2003	2010: T J Thomson, Stockton
47290	D1992		1966	2004	Converted to 57316 in 2004
47291	D1993		1966	1998	2004: C F Booth, Rotherham
47292	D1994		1966	2003	Preserved
47293	D1995		1966	1999	2007: EMR, Kingsbury
47294	D1996		1966	1996	2002: Toton Training Compound
47295	D1997		1966	2002	2011: EMR, Kingsbury
47296	D1998		1966	2001	2003: Southampton Maritime Depot
47297	D1999		1966	1999	2002: EMR, Kingsbury
47298	D1100		1966	2006	2007: C F Booth, Rotherham
47299	47216	D1866	1965	1999	2000: EWS Railway, Wigan

Class 47/3

Locos built without train heating were designated Class 47/2 under 1968 classification, then later Class 47/3 under TOPS Classification.

Latest Number Carried	Previous Number 1	Previous Number 2	Previous Number 3	Year Entered Service	Year Withdrawn	Current Status/Scrapping Details	Notes
47300	47468	D1594		1964	1995	2002: EMR, Kingsbury	
47301	D1782			1964	2001	2003: Crewe Basford Hall Yard	
47302	D1783			1964	2001	2007: T J Thomson, Stockton	
47303	47397	47303	D1784	1964	2005	2007: T J Thomson, Stockton	
47304	47392	47304	D1785	1964	1999	2000: EWS Railway, Wigan	
47305	D1786			1964	1999	2003: Crewe Basford Hall Yard	
47306	D1787			1964	2000	Preserved	
47307	D1788			1964	1999	2008: EMR, Kingsbury	
47308	D1789			1964	1999	2004: Sims Metals, Beeston	
47309	47389	47309	D1790	1964	2006	2009: T J Thomson, Stockton	
47310	D1791			1964	1999	2004: C F Booth, Rotherham	
47311	D1792			1965	1991	1993: C F Booth, Rotherham	
47312	D1793			1964	1999	2003: EWS Railway, Wigan	
47313	D1794			1964	1999	2007: EMR, Kingsbury	
47314	47387	47314	D1795	1965	1999	2008: EMR, Kingsbury	
47315	D1796			1965	1999	2000: EWS Railway, Wigan	
47316	D1797			1965	2006	2008: T J Thomson, Stockton	
47317	D1798			1965	1998	Converted to 57003 in 1998	
47318	D1799			1965	1993	2004: T J Thomson, Stockton	
47319	D1800			1965	1995	2000: Immingham Depot	
47320	D1801			1965	1993	1996: Crewe Works	
47321	D1802			1965	1995	1998: C F Booth, Rotherham	
47322	D1803			1965	1998	Converted to 57002 in 1998	
47323	D1804			1965	2000	2003: Crewe Basford Hall Yard	
47324	D1805			1965	1992	1994: C F Booth, Rotherham	
47325	D1806			1965	1996	1998: C F Booth, Rotherham	
47326	D1807			1965	1999	2006: T J Thomson, Stockton	
47327	D1808			1965	1993	1993: C F Booth, Rotherham	
47328	47396	47328	D1809	1965	1997	2005: C F Booth, Rotherham	
47329	D1810			1965	2000	Converted to 57011 in 2000	
47330	47390	47330	D1811	1965	2003	Converted to 57312 in 2003	
47331	D1812			1965	1999	2005: EMR, Kingsbury	
47332	D1813			1965	1999	Converted to 57007 in 1999	

▲ The highly unusual spectacle of a locomotive-hauled service train on the Windermere branch took place on several occasions during the summer of 2019. On 30 June 2019, 47245 has arrived at Windermere with the 17.50 from Oxenholme. **Andy Chard**

▼ 47810 is part of the varied traction fleet of Crewe-based charter operator Locomotive Services. It currently carries the number D1924 and the two-tone green livery with which it entered service in 1966. On 28 September 2019, while paired with 47614, it passes Waitby Common with the 08.08 Holyhead–Appleby "Settle to Carlisle & Coastal Statesman". **Gordon Edgar**

148

47333	D1814			1965	1995	1998: C F Booth, Rotherham	
47334	D1815			1965	2001	2005: C F Booth, Rotherham	
47335	D1816			1965	1999	2007: EMR, Kingsbury	
47336	D1817			1965	1993	1993: C F Booth, Rotherham	
47337	D1818			1965	2003	Converted to 57602 in 2003	
47338	D1819			1965	1999	2007: C F Booth, Rotherham	
47339	D1820			1965	2000	2005: C F Booth, Rotherham	
47340	D1821			1965	1998	1998: Crewe Works	
47341	D1822			1965	1996	2003: Toton Training Compound	
47342	D1823			1965	1988	1992: MC Metals, Glasgow	
47343	D1824			1965	1992	1992: MC Metals, Glasgow	
47344	D1825			1965	1999	2002: EMR, Kingsbury	
47345	D1826			1965	2001	2007: Ron Hull Jr, Rotherham	
47346	D1827			1965	1998	1998: C F Booth, Rotherham	
47347	D1828			1965	1999	Converted to 57004 in 1999	
47348	D1829			1965	2000	2007: Ron Hull Jr, Rotherham	
47349	D1830			1965	2003	Converted to 57603 in 2003	
47350	D1831			1965	1999	Converted to 57005 in 1999	
47351	D1832			1965	1997	2001: EWS Railway, Wigan	
47352	D1833			1965	1994	2000: Froddingham Depot	
47353	D1834			1965	1999	2005: C F Booth, Rotherham	
47354	D1835			1965	2000	2003: Crewe Basford Hall Yard	
47355	47391	47355	D1836	1965		West Coast Railway Co	
47356	D1875			1965	1998	Converted to 57001 in 1998	
47357	D1876			1965	2001	2001: EWS Railway, Wigan	
47358	D1877			1965	2005	2009: T J Thomson, Stockton	
47359	D1878			1965	1998	1998: C F Booth, Rotherham	
47360	D1879			1965	1999	2007: EMR, Kingsbury	
47361	D1880			1966	2001	2004: EMR, Kingsbury	
47362	D1881			1965	1999	2000: EWS Railway, Wigan	
47363	47385	47363	D1882	1965	1999	2010: C F Booth, Rotherham	
47365	D1884			1965	1998	2007: C F Booth, Rotherham	
47366	D1885			1965	1999	1999: EWS Railway, Wigan	
47367	D1886			1965	2001	Preserved	
47368	D1887			1965		West Coast Railway Co	
47369	D1888			1965	1996	1998: C F Booth, Rotherham	
47370	D1889			1965	2003	2009: T J Thomson, Stockton	
47371	D1890			1965	2004	Converted to 57313 in 2004	
47372	D1891			1965	2004	Converted to 57314 in 2004	
47373	D1892			1965	1992	1994: MC Metals, Glasgow	
47374	D1893			1965	1992	1994: C F Booth, Rotherham	
47375	D1894			1965	2009	Exported to Hungary in 2015	
47376	D1895			1965	2001	Preserved	
47377	D1896			1965	2000	2003: Crewe Basford Hall Yard	
47378	47386	47378	D1897	1965	1998	1998: C F Booth, Rotherham	
47379	D1898			1965	1999	1999: EWS Railway, Wigan	
47380	D1899			1965	1992	1994: MC Metals, Glasgow	
47381	D1900			1965	1992	1994: MC Metals, Glasgow	

Class 47/4
Locos fitted with electric heating. Class 47/4 includes 47798–47854, which were renumbered when fitted with additional fuel tanks for long range working; some later reverted to their previous numbers.

Latest Number Carried	Previous Number 1	Previous Number 2	Previous Number 3	Previous Number 4	Previous Number 5	Year Entered Service	Year Withdrawn	Scrapping Details/Current Status	Notes
47401	D1500					1962	1992	Preserved	
47402	D1501					1962	1992	Preserved	
47403	D1502					1962	1986	1994: Crewe Gresty Lane Depot	
47404	D1503					1962	1988	1990: Vic Berry, Leicester	
47405	D1504					1963	1986	1988: Crewe Works	
47406	D1505					1963	1990	1995: Froddingham Depot	
47407	D1506					1963	1990	1995: Froddingham Depot	
47408	D1507					1963	1986	1989: Vic Berry, Leicester	

47409	D1508			1963	1986	1989: Vic Berry, Leicester	
47410	D1509			1963	1987	1990: Vic Berry, Leicester	
47411	D1510			1963	1989	1994: Froddingham Depot	
47412	D1511			1963	1987	1992: C F Booth, Rotherham	
47413	D1512			1963	1991	1995: Froddingham Depot	
47414	D1513			1963	1986	1989: Vic Berry, Leicester	
47415	D1514			1963	1987	1990: Vic Berry, Leicester	
47416	D1515			1963	1986	1987: Crewe Works	
47417	D1516			1963	1992	Preserved	
47418	D1517			1963	1991	1995: Froddingham Depot	
47419	D1518			1963	1987	1990: Vic Berry, Leicester	
47420	D1519			1963	1987	1989: Vic Berry, Leicester	
47421	D1520			1963	1991	1997: Crewe Works	
47422	D1525			1963	1991	1993: C F Booth, Rotherham	
47423	D1527			1963	1992	1997: Old Oak Common Depot	
47424	D1531			1963	1991	1994: C F Booth, Rotherham	
47425	D1533			1963	1992	1997: Old Oak Common Depot	
47426	D1534			1963	1992	1997: Old Oak Common Depot	
47427	D1535			1963	1990	1992: MC Metals, Glasgow	
47428	D1536			1963	1989	1990: Vic Berry, Leicester	
47429	D1541			1963	1987	1989: Crewe Works	
47430	D1542			1963	1992	1997: Old Oak Common Depot	
47431	D1545			1963	1992	1997: Old Oak Common Depot	
47432	D1547			1963	1992	1995: Bristol Bath Road Depot	
47433	D1548			1963	1993	1996: Crewe Works	
47434	D1549			1963	1991	1993: C F Booth, Rotherham	
47435	D1550			1964	1990	1993: C F Booth, Rotherham	C1
47436	D1552			1964	1991	1993: MC Metals, Glasgow	
47437	D1553			1964	1987	1989: C F Booth, Rotherham	
47438	D1554			1964	1992	1997: Old Oak Common Depot	
47439	D1555			1964	1993	1997: Crewe Works	
47440	D1556			1964	1991	1997: Old Oak Common Depot	
47441	D1557			1964	1992	1997: Old Oak Common Depot	
47442	D1558			1964	1993	1997: Crewe Works	
47443	D1559			1964	1993	1996: Crewe Works	
47444	D1560			1964	1990	1995: Crewe Works	
47445	D1561			1964	1991	1994: C F Booth, Rotherham	
D1562				1964	1971	1971: Crewe Works	
47446	D1563			1964	1992	1997: Old Oak Common Depot	
47447	D1564			1964	1991	1994: C F Booth, Rotherham	
47448	D1565			1964	1991	1996: C F Booth, Rotherham	
47449	D1566			1964	1993	Preserved	
47450	D1567			1964	1991	1993: C F Booth, Rotherham	
47451	D1568			1964	1991	1994: C F Booth, Rotherham	
47452	D1569			1964	1991	1997: Old Oak Common Depot	
47453	D1571			1964	1992	1997: Old Oak Common Depot	
47454	D1574			1964	1991	1994: C F Booth, Rotherham	
47455	D1575			1964	1990	1995: Crewe Works	
47456	D1576			1964	1991	1993: C F Booth, Rotherham	
47457	D1577			1964	1992	1997: Old Oak Common Depot	
47458	D1578			1964	1993	1996: C F Booth, Rotherham	
47459	D1579			1964	1992	1993: C F Booth, Rotherham	
47460	D1580			1964	1992	1994: C F Booth, Rotherham	
47461	D1581			1964	1991	1993: C F Booth, Rotherham	
47462	D1582			1964	1995	2003: Toton Training Compound	
47463	D1586			1964	1995	1996: Crewe Works	
47464	D1587			1964	1986	1987: Crewe Works	
47465	D1589			1964	1991	1997: Old Oak Common Depot	
47466	D1590			1964	1991	1997: Crewe Works	
47467	D1593			1964	1998	2000: EWS Railway, Wigan	
47469	D1595			1964	1989	1989: MC Metals, Glasgow	
47470	D1596			1964	1991	1995: Crewe Works	
47471	D1598			1964	1996	2005: Ron Hull Jr, Rotherham	
47472	97472	47472	D1600	1964	1991	1997: Old Oak Common Depot	

47473	D1601				1964	1998	1998: Crewe Works
47474	D1602				1964	2000	2005: T J Thomson, Stockton
47475	D1603				1964	1999	2008: T J Thomson, Stockton
47476	D1604				1964	2000	2004: C F Booth, Rotherham
47477	D1607				1964	1992	1993: C F Booth, Rotherham
47478	D1608				1964	1995	2006: EMR, Kingsbury
47479	D1612				1964	1992	1993: C F Booth, Rotherham
47481	D1627				1964	1996	2003: Sims Metals, Beeston
47482	D1636				1964	1993	1995: Crewe Works
47483	D1637				1964	1993	1996: Crewe Works
47484	D1662				1965	1998	Preserved
47485	D1683				1963	1993	1997: Crewe Works
47486	D1689				1963	1987	1989: Vic Berry, Leicester
47487	D1707				1964	1988	1989: MC Metals, Glasgow
47488	D1713				1964		Nemesis Rail
47489	D1716				1964	1997	2010: C F Booth, Rotherham
47492	D1760				1964		West Coast Railway Co
47500	47770	47500	D1943		1966	2013	2019: West Coast Railways, Carnforth
47501	D1944				1966		Locomotive Services a)
47508	D1952				1966	1993	1995: Bristol Bath Road Depot
47509	D1953				1966	1992	1995: Bristol Bath Road Depot
47512	D1958				1967	1991	1994: C F Booth, Rotherham
47513	D1959				1967	1997	2004: C F Booth, Rotherham
47515	D1961				1968	1991	2006: Crewe Diesel Depot
47518	D1101				1966	1991	1994: MC Metals, Glasgow
47519	D1102				1966	1999	2005: T J Thomson, Stockton
47520	D1103				1966	1998	1998: C F Booth, Rotherham
47521	D1104				1966	1995	1995: Crewe Works
47522	D1105				1966	1998	2000: EWS Railway, Wigan
47523	D1106				1966	1999	2000: EWS Railway, Wigan
47524	D1107				1966	2002	2019: C F Booth, Rotherham
47525	D1108				1967	1998	2010: EMR, Kingsbury
47526	D1109				1967		West Coast Railway Co
47527	D1110				1967	1992	1995: Bristol Bath Road Depot
47528	D1111				1967	1998	2008: Ron Hull Jr, Rotherham
47529	D1551				1964	1987	1987: Crewe Works
47530	D1930				1966	1996	2001: EWS Railway, Wigan
47532	D1641				1964	1996	2001: EWS Railway, Wigan
47533	D1651				1965	1991	1995: Old Oak Common Depot
47534	D1678				1965	1991	1995: Crewe Works
47535	D1649				1965	1999	2004: Old Oak Common Depot
47536	D1655				1965	1996	2005: C F Booth, Rotherham
ADB968035	47538	D1669			1965	1990	1997: Crewe Works
47539	D1718				1964	1996	2002: EMR, Kingsbury
47540	47975	47540	D1723		1964	1998	2016: T J Thomson, Stockton
47542	D1585				1964	1989	1994: Stratford Depot
47543	D1588				1964	1998	1998: C F Booth, Rotherham
47544	D1592				1964	1990	1991: MC Metals, Glasgow
47547	D1642				1965	1996	2005: Ron Hull Jr, Rotherham
47549	D1724				1964	1991	1995: Crewe Works
47550	D1731				1964	1996	2010: EMR, Kingsbury
47555	47126	D1717			1964	1999	2000: EWS Railway, Wigan
47565	47039	D1620			1964	2000	2004: C F Booth, Rotherham
47566	47043	D1624			1964	1996	2006: C F Booth, Rotherham
47572	47168	D1763			1964	1999	2000: EWS Railway, Wigan
47574	47174	D1769			1964	1996	2005: Ron Hull Jr, Rotherham
47575	47175	D1770			1964	2001	2010: C F Booth, Rotherham
47576	47176	D1771			1964	1996	2005: C F Booth, Rotherham
47579	47793	47579	47183	D1778	1964	2004	Preserved
47580	47732	47580	47167	D1762	1964		Preserved
47584	47180	D1775			1964	2000	2002: C F Booth, Rotherham
47593	47790	47673	47593	47272	D1973	1965	Locomotive Services
47596	47255	D1933			1966	1999	Preserved
47624	47087	D1673			1965	1998	2006: C F Booth, Rotherham

47627	47273	D1974		1965	2000	2000: EWS Railway, Wigan
47628	47078	D1663		1965	1997	2006: Ron Hull Jr, Rotherham
47633	47083	D1668		1965	1990	1994: MC Metals, Glasgow
47634	47158	D1751		1964	2001	2004: EMR, Kingsbury
47635	47029	D1606		1964	2004	Preserved
47640	47244	D1921		1966		Nemesis Rail
47643	47269	D1970		1965	1991	Preserved
47645	47075	D1659		1965	1990	1992: MC Metals, Glasgow
47676	47586	47042	D1623	1964	1994	1998: C F Booth, Rotherham
47677	47617	47149	D1742	1964	1998	1998: C F Booth, Rotherham

a)   Carries the number D1944

Class 47/7 (First Batch)
Fitted with push-pull equipment.
Details as Class 47/4 except:
Maximum Speed: 100 mph.

Latest Number Carried	Previous Number 1	Previous Number 2	Year Entered Service	Year Withdrawn	Current Status/Scrapping Details	Notes
47701	47493	D1932	1966		Nemesis Rail	
47702	47504	D1947	1966	2000	2005: Toton Training Compound	
47703	47514	D1960	1967		Harry Needle Railroad Co	
47704	47495	D1937	1966	1997	2006: Ron Hull Jr, Rotherham	
47705	47554	D1957	1967	2003	Converted to 57303 in 2003	
47706	47494	D1936	1966	1995	1995: Crewe Works	
47707	47506	D1949	1966	1996	2010: C F Booth, Rotherham	
47708	47516	D1968	1965	1995	1995: Crewe Works	
47709	47499	D1942	1966	2007	2012: Eastleigh Works	
47710	47496	D1939	1966	1999	2007: EMR, Kingsbury	
47711	47498	D1941	1966	2000	2004: Toton Training Compound	
47712	47505	D1948	1966	2012	Locomotive Services	b)
47713	47510	D1954	1966	1988	1990: Vic Berry, Leicester	
47714	47511	D1955	1966		Harry Needle Railroad Co	
47715	47502	D1945	1966		Harry Needle Railroad Co	
47716	47507	D1951	1966	2007	2010: C F Booth, Rotherham	
47717	47497	D1940	1966	1996	2007: EMR, Kingsbury	

b)   Preserved locomotive on hire to Locomotive Services

Class 47/7 (Second Batch)
Fitted with additional fuel tanks for long range working. Some later reverted to their previous numbers.
Details as Class 47/4.

Latest Number Carried	Previous Number 1	Previous Number 2	Previous Number 3	Previous Number 4	Previous Number 5	Year Entered Service	Year Withdrawn	Scrapping Details/Current Status	Notes
47721	47557	47024	D1591			1964	2002	2007: EMR, Kingsbury	
47722	47558	47027	D1599			1964	2002	2007: EMR, Kingsbury	
47725	47567	47044	D1625			1964	2003	2006: C F Booth, Rotherham	
47726	47568	47045	D1626			1964	2002	2007: EMR, Kingsbury	
47727	47569	47047	D1629			1964		GB Railfreight	
47733	47582	47170	D1765			1964	2004	2008: EMR, Kingsbury	
47734	47583	47172	D1767			1964	2004	2008: EMR, Kingsbury	
47736	47587	47263	D1963			1965	2003	2007: Ron Hull Jr, Rotherham	
47737	47588	47178	D1773			1964	2004	2008: EMR, Kingsbury	
47738	47592	47171	D1766			1964	2000	2003: S Norton, Liverpool	C1
47739	47594	47035	D1615			1964		GB Railfreight	
47741	47597	47026	D1597			1964	2003	2008: EMR, Kingsbury	
47742	47598	47182	D1777			1964	2001	2007: EMR, Kingsbury	
47743	47599	47177	D1772			1964	1995	1995: Skelton Junction Sidings	
47744	47600	47250	D1927			1966		Nemesis Rail	
47745	47603	47267	D1967			1965	2000	2004: Toton Training Compound	
47746	47605	47160	D1754			1964		West Coast Railway Co	
47747	47615	47252	D1929			1966	2004	2013: C F Booth, Rotherham	
47749	47625	47076	D1660			1965		GB Railfreight	

Latest Number Carried	Previous Number 1	Previous Number 2	Previous Number 3	Previous Number 4	Previous Number 5	Year Entered Service	Year Withdrawn	Current Status/Scrapping Details	Notes
47750	47626	47082	D1667			1965	2004	2008: EMR, Kingsbury	
47756	47644	47246	D1923			1966	2003	2006: Ron Hull Jr, Rotherham	
47757	47585	47184	D1779			1964	2004	2006: T J Thomson, Stockton	
47758	47517	D1975				1965	2003	2008: EMR, Kingsbury	
47759	47559	47028	D1605			1964	2003	2008: Ron Hull Jr, Rotherham	
47760	47562	47672	47562	47036	D1617	1964		West Coast Railway Co	
47761	47564	47038	D1619			1964		Preserved	
47762	47573	47173	D1768			1964	2001	2005: C F Booth, Rotherham	
47763	47581	47169	D1764			1964	2000	2003: Motherwell Depot	
47764	47630	47041	D1622			1964	2001	2005: EMR, Kingsbury	
47765	47631	47059	D1643			1965		Preserved	
47766	47642	47040	D1621			1964	2000	2004: Toton Training Compound	
47767	47641	47086	D1672			1965	2003	2009: C F Booth, Rotherham	C1
47768	47490	D1725				1964		West Coast Railway Co	
47769	47491	D1753				1964		Harry Needle Railroad Co	
47771	47503	D1946				1966		Preserved	
47772	47537	D1657				1965		West Coast Railway Co	
47773	47541	D1755				1964		Vintage Trains	
47774	47551	47801	47551	47153	D1746	1964	2002	2006: Crewe Diesel Depot	
47775	47531	47974	47531	D1584		1964	2001	2006: Crewe Diesel Depot	
47776	47578	47181	D1776			1964		West Coast Railway Co	
47777	47636	47243	D1920			1966	2000	2004: Toton Training Compound	
47778	47606	47842	47606	47081	D1666	1965	2004	2006: EMR, Kingsbury	
47779	47612	47838	47612	47080	D1665	1965	1999	2006: EMR, Kingsbury	
47780	47618	47836	47618	47030	D1609	1964	2003	2007: EMR, Kingsbury	
47781	47653	47808	47653	47088	D1674	1965	2003	2007: EMR, Kingsbury	
47782	47824	47602	47185	D1780		1964	2003	2007: T J Thomson, Stockton	
47783	47809	47654	47056	D1640		1964	2002	2007: Ron Hull Jr, Rotherham	
47784	47819	47664	47135	D1727		1964	2004	2007: Ron Hull Jr, Rotherham	
47785	47820	47665	47232	D1909		1965		Preserved	
47786	47821	47607	47138	D1730		1964		West Coast Railway Co	
47787	47823	47610	47163	D1757		1964		West Coast Railway Co	
47788	47833	47608	47262	D1962		1965	2000	2000: EWS Railway, Wigan	
47789	47616	47671	47616	47248	D1925	1966	2004	2007: EMR, Kingsbury	
47791	47675	47595	47268	D1969		1965	2004	2013: C F Booth, Rotherham	

Class 47/4 continued

Latest Number Carried	Previous Number 1	Previous Number 2	Previous Number 3	Previous Number 4	Previous Number 5	Year Entered Service	Year Withdrawn	Current Status/Scrapping Details	Notes
47798	47834	47609	47072	D1656		1965		Preserved	
47799	47835	47620	47070	D1654		1965	2004	Preserved	
47802	47552	47259	D1950			1966		West Coast Railway Co	
47803	47553	47260	D1956			1966	1995	2007: Ron Hull Jr, Rotherham	
47804	47792	47804	47591	47265	D1965	1965		West Coast Railway Co	
47805	47650	47257	D1935			1966		Locomotive Services	c)
47806	47651	47254	D1931			1966	2003	Converted to 57309 in 2003	
47807	47652	47055	D1639			1964	2003	Converted to 57304 in 2003	
47810	47655	47247	D1924			1966		Locomotive Services	d)
47811	47656	47128	D1719			1964		Locomotive Services	
47812	47657	47239	D1916			1965		Rail Operations Group	
47813	47658	47129	D1720			1964		Rail Operations Group	
47814	47659	47242	D1919			1966	2003	Converted to 57306 in 2003	
47815	47660	47155	D1748			1964		Rail Operations Group	
47816	47661	47066	D1650			1965		Locomotive Services	
47817	47662	47032	D1611			1964	2003	Converted to 57311 in 2003	
47818	47663	47240	D1917			1965		Arlington Fleet Services	
47822	47571	47164	D1758			1964	2003	Converted to 57305 in 2003	
47825	47590	47165	D1759			1964	2001	Converted to 57601 in 2001	
47826	47637	47274	D1976			1965		West Coast Railway Co	
47827	47589	47251	D1928			1966	2002	Converted to 57302 in 2002	
47828	47629	47266	D1966			1965	2015	West Coast Railway Co	e)
47829	47619	47264	D1964			1965	2006	2013: C F Booth, Rotherham	
47830	47649	47061	D1645			1965		Freightliner	

47831	47563	47037	D1618		1964	2003	Converted to 57310 in 2003	
47832	47560	47031	D1610		1964		West Coast Railway Co	
47837	47611	47166	D1761		1964	1991	1993: C F Booth, Rotherham	
47839	47621	47136	D1728		1964	2011	2013: Eastleigh Works	
47840	47613	47077	D1661		1965	2007	Preserved	
47841	47622	47134	D1726		1964		Locomotive Services	
47843	47623	47090	D1676		1965		Rail Operations Group	
47844	47556	47020	D1583		1964	2002	2004: Crewe Works	
47845	47638	47069	D1653		1965	2002	Converted to 57301 in 2002	
47846	47647	47091	D1677		1965	2003	Converted to 57308 in 2003	
47847	47577	47179	D1774		1964		Rail Operations Group	
47848	47632	47068	D1652		1965		Rail Operations Group	
47849	47570	47048	D1630		1964	2001	2002: C F Booth, Rotherham	
47850	47648	47151	D1744		1964	1995	1997: Crewe Works	
47851	47639	47064	D1648		1965		West Coast Railway Co	
47852	47646	47074	D1658		1965	1991	1993: C F Booth, Rotherham	
47853	47614	47141	D1733		1964		Locomotive Services	f)
47854	47674	47604	47271	D1972	1965		West Coast Railway Co	
47971	97480	47480	D1616		1964	2000	2001: EMR, Kingsbury	
47972	97545	47545	D1646		1965	1998	2010: C F Booth, Rotherham	
47973	97561	47561	47034	D1614	1964	1996	1997: Crewe Works	C1
47976	47546	D1747			1964	1999	2000: EWS Railway, Wigan	
47981	47364	D1883			1965	1998	2000: EWS Railway, Wigan	

c)   Carries the number D1935
d)   Carries the number D1924
e)   Preserved locomotive on hire to WCRC
f)   Also carries the number 47614

Class 47/9
47046 was re-engined as a testbed for the forthcoming Class 56 and renumbered 47601. In 1980 it was further converted to Class 47/9 as a testbed for the forthcoming Class 58 at BR Crewe works.

Details as Class 47/0 except:
Engine: Ruston Paxman RP12RK3CT of 2355 kW (3300 hp) at 900 rpm.

Latest Number Carried	Previous Number 1	Previous Number 2	Previous Number 3	Year Entered Service	Year Withdrawn	Current Status/Scrapping Details	Notes
47901	47601	47046	D1628	1964	1990	1992: MC Metals, Glasgow	

CLASS 50   Co-Co

Built: 1967–68 by English Electric, Vulcan Foundry, Newton-le-Willows.
Engine: English Electric 16CVST of 2010 kW (2700 hp) at 850 rpm.
Transmission: Electric.
Maximum Speed: 100 mph.
Train Heating/Supply: Electric.
Train Brakes: Dual braked (air & vacuum).

C1   One cab remains
C2   Two cabs remain

Latest Number Carried	Previous Number 1	Previous Number 2	Previous Number 3	Year Entered Service	Year Withdrawn	Current Status/Scrapping Details	Notes
50001	D401			1967	1991	2002: C F Booth, Rotherham	
50002	D402			1967	1991	Preserved	
50003	D403			1968	1991	1992: MC Metals, Glasgow	
50004	D404			1967	1990	1992: C F Booth, Rotherham	
50005	D405			1968	1990	1991: Old Oak Common Depot	
50006	D406			1968	1987	1988: Vic Berry, Leicester	
50007	D407			1968	1994	GB Railfreight	a)
50008	D408			1968	1992	Preserved	
50009	D409			1968	1991	1991: Old Oak Common Depot	
50010	D410			1968	1988	1992: Plymouth Laira Depot	
50011	D411			1968	1987	1992: Crewe Works	

▲ With an output of 2700hp and a maximum speed of 100mph, Class 50s were designed to haul high-speed services over long distances. On 23 February 1988, 50019 "Ramilles" was given a comparatively undemanding duty; it is seen passing Kingkerswell with the 09.40 Newton Abbot–Paignton. **Stephen C Marshall**

▼ After BR careers that spanned 23 and 26 years respectively, 50049 & 50007 were preserved and restored by an enthusiast group, which in 2019 took the enterprising step of hiring the locomotives to the main line operator GB Railfreight. On 7 August 2020, with 50007 masquerading as 50014 "Warspite", the duo pass Elford while transferring a GWR Class 769 from Burton-on-Trent to Reading Traincare Depot. **Brad Joyce**

50012	D412			1968	1989	1989: Vic Berry, Leicester	
50013	D413			1968	1988	1989: Vic Berry, Leicester	
50014	D414			1968	1987	1989: Vic Berry, Leicester	
50015	D415			1968	1992	Preserved	
50016	D416			1968	1990	1992: C F Booth, Rotherham	
50017	D417			1968	1991	Preserved	
50018	D418			1968	1991	1993: MC Metals, Glasgow	
50019	D419			1968	1990	Preserved	
50020	D420			1968	1990	1992: C F Booth, Rotherham	
50021	D421			1968	1990	Preserved	
50022	D422			1968	1988	1989: Vic Berry, Leicester	
50023	D423			1968	1990	2004: Barrow Hill Depot	
50024	D424			1968	1991	1991: Old Oak Common Depot	
50025	D425			1968	1989	1989: Old Oak Common Depot	
50026	D426			1968	1990	Preserved	
50027	D427			1968	1991	Preserved	
50028	D428			1968	1991	1991: Old Oak Common Depot	
50029	D429			1968	1992	Preserved	
50030	D430			1968	1992	Preserved	
50031	D431			1968	1991	Preserved	
50032	D432			1968	1990	1991: Old Oak Common Depot	
50033	D433			1968	1994	Preserved	
50034	D434			1968	1990	1991: Old Oak Common Depot	
50035	D435			1968	1990	Preserved	
50036	D436			1968	1991	1992: C F Booth, Rotherham	
50037	D437			1968	1991	1992: MC Metals, Glasgow	C1
50038	D438			1968	1988	1989: Vic Berry, Leicester	
50039	D439			1968	1989	1991: Old Oak Common Depot	
50040	D440			1968	1990	2008: Sims Metals, Halesowen	
50041	D441			1968	1990	1991: Old Oak Common Depot	
50042	D442			1968	1990	Preserved	
50043	D443			1968	1991	2002: Pontypool & Blaenavon Rlwy	
50044	D444			1968	1991	Preserved	
50045	D445			1968	1990	2000: C F Booth, Rotherham	
50046	D446			1968	1992	1992: MC Metals, Glasgow	C2
50047	D447			1968	1988	1989: Vic Berry, Leicester	
50048	D448			1968	1991	1992: MC Metals, Glasgow	
50049	50149	50049	D449	1968	1991	GB Railfreight	a)
50050	D400			1967	1994	Boden Rail Engineering	

a)   Preserved locomotive on hire to GB Railfreight

CLASS 52   C-C

Built: 1961–64 by British Railways, Crewe & Swindon.
Engine: Two Bristol Siddeley Maybach MD655 of 1007 kW (1350 hp) at 1500 rpm.
Transmission: Hydraulic.
Maximum Speed: 90 mph.
Train Heating/Supply: Steam heating.
Train Brakes: Built vacuum braked and most were converted to dual braked (air & vacuum).

Latest Number Carried	Previous Number 1	Year Entered Service	Year Withdrawn	Current Status/Scrapping Details	Notes
D1000		1961	1974	1974: Swindon Works	
D1001		1962	1976	1977: Swindon Works	
D1002		1962	1974	1974: Swindon Works	
D1003		1962	1975	1977: Swindon Works	
D1004		1962	1973	1974: Swindon Works	
D1005		1962	1976	1977: Swindon Works	
D1006		1962	1975	1977: Swindon Works	
D1007		1962	1974	1975: Swindon Works	
D1008		1962	1974	1975: Swindon Works	
D1009		1962	1976	1978: Swindon Works	

D1010	1962	1977	Preserved
D1011	1962	1975	1979: Swindon Works
D1012	1962	1975	1979: Swindon Works
D1013	1962	1977	Preserved
D1014	1962	1974	1975: Swindon Works
D1015	1963	1976	Preserved
D1016	1963	1975	1977: Swindon Works
D1017	1963	1973	1975: Swindon Works
D1018	1963	1973	1974: Swindon Works
D1019	1963	1973	1974: Swindon Works
D1020	1963	1973	1974: Swindon Works
D1021	1963	1976	1979: Swindon Works
D1022	1963	1977	1978: Swindon Works
D1023	1963	1977	Preserved
D1024	1963	1973	1974: Swindon Works
D1025	1963	1975	1979: Swindon Works
D1026	1963	1975	1976: Swindon Works
D1027	1964	1975	1976: Swindon Works
D1028	1964	1976	1979: Swindon Works
D1029	1964	1974	1975: Swindon Works
D1030	1963	1976	1976: Swindon Works
D1031	1963	1975	1976: Swindon Works
D1032	1963	1973	1974: Swindon Works
D1033	1964	1976	1979: Swindon Works
D1034	1964	1975	1979: Swindon Works
D1035	1962	1975	1976: Swindon Works
D1036	1962	1976	1977: Swindon Works
D1037	1962	1976	1977: Swindon Works
D1038	1962	1973	1974: Swindon Works
D1039	1962	1973	1974: Swindon Works
D1040	1962	1976	1976: Swindon Works
D1041	1962	1977	Preserved
D1042	1962	1973	1974: Swindon Works
D1043	1962	1976	1977: Swindon Works
D1044	1962	1975	1975: Swindon Works
D1045	1962	1974	1975: Swindon Works
D1046	1962	1975	1976: Swindon Works
D1047	1963	1976	1976: Swindon Works
D1048	1962	1977	Preserved
D1049	1962	1976	1977: Swindon Works
D1050	1963	1975	1976: Swindon Works
D1051	1963	1976	1977: Swindon Works
D1052	1963	1975	1976: Swindon Works
D1053	1963	1976	1977: Swindon Works
D1054	1963	1976	1977: Swindon Works
D1055	1963	1976	1976: Swindon Works
D1056	1963	1976	1979: Swindon Works
D1057	1963	1976	1977: Swindon Works
D1058	1963	1977	1979: Swindon Works
D1059	1963	1975	1976: Swindon Works
D1060	1963	1973	1974: Swindon Works
D1061	1963	1974	1975: Swindon Works
D1062	1963	1974	Preserved
D1063	1963	1976	1977: Swindon Works
D1064	1963	1975	1977: Swindon Works
D1065	1963	1976	1977: Swindon Works
D1066	1963	1974	1975: Swindon Works
D1067	1963	1976	1976: Swindon Works
D1068	1963	1976	1977: Swindon Works
D1069	1963	1975	1977: Swindon Works
D1070	1963	1976	1979: Swindon Works
D1071	1963	1976	1978: Swindon Works
D1072	1963	1976	1977: Swindon Works
D1073	1963	1974	1975: Swindon Works

▲ D1062 "WESTERN COURIER" passes Foley Park on the Severn Valley Railway, with the 10.30 Bridgnorth–Kidderminster on 16 May 2019. **Brad Joyce**

▼ Due to a shortage of motive power during 2011, 55022 "ROYAL SCOTS GREY" was hired to haul aluminium ore trains from North Blyth to Lynemouth aluminium works. The Type 5 passes Winning signal box on 17 May 2011 with the 09.45 Lynemouth–North Blyth empties. **Gordon Edgar**

CLASS 55 Co-Co

Built: 1961–62 by English Electric, Vulcan Foundry, Newton-le-Willows.
Engine: Two Napier Deltic T18-25 of 1230 kW (1650 hp) at 1500 rpm.
Transmission: Electric.
Maximum Speed: 100 mph.
Train Heating/Supply: Built with steam heating, all later converted to dual heating.
Train Brakes: Built vacuum braked, all later converted to dual braked (air & vacuum).

C1   One cab remains

Latest Number Carried	Previous Number 1	Year Entered Service	Year Withdrawn	Current Status/Scrapping Details	Notes
55001	D9001	1961	1980	1980: Doncaster Works	
55002	D9002	1961	1982	Preserved	
55003	D9003	1961	1980	1981: Doncaster Works	
55004	D9004	1961	1981	1983: Doncaster Works	
55005	D9005	1961	1981	1983: Doncaster Works	
55006	D9006	1961	1981	1981: Doncaster Works	
55007	D9007	1961	1981	1982: Doncaster Works	
55008	D9008	1961	1981	1982: Doncaster Works	C1
55009	D9009	1961	1982	Preserved	
55010	D9010	1961	1981	1982: Doncaster Works	
55011	D9011	1961	1981	1982: Doncaster Works	
55012	D9012	1961	1981	1981: Doncaster Works	
55013	D9013	1961	1981	1982: Doncaster Works	
55014	D9014	1961	1981	1982: Doncaster Works	
55015	D9015	1961	1982	Preserved	
55016	D9016	1961		Locomotive Services	
55017	D9017	1961	1981	1983: Doncaster Works	
55018	D9018	1961	1981	1982: Doncaster Works	
55019	D9019	1961	1981	Preserved	
55020	D9020	1962	1980	1980: Doncaster Works	
55021	D9021	1962	1981	1982: Doncaster Works	C1
55022	D9000	1961		Locomotive Services	

CLASS 56 Co-Co

Built: 1976–84 by Electroputere, Craiova, Romania and BREL, Crewe & Doncaster
Engine: Ruston Paxman 16RK3CT of 2460 kW (3250 hp) at 900 rpm.
Transmission: Electric.
Maximum Speed: 80 mph.
Train Heating/Supply: None.
Train Brakes: Air.

UL   Scrapping details unconfirmed, but likely to be correct

Latest Number Carried	Previous Number 1	Year Entered Service	Year Withdrawn	Current Status/Scrapping Details	Notes
56001		1977	1996	1997: Cardiff Canton Depot	
56002		1977	1992	1994: Doncaster Carr Depot	
56004		1977	1999	2006: C F Booth, Rotherham	
56005		1977	1996	1996: C F Booth, Rotherham	
56006		1977	2003	Preserved	
56007		1977	2006	Being converted to a Class 69	
56008		1977	1992	2000: Immingham Depot	
56009	56201	1977		Awaiting Disposal	a)
56010		1977	1999	2004: C F Booth, Rotherham	
56011		1977	2001	2009: C F Booth, Rotherham	
56012		1977	1992	2000: Immingham Depot	
56013		1977	1993	2001: T J Thomson, Stockton	
56014		1977	1993	2000: Immingham Depot	
56015		1977	1993	1996: Ron Hull Jr, Rotherham	UL
56016		1977	1996	1997: Cardiff Canton Depot	

56017	1977	1992	1994: Toton Depot
56018	1977	2007	Converted to 69003 (due 2021)
56019	1977	1999	2003: Immingham Depot
56020	1977	1997	1998: C F Booth, Rotherham
56021	1977	1999	2009: T J Thomson, Stockton
56022	1977	1999	2012: EMR, Kingsbury
56023	1977	1993	2004: C F Booth, Rotherham
56024	1977	1996	1996: C F Booth, Rotherham
56025	1977	2002	2009: C F Booth, Rotherham
56026	1977	1996	1996: C F Booth, Rotherham
56027	1977	2003	2009: C F Booth, Rotherham
56028	1977	1993	1998: Crewe Works
56029	1977	1999	2007: EMR, Kingsbury
56030	1977	1993	1998: Crewe Works
56031	1977	2006	Converted to 69001 (due 2021)
56032	1977		GB Railfreight
56033	1977	2003	2010: EMR, Kingsbury
56034	1977	1999	2007: C F Booth, Rotherham
56035	1977	1999	2000: EWS Railway, Wigan
56036	1978	2000	2006: C F Booth, Rotherham
56037	1978	2003	Being converted to a Class 69
56038	1978	2006	Being converted to a Class 69
56039	1978	1999	2004: T J Thomson, Stockton
56040	1978	2000	2011: T J Thomson, Stockton
56041	1978	2003	2011: EMR, Attercliffe
56042	1978	1991	1994: Toton Depot
56043	1978	2000	2009: C F Booth, Rotherham
56044	1978	2000	2007: C F Booth, Rotherham
56046	1978	2002	2012: EMR, Kingsbury
56047	1978	1999	2003: Immingham Depot
56048	1978	2002	2010: EMR, Kingsbury
56049	1978		Colas Rail
56050	1978	1999	2004: C F Booth, Rotherham
56051	1978		Colas Rail
56052	1978	1999	2009: C F Booth, Rotherham
56053	1978	1999	2011: EMR, Attercliffe
56054	1979	2003	2011: T J Thomson, Stockton
56055	1979	2003	2011: EMR, Attercliffe
56056	1979	2004	2010: EMR, Kingsbury
56058	1979	2006	2012: EMR, Kingsbury
56059	1979	2006	2011: T J Thomson, Stockton
56060	1979	2006	Being converted to a Class 69
56061	1979	1999	2006: T J Thomson, Stockton
56062	1979	2004	2010: EMR, Kingsbury
56063	1979	2002	2007: C F Booth, Rotherham
56064	1979	2000	2009: C F Booth, Rotherham
56065	1979	2006	Being converted to a Class 69
56066	1979	1999	2005: Ron Hull Jr, Rotherham
56067	1979	2003	2011: T J Thomson, Stockton
56068	1979	2003	2010: EMR, Kingsbury
56069	1979	2007	Converted to 69004 (due 2021)
56070	1979	2004	2011: T J Thomson, Stockton
56071	1979	2006	2011: T J Thomson, Stockton
56072	1980	2004	2010: EMR, Attercliffe
56073	1980	2002	2012: EMR, Kingsbury
56074	1980	2006	2014: Ron Hull Jr, Rotherham
56075	1980	1999	2004: C F Booth, Rotherham
56076	1980	2000	2009: C F Booth, Rotherham
56077	1980		GB Railfreight
56078	1980		Colas Rail
56079	1980	1999	2010: EMR, Kingsbury
56080	1980	2002	2003: Cardiff Cathays Depot
56081	1980		GB Railfreight
56082	1980	1999	2009: C F Booth, Rotherham

56083		1980	2003	2011: T J Thomson, Stockton	
56084		1980	2000	2009: C F Booth, Rotherham	
56085		1981	2002	2011: EMR, Hartlepool	
56086		1980	1999	2013: EMR, Kingsbury	
56087		1980		Colas Rail	
56088		1981	2004	2011: EMR, Hartlepool	
56089		1981	2002	2009: C F Booth, Rotherham	
56090		1981		Colas Rail	
56091		1981		DC Rail	
56092		1981	1999	2001: EWS Railway, Wigan	
56093		1981	1999	2010: EMR, Attercliffe	
56094		1981		Colas Rail	
56095		1981	2006	2011: T J Thomson, Stockton	
56096		1981		Colas Rail	
56097		1981	1999	Preserved	
56098		1981		GB Railfreight	
56099		1981	2003	2010: EMR, Attercliffe	
56100		1981	2003	2010: EMR, Kingsbury	
56101		1981	2000	Exported to Hungary in 2012	
56102		1981	2003	2010: EMR, Hartlepool	
56103		1981		DC Rail	
56104		1982		GB Railfreight	
56105		1982		Colas Rail	
56106		1982		GB Railfreight	b)
56107		1982	2004	2011: T J Thomson, Stockton	
56108		1982	1999	2011: EMR, Hartlepool	
56109		1982	2003	2011: T J Thomson, Stockton	
56110		1982	2002	2011: EMR, Attercliffe	
56111		1982	2003	2011: EMR, Hartlepool	
56112		1982	2003	2012: EMR, Kingsbury	
56113		1982		Colas Rail	
56114		1983	2003	2012: EMR, Kingsbury	
56115		1983	2006	Exported to Hungary in 2012	c)
56116		1983	2002	2011: EMR, Kingsbury	
56117		1983	2006	Exported to Hungary in 2013	
56118		1983	2006	2009: C F Booth, Rotherham	
56119		1983	2004	2011: EMR, Attercliffe	
56120		1983	2003	2011: T J Thomson, Stockton	
56121		1983	1999	2005: C F Booth, Rotherham	
56122		1983	1992	1998: C F Booth, Rotherham	
56123		1983	1999	2003: Immingham Depot	
56126		1983	1999	2001: EWS Railway, Wigan	
56127		1983	2002	2010: EMR, Hartlepool	
56128		1983	1999	Being converted to a Class 69	
56129		1984	2003	2011: EMR, Hartlepool	
56130		1984	1999	2004: C F Booth, Rotherham	
56131		1984	2002	2007: C F Booth, Rotherham	
56132		1984	2000	2006: C F Booth, Rotherham	
56133		1984	2004	2012: EMR, Kingsbury	
56134		1984	2002	2010: C F Booth, Rotherham	
56135		1984	1999	2003: Immingham Depot	
56301	56045	1978		UK Rail Leasing	d)
56302	56124	1983		Colas Rail	
56303	56125	1983		GB Railfreight	
56311	56057	1979	2014	Converted to 69002 (due 2021)	
56312	56003	1977		GB Railfreight	

a) At EMD Longport
b) One cab has been removed
c) Involved in a serious collision abroad in November 2016
d) Preserved locomotive on hire to UK Rail Leasing

▲ Colas Rail's 56078 approaches Alsager foot crossing with a short rake of wagons that it is transferring from Crewe Basford Hall to Pinnox Branch Esso Sidings near Longport on 29 May 2020. **Brad Joyce**

▼ With 57604 just visible on the front, 57604 brings up the rear of 07.15 Paddington–Reading Traincare Depot empty coaching stock working on 25 June 2018. The train is taking a circuitous route via the Chiltern Line and has just passed through Princes Risborough. **Geoff Plumb**

CLASS 57 Co-Co

Built: 1964–67 as Class 47 (see Class 47) and converted to Class 57 1998–2004 by Brush Traction, Loughborough.
Transmission: Electric.
Train Brakes: Air.

Class 57/0
Engine: General Motors 12 645 E3 of 1860 kW (2500 hp) at 904 rpm.
Maximum Speed: 75 mph.
Train Heating/Supply: None.

Latest Number Carried	Previous Number 1	Year Entered Service	Year Withdrawn	Current Status/Scrapping Details	Notes
57001	47356	1998		West Coast Railway Co	
57002	47322	1998		Direct Rail Services	
57003	47317	1999		Direct Rail Services	
57004	47347	1999		Direct Rail Services	
57005	47350	1999		West Coast Railway Co	
57006	47187	1999		West Coast Railway Co	
57007	47332	1999		Direct Rail Services	
57008	47060	1999		Direct Rail Services	
57009	47079	1999		Direct Rail Services	
57010	47231	2000		Direct Rail Services	
57011	47329	2000		Direct Rail Services	
57012	47204	2000		Direct Rail Services	

Class 57/3
Engine: General Motors 12 645 F3B of 2050 kW (2750 hp) at 954 rpm.
Maximum Speed: 95 mph.
Train Heating/Supply: Electric.

Latest Number Carried	Previous Number 1	Year Entered Service	Year Withdrawn	Current Status/Scrapping Details	Notes
57301	47845	2002		Rail Operations Group	a)
57302	47827	2002		Direct Rail Services	
57303	47705	2003		Rail Operations Group	a)
57304	47807	2003		Direct Rail Services	
57305	47822	2003		Rail Operations Group	a)
57306	47814	2003		Direct Rail Services	
57307	47225	2003		Direct Rail Services	
57308	47846	2003		Direct Rail Services	
57309	47806	2003		Direct Rail Services	
57310	47831	2003		Rail Operations Group	a)
57311	47817	2003		Direct Rail Services	
57312	47330	2003		Rail Operations Group	a)
57313	47371	2004		West Coast Railway Co	
57314	47372	2004		West Coast Railway Co	
57315	47234	2004		West Coast Railway Co	
57316	47290	2004		West Coast Railway Co	

a)   DRS Locomotive on hire to ROG

Class 57/6
Engine: General Motors 12 645 E3 of 1860 kW (2500 hp) at 904 rpm.
Maximum Speed: 95 mph.
Train Heating/Supply: Electric.

Latest Number Carried	Previous Number 1	Year Entered Service	Year Withdrawn	Current Status/Scrapping Details	Notes
57601	47825	2001		West Coast Railway Co	
57602	47337	2003		Great Western Railway	
57603	47349	2003		Great Western Railway	
57604	47209	2004		Great Western Railway	
57605	47206	2004		Great Western Railway	

CLASS 58 Co-Co

Built: 1983–87 by BREL, Doncaster.
Engine: Ruston Paxman 12RK3ACT of 2460 kW (3300 hp) at 1000 rpm.
Transmission: Electric.
Maximum Speed: 80 mph.
Train Heating/Supply: None.
Train Brakes: Air.

C1   One cab remains
ES   Locomotive exported and subsequently scrapped

Latest Number Carried	Previous Number 1	Year Entered Service	Year Withdrawn	Current Status/Scrapping Details	Notes
58001		1983	1999	Exported to France in 2009	
58002		1983	2000	2013: Eastleigh Depot	
58003		1983	1999	2010: EMR, Kingsbury	
58004		1983	2006	Exported to France in 2009	
58005		1983	2000	Exported to France in 2009	
58006		1983	2000	Exported to France in 2009	
58007		1983	2000	Exported to France in 2009	
58008		1983	1999	2016: Eastleigh Works	C1
58009		1984	2002	Exported to France in 2009	
58010		1984	1999	Exported to France in 2009	
58011		1984	2000	Exported to France in 2009	
58012		1984	1999	Preserved	
58013		1984	2001	Exported to France in 2009	
58014		1984	2000	2010: EMR, Kingsbury	
58015		1984	2011	2020: Manforte Del Cid, Spain	ES
58016		1984	2006	Preserved	
58017		1984	1999	2014: Eastleigh Depot	
58018		1984	1999	Exported to France in 2009	

▲ West Coast Railway Company's **57313** "Scarborough Castle" and **57601** "Windsor Castle" head north through Stafford with an empty coaching stock working from Southall to Carnforth on 16 March 2020. **Brad Joyce**

Number	Built	Withdrawn	Current Status/Scrapping Details	Notes
58019	1984	2001	2010: EMR, Kingsbury	
58020	1984	2011	2020: Manforte Del Cid, Spain	ES
58021	1984	2002	Exported to France in 2009	
58022	1984	1999	Preserved	a)
58023	1984	1999	Preserved	
58024	1984	2011	2020: Manforte Del Cid, Spain	ES
58025	1985	2004	Exported to Spain in 2004	
58026	1985	2002	Exported to France in 2009	
58027	1985	1999	Exported to Spain in 2008	
58028	1985	1999	2010: EMR, Kingsbury	
58029	1985	2011	2020: Manforte Del Cid, Spain	ES
58030	1985	2011	2020: Manforte Del Cid, Spain	ES
58031	1985	2011	2020: Manforte Del Cid, Spain	ES
58032	1985	1999	Exported to France in 2009	
58033	1985	2002	Exported to France in 2009	
58034	1985	1999	Exported to France in 2009	
58035	1986	1999	Exported to France in 2009	
58036	1986	2000	Exported to France in 2009	
58037	1986	2002	2013: Eastleigh Depot	
58038	1986	1999	Exported to the Netherlands in 2008	b)
58039	1986	2003	Exported to the Netherlands in 2009	b)
58040	1986	1999	Exported to France in 2009	
58041	1986	2011	Exported to Spain in 2003	
58042	1986	2002	Exported to France in 2009	
58043	1986	2011	2020: Manforte Del Cid, Spain	ES
58044	1986	2003	Exported to the Netherlands in 2009	b)
58045	1986	2002	2010: EMR, Kingsbury	
58046	1986	2000	Exported to France in 2009	
58047	1986	2011	2020: Manforte Del Cid, Spain	ES
58048	1986	2000	Preserved	
58049	1986	2002	Exported to France in 2009	
58050	1987	2002	Exported to Spain in 2008	

a)   Frame of 58022 to be used for replica LMS 10000 build
b)   Transferred to France in 2009

CLASS 59   Co-Co

Built: 1985 (59001–59004) and 1989 (59005) by General Motors, La Grange, Illinois, USA.
1990 (59101–59104), 1994 (59201) and 1995 (59202–59206) by General Motors, London, Canada.
Engine: General Motors 16-645E3C two stroke of 2460 kW (3300 hp) at 904 rpm.
Transmission: Electric.
Maximum Speed: 60 mph.
Train Heating/Supply: None.
Train Brakes: Air.

Class 59/0

Latest Number Carried	Previous Number 1	Year Entered Service	Year Withdrawn	Current Status/Scrapping Details	Notes
59001		1986		Freightliner	
59002		1986		Freightliner	
59003		1986		GB Railfreight	
59004		1986		Freightliner	
59005		1989		Freightliner	

Class 59/1
Details as Class 59/0.

Latest Number Carried	Previous Number 1	Year Entered Service	Year Withdrawn	Current Status/Scrapping Details	Notes
59101		1990		Freightliner	
59102		1990		Freightliner	
59103		1990		Freightliner	
59104		1990		Freightliner	

▲ Still adorned with the original Railfreight livery in which it entered service two years earlier, on 30 June 1987, 58034 "Bassetlaw" heads south through Kings Sutton with a lengthy rake of loaded MGR wagons which are destined for Didcot Power Station. **Stephen Dance**

▼ American-built 59004 was one of the original four Class 59s that arrived in the UK in January 1986. On 10 September 2015, while carrying its second name "PAUL A HAMMOND", the 3300hp locomotive passes Kensington Olympia with a loaded aggregate working from Acton to Crawley. **Brad Joyce**

Class 59/2
Details as Class 59/0 except:
Maximum Speed: 75 mph.

Latest Number Carried	Previous Number 1	Year Entered Service	Year Withdrawn	Current Status/Scrapping Details	Notes
59201		1994		Freightliner	
59202		1995		Freightliner	
59203		1995		Freightliner	
59204		1995		Freightliner	
59205		1995		Freightliner	
59206		1995		Freightliner	

CLASS 60 Co-Co

Built: 1989–93 by Brush Traction, Loughborough.
Engine: Mirlees 8MB275T of 2310 kW (3100 hp) at 1000 rpm.
Transmission: Electric.
Maximum Speed: 62 mph.
Train Heating/Supply: None.
Train Brakes: Air.

Latest Number Carried	Previous Number 1	Year Entered Service	Year Withdrawn	Current Status/Scrapping Details	Notes
60001		1991		DB Cargo	
60002		1992		GB Railfreight	
60003		1992		DB Cargo	
60004		1991		GB Railfreight	
60005		1991		DB Cargo	
60006		1991	2006	2020: Toton Depot	
60007		1993		DB Cargo	
60008		1992		GB Railfreight	
60009		1993		DB Cargo	
60010		1991		DB Cargo	
60011		1991		DB Cargo	
60012		1991		DB Cargo	
60013		1993		DB Cargo	
60014		1993		GB Railfreight	
60015		1993		DB Cargo	
60017		1990		DB Cargo	
60018		1990		GB Railfreight	
60019		1990		DB Cargo	
60020		1991		DB Cargo	
60021		1990		GB Railfreight	
60022		1991		DB Cargo	
60023		1990		DB Cargo	
60024		1990		DB Cargo	
60025		1990		DB Cargo	
60026		1990		GB Railfreight	
60027		1991		DB Cargo	
60028		1990		DC Rail	
60029		1990		DC Rail	
60030		1990		DB Cargo	
60031		1991		DB Cargo	
60032		1990		DB Cargo	
60033		1991		DB Cargo	
60034		1990		DB Cargo	
60035		1991		DB Cargo	
60036		1991		DB Cargo	
60037		1991		DB Cargo	
60038		1991		DB Cargo	
60039		1991		DB Cargo	

60040		1992	DB Cargo
60041		1991	DB Cargo
60042		1991	DB Cargo
60043		1991	DB Cargo
60044		1991	DB Cargo
60045		1991	DB Cargo
60046		1991	DC Rail
60047		1991	GB Railfreight
60048		1991	DB Cargo
60049		1991	DB Cargo
60050		1991	Preserved
60051		1991	DB Cargo
60052		1991	DB Cargo
60053		1991	DB Cargo
60054		1991	DB Cargo
60055		1991	DC Rail
60056		1991	GB Railfreight
60057		1991	DB Cargo
60058		1991	DB Cargo
60059		1991	DB Cargo
60060		1991	Preserved
60061		1991	DB Cargo
60062		1991	DB Cargo
60063		1991	DB Cargo
60064		1991	DB Cargo
60065		1991	DB Cargo
60066		1991	DB Cargo
60067		1991	DB Cargo
60068		1991	DB Cargo
60069		1991	DB Cargo
60070		1991	DB Cargo
60071		1991	DB Cargo
60072		1991	DB Cargo
60073		1991	DB Cargo
60074		1991	DB Cargo
60075		1991	DB Cargo
60076		1991	GB Railfreight
60077		1991	DB Cargo
60078		1991	DB Cargo
60079		1992	DB Cargo
60080		1991	DB Cargo
60081		1991	Locomotive Services
60082		1991	DB Cargo
60083		1992	DB Cargo
60084		1993	DB Cargo
60085		1991	GB Railfreight
60086		1992	Preserved
60087		1991	GB Railfreight
60088		1992	DB Cargo
60089		1992	DB Cargo
60090		1992	DB Cargo
60091		1992	DB Cargo
60092		1992	DB Cargo
60093		1992	DB Cargo
60094		1992	DB Cargo
60095		1992	GB Railfreight
60096		1992	GB Railfreight
60097		1992	DB Cargo
60098		1992	DB Cargo
60099		1992	DB Cargo
60100		1992	DB Cargo
60500	60016	1993	DB Cargo

▲ On 28 June 2019, DB Cargo's 60015 approaches South Staffordshire Junction with a heavy steel train which originated at Wolverhampton Steel Terminal and is heading for Immingham Sorting Sidings. **Brad Joyce**

▼ 66727 "Maritime One" is one of several locomotives that GB Railfreight have painted in this striking Maritime blue livery. It heads south from Blea Moor Sidings near Ribblehead on 8 August 2017, making its way from Acrow Quarry to the stone terminal at Pendleton, Salford. **Liam Barnes**

CLASS 66   Co-Co

Built: 1998–2016 by General Motors, London, Canada.
Engine: General Motors 12N-710G3B-EC two stroke of 2385 kW (3200 hp) at 904 rpm (Class 66/0, 66501–66572, 66/6, 66717–66671, 66733–66746, 66750–66751 and 66/8).
General Motors EMD 12N-710G3B-T2 two stroke of 2420 kW (3245 hp) at 904 rpm (Class 66/3, 66/4, 66585–66599, 66718–66732, 66747–66749, 66752–66779, 66/9 and 66953–66957 which are 66/5s).
Transmission: Electric.
Maximum Speed: 65 mph (Class 66/6) and 75 mph (others).
Train Heating/Supply: None.
Train Brakes: Air.

Latest Number Carried	Previous Number 1	Previous Number 2	Year Entered Service	Year Withdrawn	Current Status/Scrapping Details	Notes
66001			1998		DB Cargo	
66002			1998		DB Cargo	
66003			1998		DB Cargo	
66004			1998		DB Cargo	
66005			1998		DB Cargo	
66006			1998		DB Cargo	
66007			1998		DB Cargo	
66009			1998		DB Cargo	
66010			1998		Exported	
66011			1998		DB Cargo	
66012			1998		DB Cargo	
66013			1998		DB Cargo	
66014			1998		DB Cargo	
66015			1998		DB Cargo	
66017			1998		DB Cargo	
66018			1998		DB Cargo	
66019			1998		DB Cargo	
66020			1998		DB Cargo	
66021			1998		DB Cargo	
66022			1998		Exported	
66023			1998		DB Cargo	
66024			1998		DB Cargo	
66025			1998		DB Cargo	
66026			1998		Exported	
66027			1998		DB Cargo	
66028			1998		Exported	
66029			1998		Exported	
66030			1998		DB Cargo	
66031			1998		Direct Rail Services	a)
66032			1998		Exported	
66033			1998		Exported	
66034			1998		DB Cargo	
66035			1998		DB Cargo	
66036			1998		Exported	
66037			1998		DB Cargo	
66038			1998		Exported	
66039			1998		DB Cargo	
66040			1998		DB Cargo	
66041			1998		DB Cargo	
66042			1998		Exported	
66043			1998		DB Cargo	
66044			1998		DB Cargo	
66045			1998		Exported	
66047			1999		DB Cargo	
66048			1999		DB Cargo	b)
66049			1999		Exported	
66050			1999		DB Cargo	
66051			1999		DB Cargo	

66052	1999	Exported	
66053	1999	DB Cargo	
66054	1999	DB Cargo	
66055	1999	DB Cargo	
66056	1999	DB Cargo	
66057	1999	DB Cargo	
66059	1999	DB Cargo	
66060	1999	DB Cargo	
66061	1999	DB Cargo	
66062	1999	Exported	
66063	1999	DB Cargo	
66064	1999	Exported	
66065	1999	DB Cargo	
66066	1999	DB Cargo	
66067	1999	DB Cargo	
66068	1999	DB Cargo	
66069	1999	DB Cargo	
66070	1999	DB Cargo	
66071	1999	Exported	
66072	1999	Exported	
66073	1999	Exported	
66074	1999	DB Cargo	
66075	1999	DB Cargo	
66076	1999	DB Cargo	
66077	1999	DB Cargo	
66078	1999	DB Cargo	
66079	1999	DB Cargo	
66080	1999	DB Cargo	
66082	1999	DB Cargo	
66083	1999	DB Cargo	
66084	1999	DB Cargo	
66085	1999	DB Cargo	
66086	1999	DB Cargo	
66087	1999	DB Cargo	
66088	1999	DB Cargo	
66089	1999	DB Cargo	
66090	1999	DB Cargo	
66091	1999	Direct Rail Services	a)
66092	1999	DB Cargo	
66093	1999	DB Cargo	
66094	1999	DB Cargo	
66095	1999	DB Cargo	
66096	1999	DB Cargo	
66097	1999	DB Cargo	
66098	1999	DB Cargo	
66099	1999	DB Cargo	
66100	1999	DB Cargo	
66101	1999	DB Cargo	
66102	1999	DB Cargo	
66103	1999	DB Cargo	
66104	1999	DB Cargo	
66105	1999	DB Cargo	
66106	1999	DB Cargo	
66107	1999	DB Cargo	
66108	1999	Direct Rail Services	a)
66109	1999	DB Cargo	
66110	1999	DB Cargo	
66111	1999	DB Cargo	
66112	1999	DB Cargo	
66113	1999	DB Cargo	
66114	1999	DB Cargo	
66115	1999	DB Cargo	
66116	1999	DB Cargo	
66117	1999	DB Cargo	

66118	1999	DB Cargo	
66119	1999	DB Cargo	
66120	1999	DB Cargo	
66121	1999	DB Cargo	
66122	1999	Direct Rail Services	a)
66123	1999	Exported	
66124	1999	DB Cargo	
66125	1999	DB Cargo	
66126	1999	Direct Rail Services	a)
66127	1999	DB Cargo	
66128	1999	DB Cargo	
66129	1999	DB Cargo	
66130	1999	DB Cargo	
66131	1999	DB Cargo	
66133	1999	DB Cargo	
66134	1999	DB Cargo	
66135	1999	DB Cargo	
66136	1999	DB Cargo	
66137	1999	DB Cargo	
66138	1999	DB Cargo	
66139	1999	DB Cargo	
66140	1999	DB Cargo	
66142	1999	DB Cargo	
66143	1999	DB Cargo	
66144	1999	DB Cargo	
66145	1999	DB Cargo	
66146	1999	Exported	
66147	1999	DB Cargo	
66148	1999	DB Cargo	
66149	1999	DB Cargo	
66150	1999	DB Cargo	
66151	1999	DB Cargo	
66152	1999	DB Cargo	
66153	1999	Exported	
66154	2000	DB Cargo	
66155	2000	DB Cargo	
66156	1999	DB Cargo	
66157	1999	Exported	
66158	1999	DB Cargo	
66159	1999	Exported	
66160	1999	DB Cargo	
66161	1999	DB Cargo	
66162	1999	DB Cargo	
66163	1999	Exported	
66164	1999	DB Cargo	
66165	1999	DB Cargo	
66166	1999	Exported	
66167	1999	DB Cargo	
66168	1999	DB Cargo	
66169	1999	DB Cargo	
66170	1999	DB Cargo	
66171	1999	DB Cargo	
66172	1999	DB Cargo	
66173	1999	Exported	
66174	1999	DB Cargo	
66175	1999	DB Cargo	
66176	1999	DB Cargo	
66177	1999	DB Cargo	
66178	1999	Exported	
66179	1999	Exported	
66180	1999	Exported	
66181	1999	DB Cargo	
66182	1999	DB Cargo	
66183	1999	DB Cargo	

66185	1999	DB Cargo
66186	1999	DB Cargo
66187	1999	DB Cargo
66188	1999	DB Cargo
66189	1999	Exported
66190	2000	Exported
66191	2000	Exported
66192	2000	DB Cargo
66193	2000	Exported
66194	2000	DB Cargo
66195	2000	Exported
66196	2000	Exported
66197	2000	DB Cargo
66198	2000	DB Cargo
66199	2000	DB Cargo
66200	2000	DB Cargo
66201	2000	Exported
66202	2000	Exported
66203	2000	Exported
66204	2000	Exported
66205	2000	Exported
66206	2000	DB Cargo
66207	2000	DB Cargo
66208	2000	Exported
66209	2000	Exported
66210	2000	Exported
66211	2000	Exported
66212	2000	Exported
66213	2000	Exported
66214	2000	Exported
66215	2000	Exported
66216	2000	Exported
66217	2000	Exported
66218	2000	Exported
66219	2000	Exported
66220	2000	Exported
66221	2000	DB Cargo
66222	2000	Exported
66223	2000	Exported
66224	2000	Exported
66225	2000	Exported
66226	2000	Exported
66227	2000	Exported
66228	2000	Exported
66229	2000	Exported
66230	2000	DB Cargo
66231	2000	Exported
66232	2000	Exported
66233	2000	Exported
66234	2000	Exported
66235	2000	Exported
66236	2000	Exported
66237	2000	Exported
66239	2000	Exported
66240	2000	Exported
66241	2000	Exported
66242	2000	Exported
66243	2000	Exported
66244	2000	Exported
66245	2000	Exported
66246	2000	Exported
66247	2000	Exported
66248	2000	Exported
66249	2000	Exported

66301	2008		Direct Rail Services
66302	2008		Direct Rail Services
66303	2008		Direct Rail Services
66304	2008		Direct Rail Services
66305	2008		Direct Rail Services
66411	2006		Exported
66412	2006		Exported
66413	2006		Freightliner
66414	2006		Freightliner
66415	2006		Freightliner
66416	2006		Freightliner
66417	2006		Exported
66418	2006		Freightliner
66419	2006		Freightliner
66420	2006		Freightliner
66421	2007		Direct Rail Services
66422	2007		Direct Rail Services
66423	2007		Direct Rail Services
66424	2007		Direct Rail Services
66425	2007		Direct Rail Services
66426	2007		Direct Rail Services
66427	2007		Direct Rail Services
66428	2007		Direct Rail Services
66429	2007		Direct Rail Services
66430	2007		Direct Rail Services
66431	2008		Direct Rail Services
66432	2008		Direct Rail Services
66433	2008		Direct Rail Services
66434	2008		Direct Rail Services
66501	1999		Freightliner
66502	1999		Freightliner
66503	1999		Freightliner
66504	1999		Freightliner
66505	1999		Freightliner
66506	2000		Freightliner
66507	2000		Freightliner
66508	2000		Freightliner
66509	2000		Freightliner
66510	2000		Freightliner
66511	2000		Freightliner
66512	2000		Freightliner
66513	2000		Freightliner
66514	2000		Freightliner
66515	2000		Freightliner
66516	2000		Freightliner
66517	2000		Freightliner
66518	2000		Freightliner
66519	2000		Freightliner
66520	2000		Freightliner
66521	2000	2001	2006: C F Booth, Rotherham
66522	2000		Freightliner
66523	2000		Freightliner
66524	2000		Freightliner
66525	2000		Freightliner
66526	2001		Freightliner
66527	2001		Exported
66528	2001		Freightliner
66529	2001		Freightliner
66530	2001		Exported
66531	2001		Freightliner
66532	2001		Freightliner
66533	2001		Freightliner
66534	2001		Freightliner
66535	2001		Exported

66536	2001	Freightliner
66537	2001	Freightliner
66538	2001	Freightliner
66539	2001	Freightliner
66540	2001	Freightliner
66541	2001	Freightliner
66542	2001	Freightliner
66543	2001	Freightliner
66544	2001	Freightliner
66545	2001	Freightliner
66546	2001	Freightliner
66547	2001	Freightliner
66548	2001	Freightliner
66549	2001	Freightliner
66550	2001	Freightliner
66551	2001	Freightliner
66552	2001	Freightliner
66553	2001	Freightliner
66554	2002	Freightliner
66555	2002	Freightliner
66556	2002	Freightliner
66557	2002	Freightliner
66558	2002	Freightliner
66559	2002	Freightliner
66560	2002	Freightliner
66561	2002	Freightliner
66562	2002	Freightliner
66563	2003	Freightliner
66564	2003	Freightliner
66565	2003	Freightliner
66566	2003	Freightliner

▲ On 28 March 2018, 66782 makes its way along the Rylstone branch and towards Skipton with a loaded limestone train from Swinden Quarry that is destined for the Hunslet Tilcon terminal to the east of Leeds.
Liam Barnes

66567	2003	Freightliner
66568	2003	Freightliner
66569	2003	Freightliner
66570	2003	Freightliner
66571	2003	Freightliner
66572	2003	Freightliner
66582	2007	Exported
66583	2007	Exported
66584	2007	Exported
66585	2007	Freightliner
66586	2007	Exported
66587	2007	Freightliner
66588	2007	Freightliner
66589	2007	Freightliner
66590	2007	Freightliner
66591	2007	Freightliner
66592	2007	Freightliner
66593	2007	Freightliner
66594	2007	Freightliner
66595	2008	Exported
66596	2008	Freightliner
66597	2008	Freightliner
66598	2008	Freightliner
66599	2008	Freightliner
66601	2000	Freightliner
66602	2000	Freightliner
66603	2000	Freightliner
66604	2000	Freightliner
66605	2000	Freightliner
66606	2000	Freightliner
66607	2002	Freightliner
66608	2002	Exported
66609	2002	Exported
66610	2002	Freightliner
66611	2002	Exported
66612	2002	Exported
66613	2003	Freightliner
66614	2003	Freightliner
66615	2003	Freightliner
66616	2003	Freightliner
66617	2003	Freightliner
66618	2003	Freightliner
66619	2005	Freightliner
66620	2005	Freightliner
66621	2005	Freightliner
66622	2005	Freightliner
66623	2007	Freightliner
66624	2007	Exported
66625	2007	Exported
66701	2001	GB Railfreight
66702	2001	GB Railfreight
66703	2001	GB Railfreight
66704	2001	GB Railfreight
66705	2001	GB Railfreight
66706	2001	GB Railfreight
66707	2001	GB Railfreight
66708	2002	GB Railfreight
66709	2002	GB Railfreight
66710	2002	GB Railfreight
66711	2002	GB Railfreight
66712	2002	GB Railfreight
66713	2003	GB Railfreight
66714	2003	GB Railfreight
66715	2003	GB Railfreight

66716			2003		GB Railfreight
66717			2003		GB Railfreight
66718			2006		GB Railfreight
66719			2006		GB Railfreight
66720			2006		GB Railfreight
66721			2006		GB Railfreight
66722			2006		GB Railfreight
66723			2006		GB Railfreight
66724			2006		GB Railfreight
66725			2006		GB Railfreight
66726			2006		GB Railfreight
66727			2006		GB Railfreight
66728			2008		GB Railfreight
66729			2008		GB Railfreight
66730			2008		GB Railfreight
66731			2008		GB Railfreight
66732			2008		GB Railfreight
66733	66401		2003		GB Railfreight
66734	66402		2003	2012	2013: Lineside at Loch Treig
66735	66403		2003		GB Railfreight
66736	66404		2003		GB Railfreight
66737	66405		2003		GB Railfreight
66738	66578		2005		GB Railfreight
66739	66579		2005		GB Railfreight
66740	66580		2005		GB Railfreight
66741	66581		2005		GB Railfreight
66742	66841	66406	2003		GB Railfreight
66743	66842	66407	2003		GB Railfreight
66744	66843	66408	2003		GB Railfreight
66745	66844	66409	2003		GB Railfreight
66746	66845	66410	2003		GB Railfreight
66747			2012		GB Railfreight
66748			2012		GB Railfreight
66749			2012		GB Railfreight
66750			2013		GB Railfreight
66751			2013		GB Railfreight
66752			2014		GB Railfreight
66753			2014		GB Railfreight
66754			2014		GB Railfreight
66755			2014		GB Railfreight
66756			2014		GB Railfreight
66757			2014		GB Railfreight
66758			2014		GB Railfreight
66759			2014		GB Railfreight
66760			2014		GB Railfreight
66761			2014		GB Railfreight
66762			2014		GB Railfreight
66763			2014		GB Railfreight
66764			2014		GB Railfreight
66765			2014		GB Railfreight
66766			2014		GB Railfreight
66767			2014		GB Railfreight
66768			2014		GB Railfreight
66769			2014		GB Railfreight
66770			2014		GB Railfreight
66771			2014		GB Railfreight
66772			2014		GB Railfreight
66773			2016		GB Railfreight
66774			2016		GB Railfreight
66775			2016		GB Railfreight
66776			2016		GB Railfreight
66777			2016		GB Railfreight
66778			2016		GB Railfreight
66779			2016		GB Railfreight

66780	66008	1998	GB Railfreight	
66781	66016	1998	GB Railfreight	
66782	66046	1999	GB Railfreight	
66783	66058	1999	GB Railfreight	
66784	66081	1999	GB Railfreight	
66785	66132	1999	GB Railfreight	
66786	66141	1999	GB Railfreight	
66787	66184	1999	GB Railfreight	
66788	66238	2000	GB Railfreight	
66789	66250	2000	GB Railfreight	
66790	T66 403	2018	GB Railfreight	c)
66791	T66 404	2019	GB Railfreight	d)
66792	T66 405	2019	GB Railfreight	d)
66793	29004	2021	GB Railfreight	e)
66794	29005	2021	GB Railfreight	e)
66795	561-05	2021	GB Railfreight	f)
66796	513-10	2021	GB Railfreight	g)
66797	513-09	2021	GB Railfreight	f)
66846	66573	2003	Colas Rail	
66847	66574	2003	Colas Rail	
66848	66575	2004	Colas Rail	
66849	66576	2004	Colas Rail	
66850	66577	2004	Colas Rail	
66951		2004	Freightliner	
66952		2004	Freightliner	
66953		2008	Freightliner	
66954		2008	Exported	
66955		2008	Freightliner	
66956		2008	Freightliner	
66957		2008	Freightliner	

a) DB Cargo locomotive on hire to DRS
b) Stored at Longport after derailment accident
c) Locomotive imported from Sweden in 2018
d) Locomotive imported from Sweden in 2019
e) Locomotive imported from Germany during 2020
f) Locomotive imported from Germany during 2021
g) Locomotive due to be imported during 2021

CLASS 67   Bo-Bo

Built: 1999–2000 by Alstom, Valencia, Spain.
Engine: GM 12N-710G3B-EC two stroke of 2460 kW (3300 hp) at 904 rpm.
Transmission: Electric.
Maximum Speed: 125 mph.
Train Heating/Supply: Electric.
Train Brakes: Air.

Latest Number Carried	Previous Number 1	Year Entered Service	Year Withdrawn	Current Status/Scrapping Details	Notes
67001		2000		DB Cargo	
67002		2000		DB Cargo	
67003		1999		DB Cargo	
67004		2000		DB Cargo	
67005		2000		DB Cargo	
67006		2000		DB Cargo	
67007		2000		DB Cargo	
67008		2000		Transport for Wales	a)
67009		2000		DB Cargo	
67010		2000		Transport for Wales	a)
67011		2000		DB Cargo	
67012		2000		DB Cargo	
67013		2000		DB Cargo	

67014	2000	DB Cargo	
67015	2000	DB Cargo	
67016	2000	DB Cargo	
67017	2000	Transport for Wales	a)
67018	2000	DB Cargo	
67019	2000	DB Cargo	
67020	2000	DB Cargo	
67021	2000	DB Cargo	
67022	2000	DB Cargo	
67023	2000	Colas Rail	
67024	2000	DB Cargo	
67025	2000	Transport for Wales	a)
67026	2000	DB Cargo	
67027	2000	Colas Rail	
67028	2000	DB Cargo	
67029	2000	DB Cargo	
67030	2000	DB Cargo	

a)   DB Cargo locomotive on hire to Transport for Wales

▲ With 67006 "Royal Sovereign" out of sight on the front, 67026 "Diamond Jubilee" brings up the rear of the 07.15 London Victoria–Runcorn on 14 April 2012. This special service was running in connection with the Grand National and is seen passing Old Linslade on the West Coast Main Line.

Geoff Plumb

CLASS 68 Bo-Bo

Built: 2012–17 by Vossloh, Valencia, Spain.
Engine: Caterpillar C175-16 of 2800 kW (3750 hp) at 1740 rpm.
Transmission: Electric.
Maximum Speed: 100 mph.
Train Heating/Supply: Electric.
Train Brakes: Air.

Latest Number Carried	Previous Number 1	Year Entered Service	Year Withdrawn	Current Status/Scrapping Details	Notes
68001		2014		Direct Rail Services	
68002		2014		Direct Rail Services	
68003		2014		Direct Rail Services	
68004		2014		Direct Rail Services	
68005		2014		Direct Rail Services	
68006		2014		Direct Rail Services	
68007		2014		Direct Rail Services	
68008		2014		Direct Rail Services	
68009		2014		Direct Rail Services	
68010		2014		Direct Rail Services	
68011		2014		Direct Rail Services	
68012		2014		Direct Rail Services	
68013		2014		Direct Rail Services	
68014		2014		Direct Rail Services	
68015		2014		Direct Rail Services	
68016		2015		Direct Rail Services	
68017		2015		Direct Rail Services	
68018		2015		Direct Rail Services	
68019		2015		TransPennine Express	
68020		2016		TransPennine Express	
68021		2016		TransPennine Express	
68022		2016		TransPennine Express	
68023		2016		TransPennine Express	
68024		2016		TransPennine Express	
68025		2016		TransPennine Express	
68026		2017		TransPennine Express	
68027		2017		TransPennine Express	
68028		2017		TransPennine Express	
68029		2017		TransPennine Express	
68030		2017		TransPennine Express	
68031		2017		TransPennine Express	
68032		2017		TransPennine Express	
68033		2017		Direct Rail Services	a)
68034		2017		Direct Rail Services	a)

a)   TransPennine Express spare locomotive

CLASS 69 Co-Co

Built: 1976–84 by Electroputere, Craiova, Romania and BREL, Crewe & Doncaster as Class 56 (see Class 56) and converted to Class 69 2019–2021 by ElectroMotive Diesel Services, Longport.
Engine: General Motors 12N-710G3B-T2 two stroke of 2385 kW (3200 hp) at 904 rpm.
Transmission: Electric.
Maximum Speed: 75 mph.
Train Heating / Supply: None.
Train Brakes: Air.

Latest Number Carried	Previous Number 1	Year Entered Service	Year Withdrawn	Current Status/Scrapping Details	Notes
69001	56031	N/A		GB Railfreight	a)
69002	56311	N/A		GB Railfreight	a)
69003	56018	N/A		GB Railfreight	a)
69004	56069	N/A		GB Railfreight	a)

▲ Before it was acquired by Colas Rail in 2016, 67027 was branded with the unmissable red of DB Schenker (now DB Cargo). It leaves Bradford Interchange with the 16.16 Leeds–Hebden Bridge additional service in connection with a cycling event that took place on 7 June 2014. **Gavin Morrison**

▼ 68008 is one of the eight Direct Rail Services-owned locomotives (68008–68015) that regularly ply their trade on the Chiltern route between London and the West Midlands. On 17 September 2020, it passes Kings Sutton with the 16.15 London Marylebone–Kidderminster. **Ken Davies**

69005	56007 (TBC)	N/A	GB Railfreight	a)
69006	56128 (TBC)	N/A	GB Railfreight	a)
69007	56037 (TBC)	N/A	GB Railfreight	a)
69008	56038 (TBC)	N/A	GB Railfreight	a)
69009	56060 (TBC)	N/A	GB Railfreight	a)
69010	56065 (TBC)	N/A	GB Railfreight	a)

a)   Due to enter service in 2021

CLASS 70   DIESEL   Co-Co

Built: 2009–17 by General Electric, Erie, Pennsylvania, USA and TULOMSAS, Eskisehir, Turkey (70801).
Engine: General Electric Powerhaul P616LDA1 of 2848 kW (3820 hp) at 1500 rpm.
Transmission: Electric.
Maximum Speed: 75mph.
Train Heating / Supply: None.
Train Brakes: Air.

Latest Number Carried	Previous Number 1	Year Entered Service	Year Withdrawn	Current Status/Scrapping Details	Notes
70001		2009		Freightliner	
70002		2009		Freightliner	
70003		2009		Freightliner	
70004		2009		Freightliner	
70005		2009		Freightliner	
70006		2009		Freightliner	
70007		2011		Freightliner	
70008		2011		Freightliner	
70009		2011		Freightliner	
70010		2011		Freightliner	
70011		2011		Freightliner	
70012		n/a		Exported	a)
70013		2011		Freightliner	
70014		2011		Freightliner	
70015		2011		Freightliner	
70016		2011		Freightliner	
70017		2012		Freightliner	
70018		2012		Freightliner	
70019		2012		Freightliner	
70020		2012		Freightliner	
70801	70099	2012		Colas Rail	
70802		2014		Colas Rail	
70803		2014		Colas Rail	
70804		2014		Colas Rail	
70805		2014		Colas Rail	
70806		2014		Colas Rail	
70807		2014		Colas Rail	
70808		2014		Colas Rail	
70809		2014		Colas Rail	
70810		2014		Colas Rail	
70811		2017		Colas Rail	
70812		2017		Colas Rail	
70813		2017		Colas Rail	
70814		2017		Colas Rail	
70815		2017		Colas Rail	
70816		2017		Colas Rail	
70817		2017		Colas Rail	

a)   Damaged during unloading in 2011 and returned to USA

▲ 69001 breaks new ground on 15 February 2021 as it undergoes the first test working of the new class. The former 56031 passes Northwood Lane while hauling a Shark brakevan between Kidderminster and Highley on the Severn Valley Railway. **Jack Boskett**

▼ Freightliner's 70001 passes Slindon in Staffordshire with the 13.00 intermodal service from Southampton to Trafford Park on 14 September 2020. **Andy Chard**

3. ELECTRIC LOCOMOTIVES

3.1. ELECTRIC LOCOMOTIVES WITH PRE-TOPS CLASSIFICATION

CLASS ES1   Bo-Bo

Built: 1903 by North Eastern Railway.
Electric Supply System: 600 V DC overhead or third rail.
Power Output: 477 kW (640 hp).
Maximum Speed: 25 mph.
Train Heating/Supply: None.

Latest Number Carried	Previous Number 1	Previous Number 2	Year Entered Service	Year Withdrawn	Current Status/Scrapping Details	Notes
26500	6480	1	1903	1964	Preserved	
26501	6481	2	1903	1964	1966: W Willoughby, Choppington	

CLASS EB1   Bo-Bo

Built: 1915–20 by North Eastern Railway.
Electric Supply System: 1500 V DC overhead.
Power Output: 205 kW (1100 hp).
Maximum Speed: 45 mph.
Train Heating/Supply: None.

Latest Number Carried	Previous Number 1	Previous Number 2	Year Entered Service	Year Withdrawn	Current Status/Scrapping Details	Notes
26502	6490		1915	1950	1951: Wanty & Co, Sheffield	
26503	6491		1915	1950	1951: Wanty & Co, Sheffield	
26504	6492		1915	1950	1950: Darlington Works	
26505	6493		1915	1950	1951: Wanty & Co, Sheffield	
26506	6494		1915	1950	1951: Wanty & Co, Sheffield	
26507	6495		1915	1950	1951: Wanty & Co, Sheffield	
26508	6496		1915	1950	1951: Wanty & Co, Sheffield	
26509	6497		1915	1950	1951: Wanty & Co, Sheffield	
100	26510	6498	1915	1950	1964: Doncaster Works	
26511	6499		1920	1950	1951: Wanty & Co, Sheffield	
26600	26999	6999	1922	1950	1951: Wanty & Co, Sheffield	

▲ The North Eastern Railway's two Class ES1 DC electric locomotives were built in 1903, making them the oldest entries within this book. 26501 is seen at Trafalgar Yard in Manors, Newcastle on 2 October 1963, 60 years after it entered service and less than a year before it would be withdrawn. Its primary duty was moving freight between there and Newcastle Quayside Yard.

Neville Simms/Ranwell Collection/Rail Photoprints

▼ Many decades before its American-built diesel namesake was conceived, the Class 70 was an early electric class that could draw power from the third rail or overhead electric wires. 20002 is seen stabled at Redhill on 21 December 1968; it would be withdrawn the next day and be scrapped by J Cashmore of Newport in September 1969. **Ronald F. Collen-Jones/Rail Photoprints**

3.2. ELECTRIC LOCOMOTIVES WITH TOPS CLASSIFICATION

CLASS 70   ELECTRIC   Co-Co

Built: 1941–48 by Southern Railway, Ashford and British Railways, Brighton.
Electric Supply System: 660–750 V DC third rail or overhead.
Power Output: 1097 kW (1470 hp).
Maximum Speed: 75 mph.
Train Heating/Supply: Steam heating.
Train Brakes: Vacuum.

Latest Number Carried	Previous Number 1	Year Entered Service	Year Withdrawn	Current Status/Scrapping Details	Notes
20001	CC1	1941	1969	1969: J Cashmore, Newport	
20002	CC2	1945	1968	1969: J Cashmore, Newport	
20003		1948	1968	1969: G Cohen, Kettering	

CLASS 71   Bo-Bo

Built: 1958–60 by British Railways, Doncaster Works.
Electric Supply System: 660–750 V DC third rail or overhead.
Power Output: 1715 kW (2300 hp).
Maximum Speed: 90 mph.
Train Heating/Supply: Electric.
Train Brakes: Dual braked (air & vacuum).

Latest Number Carried	Previous Number 1	Previous Number 2	Year Entered Service	Year Withdrawn	Current Status/Scrapping Details	Notes
E5024	E5000		1958	1968	Converted to Class 74 E6104 in 1968	
71001	E5001		1959	1977	Preserved	
71002	E5002		1959	1977	1979: J Cashmore, Newport	
E5003[1]			1959	1968	Converted to Class 74 E6107 in 1968	a)
71004	E5004		1959	1977	1980: Doncaster Works	
E5005[1]			1959	1968	Converted to Class 74 E6108 in 1968	b)
E5006[1]			1959	1967	Converted to Class 74 E6103 in 1967	c)
71007	E5007		1959	1977	1978: J Cashmore, Newport	
71008	E5008		1959	1977	1978: J Cashmore, Newport	
71009	E5009		1959	1977	1979: Doncaster Works	
71010	E5010		1959	1977	1979: Doncaster Works	
71011	E5011		1959	1977	1979: Doncaster Works	
71012	E5012		1959	1977	1978: J Cashmore, Newport	
71013	E5013		1959	1977	1979: Doncaster Works	
71014	E5014		1960	1977	1979: Doncaster Works	
E5015			1960	1968	Converted to Class 74 E6101 in 1968	
E5016			1960	1967	Converted to Class 74 E6102 in 1967	
E5017			1960	1968	Converted to Class 74 E6109 in 1968	
71003	E5003[2]	E5018	1960	1977	1980: Doncaster Works	d)
E5019			1960	1968	Converted to Class 74 E6105 in 1968	
71005	E5005[2]	E5020	1960	1977	1978: J Cashmore, Newport	e)
E5021			1960	1968	Converted to Class 74 E6110 in 1968	
71006	E5006[2]	E5022	1960	1977	1978: J Cashmore, Newport	f)
E5023			1960	1968	Converted to Class 74 E6106 in 1968	

a)   First of 2 locomotives to be numbered E5003
b)   First of 2 locomotives to be numbered E5005
c)   First of 2 locomotives to be numbered E5006
d)   Second of 2 locomotives to be numbered E5003
e)   Second of 2 locomotives to be numbered E5005
f)   Second of 2 locomotives to be numbered E5006

▲ From left to right 71003, 71010 and 71011 are seen to the west of Ashford in July 1977. The trio had been there since February 1977 and would lay dormant until they were formally withdrawn in November 1977. By mid-1977, a handful of the class had already been withdrawn and the remainder would follow before the year ended. **Ian Mortimer**

▼ The sole surviving Class 71 E5001 belongs to the National Collection of preserved railway vehicles. On 12 September 1992, it returned to the main line, working Hertfordshire Railtours' "Royal Wessex" which made a return trip from London Waterloo to Bournemouth; the charter is seen passing St Denys. **Gavin Morrison**

CLASS 73   Bo-Bo

Built: 1962–67 by British Railways, Eastleigh Works (73001–73006) and English Electric, Vulcan Foundry, Newton-le-Willows (all except 73001–73006).
Diesel Engine: English Electric 4SRKT of 447 kW (600 hp) at 850 rpm.
Electric Supply System: 660–750 V DC third rail.
Power Output: Electric 1060 kW (1420 hp).
Maximum Speed: 80 mph.
Train Heating/Supply: Electric.
Train Brakes: Triple braked (air, vacuum and electro-pneumatic).

Class 73/0

Latest Number Carried	Previous Number 1	Previous Number 2	Previous Number 3	Year Entered Service	Year Withdrawn	Current Status/Scrapping Details	Notes
73001	73901	73001	E6001	1962	2000	Locomotive Services	
73002	E6002			1962	1995	Locomotive Services	
73003	E6003			1962	1996	Preserved	
73004	E6004			1962	1991	2004: EMR, Kingsbury	
73005	E6005			1962	2015	Converted to 73966 in 2015	

Class 73/1
Details as Class 73/0 except:

Maximum Speed: 90 mph.

Latest Number Carried	Previous Number 1	Previous Number 2	Previous Number 3	Year Entered Service	Year Withdrawn	Current Status/Scrapping Details	Notes
73101	73100	73101	E6007	1965		GB Railfreight	
73103	E6009			1965	2016	Converted to 73970 in 2016	
73104	E6010			1965	2015	Converted to 73951 in 2015	
73105	E6011			1965	2016	Converted to 73969 in 2016	
73106	E6012			1965	2000	2004: C F Booth, Rotherham	
73107	E6013			1965		GB Railfreight	
73108	E6014			1966	2002	2004: C F Booth, Rotherham	
73109	E6015			1966		GB Railfreight	
73110	E6016			1966		GB Railfreight	
73111	E6017			1966	1991	1997: Stewarts Lane Depot	
73114	E6020			1966		Nemesis Rail	
73115	E6021			1966	1982	1982: Selhurst Depot	
73117	E6023			1966	2015	Converted to 73968 in 2015	
73118	E6024			1966		Preserved	
73119	E6025			1966		GB Railfreight	
E6027				1966	1972	1973: Slade Green Depot	
73126	E6033			1966	1999	2009: C F Booth, Rotherham	
73128	E6035			1966		GB Railfreight	
73129	E6036			1966	2002	Preserved	
73130	E6037			1966		Preserved	
73131	E6038			1966	2003	2004: C F Booth, Rotherham	
73132	E6039			1966	2003	2006: Ron Hull Jr, Rotherham	
73133	E6040			1966		Transmart Trains	
73134	E6041			1966		GB Railfreight	
73136	E6043			1966		GB Railfreight	
73138	E6045			1966		Network Rail	
73139	E6046			1966		GB Railfreight	
73140	E6047			1966	1998	Preserved	
73141	E6048			1966		GB Railfreight	
73201	73142	E6049		1967		GB Railfreight	
73202	73137	E6044		1966		Southern	
73203	73127	E6034		1966	2001	2010: Sims Metals, Halesowen	
73204	73125	E6032		1966	2014	Converted to 73962 in 2014	
73205	73124	E6031		1966	2015	Converted to 73964 in 2015	
73206	73123	E6030		1966	2014	Converted to 73963 in 2014	
73207	73122	E6029		1966	2016	Converted to 73971 in 2016	
73208	73121	E6028		1966	2015	Converted to 73965 in 2015	

▲ After being confined to BR's Southern Region for decades, Class 73s now make periodic visits to the North-West on test train duties. On 28 August 2017, GB Railfreight's 73961 (front) & 73963 pass Mobberley on the mid-Cheshire Line, while working the 13.13 Derby RTC–Crewe.　**Ken Davies**

▼ 73142 and two parcel vans sit in the once extensive Bricklayers Arms Goods Depot on 11 March 1978. This location was accessed by a spur which began near South Bermondsey station and ran east for over a mile. The depot and spur closed in 1981.　**Ian Mortimer**

73209	73120	E6026	1966	2014	Converted to 73961 in 2014
73210	73116	E6022	1966	2002	Preserved
73211	73113	E6019	1966	2014	Converted to 73952 in 2014
73212	73102	E6008	1965		GB Railfreight
73213	73112	E6018	1966		GB Railfreight
73235	73135	E6042	1966		South Western Railway
73906	73006	E6006	1962	2015	Converted to 73967 in 2015

Class 73/9 (RVEL)

Rebuilt: 2013–15 by RVEL Derby.
Diesel Engine: Two Cummins QSK19 of 560 kW (750 hp) at 1800 rpm (total 1120 kW, 1500 hp).
Electric Supply System: 750 V DC Third Rail.
Power Output: Electric 1060 kW (1420 hp).
Train Heating/Supply: Not fitted.
Train Brakes: Air.

Latest Number Carried	Previous Number 1	Year Entered Service	Year Withdrawn	Current Status/Scrapping Details	Notes
73951	73104	2015		Network Rail	
73952	73211	2014		Network Rail	

Class 73/9 (GBRf)

Rebuilt: 2014–16 by Brush, Loughborough.
Diesel Engine: MTU 8V4000 R43L of 1195 kW (1600 hp) at 1800 rpm.
Electric Supply System: 750 V DC Third Rail.
Power Output: Electric 1060 kW (1420 hp).
Train Heating/Supply: Electric.
Train Brakes: Air.

Latest Number Carried	Previous Number 1	Year Entered Service	Year Withdrawn	Current Status/Scrapping Details	Notes
73961	73209	2014		GB Railfreight	
73962	73204	2014		GB Railfreight	
73963	73206	2014		GB Railfreight	
73964	73205	2015		GB Railfreight	
73965	73208	2015		GB Railfreight	
73966	73005	2015		GB Railfreight	
73967	73906	2015		GB Railfreight	
73968	73117	2015		GB Railfreight	
73969	73105	2016		GB Railfreight	
73970	73103	2016		GB Railfreight	
73971	73207	2016		GB Railfreight	

CLASS 74

10 Locomotives were converted from Class 71 locomotives to Class 74 electro-diesel locomotives. Overhead supply equipment removed.

Technical details as Class 71 except:
Conversions Completed: 1967–68
Engine: Paxman 6YJXL of 485 kW (650 hp).

Latest Number Carried	Previous Number 1	Year Entered Service	Year Withdrawn	Current Status/Scrapping Details	Notes
74001	E6101	1968	1977	1978: Bird Group, Long Marston	
74002	E6102	1967	1977	1977: J Cashmore, Newport	
74003	E6103	1967	1977	1981: J Cashmore, Newport	
74004	E6104	1968	1977	1978: Bird Group, Long Marston	
74005	E6105	1968	1977	1981: Fratton Depot	
74006	E6106	1968	1976	1977: G Cohen, Kettering	
74007	E6107	1968	1977	1978: Bird Group, Long Marston	
74008	E6108	1968	1977	1978: Bird Group, Long Marston	
74009	E6109	1968	1977	1978: Bird Group, Long Marston	
74010	E6110	1968	1977	1979: Doncaster Works	

▲ The electro-diesel Class 74s were created when ten Class 71s had their overhead electric equipment removed and Paxman engines fitted. 74004 passes through Southampton on 15 October 1977; to its left 31421 approaches with the 09.19 Bristol Temple Meads–Portsmouth Harbour.

Stephen C Marshall

▼ 76023 & 73010 wait in Tinsley Yard, before taking over "The Pennine Rambler" railtour, which they will escort across the Pennines via the Woodhead Route on 7 October 1978. **Gordon Edgar**

CLASS 76 Bo+Bo

Built: 1941–53 by LNER at Doncaster Works and British Railways, Gorton Works.
Electric Supply System: 1500V DC overhead.
Power Output: 970 kW (1300 hp).
Maximum Speed: 65 mph.
Train Heating/Supply: E26000/E26050–057 were built with steam heating. It was also later fitted to E26020/E26046–049.
Train Brakes: Built vacuum braked some were later converted to air or dual (air & vacuum).

C1 One cab remains
UL Scrapping details unconfirmed, but likely to be correct

Latest Number Carried	Previous Number 1	Previous Number 2	Year Entered Service	Year Withdrawn	Current Status/Scrapping Details	Notes
26000	6000	6701	1941	1970	1972: Crewe Works	UL
76001	26001		1950	1980	1983: C F Booth, Rotherham	
76002	26002		1950	1978	1984: C F Booth, Rotherham	
76003²	76036¹	26036	1952	1981	1983: Vic Berry, Leicester	a)
76004	26004		1951	1978	1984: C F Booth, Rotherham	
26005			1951	1970	1971: Crewe Works	
76006	26006		1951	1981	1983: C F Booth, Rotherham	
76007	26007		1951	1981	1983: C F Booth, Rotherham	
76008	26008		1951	1981	1983: C F Booth, Rotherham	
76009	26009		1951	1981	1983: C F Booth, Rotherham	
76010	26010		1951	1981	1983: C F Booth, Rotherham	
76011	26011		1951	1981	1983: C F Booth, Rotherham	
76012	26012		1951	1981	1983: C F Booth, Rotherham	
76013	26013		1951	1981	1983: C F Booth, Rotherham	
76014	26014		1951	1981	1983: C F Booth, Rotherham	
76015	26015		1951	1981	1983: C F Booth, Rotherham	
76016	26016		1951	1981	1983: C F Booth, Rotherham	
26017			1951	1970	1971: Reddish Depot	UL
26019			1951	1971	1972: Crewe Works	
76020	26020		1951	1977	Preserved	
76021	26021		1951	1981	1983: C F Booth, Rotherham	
76022	26022		1951	1981	1983: C F Booth, Rotherham	
76023	26023		1951	1981	1983: C F Booth, Rotherham	
76024	26024		1951	1981	1983: C F Booth, Rotherham	
76025	26025		1952	1981	1983: C F Booth, Rotherham	
76026	26026		1952	1981	1983: C F Booth, Rotherham	
76027	26027		1952	1981	1983: C F Booth, Rotherham	
76028	26028		1952	1981	1983: C F Booth, Rotherham	
76029	26029		1951	1981	1983: Coopers Metals, Sheffield	
76030	26030		1951	1971	1983: C F Booth, Rotherham	
26031			1952	1981	1972: Crewe Works	
76031	76044	26044	1952	1981	1984: Coopers Metals, Sheffield	
76032	26032		1952	1981	1983: Coopers Metals, Sheffield	
76033	26033		1952	1981	1983: Coopers Metals, Sheffield	
76034	26034		1952	1981	1983: C F Booth, Rotherham	
26035			1952	1970	1971: Reddish Depot	UL
76035	76018	26018	1951	1981	1983: C F Booth, Rotherham	
76036²	76003¹	26003	1950	1981	1983: C F Booth, Rotherham	b)
76037	26037		1952	1981	1983: Vic Berry, Leicester	
76038²	76050	26050	1952	1981	1983: C F Booth, Rotherham	c)
76039²	76048¹	26048	1952	1981	1983: C F Booth, Rotherham	C1 d)
76040	26040		1952	1981	1983: Vic Berry, Leicester	
76041	26041		1952	1980	1983: C F Booth, Rotherham	
26042			1952	1970	1971: Reddish Depot	UL
76043	26043		1952	1978	1984: C F Booth, Rotherham	
26045			1952	1971	1972: Crewe Works	
76046	26046		1952	1980	1983: C F Booth, Rotherham	
76047	26047		1952	1980	1983: C F Booth, Rotherham	
76048²	76039¹	26039	1952	1977	1984: C F Booth, Rotherham	C1 e)

76049	26049		1952	1980	1983: C F Booth, Rotherham	
76050	76038[1]	26038	1952	1977	1984: C F Booth, Rotherham	f)
76051	26051		1953	1981	1983: C F Booth, Rotherham	
76052	26052		1953	1978	1984: C F Booth, Rotherham	
76053	26053		1953	1980	1983: C F Booth, Rotherham	
76054	26054		1953	1981	1983: C F Booth, Rotherham	
76055	26055		1953	1977	1984: C F Booth, Rotherham	
76056	26056		1953	1978	1983: Reddish Depot	
76057	26057		1953	1977	1983: Reddish Depot	

a) Second of 2 locomotives to be numbered 76003. First of 2 locomotives to be numbered 76036

b) Second of 2 locomotives to be numbered 76036. First of 2 locomotives to be numbered 76003

c) Second of 2 locomotives to be numbered 76038

d) Second of 2 locomotives to be numbered 76039. First of 2 locomotives to be numbered 76048

e) Second of 2 locomotives to be numbered 76048. First of 2 locomotives to be numbered 76039

f) First of 2 locomotives to be numbered 76038

CLASS 77 (EM2) Co-Co

Built: 1953–54 by British Railways, Gorton Works.
Electric Supply System: 1500V DC overhead.
Power Output: 1716 kW (2300 hp).
Maximum Speed: 90 mph.
Train Heating/Supply: Steam.
Train Brakes: Vacuum.

ES   Locomotive exported and subsequently scrapped

After withdrawal from BR in 1968, all seven locos were exported to the Netherlands where four were subsequently scrapped. Two later returned to the UK, where they are now preserved.

Latest Number Carried	Previous Number 1	Previous Number 2	Year Entered Service	Year Withdrawn	Current Status/Scrapping Details	Notes
1502	E27000	27000	1953	1968	Preserved	
1505	E27001	27001	1954	1968	Preserved	
1506	E27002	27002	1954	1968	1985: Tilburg Works, Netherlands	ES
1501	E27003	27003	1954	1968	Exported to the Netherlands in 1969	
1503	E27004	27004	1954	1968	1986: Tilburg Works, Netherlands	ES
E27005	27005		1954	1968	1971: Tilburg Works, Netherlands	ES
1504	E27006	27006	1954	1968	1986: Tilburg Works, Netherlands	ES

CLASS 81 Bo-Bo

Built: 1959–64 by Birmingham Railway Carriage and Wagon Company.
Electric Supply System: 25 kV AC overhead.
Power Output: 2390 kW (3200 hp).
Maximum Speed: 100 mph.
Train Heating/Supply: Electric.
Train Brakes: Built vacuum braked, most converted to dual braked (air & vacuum brakes).

Latest Number Carried	Previous Number 1	Previous Number 2	Year Entered Service	Year Withdrawn	Current Status/Scrapping Details	Notes
81001	E3001		1959	1984	1986: Crewe Works	
E3002			1960	1968	1969: Crewe Works	
81002	E3003		1960	1990	Preserved	
81003	E3004		1960	1988	1992: Coopers Metals, Attercliffe	
81004	E3005		1960	1990	1992: MC Metals, Glasgow	
81005	E3006		1960	1989	1992: Coopers Metals, Attercliffe	
81006	E3007		1960	1988	1992: Coopers Metals, Attercliffe	
81007	E3008		1960	1989	1992: Coopers Metals, Attercliffe	

▲ BR sold all seven of the Class 77s to the Dutch national operator Nederlandse Spoorwegen and they were exported in 1968. 1503, which is the former E27004, stops at Eindhoven with a Rotterdam to Venlo express service on 15 July 1972. The locomotive was later withdrawn and scrapped at Tilberg Works in the Netherlands. **Gordon Edgar**

▼ 81002 approaches Crewe Basford Hall with a BOC tank train on 31 May 1983. **Gavin Morrison**

E3009			1960	1968	1968: Crewe Works
81008	E3010		1960	1988	1991: Coopers Metals, Attercliffe
81009	E3011		1960	1990	1992: Coopers Metals, Attercliffe
81010	E3012		1960	1990	1992: Coopers Metals, Attercliffe
81011	E3013		1960	1989	1991: Coopers Metals, Attercliffe
81012	E3014		1960	1991	1992: Coopers Metals, Attercliffe
81013	E3015		1960	1989	1991: Coopers Metals, Attercliffe
81014	E3016		1961	1988	1991: Coopers Metals, Attercliffe
81015	E3017		1961	1984	1992: MC Metals, Glasgow
81016	E3018		1961	1983	1985: Crewe Works
E3019			1961	1971	1971: Crewe Works
81017	E3020		1961	1991	1992: Coopers Metals, Attercliffe
81018	E3021		1961	1986	1992: MC Metals, Glasgow
81019	E3022		1961	1989	1991: Coopers Metals, Attercliffe
81020	E3023		1961	1987	1991: Coopers Metals, Attercliffe
81021	E3096	E3301	1962	1987	1992: MC Metals, Glasgow
81022	E3097		1964	1987	1988: Crewe Works

CLASS 82   Bo-Bo

Built: 1960–62 by Beyer Peacock & Co., Manchester
Electric Supply System: 25 kV AC overhead.
Power Output: 2460 kW (3300 hp).
Maximum Speed: 100 mph.
Train Heating/Supply: Electric.
Train Brakes: Built vacuum braked, most converted to dual braked (air & vacuum).

UL   Scrapping details unconfirmed, but likely to be correct

Latest Number Carried	Previous Number 1	Year Entered Service	Year Withdrawn	Current Status/Scrapping Details	Notes
E3046		1960	1971	1971: Crewe Works	
82001	E3047	1960	1983	1985: Vic Berry, Leicester	
82002	E3048	1960	1983	1984: Vic Berry, Leicester	
82003	E3049	1960	1983	1993: C F Booth, Rotherham	
82004	E3050	1960	1983	1984: Vic Berry, Leicester	
82005	E3051	1960	1987	1993: C F Booth, Rotherham	
82006	E3052	1960	1983	1984: Vic Berry, Leicester	
82007	E3053	1962	1983	1984: Vic Berry, Leicester	
82008	E3054	1961	1987	Preserved	
E3055		1962	1969	1970: Crewe Works	UL

CLASS 83   Bo-Bo

Built: 1960–62 by English Electric, Vulcan Foundry, Newton-le-Willows.
Electric Supply System: 25 kV AC overhead.
Power Output: 2200 kW (2950 hp).
Maximum Speed: 100 mph.
Train Heating/Supply: Electric.
Train Brakes: Built vacuum braked, all converted to dual braked (air & vacuum).

Latest Number Carried	Previous Number 1	Previous Number 2	Year Entered Service	Year Withdrawn	Current Status/Scrapping Details	Notes
83001	E3024		1960	1983	1984: Vic Berry, Leicester	
83002	E3025		1960	1983	1984: Vic Berry, Leicester	
83003	E3026		1960	1975	1975: Crewe Works	
83004	E3027		1960	1978	1978: Willesden Depot	
83005	E3028		1960	1983	1984: Vic Berry, Leicester	
83006	E3029		1960	1983	1984: Vic Berry, Leicester	
83007	E3030		1960	1983	1984: Vic Berry, Leicester	
83008	E3031		1960	1983	1984: Vic Berry, Leicester	
83009	E3032		1960	1989	1993: MC Metals, Glasgow	
83010	E3033		1960	1983	1984: Vic Berry, Leicester	

▲ Prior to becoming Class 84s, the ten North British pilot scheme AC electric locomotives were given the classification AL4. A few months before it was withdrawn, 84003 was captured at Birmingham New Street station on 25 August 1980. **Gavin Morrison**

▼ E3057, which would become 85002 in 1974, arrives at Garston on an unknown date during 1962. It is hauling a consignment of new cars from the nearby Ford plant at Halewood. **Colin Whitfield/Rail Photoprints**

83011	E3034		1961	1983	1984: Vic Berry, Leicester
83012	E3035		1961	1989	Preserved
83013	E3098	E3303	1961	1983	1984: Vic Berry, Leicester
83014	E3099	E3304	1961	1983	1984: Vic Berry, Leicester
83015	E3100		1962	1988	1993: MC Metals, Glasgow

CLASS 84   Bo-Bo

Built: 1960–61 by North British Locomotive Company, Glasgow.
Electric Supply System: 25 kV AC overhead.
Power Output: 2312 kW (3100 hp).
Maximum Speed: 100 mph.
Train Heating/Supply: Electric.
Train Brakes: Built vacuum braked, all converted to dual braked (air & vacuum).

C1   One cab remains
SP   Locomotive was not self-propelled whilst in departmental use

Latest Number Carried	Previous Number 1	Previous Number 2	Year Entered Service	Year Withdrawn	Current Status/Scrapping Details	Notes
84001	E3036		1960	1979	Preserved	
84002	E3037		1960	1980	1982: Texas Metals, Hyde	
84003	E3038		1960	1980	1986: Vic Berry, Leicester	
84004	E3039		1960	1977	1985: Bird Group, Long Marston	
84005	E3040		1960	1977	1985: Bird Group, Long Marston	
84006	E3041		1960	1978	1979: Crewe Gresty Lane Depot	
84007	E3042		1960	1977	1979: Crewe Gresty Lane Depot	
84008	E3043		1960	1979	1988: Crewe Works	
ADB968021	84009	E3044	1960	1995	1995: Gwent Demolition, Margam	C1 SP
84010	E3045		1961	1980	1982: Texas Metals, Hyde	

CLASS 85   Bo-Bo

Built: 1961–64 by British Railways, Doncaster Works.
Electric Supply System: 25 kV AC overhead.
Power Output: 2390 kW (3200 hp).
Maximum Speed: 100 mph.
Train Heating/Supply: Electric.
Train Brakes: Built vacuum braked, all converted to dual braked (air & vacuum).

Latest Number Carried	Previous Number 1	Previous Number 2	Previous Number 3	Year Entered Service	Year Withdrawn	Current Status/Scrapping Details	Notes
85001	E3056			1961	1985	1989: MC Metals, Glasgow	
85002	E3057			1961	1989	1992: MC Metals, Glasgow	
85005	E3060			1961	1990	1993: MC Metals, Glasgow	
85006	85101	85006	E3061	1961	1992	Preserved	
85008	E3063			1961	1990	1993: MC Metals, Glasgow	
85013	E3068			1962	1990	1993: MC Metals, Glasgow	
85014	E3069			1962	1989	1992: MC Metals, Glasgow	
85015	E3070			1962	1990	1992: MC Metals, Glasgow	
85017	E3072			1962	1987	1993: MC Metals, Glasgow	
85018	E3073			1963	1991	1992: MC Metals, Glasgow	
85019	E3074			1962	1989	1990: Vic Berry, Leicester	
85020	E3075			1963	1990	1993: MC Metals, Glasgow	
85022	E3077			1963	1989	1993: MC Metals, Glasgow	
85023	E3078			1963	1990	1992: MC Metals, Glasgow	
85025	E3080			1963	1990	1991: Vic Berry, Leicester	
85026	E3081			1963	1990	1993: MC Metals, Glasgow	
85027	E3082			1963	1983	1985: Crewe Works	
85028	E3083			1963	1990	1994: MC Metals, Glasgow	
85029	E3084			1964	1988	1993: MC Metals, Glasgow	
85030	E3085			1964	1990	1992: MC Metals, Glasgow	
85031	E3086			1962	1990	1992: MC Metals, Glasgow	

85033	E3088		1963	1984	1985: Crewe Works
85034	E3089		1963	1990	1993: MC Metals, Glasgow
85037	E3092		1964	1990	1992: MC Metals, Glasgow
85038	E3093		1963	1990	1992: MC Metals, Glasgow
85039	E3094		1964	1987	1989: MC Metals, Glasgow
85040	E3095		1964	1991	1993: MC Metals, Glasgow
85102	85009	E3064	1961	1991	1992: MC Metals, Glasgow
85103	85010	E3065	1961	1991	1992: MC Metals, Glasgow
85104	85012	E3067	1962	1991	1993: MC Metals, Glasgow
85105	85016	E3071	1962	1991	1992: MC Metals, Glasgow
85106	85021	E3076	1963	1990	1992: MC Metals, Glasgow
85107	85024	E3079	1963	1990	1993: MC Metals, Glasgow
85108	85032	E3087	1962	1991	1992: MC Metals, Glasgow
85109	85035	E3090	1963	1991	1992: MC Metals, Glasgow
85110	85036	E3091	1963	1991	1992: MC Metals, Glasgow
85111	85004	E3059	1961	1990	1992: MC Metals, Glasgow
85112	85007	E3062	1961	1991	1993: MC Metals, Glasgow
85113	85003	E3058	1961	1991	1993: MC Metals, Glasgow
85114	85011	E3066	1962	1991	1993: MC Metals, Glasgow

▲ 86622 & 86613 speed round the curve at Whitmore, Staffordshire with the 06.15 Trafford Park–Felixstowe intermodal service on 21 July 2020. **Brad Joyce**

CLASS 86   Bo-Bo

Built: 1965–66 by British Railways, Doncaster Works and English Electric, Vulcan Foundry, Newton-le-Willows.
Electric Supply System: 25 kV AC overhead.
Power Output: 2680 kW (3600 hp).
Maximum Speed: 100 mph.
Train Heating/Supply: Electric.
Train Brakes: Dual braked (vacuum and air).

C1   One cab remains

Class 86/0
Locos as built to technical specification above. All locos subsequently modified and renumbered - see below.

Class 86/1
Fitted with new bogies.
Details as Class 86/0 except:
Power Output: 5860 kW (5000 hp).
Maximum Speed: 110 mph.

Latest Number Carried	Previous Number 1	Previous Number 2	Year Entered Service	Year Withdrawn	Current Status/Scrapping Details	Notes
86101	86201	E3191	1965		Locomotive Services	
86102	86202	E3150	1966	2002	2005: Ministry of Defence, Caerwent	
86103	86203	E3143	1966	1995	2002: Immingham Railfreight Term.	

Class 86/2
Fitted with flexicoil suspension.
Details as Class 86/0 except:
Power Output: 3010 kW (4040 hp).

Latest Number Carried	Previous Number 1	Previous Number 2	Previous Number 3	Previous Number 4	Year Entered Service	Year Withdrawn	Scrapping Details/Current Status	Notes
86204	E3173				1965	1998	2003: Immingham Railfreight Term.	
86206	E3184				1965	2002	2004: Sims Metals, Cardiff	
86207	E3179				1965	2002	2006: Ron Hull Jr, Rotherham	
86208	E3141				1966	2000	2003: Crewe Electric Depot	
86209	E3125				1965	2004	2005: Boreham Scrap Co, Chelmsford	
86211	E3147				1966	1986	1987: Crewe Works	
86212	E3151				1966	2003	2011: EMR, Kingsbury	
86213	E3193				1965	1998	Exported	
86214	E3106				1965	2002	2006: Ron Hull Jr, Rotherham	
86215	E3165				1965	2004	Exported	
86216	E3166				1965	1998	2003: Immingham Railfreight Term.	
86217	86504	86217	E3177		1965	2004	Exported	
86218	E3175				1965	2004	Exported	
86219	E3196				1965	1996	2002: Immingham Railfreight Term.	
86220	E3156				1966	2002	2003: Immingham Railfreight Term.	
86221	E3132				1965	2003	2003: Immingham Railfreight Term.	
86222	86502	86222	E3131		1966	2002	2003: Immingham Railfreight Term.	
86223	E3158				1966	2004	2011: EMR, Kingsbury	
86224	E3134				1965	2002	2006: Ron Hull Jr, Rotherham	
86225	E3164				1965	2002	2006: Ron Hull Jr, Rotherham	
86226	E3162				1965	2002	2011: EMR, Kingsbury	
86227	E3117				1965	2004	2005: Ron Hull Jr, Rotherham	
86228	E3167				1965	2003	Exported	
86229	E3119				1965	2003	2020: Sandbach Car & Commercial	
86230	E3168				1965	2004	2011: EMR, Kingsbury	
86231	E3126				1965	2002	Exported	
86232	E3113				1965	2005	Exported	
86233	86506	86233	E3172		1965	2003	Exported	
86234	E3155				1966	2005	Exported	
86235	E3194				1966	2005	Exported	

86236	E3133					1965	2002	2003: Immingham Railfreight Term.	
86237	E3197					1966	2004	2004: Sims Metals, Cardiff	
86238	E3116					1965	2004	2005: Boreham Scrap Co, Chelmsford	
86239	86507	86239	E3169			1965	1996	1997: Crewe Electric Depot	
86240	E3127					1965	2002	2005: Ron Hull Jr, Rotherham	
86241	86508	86241	E3121			1965	2000	2003: Crewe Electric Depot	
86242	E3138					1966	2004	Exported	
86243	E3181					1965	2002	2004: C F Booth, Rotherham	
86244	E3178					1965	2002	2003: Immingham Railfreight Term.	
86245	E3182					1965	2003	2010: EMR, Kingsbury	
86246	86505	86246	E3149			1966	2004	2017: C F Booth, Rotherham	
86247	E3192					1965	2003	2015: Crewe Basford Hall Yard	C1
86248	E3107					1965	2002	Exported	
86249	E3161					1965	2003	2005: Ministry of Defence, Caerwent	
86250	E3189					1965	2004	Exported	
86251	E3183					1965	2002	Freightliner	
86252	E3101					1965	2002	2002: Immingham Railfreight Term.	
86254	86047	E3142				1966	2002	2004: C F Booth, Rotherham	
86255	86042	E3154				1966	1998	2002: Immingham Railfreight Term.	
86256	86040	E3135				1966	2002	2006: Ron Hull Jr, Rotherham	
86257	86043	E3139				1966	2002	2003: Immingham Railfreight Term.	
86258	86501[1]	86258	86046	E3140		1966	2002	2009: EMR, Kingsbury	a)
86259	86045	E3137				1966		Preserved	
86261	86041	E3118				1965	2002	2004: C F Booth, Rotherham	

a) First of 2 locomotives to be numbered 86501

Class 86/4
Details as Class 86/2 except:
Power Output: 2680 kW (3600 hp).

Latest Number Carried	Previous Number 1	Previous Number 2	Previous Number 3	Previous Number 4	Previous Number 5	Year Entered Service	Year Withdrawn	Scrapping Details/Current Status	Notes
86401	86001	E3199				1966		West Coast Railway Co	
86416	86616	86416	86316	86016	E3109	1965	2002	2005: C F Booth, Rotherham	
86417	86317	86017	E3146			1966	2001	2004: C F Booth, Rotherham	
86419	86319	86019	E3120			1965	1999	2003: Crewe Electric Depot	
86424	86324	86024	E3111			1965	2002	Exported	
86425	86325	86025	E3186			1965	2002	2005: C F Booth, Rotherham	
86426	86326	86026	E3195			1965	2004	2005: C F Booth, Rotherham	
86429	86329	86029	E3200			1966	1986	1987: Crewe Works	
86430	86030	E3105				1965	2004	2005: C F Booth, Rotherham	

Class 86/6
Electric Train Supply isolated.
Details as Class 86/2 except:
Maximum Speed: 75 mph.

Latest Number Carried	Previous Number 1	Previous Number 2	Previous Number 3	Previous Number 4	Previous Number 5	Year Entered Service	Year Withdrawn	Scrapping Details/Current Status	Notes
86602	86402	86002	E3170			1965	2005	2010: Crewe LNWR Depot	
86603	86403	86003	E3115			1965	1999	2005: C F Booth, Rotherham	
86604	86404	86004	E3103			1965		Freightliner	
86605	86405	86605	86405	86005	E3185	1965		Freightliner	
86606	86406	86006	E3112			1965	2003	2007: Ron Hull Jr, Rotherham	
86607	86407	86007	E3176			1965		Freightliner	
86608	86501[2]	86408	86002	E3180		1965		Freightliner	b)
86609	86409	86009	E3102			1965		Freightliner	
86610	86410	86010	E3104			1965		Freightliner	
86611	86411	86611	86411	86311	86011	1965	2003	2005: Crewe Works	c)
86612	86412	86312	86012	E3122		1965		Freightliner	
86613	86413	86313	86013	E3128		1965		Freightliner	
86614	86414	86614	86414	86314	86014	1966		Freightliner	d)
86615	86415	86615	86415	86315	86015	1965	2005	2007: Ron Hull Jr, Rotherham	e)
86618	86418	86318	86018	E3163		1965	2001	2005: C F Booth, Rotherham	

86620	86420	86320	86020	E3114		1965	2005	2007: Ron Hull Jr, Rotherham
86621	86421	86321	86021	E3157		1966	2011	2013: Crewe LNWR Depot
86622	86422	86322	86022	E3174		1965		Freightliner
86623	86423	86323	86023	E3152		1966	2003	2010: Crewe LNWR Depot
86627	86427	86327	86027	E3110		1965		Freightliner
86628	86428	86628	86428	86328	86028	1966		Freightliner f)
86631	86431	86631	86431	86031	E3188	1965	2003	2005: Crewe Works
86632	86432	86032	E3148			1966		Freightliner
86633	86433	86033	E3198			1966	2004	2013: Crewe LNWR Depot
86634	86434	86004	E3187			1965	2002	2005: C F Booth, Rotherham
86635	86435	86035	E3124			1965	2004	2013: Crewe LNWR Depot
86636	86436	86036	E3160			1966	2000	2005: C F Booth, Rotherham
86637	86437	86037	E3130			1965		Freightliner
86638	86438	86038	E3108			1965		Freightliner
86639	86439	86039	E3153			1966		Freightliner

b) Second of 2 locomotives to be numbered 86501
c) Also carried previous number 6: E3171
d) Also carried previous number 6: E3145
e) Also carried previous number 6: E3123
f) Also carried previous number 6: E3159

▲ 87002 "Royal Sovereign" is now the only operational Class 87 in Britain. On 25 June 2020, it is about to pass through Winsford, with Class 47 D1935 (47805) tucked behind dead in tow, while transferring an empty rake of charter coaches from Carlisle to Crewe. **Brad Joyce**

Class 86/7
Refurbished locos.
Details as Class 86/2 except:
Maximum Speed: 110 mph.

Latest Number Carried	Previous Number 1	Previous Number 2	Previous Number 3	Year Entered Service	Year Withdrawn	Current Status/Scrapping Details	Notes
86701	86503	86205	E3129	1965	2016	Exported	
86702	86260	86048	E3144	1966	2016	Exported	

Class 86/9
Rebuilt locos. Electric Train Supply isolated.
Details as Class 86/2 except:
Maximum Speed: 60 mph.

Latest Number Carried	Previous Number 1	Previous Number 2	Previous Number 3	Year Entered Service	Year Withdrawn	Current Status/Scrapping Details	Notes
86901	86253	86044	E3136	1965	2011	2018: Sandbach Car & Commercial	
86902	86210	E3190		1965	2011	2016: C F Booth, Rotherham	

CLASS 87 Bo-Bo

Built: 1973–75 by BREL, Crewe Works.
Electric Supply System: 25 kV AC overhead.
Power Output: 3730 kW (5000 hp).
Maximum Speed: 110 mph.
Train Heating/Supply: Electric.
Train Brakes: Air.

Class 87/0

Latest Number Carried	Previous Number 1	Year Entered Service	Year Withdrawn	Current Status/Scrapping Details	Notes
87001		1973	2005	Preserved	
87002		1973		Locomotive Services	
87003		1973	2005	Exported	
87004		1973	2005	Exported	
87005		1973	2003	2005: Ministry of Defence, Caerwent	
87006		1973	2006	Exported	
87007		1973	2007	Exported	
87008		1973	2006	Exported	
87009		1973	2004	Exported	
87010		1973	2005	Exported	
87011		1974	2003	2011: EMR, Kingsbury	
87012		1974	2006	Exported	
87013		1974	2005	Exported	
87014		1974	2005	Exported	
87015		1974	2004	2005: Ministry of Defence, Caerwent	
87016		1974	2004	2004: Ministry of Defence, Caerwent	
87017		1974	2003	Exported	
87018		1974	2004	2010: EMR, Kingsbury	
87019		1974	2006	Exported	
87020		1974	2003	Exported	
87021		1974	2005	2010: EMR, Kingsbury	
87022		1974	2008	Exported	
87023		1974	2005	Exported	
87024		1974	2004	2005: Ministry of Defence, Caerwent	
87025		1974	2004	Exported	
87026		1974	2006	Exported	
87027		1974	2004	2010: EMR, Kingsbury	
87028		1974	2007	Exported	

87029		1974	2004	Exported
87030		1974	2005	2011: EMR, Kingsbury
87031		1974	2005	2010: EMR, Kingsbury
87032		1974	2004	2010: EMR, Kingsbury
87033		1974	2005	Exported
87034		1974	2003	Exported
87035		1974	2005	Preserved

Class 87/1
Fitted with thyristor power control system.
Details as Class 87/0.

Latest Number Carried	Previous Number 1	Year Entered Service	Year Withdrawn	Current Status/Scrapping Details	Notes
87101		1975	1999	2002: Barrow Hill Depot	

CLASS 88   Bo-Bo

Built: 2015–16 by Stadler, Valencia, Spain.
Diesel Engine: Caterpillar C27 of 708 kW (950 hp) at 1750 rpm.
Electric Supply System: 25 kV AC overhead.
Power Output: 4000 kW (5360 hp).
Maximum Speed: 100 mph.
Train Heating/Supply: Electric.
Train Brakes: Air.

Latest Number Carried	Previous Number 1	Year Entered Service	Year Withdrawn	Current Status/Scrapping Details	Notes
88001		2017		Direct Rail Services	
88002		2017		Direct Rail Services	
88003		2017		Direct Rail Services	
88004		2017		Direct Rail Services	
88005		2017		Direct Rail Services	
88006		2017		Direct Rail Services	
88007		2017		Direct Rail Services	
88008		2017		Direct Rail Services	
88009		2017		Direct Rail Services	
88010		2017		Direct Rail Services	

CLASS 89   Co-Co

Built: 1987 by BREL, Crewe Works.
Electric Supply System: 25 kV AC overhead.
Power Output: 4350 kW (5850 hp).
Maximum Speed: 125 mph.
Train Heating/Supply: Electric.
Train Brakes: Air.

Latest Number Carried	Previous Number 1	Year Entered Service	Year Withdrawn	Current Status/Scrapping Details	Notes
89001		1987	2002	Preserved	

▲ On 30 August 2018, 88002 "Prometheus" and 88005 "Minerva" pass Valley on western Anglesey with a light load consisting of two nuclear flasks. **Liam Barnes**

▼ The sole Class 89 AC electric locomotive was built by BR in 1986 and went on to have several intermittent stints of main line operation. While it was in service for the operator GNER, 89001 is seen inside Bounds Green depot in North London on 19 April 1997. It is currently under overhaul and when this has been completed, it will return to main line traffic once again. **Geoff Plumb**

CLASS 90 Bo-Bo

Built: 1987–90 by BREL, Crewe Works.
Electric Supply System: 25 kV AC overhead.
Power Output: 3730 kW (5000 hp).
Maximum Speed: 110 mph.
Train Heating/Supply: Electric.
Train Brakes: Air.

Latest Number Carried	Previous Number 1	Previous Number 2	Previous Number 3	Year Entered Service	Year Withdrawn	Current Status/Scrapping Details	Notes
90001				1988		Locomotive Services	
90002				1988		Locomotive Services	
90003				1988		Freightliner	
90004				1988		Freightliner	
90005				1988		Freightliner	
90006				1988		Freightliner	
90007				1988		Freightliner	
90008				1988		Freightliner	
90009				1988		Freightliner	
90010				1988		Freightliner	
90011				1988		Freightliner	
90012				1988		Freightliner	
90013				1988		Freightliner	
90014				1988		Freightliner	
90015				1988		Freightliner	
90016				1988		Freightliner	
90017				1988		DB Cargo	
90018				1988		DB Cargo	
90019				1989		DB Cargo	
90020				1989		DB Cargo	
90021	90221	90021		1989		DB Cargo	
90022	90222	90022		1989		DB Cargo	
90023	90223	90023		1989		DB Cargo	
90024	90224	90024		1989		DB Cargo	
90025	90225	90125	90025	1989		DB Cargo	
90026	90126	90026		1989		DB Cargo	
90027	90227	90127	90027	1989		DB Cargo	
90028	90128	90028		1989		DB Cargo	
90029	90129	90029		1989		DB Cargo	
90030	90130	90030		1989		DB Cargo	
90031	90131	90031		1989		DB Cargo	
90032	90132	90032		1989		DB Cargo	
90033	90233	90133	90033	1989		DB Cargo	
90034	90134	90034		1989		DB Cargo	
90035	90135	90035		1989		DB Cargo	
90036	90136	90036		1990		DB Cargo	
90037	90137	90037		1990		DB Cargo	
90038	90238	90138	90038	1990		DB Cargo	
90039	90239	90139	90039	1990		DB Cargo	
90040	90140	90040		1990		DB Cargo	
90041	90141	90041		1990		Freightliner	
90042	90142	90042		1990		Freightliner	
90043	90143	90043		1990		Freightliner	
90044	90144	90044		1990		Freightliner	
90045	90145	90045		1990		Freightliner	
90046	90146	90046		1990		Freightliner	
90047	90147	90047		1990		Freightliner	
90048	90148	90048		1990		Freightliner	
90049	90149	90049		1990		Freightliner	
90050	90150	90050		1990		Freightliner	

▲ 90001 is one of many locomotives that have moved between operators since the last edition of this book; it was acquired by the Crewe-based charter operator Locomotive Services during 2020. On 25 September 2020, the class pioneer passes Heamies Farm with the London Euston–Mossend Down Yard leg of a private charter operated by its new owner. **Brad Joyce**

▼ The unique livery of 91111 "For the Fallen" blends in with its surroundings at Leeds on 18 January 2020. It sits on the rear of the 14.45 to Peterborough, which on this occasion was not proceeding to London King's Cross due to engineering work. **Andy Chard**

CLASS 91 Bo-Bo

Built: 1988–91 by BREL, Crewe Works.
Electric Supply System: 25 kV AC overhead.
Power Output: 4540 kW (6090 hp).
Maximum Speed: 140 mph, restricted to 125 mph or 110 mph when running blunt end first.
Train Heating/Supply: Electric.
Train Brakes: Air.

Latest Number Carried	Previous Number 1	Year Entered Service	Year Withdrawn	Current Status/Scrapping Details	Notes
91101	91001	1988		LNER	
91102	91002	1988		Stored	
91103	91003	1988		Stored	
91104	91004	1988		Stored	
91105	91005	1988		LNER	
91106	91006	1988		LNER	
91107	91007	1988		LNER	
91108	91008	1988		Stored	
91109	91009	1988		LNER	
91110	91010	1989		LNER	
91111	91011	1990		LNER	
91112	91012	1990		Stored	
91113	91013	1990		Stored	
91114	91014	1990		LNER	
91115	91015	1990		Stored	
91116	91016	1990		Stored	
91117	91017	1990		Europhoenix	
91118	91018	1990		Stored	
91119	91019	1990		LNER	
91120	91020	1990		Europhoenix	

▲ In late 2018 91119 "Bounds Green INTERCITY Depot 1977-2017" was repainted into the InterCity livery that it carried when it first entered traffic in 1990. On 19 December 2018, the former 91019 passes Spittal and nears its destination with the 07.30 London King's Cross–Edinburgh. **Keith Sanders**

91121	91021	1990	Stored	
91122	91022	1990	Rail Operations Group	
91124	91024	1990	LNER	
91125	91025	1990	Stored	
91126	91026	1990	Stored	
91127	91027	1990	LNER	
91128	91028	1990	Rail Operations Group	
91129	91029	1991	Stored	
91130	91030	1991	LNER	
91131	91031	1991	Stored	
91132	91023	1990	Stored	

CLASS 92   Co-Co

Built: 1993–96 by Brush Traction, Loughborough.
Electric Supply System: 25 kV AC overhead or 750 V DC third rail.
Power Output: 5040 kW (6760 hp) on AC overhead and 4000 kW (5360 hp) on DC third rail.
Maximum Speed: 140 mph.
Train Heating/Supply: Electric.
Train Brakes: Air.

Latest Number Carried	Previous Number 1	Year Entered Service	Year Withdrawn	Current Status/Scrapping Details	Notes
92001		1994		Exported	
92002		1993		Exported	
92003		1994		Exported	
92004		1994		DB Cargo	
92005		1994		Exported	
92006		1994		GB Railfreight	
92007		1994		DB Cargo	
92008		1994		DB Cargo	
92009		1994		DB Cargo	
92010		1994		GB Railfreight	
92011		1994		DB Cargo	
92012		1994		Exported	
92013		1994		DB Cargo	
92014		1994		GB Railfreight	
92015		1994		DB Cargo	
92016		1994		DB Cargo	
92017		1994		DB Cargo	
92018		1994		GB Railfreight	
92019		1994		DB Cargo	
92020		1994		GB Railfreight	
92021		1995		GB Railfreight	
92022		1995		Exported	
92023		1995		GB Railfreight	
92024		1995		Exported	
92025		1995		Exported	
92026		1995		Exported	
92027		1995		Exported	
92028		1995		GB Railfreight	
92029		1995		DB Cargo	
92030		1995		Exported	
92031		1995		DB Cargo	
92032		1995		GB Railfreight	
92033		1995		GB Railfreight	
92034		1995		Exported	
92035		1995		DB Cargo	
92036		1995		DB Cargo	

92037	1995	DB Cargo
92038	1995	GB Railfreight
92039	1995	Exported
92040	1995	GB Railfreight
92041	1995	DB Cargo
92042	1995	DB Cargo
92043	1995	GB Railfreight
92044	1995	GB Railfreight
92045	1995	GB Railfreight
92046	1996	GB Railfreight

▲ Class 92s can draw power from both AC overhead electric wires and the DC third rail electric network. On 6 April 2019, GB Railfreight's 92020 passes Heamies Farm, Staffordshire with a Garston to Wembley working. **Brad Joyce**

APPENDIX I: LOCOMOTIVE SUMMARY AND CLASSIFICATION INDEX

The following is a list of all locomotives by classification, in the order that they are listed in this book. It shows the total number produced and the number ranges for each locomotive classification.

Class Category	No. of Locos	TOPS Number Range	1957 Numbers	1948 Numbers	Notes
Experimental Shunters	7		D0226–D0227, D9998 & 4 with names only		
Experimental Diesel Mainline Locos	14		D0260, Deltic, D1200, DP2, D9, DHP1, HS4000	10000–10800	
Experimental Gas Turbine Locos	3		GT3	18000 & 18100	
Experimental Electric Mainline Locos	1		E2001		
Purpose Built Departmental Locos (with TOPS No.)	21	97020–97654	20, 56, 82–87, DS1169, ED1–ED7 & PWM650–PWM654		
Standard Locos–Unclassified Shunters	23		11001, 11104 & 15107		Also LMS Numbers 1831–7068
Standard Loocs with no TOPS class					
Class D1/1 (0-4-0 Hunslet Shunter)	3		D2950–D2952	11500–11502	
Class D1/3 (0-4-0 Ruston & Hornsby Shunter)	2		D2957–D2958	11507–11508	
Class D2/1 (0-4-0 North British Shunter)	8		D2700–D2707	11700–11707	
Class D2/5 (0-6-0 Andrew Barclay Shunter, differs to Class 05)	10		D2400–D2409	11177–11186	
Class D2/7 (0-6-0 Hudswell Clarke Shunter)	10		D2500–D2509	11116–11148	
Class D2/10 (0-4-0 North British Shunter)	73		D2708–D2780	11709–11719	Not all were given 1948 Numbers
Class D2/11 (0-4-0 Beyer Peacock / Brush Shunter)	1		D2999		
Class D2/12 (0-4-0 Huswell Clarke Shunter)	10		D2510–D2519		
Class D3/1 (0-4-0 North British Shunter)	14		D2900–D2913		
Class D3/3 (0-6-0 British Rail Shunter)	10		D3117–D3126	13117–13126	
Class D3/5 (0-6-0 British Rail Shunter)	15		D3152–D3166	13152–13166	
Class D3/6 (0-6-0 LMS Shunter)	11			12000–12002	Also LMS Numbers 7069–7079
Class D3/7 (0-6-0 LMS Shunter)	40			12003–12032	Also LMS Numbers 7080–7119
Class D3/9 (0-6-0 LNER Shunter)	4			15000–15003	Also LNER Numbers 8000–8003
Class D3/10 (0-6-0 Great Western Shunter)	1			15100	
Class D3/11 (0-6-0 English Electric Shunter)	6			15101–15106	
Class D3/12 (0-6-0 Southern Railway Shunter)	3			15201–15203	
Class D3/14 (0-6-0 LNER / Brush Shunter)	1			15004	
Standard Locos with TOPS Class					
Class 01	5		D2953–D2956 (2)	81 & 11503–11506	
Class 02	20	02001–02004	D2850–D2869		Not all were given TOPS numbers
Class 03	230	03004–03399	D2000–D2399	11187–11211	Not all were given TOPS numbers
Class 04	142	04110	D2200–D2341	11100–11229	
Class 05	69	05001	D2550–D2618	11136–11176	

Class	Built	TOPS numbers	D-numbers	Other numbers	Notes
Class 06	35	06001–06010	D2411–D2444		Not all were given TOPS numbers
Class 07	14	07001–07013	D2985–D2998		Not all were given TOPS numbers
Class 08	996	08001–08995	D2400–D4192	11116–15206	
Class 09	38	09001–09205	D3536–D4114		
Class 10	146		D3137–D4094	13137–13151	
Class 11	106			12033–12138	
Class 12	26			15211–15236	
Class 13	3	13001–13003	D4500–D4502		
Class 14	56		D9500–D9555		
Class 15	44		D8200–D8243		
Class 16	10		D8400–D8409		
Class 17	117		D8500–D8616		
Class 20	228	20001–20906	D8000–D8327		
Class 21 (& 29)	58		D6100–D6157		
Class 22	58		D6300–D6357		
Class 23	11		D5900–D5910		
Class 24	151	24001–24150	D5000–D5150		Not all were given TOPS numbers
Class 25	327	25001–25912	D5151–D5299 & D7500–D7677		Not all were given TOPS numbers
Class 26	47	26001–26046	D5300–D5346		Not all were given TOPS numbers
Class 27	69	27001–27212	D5347–D5414		Not all were given TOPS numbers
Class 28	20		D5700–D5719		
Class 31 (& 30)	263	31001–31970	D5500–D5862		
Class 33	98	33001–33212	D6500–D6597		Not all were given TOPS numbers
Class 35	101		D7000–D7100		
Class 37	309	37001–97304	D6600–D6999		Not all were given TOPS numbers
Class 40	200	40001–40199	D200–D399		Not all were given TOPS numbers
Class 41	5		D600–D604		
Class 41 HST	2	41001–41002			
Class 42	38		D800–D870		
Class 43	33		D833–D865		
Class 43 HST	197	43002–43484			
Class 44	10	44001–44010	D1–D10		
Class 45	127	45001–45150	D11–D137		
Class 46	56	46001–46056	D138–D193		
Class 47	512	47001–47981	D1100–D1999		
Class 50	50	50001–50149	D400–D449		
Class 52	74		D1000–D1073		
Class 55	22	55001–55022	D9000–D9021		
Class 56	135	56001–56312			
Class 57	33	57001–57605			
Class 58	50	58001–58050			
Class 59	15	59001–59206			
Class 60	100	60001–60500			
Class 66	493	66001–66957			
Class 67	30	67001–67030			

Class 68	34	68001–68034			
Class 69	10	69001–69010			
Class 70 (Diesel)	37	70001–80817			
Class 70 (Electric)	3			20001–20003	
Class 71	24	71001–71014	E5000–E5023		Not all were given TOPS numbers
Class 73	49	73001–73901	E6001–E6049		
Class 73/9	13	73951–73971			
Class 74	10	74001–74010	E6101–E6110		
Class 76	58	76001–76057		26000–26057	
Class ES1 (NER Bo-Bo Electric)	2			26500–26501	
Class EB1 (NER Bo-Bo Electric)	10			26502–26511	
Class EE1 (NER Bo-Bo Electric)	1			26600	
Class 77 (EM2)	7		E27000–E27006	27000–27006	
Class 81	25	81001–81022	E3001–E3097		Not all were given TOPS numbers
Class 82	10	82001–82008	E3046–E3055		Not all were given TOPS numbers
Class 83	15	83001–83015	E3024–E3100		
Class 84	10	84001–84010	E3036–E3045		
Class 85	40	85001–85114	E3056–E3095		
Class 86	100	86001–86902	E3101–E3200		
Class 87	36	87001–87101			
Class 88	10	88001–88010			
Class 89	1	89001–89001			
Class 90	50	90001–90239			
Class 91	31	91001–91132			
Class 92	46	92001–92046			

▲ Colas Rail's **37254** "Cardiff Canton" and **37099** "MERL EVANS 1947–2016" bring the **18.38** Crewe–Crewe Network Rail infrastructure monitoring service through Chassen Park during the evening of 6 August 2020. **Andy Chard**

APPENDIX II: MULTIPLE TOPS NUMBERS

This Appendix lists all previously carried TOPS numbers and shows the latest TOPS number under which the locomotive is listed in this book. Where a locomotive has two or more previously carried TOPS numbers, there are multiple entries for such locomotives. For example, 47780 has previously carried three different TOPS numbers (47030, 47618 and 47836), therefore each of these three previously carried numbers are listed, each entry referring to 47780 where the locomotive can be found in this book. Locomotives that have only carried one TOPS number are not included in Appendix II.

Previous TOPS No.	TOPS No. Listed Under	Class
03901	03128	03
08111	ADB968012	08
08117	ADB968010	08
08119	ADB968011	08
08203	08991	08
08259	08992	08
08267	97801	08
08421	09201	09
08462	08994	08
08592	08993	08
08620	09205	09
08687	08995	08
08717	09204	09
08732	09202	09
08749	09104	09
08759	09106	09
08766	09103	09
08781	09203	09
08832	09102	09
08833	09101	09
08835	09105	09
08845	09107	09
20041	20904	20
20042	20312	20
20047	20301 (2)	20
20060	20902	20
20075	20309	20
20083	20903	20
20084	20302 (2)	20
20095	20305 (2)	20
20101	20901	20
20102	20311	20
20104	20315	20
20117	20314	20
20120	20304 (2)	20
20127	20303 (2)	20
20128	20307 (2)	20
20131	20306 (2)	20
20187	20308	20
20190	20310	20
20194	20313	20
20219	20906	20
20225	20905	20
20301	20023	20
20302	20059	20
20303	20134	20
20304	20168	20
20305	20172	20
20306	20173	20
20307	20313	20
20308	20196	20
24054	ADB968008	24
24061	RDB968007	24
24142	ADB968009	24
25131	97202	25
25262	25901	25
25268	25902	25
25276	25903	25
25283	25904	25
25286	25905	25
25296	25906	25
25297	25907	25
25305	97251	25
25307	25908	25
25309	25909	25
25310	97250	25
25314	97252	25
25315	25910	25
25316	25911	25
25322	25912	25
26001	76001	76
26002	76002	76
26004	76004	76
26006	76006	76
26007	76007	76
26008	76008	76
26009	76009	76
26010	76010	76
26011	76011	76
26012	76012	76
26013	76013	76
26014	76014	76
26015	76015	76
26016	76016	76
26020	76020	76
26021	76021	76
26022	76022	76
26023	76023	76
26024	76024	76
26025	76025	76
26026	76026	76
26027	76027	76
26028	76028	76
26029	76029	76
26030	76030	76
26032	76032	76
26033	76033	76
26034	76034	76
26037	76037	76
26040	76040	76
26041	76041	76
26043	76043	76
26046	76046	76
26047	76047	76
26049	76049	76
26051	76051	76
26052	76052	76
26053	76053	76
26054	76054	76
26055	76055	76
26056	76056	76
26057	76057	76
27024	ADB968028	27
27045	27101	27
27046	27102	27
27048	27104	27
27049	27105	27
27103	27066	27
27103 (2)	27047	27
27106	27050	27
27107	27051	27
27108	27052	27
27109	27053	27
27110	27054	27
27111	27055	27
27112	27056	27
27113	ADB968025	27
27114	27208	27
27115	27063	27
27116	27064	27
27117	27065	27
27118	27047	27
27119	27201	27
27120	27202	27
27121	27203	27
27122	27058	27
27123	27059	27
27124	27206	27
27204	27058	27
27205	27059	27
27207	ADB968025	27
27209	27063	27
27210	27064	27
27211	27065	27
27212	27066	27
31002	ADB968014	31
31008	ADB968016	31
31013	ADB968013	31
31014	ADB968015	31
31114	31553	31
31115	31466	31
31129	31461	31
31133	31450	31
31137	31444	31
31139	31538	31
31140	31421	31
31148	31548	31
31151	31436	31
31153	31432	31
31157	31524	31
31161	31400	31
31169	31457	31
31172	31420	31
31177	31443	31
31179	31435	31
31182	31437	31
31186	31601	31
31191	31602	31
31193	31426	31
31194	31427	31
31197	31423	31
31204	31440	31
31211	31428	31
31213	31465	31
31216	31467	31
31220	31541	31
31228	31454	31
31236	31433	31
31239	31439	31
31246	31455	31
31251	31442	31
31253	31531	31
31256	31459	31
31258	31434	31
31265	31530	31
31266	31460	31
31269	31429	31
31274	31425	31
31277	31569	31
31279	31452	31
31291	31556	31
31295	31547	31
31297	31563	31
31298	97203	31
31300	31545	31
31303	31558	31
31307	31549	31
31310	31422	31
31315	31462	31
31316	31546	31
31318	31551	31
31321	31468	31
31325	31464	31
31326	31970	31
31414	31514	31
31416	31516	31
31419	31519	31
31424	31524	31
31430	31530	31
31431	31531	31
31438	31538	31
31441	31541	31
31445	31545	31
31446	31546	31
31447	31547	31
31448	31548	31
31449	31549	31
31451	31551	31
31453	31553	31
31456	31556	31
31458	31558	31
31463	31563	31
31469	31569	31
31507	31407	31
31511	31411	31
31512	31412	31
31522	31422	31
31526	31426	31
31533	31433	31
31537	31437	31
31544	31444	31
31552	31452	31
31554	31454	31
31555	31455	31
31565	31465	31
31568	31468	31
33302	33205	33
37001	37707	37

37002	37351	37	37143	37800	37	37274	37402	37	47029	47635	47
37005	37601	37	37145	37382	37	37274 (2)	37308	37	47030	47780	47
37006	37798	37	37147	37371	37	37276	37413	37	47031	47832	47
37007	37604	37	37148	37902	37	37277	37415	37	47032	47817	47
37008	37352	37	37149	37892	37	37279	37424	37	47034	47973	47
37009	37340	37	37150	37901	37	37281	37428	37	47035	47739	47
37014	37709	37	37151	37667	37	37282	37405	37	47036	47760	47
37015	37341	37	37155	37897	37	37283	37895	37	47037	47831	47
37016	37706	37	37157	37695	37	37284	37381	37	47038	47761	47
37017	37503	37	37159	37372	37	37285	37335	37	47039	47565	47
37018	37517	37	37160	37373	37	37286	37404	37	47040	47766	47
37020	37702	37	37161	37899	37	37287	37414	37	47041	47764	47
37021	37715	37	37163	37802	37	37288	37427	37	47042	47676	47
37022	37608	37	37164	37675	37	37289	37408	37	47043	47566	47
37024	37714	37	37166	37891	37	37290	37411	37	47044	47725	47
37027	37519	37	37167	37383	37	37291	37419	37	47045	47726	47
37028	37505	37	37168	37890	37	37292	37425	37	47046	47901	47
37030	37701	37	37169	37674	37	37295	37406	37	47047	47727	47
37033	37719	37	37170	97302	37	37296	37423	37	47048	47849	47
37034	37704	37	37171	37611	37	37297	37420	37	47055	47807	47
37036	37605	37	37172	37686	37	37299	37426	37	47056	47783	47
37039	37603	37	37173	37801	37	37300	37429	37	47059	47765	47
37041	37520	37	37176	37883	37	37301	37412	37	47060	57008	57
37043	37354	37	37177	37885	37	37302	37416	37	47061	47830	47
37044	37710	37	37178	97303	37	37303	37333	37	47064	47851	47
37045	37355	37	37179	37612	37	37304	37334	37	47066	47816	47
37049	37343	37	37180	37886	37	37305	37407	37	47068	47848	47
37050	37717	37	37181	37610	37	37306	37273 (2)	37	47069	47845	47
37052	37713	37	37182	37670	37	37307	37403	37	47070	47799	47
37053	37344	37	37183	37884	37	37310	37152	37	47072	47798	47
37056	37513	37	37186	37898	37	37311	37156	37	47074	47852	47
37060	37705	37	37187	37683	37	37312	37137	37	47075	47645	47
37061	37799	37	37189	37672	37	37313	37382	37	47076	47749	47
37064	37515	37	37192	37694	37	37314	37190	37	47077	47840	47
37067	37703	37	37193	37375	37	37320	37026	37	47078	47628	47
37068	37356	37	37195	37689	37	37321	37037	37	47079	57009	57
37076	37518	37	37199	37376	37	37322	37343	37	47080	47779	47
37079	37357	37	37200	37377	37	37323	37088	37	47081	47778	47
37081	37797	37	37202	37331	37	37324	37099	37	47082	47750	47
37082	37602	37	37204	37378	37	37325	37108	37	47083	47633	47
37084	37718	37	37205	37688	37	37326	37111	37	47086	47767	47
37085	37711	37	37206	37906	37	37353	37032	37	47087	47624	47
37086	37516	37	37208	37803	37	37374	37165	37	47088	47781	47
37089	37708	37	37210	37693	37	37380	37259	37	47090	47843	47
37090	37606	37	37217	97304	37	37501	37601	37	47091	47846	47
37091	37358	37	37224	37680	37	37502	37602	37	47126	47555	47
37093	37509	37	37226	37379	37	37504	37603	37	47128	47811	47
37094	37716	37	37228	37696	37	37506	37604	37	47129	47813	47
37100	97301	37	37231	37896	37	37507	37605	37	47134	47841	47
37101	37345	37	37233	37889	37	37508	37606	37	47135	47784	47
37102	37712	37	37234	37685	37	37511	37607	37	47136	47839	47
37103	37607	37	37236	37682	37	37512	37608	37	47138	47786	47
37105	37796	37	37237	37893	37	37514	37609	37	47141	47853	47
37112	37510	37	37239	37332	37	37687	37610	37	47149	47677	47
37115	37609	37	37243	37697	37	37690	37611	37	47151	47850	47
37117	37521	37	37246	37698	37	37691	37612	37	47153	47774	47
37118	37359	37	37247	37671	37	40060	97405	40	47155	47815	47
37119	37350	37	37249	37903	37	41001	43000	41	47158	47634	47
37120	37887	37	37253	37699	37	41002	ADB975813	41	47160	47746	47
37121	37677	37	37256	37678	37	45017	ADB968024	45	47163	47787	47
37122	37692	37	37257	37668	37	45022	97409	45	47164	47822	47
37123	37679	37	37258	37384	37	45029	97410	45	47165	47825	47
37124	37894	37	37265	37430	37	45034	97411	45	47166	47837	47
37125	37904	37	37266	37422	37	45040	97412	45	47167	47580	47
37126	37676	37	37267	37421	37	45054	45150	45	47168	47572	47
37127	37370	37	37268	37401	37	45066	97413	45	47169	47763	47
37128	37330	37	37269	37417	37	46035	97403	46	47170	47733	47
37129	37669	37	37270	37409	37	46045	97404	46	47171	47738	47
37130	37681	37	37271	37418	37	47020	47844	47	47172	47734	47
37132	37673	37	37271 (2)	37333	37	47024	47721	47	47173	47762	47
37134	37684	37	37272	37431	37	47026	47741	47	47174	47574	47
37135	37888	37	37272 (2)	37334	37	47027	47722	47	47175	47575	47
37136	37905	37	37273	37410	37	47028	47759	47	47176	47576	47

47177	47743	47	47398	47152	47	47606	47778	47	47823	47787	47
47178	47737	47	47399	47150	47	47607	47786	47	47824	47782	47
47179	47847	47	47468	47300	47	47608	47788	47	47825	57301	57
47180	47584	47	47480	47971	47	47609	47798	47	47827	57302	57
47181	47776	47	47490	47768	47	47610	47787	47	47831	57310	57
47182	47742	47	47491	47769	47	47611	47837	47	47833	47788	47
47183	47579	47	47493	47701	47	47612	47779	47	47834	47798	47
47184	47757	47	47494	47706	47	47613	47840	47	47835	47799	47
47185	47782	47	47495	47704	47	47614	47853	47	47836	47780	47
47187	57006	57	47496	47710	47	47615	47747	47	47838	47779	47
47204	57012	57	47497	47717	47	47616	47789	47	47842	47778	47
47206	57605	57	47498	47711	47	47617	47677	47	47845	57301	57
47209	57604	57	47499	47709	47	47618	47780	47	47846	57308	57
47216	47299	47	47502	47715	47	47619	47829	47	47974	47775	47
47225	57307	57	47503	47771	47	47620	47799	47	47975	47540	47
47231	57010	57	47504	47702	47	47621	47839	47	50149	50049	50
47232	47785	47	47505	47712	47	47622	47841	47	56003	56312	56
47234	57315	57	47506	47707	47	47623	47843	47	56045	56301	56
47239	47812	47	47507	47716	47	47625	47749	47	56057	56311	56
47240	47818	47	47510	47713	47	47626	47750	47	56124	56302	56
47242	47814	47	47511	47714	47	47629	47828	47	56125	56303	56
47243	47777	47	47514	47703	47	47630	47764	47	56201	56009	56
47244	47640	47	47516	47708	47	47631	47765	47	60016	60500	60
47246	47756	47	47517	47758	47	47632	47848	47	66008	66780	66
47247	47810	47	47531	47775	47	47636	47777	47	66016	66781	66
47248	47789	47	47537	47772	47	47637	47826	47	66046	66782	66
47250	47744	47	47538	ADB968035	47	47638	47845	47	66058	66783	66
47251	47827	47	47541	47773	47	47639	47851	47	66081	66784	66
47252	47747	47	47545	47972	47	47641	47767	47	66081	66784	66
47254	47806	47	47546	47976	47	47642	47766	47	66141	66786	66
47255	47596	47	47551	47774	47	47644	47756	47	66184	66787	66
47257	47805	47	47552	47802	47	47646	47852	47	66238	66788	66
47259	47802	47	47553	47803	47	47647	47846	47	66250	66789	66
47260	47803	47	47554	47705	47	47648	47850	47	66401	66733	66
47262	47788	47	47556	47844	47	47649	47830	47	66402	66734	66
47263	47736	47	47557	47721	47	47650	47805	47	66403	66735	66
47264	47829	47	47558	47722	47	47651	47806	47	66404	66736	66
47265	47804	47	47559	47759	47	47652	47807	47	66405	66737	66
47266	47828	47	47560	47832	47	47653	47781	47	66406	66742	66
47267	47745	47	47561	47973	47	47654	47783	47	66407	66743	66
47268	47791	47	47562	47760	47	47655	47810	47	66408	66744	66
47269	47643	47	47563	47831	47	47656	47811	47	66409	66745	66
47271	47854	47	47564	47761	47	47657	47812	47	66410	66746	66
47272	47593	47	47567	47725	47	47658	47813	47	66573	66846	66
47273	47627	47	47568	47726	47	47659	47814	47	66574	66847	66
47274	47826	47	47569	47727	47	47660	47815	47	66575	66848	66
47290	57316	57	47570	47849	47	47661	47816	47	66576	66849	66
47317	57003	57	47571	47822	47	47662	47817	47	66577	66850	66
47322	57002	57	47573	47762	47	47663	47818	47	66578	66738	66
47329	57011	57	47577	47847	47	47664	47784	47	66579	66739	66
47330	57312	57	47578	47776	47	47665	47785	47	66580	66740	66
47332	57007	57	47581	47763	47	47671	47789	47	66581	66741	66
47337	57602	57	47582	47733	47	47672	47760	47	66841	66742	66
47347	57004	57	47583	47734	47	47673	47593	47	66842	66743	66
47349	57603	57	47585	47757	47	47674	47854	47	66843	66744	66
47350	57005	57	47586	47676	47	47675	47791	47	66844	66745	66
47356	57001	57	47587	47736	47	47705	57303	57	66845	66746	66
47364	47981	47	47588	47737	47	47732	47580	47	70099	70801	70
47371	57313	57	47589	47827	47	47770	47500	47	73005	73966	73/9
47372	57314	57	47590	47825	47	47790	47593	47	73006	73906	73
47384	47226	47	47591	47804	47	47792	47804	47	73100	73101	73
47385	47363	47	47592	47738	47	47793	47579	47	73102	73212	73
47386	47378	47	47594	47739	47	47801	47774	47	73103	73970	73/9
47387	47314	47	47595	47791	47	47806	57309	57	73104	73951	73/9
47388	47204	47	47597	47741	47	47807	57304	57	73105	73969	73/9
47389	47309	47	47598	47742	47	47808	47781	47	73112	73213	73
47390	47330	47	47599	47743	47	47809	47783	47	73113	73211	73
47391	47355	47	47600	47744	47	47814	57306	57	73116	73210	73
47393	47209	47	47601	47901	47	47817	57311	57	73117	73968	73/9
47394	47211	47	47602	47782	47	47819	47784	47	73120	73209	73
47395	47205	47	47603	47745	47	47820	47785	47	73120	73209	73
47396	47328	47	47604	47854	47	47821	47786	47	73121	73208	73
47397	47303	47	47605	47746	47	47822	57305	57	73122	73207	73

73123	73206	73	86021	86621	86	86409	86609	86	90221	90021	90			
73124	73205	73	86022	86622	86	86410	86610	86	90222	90022	90			
73125	73204	73	86023	86623	86	86411	86611	86	90223	90023	90			
73127	73203	73	86024	86424	86	86412	86612	86	90224	90024	90			
73135	73235	73	86025	86425	86	86413	86613	86	90227	90027	90			
73137	73202	73	86026	86426	86	86414	86614	86	90233	90033	90			
73142	73201	73	86027	86627	86	86415	86615	86	90238	90038	90			
73204	73962	73/9	86028	86628	86	86418	86618	86	90239	90039	90			
73205	73964	73/9	86029	86429	86	86420	86620	86	91001	91101	91			
73206	73963	73/9	86030	86430	86	86421	86621	86	91002	91102	91			
73207	73971	73/9	86031	86631	86	86422	86622	86	91003	91103	91			
73208	73965	73/9	86032	86632	86	86423	86623	86	91004	91104	91			
73209	73961	73/9	86033	86633	86	86427	86627	86	91005	91105	91			
73211	73952	73/9	86035	86635	86	86428	86628	86	91006	91106	91			
73901	73001	73	86036	86636	86	86431	86631	86	91007	91107	91			
73906	73967	73/9	86037	86637	86	86432	86632	86	91008	91108	91			
76003	76036 (2)	76	86038	86638	86	86433	86633	86	91009	91109	91			
76018	76035	76	86039	86639	86	86434	86634	86	91010	91110	91			
76036	76003 (2)	76	86040	86256	86	86435	86635	86	91011	91111	91			
76038	76050	76	86041	86261	86	86436	86636	86	91012	91112	91			
76039	76048 (2)	76	86042	86255	86	86437	86637	86	91013	91113	91			
76044	76031	76	86043	86257	86	86438	86638	86	91014	91114	91			
76048	76039 (2)	76	86044	86901	86	86439	86639	86	91015	91115	91			
76050	76038 (2)	76	86045	86259	86	86501	86258	86	91016	91116	91			
84009	ADB968021	84	86046	86258	86	86501 (2)	86608	86	91017	91117	91			
85003	85113	85	86047	86254	86	86502	86222	86	91018	91118	91			
85004	85111	85	86048	86702	86	86503	86701	86	91019	91119	91			
85007	85112	85	86201	86101	86	86504	86217	86	91020	91120	91			
85009	85102	85	86202	86102	86	86505	86246	86	91021	91121	91			
85010	85103	85	86203	86103	86	86506	86233	86	91022	91122	91			
85011	85114	85	86205	86701	86	86507	86239	86	91023	91132	91			
85012	85104	85	86210	86902	86	86508	86241	86	91024	91124	91			
85016	85105	85	86253	86901	86	86616	86416	86	91025	91125	91			
85021	85106	85	86260	86702	86	90125	90025	90	91026	91126	91			
85024	85107	85	86311	86611	86	90126	90026	90	91027	91127	91			
85032	85108	85	86312	86612	86	90127	90027	90	91028	91128	91			
85035	85109	85	86313	86613	86	90128	90028	90	91029	91129	91			
85036	85110	85	86314	86614	86	90129	90029	90	91030	91130	91			
85101	85006	85	86315	86615	86	90130	90030	90	91031	91131	91			
86001	86401	86	86316	86416	86	90131	90031	90	97201	RDB968007	24			
86002	86602	86	86317	86417	86	90132	90032	90	97204	31970	31			
86002	86608	86	86318	86618	86	90133	90032	90	97406	40135	40			
86003	86603	86	86319	86419	86	90133	90033	90	97407	40012	40			
86004	86604	86	86320	86620	86	90134	90034	90	97408	40118	40			
86004	86634	86	86321	86621	86	90135	90035	90	97472	47472	47			
86005	86605	86	86322	86622	86	90136	90036	90	97480	47971	47			
86006	86606	86	86323	86623	86	90137	90037	90	97545	47972	47			
86007	86607	86	86324	86424	86	90138	90038	90	97561	47973	47			
86009	86609	86	86325	86425	86	90139	90039	90	97800	08600	08			
86010	86610	86	86326	86426	86	90140	90040	90	97803	05001	05			
86011	86611	86	86327	86627	86	90141	90041	90	97804	06003	06			
86012	86612	86	86328	86628	86	90142	90042	90	97806	09017	09			
86013	86613	86	86329	86429	86	90143	90043	90	PWM650	97650	97			
86014	86614	86	86402	86602	86	90144	90044	90	PWM651	97651	97			
86015	86615	86	86403	86603	86	90145	90045	90	PWM652	97652	97			
86016	86416	86	86404	86604	86	90146	90046	90	PWM653	97653	97			
86017	86417	86	86405	86605	86	90147	90047	90	PWM654	97654	97			
86018	86618	86	86406	86606	86	90148	90048	90	RDB968020	97801	08			
86019	86419	86	86407	86607	86	90149	90049	90	TDB968030	33018	33			
86020	86620	86	86408	86608	86	90150	90050	90						

APPENDIX III: 1948 BR NUMBER & 1957 BR NUMBER SERIES INDEX

This appendix lists all locomotives that carried a 1948 BR Number or 1957 BR Number and were subsequently given a different number, under which they are listed in this book. The 1948 numbers show the subsequently-carried 1957 number (where the locomotive was not given a TOPS number) or TOPS number, under which it can be found in this book; the 1957 numbers show the TOPS number under which it can be found in this book. Locomotives that only carried one 1948 or one 1957 number throughout their lives are not listed in this Appendix, as they are listed under that one number.

There are a small number of locomotives where the "Number Loco is listed by" is not the latest number carried, but a previously carried number, to which it is more logical to refer, such as for some industrial or departmental renumberings. For example, for D8066 it refers to 20066 rather than the last carried number 82. Locomotives renumbered into the departmental 97xxx series have their service TOPS number shown in parentheses to indicate the class of locomotive under which the locomotives' entries can be found. Such locomotives are listed under their 97xxx departmental series number.

Previously carried 1948 No.	Number Loco is listed by
11100	D2200
11101	D2201
11102	D2202
11103	D2203
11105	D2204
11106	D2205
11107	D2206
11108	D2207
11109	D2208
11110	D2209
11111	D2210
11112	D2211
11113	D2212
11114	D2213
11115	D2214
11116	D2500
11117	D2501
11118	D2502
11119	D2503
11120	D2504
11121	D2215
11122	D2216
11123	D2217
11124	D2218
11125	D2219
11126	D2220
11127	D2221
11128	D2222
11129	D2223
11130	D2224
11131	D2225
11132	D2226
11133	D2227
11134	D2228
11135	D2229
11136	D2550
11137	D2551
11138	D2552
11139	D2553
11140	05001
11141	D2555
11142	D2556
11143	D2557
11144	D2505
11145	D2506
11146	D2507
11147	D2508
11148	D2509
11149	D2230
11150	D2231
11151	D2232
11152	D2233
11153	D2234
11154	D2235
11155	D2236
11156	D2237
11157	D2238
11158	D2239
11159	D2240
11160	D2241
11161	D2558
11162	D2559
11163	D2560
11164	D2561
11165	D2562
11166	D2563
11167	D2564
11168	D2565
11169	D2566
11170	D2567
11171	D2568
11172	D2569
11173	D2570
11174	D2571
11175	D2572
11176	D2573
11177	D2400
11178	D2401
11179	D2402
11180	D2403
11181	D2404
11182	D2405
11183	D2406
11184	D2407
11185	D2408
11186	D2409
11187	D2000
11188	D2001
11189	D2002
11190	D2003
11191	03004
11192	03005
11193	D2006
11194	03007
11195	03008
11196	03009
11197	03010
11198	D2011
11199	03012
11200	03013
11201	03014
11202	03015
11203	03016
11204	03017
11205	03018
11206	D2019
11207	03020
11208	03021
11209	03022
11210	03023
11211	D2024
11212	D2242
11213	D2243
11214	D2244
11215	D2245
11216	D2246
11217	D2247
11218	D2248
11219	D2249
11220	D2250
11221	D2251
11222	D2252
11223	D2253
11224	D2254
11225	D2255
11226	D2256
11227	D2257
11228	D2258
11229	D2259
11500	D2950
11501	D2951
11502	D2952
11503	D2953
11504	01001
11505	01002
11506	D2956
11507	D2957
11508	D2958
11700	D2700
11701	D2701
11702	D2702
11703	D2703
11704	D2704
11705	D2705
11706	D2706
11707	D2707
11708	D2708
11709	D2709
11710	D2710
11711	D2711
11712	D2712
11713	D2713
11714	D2714
11715	D2715
11716	D2716
11717	D2717
11718	D2718
11719	D2719
12082	12049 (2)
13000	D3000
13001	D3001
13002	D3002
13003	D3003
13004	08001
13005	08002
13006	D3006
13007	08003
13008	08004
13009	08005
13010	08006
13011	D3011
13012	08007
13013	D3013
13014	D3014
13015	08008
13016	08009
13017	08010
13018	08011
13019	08012
13020	08013
13021	08014
13022	08015
13023	08016
13024	08017
13025	08018
13026	D3026
13027	08019
13028	08020
13029	08021
13030	08022
13031	08023
13032	08024
13033	08025
13034	D3034
13035	D3035
13036	08026
13037	D3035
13038	D3038
13039	08027
13040	08028
13041	08029
13042	08030
13043	08031
13044	08032
13045	D3045
13046	08033
13047	08034
13048	08035
13049	08036
13050	08037
13051	08038
13052	08039
13053	08040
13054	08041
13055	08042
13056	08043
13057	08044
13058	08045
13059	08046
13060	08047
13061	08048
13062	08049
13063	08050
13064	08051
13065	08052
13066	08053
13067	08054
13068	08055
13069	D3069
13070	08056
13071	08057
13072	08058
13073	08059
13074	08060
13075	08061
13076	08062
13077	08063
13078	D3078
13079	08064
13080	08065
13081	08066
13082	08067

13083 08068	13151 D3151	13219 08151	13286 08216	13353 08283
13084 08069	13152 D3152	13220 08152	13287 08217	13354 08284
13085 08070	13153 D3153	13221 08153	13288 08218	13355 08285
13086 08071	13154 D3154	13222 08154	13289 08219	13356 08286
13087 08072	13155 D3155	13223 08155	13290 08220	13357 08287
13088 08073	13156 D3156	13224 08156	13291 08221	13363 08293
13089 08074	13157 D3157	13225 08157	13292 08222	13364 08294
13090 08075	13158 D3158	13226 08158	13293 08223	13365 08295
13091 08076	13159 D3159	13227 08159	13294 08224	13366 08296
13092 D3092	13160 D3160	13228 08160	13295 08225	26001 76001
13093 D3093	13161 D3161	13229 08161	13296 08226	26002 76002
13094 D3094	13162 D3162	13230 08162	13297 08227	26003 76036 (2)
13095 D3095	13163 D3163	13231 08163	13298 08228	26004 76004
13096 D3096	13164 D3164	13232 08164	13299 08229	26006 76006
13097 D3097	13165 D3165	13233 08165	13300 08230	26007 76007
13098 D3098	13166 D3166	13234 08166	13301 08231	26008 76008
13099 D3099	13167 08102	13235 08167	13302 08232	26009 76009
13100 D3100	13168 08103	13236 08168	13303 08233	26010 76010
13101 D3101	13169 08104	13237 08169	13304 08234	26011 76011
13102 08077	13170 08105	13238 08170	13305 08235	26012 76012
13103 08078	13171 08106	13239 08171	13306 08236	26013 76013
13104 08079	13172 D3172	13240 08172	13307 08237	26014 76014
13105 08080	13173 08107	13241 08173	13308 08238	26015 76015
13106 08081	13174 08108	13242 08174	13309 08239	26016 76016
13107 08082	13175 08109	13243 08175	13310 08240	26018 76035
13108 08083	13176 08110	13244 08176	13311 08241	26020 76020
13109 08084	13177 08111	13245 08177	13312 08242	26021 76021
13110 08085	13178 08112	13246 08178	13313 08243	26022 76022
13111 08086	13179 08113	13247 08179	13314 08244	26023 76023
13112 08087	13180 08114	13248 08180	13315 08245	26024 76024
13113 08088	13181 08115	13249 08181	13316 08246	26025 76025
13114 08089	13182 08116	13250 08182	13317 08247	26026 76026
13115 08090	13183 D3183	13251 08183	13318 08248	26027 76027
13116 08091	13184 08117	13252 08184	13319 08249	26028 76028
13117 D3117	13185 08118	13253 08185	13320 08250	26029 76029
13118 D3118	13186 08119	13254 08186	13321 08251	26030 76030
13119 D3119	13187 08120	13255 D3255	13322 08252	26032 76032
13120 D3120	13188 08121	13256 08187	13323 08253	26033 76033
13121 D3121	13189 08122	13257 08188	13324 08254	26034 76034
13122 D3122	13190 08123	13258 08189	13325 08255	26036 76003 (2)
13123 D3123	13191 08124	13259 08190	13326 08256	26037 76037
13124 D3124	13192 08125	13260 08191	13327 08257	26038 76050
13125 D3125	13193 D3193	13261 D3261	13328 08258	26039 76048 (2)
13126 D3126	13194 08126	13262 08192	13329 08992	26040 76040
13127 08092	13195 08127	13263 08193	13330 08260	26041 76041
13128 08093	13196 08128	13264 08194	13331 08261	26043 76031
13129 08094	13197 08129	13265 08195	13332 08262	26044 76031
13130 08095	13198 08130	13266 08196	13333 08263	26046 76046
13131 08096	13199 08131	13267 08197	13334 08264	26047 76047
13132 08097	13200 08132	13268 08198	13335 08265	26048 76039 (2)
13133 08098	13201 08133	13269 08199	13336 08266	26049 76049
13134 08099	13202 08134	13270 08200	13337 8267	26050 76038 (2)
13135 08100	13203 08135	13271 08201	13338 08268	26051 76051
13136 08101	13204 08136	13272 08202	13339 08269	26052 76052
13137 D3137	13205 08137	13273 08991	13340 08270	26053 76053
13138 D3138	13206 08138	13274 08204	13341 08271	26054 76054
13139 D3139	13207 08139	13275 08205	13342 08272	26055 76055
13140 D3140	13208 08140	13276 08206	13343 08273	26056 76056
13141 D3141	13209 08141	13277 08207	13344 08274	26057 76057
13142 D3142	13210 08142	13278 08208	13345 08275	27000 E27000
13143 D3143	13211 08143	13279 08209	13346 08276	27001 E27001
13144 D3144	13212 08144	13280 08210	13347 08277	27002 E27002
13145 D3145	13213 08145	13281 08211	13348 08278	27003 E27003
13146 D3146	13214 08146	13282 08212	13349 08279	27004 E27004
13147 D3147	13215 08147	13283 08213	13350 08280	27005 E27005
13148 D3148	13216 08148	13284 08214	13351 08281	27006 E27006
13149 D3149	13217 08149	13285 08215	13352 08282	81 D2956 (2)
13150 D3150	13218 08150			

Previous Number 1957 Number	Loco is listed by	Previous Number 1957 Number	Loco is listed by	Previous Number 1957 Number	Loco is listed by	Previous Number 1957 Number	Loco is listed by	Previous Number 1957 Number	Loco is listed by
D1	44001	D33	45019	D68	45046	D103	45062	D138	46001
D2	44002	D34	45119	D69	45047	D104	45063	D139	46002
D3	44003	D35	45117	D70	45048	D105	45064	D140	46003
D4	44004	D36	45031	D71	45049	D106	45106	D141	46004
D5	44005	D37	45009	D72	45050	D107	45120	D142	46005
D6	44006	D38	45032	D73	45110	D108	45012	D143	46006
D7	44007	D39	45033	D74	45051	D109	45139	D144	46007
D8	44008	D40	45133	D75	45052	D110	45065	D145	46008
D9	44009	D41	45147	D76	45053	D111	45129	D146	46009
D10	44010	D42	97411 (45034)	D77	45004	D112	45010	D147	46010
D11	45122	D43	45107	D78	45150	D113	45128	D148	46011
D12	45011	D44	45035	D79	45005	D114	97413 (45066)	D149	46012
D13	45001	D45	45036	D80	45113	D115	45067	D150	46013
D14	45015	D46	45037	D81	45115	D116	45103	D151	46014
D15	45018	D47	45116	D82	45141	D117	45130	D152	46015
D16	45016	D48	45038	D83	45142	D118	45068	D153	46016
D17	45024	D49	45039	D84	45055	D119	45007	D154	46017
D18	45121	D50	97412 (45040)	D85	45109	D120	45108	D155	46018
D19	45025	D51	45102	D86	45105	D121	45069	D156	46019
D20	45013	D52	45123	D87	45127	D122	45070	D157	46020
D21	45026	D53	45041	D88	45136	D123	45125	D158	46021
D22	45132	D54	45023	D89	45006	D124	45131	D159	46022
D23	968024 (45017)	D55	45144	D90	45008	D125	45071	D160	46023
D24	45027	D56	45137	D91	45056	D126	45134	D161	46024
D25	45021	D57	45042	D92	45138	D127	45072	D162	46025
D26	45020	D58	45043	D93	45057	D128	45145	D163	46026
D27	45028	D59	45104	D94	45114	D129	45073	D164	46027
D28	45124	D60	97409 (45022)	D95	45054	D130	45148	D165	46028
D29	45002	D61	45112	D96	45101	D131	45074	D166	46029
D30	97410 (45029)	D62	45143	D97	45058	D132	45075	D167	46030
D31	45030	D63	45044	D98	45059	D133	45003	D168	46031
D32	45126	D64	45045	D99	45135	D134	45076	D169	46032
		D65	45111	D100	45060	D135	45149	D170	46033
		D66	45146	D101	45061	D136	45077	D171	46034
		D67	45118	D102	45140	D137	45014	D172	97403 (46035)

▲ The Class 97 identity is used for departmental (non-revenue earning) locomotives. The 97 prefix has been assigned to a great variety of traction, most of which is technically a member of another class. The former 06003, which became 97804 in 1981, enjoys some attention during Reading Traction Maintenance Depot's open day on 12 June 1985. **Gordon Edgar**

D173	46036	D252	40052	D326	40126	D399	40199	D1510	47411
D174	46037	D253	40053	D327	40127	D400	50050	D1511	47412
D175	46038	D254	40054	D328	40128	D401	50001	D1512	47413
D176	46039	D255	40055	D329	40129	D402	50002	D1513	47414
D177	46040	D256	40056	D330	40130	D403	50003	D1514	47415
D178	46041	D257	40057	D331	40131	D404	50004	D1515	47416
D179	46042	D258	40058	D332	40132	D405	50005	D1516	47417
D180	46043	D259	40059	D333	40133	D406	50006	D1517	47418
D181	46044	D260	97405 (40060)	D334	40134	D407	50007	D1518	47419
D182	97404 (46045)	D261	40061	D335	40135	D408	50008	D1519	47420
D183	46046	D262	40062	D336	40136	D409	50009	D1520	47421
D184	46047	D263	40063	D337	40137	D410	50010	D1521	47001
D185	46048	D264	40064	D338	40138	D411	50011	D1522	47002
D186	46049	D265	40065	D339	40139	D412	50012	D1523	47003
D187	46050	D266	40066	D340	40140	D413	50013	D1524	47004
D188	46051	D267	40067	D341	40141	D414	50014	D1525	47422
D189	46052	D268	40068	D342	40142	D415	50015	D1526	47005
D190	46053	D269	40069	D343	40143	D416	50016	D1527	47423
D191	46054	D270	40070	D344	40144	D417	50017	D1528	47006
D192	46055	D271	40071	D345	40145	D418	50018	D1529	47007
D193	46056	D272	40072	D346	40146	D419	50019	D1530	47008
D200	40122	D273	40073	D347	40147	D420	50020	D1531	47424
D201	40001	D274	40074	D348	40148	D421	50021	D1532	47009
D202	40002	D275	40075	D349	40149	D422	50022	D1533	47425
D203	40003	D276	40076	D350	40150	D423	50023	D1534	47426
D204	40004	D277	40077	D351	40151	D424	50024	D1535	47427
D205	40005	D278	40078	D352	40152	D425	50025	D1536	47428
D206	40006	D279	40079	D353	40153	D426	50026	D1537	47010
D207	40007	D280	40080	D354	40154	D427	50027	D1538	47011
D208	40008	D281	40081	D355	40155	D428	50028	D1539	47012
D209	40009	D282	40082	D356	40156	D429	50029	D1540	47013
D210	40010	D283	40083	D357	40157	D430	50030	D1541	47429
D211	40011	D284	40084	D358	40158	D431	50031	D1542	47430
D212	40012	D285	40085	D359	40159	D432	50032	D1543	47014
D213	40013	D286	40086	D360	40160	D433	50033	D1544	47015
D214	40014	D287	40087	D361	40161	D434	50034	D1545	47431
D215	40015	D288	40088	D362	40162	D435	50035	D1546	47016
D216	40016	D289	40089	D363	40163	D436	50036	D1547	47432
D217	40017	D290	40090	D364	40164	D437	50037	D1548	47433
D218	40018	D291	40091	D365	40165	D438	50038	D1549	47434
D219	40019	D292	40092	D366	40166	D439	50039	D1550	47435
D220	40020	D293	40093	D367	40167	D440	50040	D1551	47529
D221	40021	D294	40094	D368	40168	D441	50041	D1552	47436
D222	40022	D295	40095	D369	40169	D442	50042	D1553	47437
D223	40023	D296	40096	D370	40170	D443	50043	D1554	47438
D224	40024	D297	40097	D371	40171	D444	50044	D1555	47439
D225	40025	D298	40098	D372	40172	D445	50045	D1556	47440
D226	40026	D299	40099	D373	40173	D446	50046	D1557	47441
D227	40027	D300	40100	D374	40174	D447	50047	D1558	47442
D228	40028	D301	40101	D375	40175	D448	50048	D1559	47443
D229	40029	D302	40102	D376	40176	D449	50049	D1560	47444
D230	40030	D303	40103	D377	40177	D1100	47298	D1561	47445
D231	40031	D304	40104	D378	40178	D1101	47518	D1563	47446
D232	40032	D305	40105	D379	40179	D1102	47519	D1564	47447
D233	40033	D306	40106	D380	40180	D1103	47520	D1565	47448
D234	40034	D307	40107	D381	40181	D1104	47521	D1566	47449
D235	40035	D308	40108	D382	40182	D1105	47522	D1567	47450
D236	40036	D309	40109	D383	40183	D1106	47523	D1568	47451
D237	40037	D310	40110	D384	40184	D1107	47524	D1569	47452
D238	40038	D311	40111	D385	40185	D1108	47525	D1570	47017
D239	40039	D312	40112	D386	40186	D1109	47526	D1571	47453
D240	40040	D313	40113	D387	40187	D1110	47527	D1572	47018
D241	40041	D314	40114	D388	40188	D1111	47528	D1573	47019
D242	40042	D315	40115	D389	40189	D1500	47401	D1574	47454
D243	40043	D316	40116	D390	40190	D1501	47402	D1575	47455
D244	40044	D317	40117	D391	40191	D1502	47403	D1576	47456
D245	40045	D318	40118	D392	40192	D1503	47404	D1577	47457
D246	40046	D319	40119	D393	40193	D1504	47405	D1578	47458
D247	40047	D320	40120	D394	40194	D1505	47406	D1579	47459
D248	40048	D321	40121	D395	40195	D1506	47407	D1580	47460
D249	40049	D323	40123	D396	40196	D1507	47408	D1581	47461
D250	40050	D324	40124	D397	40197	D1508	47409	D1582	47462
D251	40051	D325	40125	D398	40198	D1509	47410	D1583	47844

D1584 47775	D1657 47772	D1731 47550	D1805 47324	D1878 47359
D1585 47542	D1658 47852	D1732 47140	D1806 47325	D1879 47360
D1586 47463	D1659 47645	D1733 47853	D1807 47326	D1880 47361
D1587 47464	D1660 47749	D1735 47142	D1808 47327	D1881 47362
D1588 47543	D1661 47840	D1736 47143	D1809 47328	D1882 47363
D1589 47465	D1662 47484	D1737 47144	D1810 47329	D1883 47981
D1590 47466	D1663 47628	D1738 47145	D1811 47330	D1884 47365
D1591 47721	D1664 47079	D1739 47146	D1812 47331	D1885 47366
D1592 47544	D1665 47779	D1740 47147	D1813 47332	D1886 47367
D1593 47467	D1666 47778	D1741 47148	D1814 47333	D1887 47368
D1594 47300	D1667 47750	D1742 47677	D1815 47334	D1888 47369
D1595 47469	D1668 47633	D1743 47150	D1816 47335	D1889 47370
D1596 47470	D1669 968035 (47538)	D1744 47850	D1817 47336	D1890 47371
D1597 47741	D1670 47085	D1745 47152	D1818 47337	D1891 47372
D1598 47471	D1672 47767	D1746 47774	D1819 47338	D1892 47373
D1599 47722	D1673 47624	D1747 47976	D1820 47339	D1893 47374
D1600 47472	D1674 47781	D1748 47815	D1821 47340	D1894 47375
D1601 47473	D1675 47089	D1749 47156	D1822 47341	D1895 47376
D1602 47474	D1676 47843	D1750 47157	D1823 47342	D1896 47377
D1603 47475	D1677 47846	D1751 47634	D1824 47343	D1897 47378
D1604 47476	D1678 47534	D1752 47159	D1825 47344	D1898 47379
D1605 47759	D1679 47093	D1753 47769	D1826 47345	D1899 47380
D1606 47635	D1680 47094	D1754 47746	D1827 47346	D1900 47381
D1607 47477	D1681 47095	D1755 47773	D1828 47347	D1901 47225
D1608 47478	D1682 47096	D1756 47162	D1829 47348	D1902 47226
D1609 47780	D1683 47485	D1757 47787	D1830 47349	D1903 47227
D1610 47832	D1684 47097	D1758 47822	D1831 47350	D1904 47228
D1611 47817	D1685 47098	D1759 47825	D1832 47351	D1905 47229
D1612 47479	D1686 47099	D1760 47492	D1833 47352	D1906 47230
D1613 47033	D1687 47100	D1761 47837	D1834 47353	D1907 47231
D1614 47973	D1688 47101	D1762 47580	D1835 47354	D1909 47785
D1615 47739	D1689 47486	D1763 47572	D1836 47355	D1910 47233
D1616 47971	D1690 47102	D1764 47763	D1837 47187	D1911 47234
D1617 47760	D1691 47103	D1765 47733	D1838 47188	D1912 47235
D1618 47831	D1692 47104	D1766 47738	D1839 47189	D1913 47236
D1619 47761	D1693 47105	D1767 47734	D1840 47190	D1914 47237
D1620 47565	D1694 47106	D1768 47762	D1841 47191	D1915 47238
D1621 47766	D1695 47107	D1769 47574	D1842 47192	D1916 47812
D1622 47764	D1696 47108	D1770 47575	D1843 47193	D1917 47818
D1623 47676	D1697 47109	D1771 47576	D1844 47194	D1918 47241
D1624 47566	D1698 47110	D1772 47743	D1845 47195	D1919 47814
D1625 47725	D1699 47111	D1773 47737	D1846 47196	D1920 47777
D1626 47726	D1700 47112	D1774 47847	D1847 47197	D1921 47640
D1627 47481	D1701 47113	D1775 47584	D1848 47198	D1922 47245
D1628 47901	D1702 47114	D1776 47776	D1849 47199	D1923 47756
D1629 47727	D1703 47115	D1777 47742	D1850 47200	D1924 47810
D1630 47849	D1704 47116	D1778 47579	D1851 47201	D1925 47789
D1631 47049	D1705 47117	D1779 47757	D1852 47202	D1926 47249
D1632 47050	D1706 47118	D1780 47782	D1853 47203	D1927 47744
D1633 47051	D1707 47487	D1781 47186	D1854 47204	D1928 47827
D1634 47052	D1708 47119	D1782 47301	D1855 47205	D1929 47747
D1635 47053	D1709 47120	D1783 47302	D1856 47206	D1930 47530
D1636 47482	D1710 47121	D1784 47303	D1857 47207	D1931 47806
D1637 47483	D1711 47122	D1785 47304	D1858 47208	D1932 47701
D1638 47054	D1712 47123	D1786 47305	D1859 47209	D1933 47596
D1639 47807	D1713 47488	D1787 47306	D1860 47210	D1934 47256
D1640 47783	D1714 47124	D1788 47307	D1861 47211	D1935 47805
D1641 47532	D1715 47125	D1789 47308	D1862 47212	D1936 47706
D1642 47547	D1716 47489	D1790 47309	D1863 47213	D1937 47704
D1643 47765	D1717 47555	D1791 47310	D1864 47214	D1938 47258
D1644 47060	D1718 47539	D1792 47311	D1865 47215	D1939 47710
D1645 47830	D1719 47811	D1793 47312	D1866 47299	D1940 47717
D1646 47972	D1720 47813	D1794 47313	D1867 47217	D1941 47711
D1647 47063	D1721 47130	D1795 47314	D1868 47218	D1942 47709
D1648 47851	D1722 47131	D1796 47315	D1869 47219	D1943 47500
D1649 47535	D1723 47540	D1797 47316	D1870 47220	D1944 47501
D1650 47816	D1724 47549	D1798 47317	D1871 47221	D1945 47715
D1651 47533	D1725 47768	D1799 47318	D1872 47222	D1946 47771
D1652 47848	D1726 47841	D1800 47319	D1873 47223	D1947 47702
D1653 47845	D1727 47784	D1801 47320	D1874 47224	D1948 47712
D1654 47799	D1728 47839	D1802 47321	D1875 47356	D1949 47707
D1655 47536	D1729 47137	D1803 47322	D1876 47357	D1950 47802
D1656 47798	D1730 47786	D1804 47323	D1877 47358	D1951 47716

1952 47508	D2050 03050	D2163 03163	D3029 08021	D3129 08094
1953 47509	D2055 03055	D2164 03164	D3030 08022	D3130 08095
1954 47713	D2056 03056	D2165 03165	D3031 08023	D3131 08096
1955 47714	D2058 03058	D2166 03166	D3032 08024	D3132 08097
1956 47803	D2059 03059	D2167 03167	D3033 08025	D3133 08098
1957 47705	D2060 03060	D2168 03168	D3036 08026	D3134 08099
1958 47512	D2061 03061	D2169 03169	D3039 08027	D3135 08100
1959 47513	D2062 03062	D2170 03170	D3040 08028	D3136 08101
1960 47703	D2063 03063	D2171 03171	D3041 08029	D3167 08102
1961 47515	D2064 03064	D2172 03172	D3042 08030	D3168 08103
1962 47788	D2066 03066	D2174 03174	D3043 08031	D3169 08104
1963 47736	D2067 03067	D2175 03175	D3044 08032	D3170 08105
1964 47829	D2068 03068	D2179 03179	D3046 08033	D3171 08106
1965 47804	D2069 03069	D2180 03180	D3047 08034	D3173 08107
1966 47828	D2072 03072	D2189 03189	D3048 08035	D3174 08108
1967 47745	D2073 03073	D2196 03196	D3049 08036	D3175 08109
1968 47708	D2075 03075	D2197 03197	D3050 08037	D3176 08110
1969 47791	D2076 03076	D2310 04110	D3051 08038	D3177 08111
1970 47643	D2078 03078	D2370 03370	D3052 08039	D3178 08112
1971 47270	D2079 03079	D2371 03371	D3053 08040	D3179 08113
1972 47854	D2080 03080	D2382 03382	D3054 08041	D3180 08114
1973 47790	D2081 03081	D2386 03386	D3055 08042	D3181 08115
1974 47627	D2084 03084	D2389 03389	D3056 08043	D3182 08116
1975 47758	D2086 03086	D2397 03397	D3057 08044	D3184 08117
1976 47826	D2089 03089	D2399 03399	D3058 08045	D3185 08118
1977 47275	D2090 03090	D2413 06001	D3059 08046	D3186 08119
1978 47276	D2091 03091	D2414 06002	D3060 08047	D3187 08120
1979 47277	D2092 03092	D2420 97804 (06003)	D3061 08048	D3188 08121
1980 47278	D2094 03094	D2421 06004	D3062 08049	D3189 08122
1981 47279	D2095 03095	D2422 06005	D3063 08050	D3190 08123
1982 47280	D2096 03096	D2423 06006	D3064 08051	D3191 08124
1983 47281	D2097 03097	D2426 06007	D3065 08052	D3192 08125
1984 47282	D2098 03098	D2437 06008	D3066 08053	D3194 08126
1985 47283	D2099 03099	D2440 06009	D3067 08054	D3195 08127
1986 47284	D2102 03102	D2444 06010	D3068 08055	D3196 08128
1987 47285	D2103 03103	D2554 05001	D3070 08056	D3197 08129
1988 47286	D2104 03104	D2851 02001	D3071 08057	D3198 08130
1989 47287	D2105 03105	D2852 02002	D3072 08058	D3199 08131
1990 47288	D2106 03106	D2853 02003	D3073 08059	D3200 08132
1991 47289	D2107 03107	D2856 02004	D3074 08060	D3201 08133
1992 47290	D2108 03108	D2954 01001	D3075 08061	D3202 08134
1993 47291	D2109 03109	D2955 01002	D3076 08062	D3203 08135
1994 47292	D2110 03110	D2985 07001	D3077 08063	D3204 08136
1995 47293	D2111 03111	D2986 07002	D3079 08064	D3205 08137
1996 47294	D2112 03112	D2987 07003	D3080 08065	D3206 08138
1997 47295	D2113 03113	D2989 07005	D3081 08066	D3207 08139
1998 47296	D2118 03118	D2990 07006	D3082 08067	D3208 08140
1999 47297	D2119 03119	D2991 07007	D3083 08068	D3209 08141
2004 03004	D2120 03120	D2993 07009	D3084 08069	D3210 08142
2005 03005	D2121 03121	D2994 07010	D3085 08070	D3211 08143
2007 03007	D2128 03128	D2995 07011	D3086 08071	D3212 08144
2008 03008	D2129 03129	D2996 07012	D3087 08072	D3213 08145
2009 03009	D2134 03134	D2997 07013	D3088 08073	D3214 08146
2010 03010	D2135 03135	D3004 08001	D3089 08074	D3215 08147
2012 03012	D2137 03137	D3005 08002	D3090 08075	D3216 08148
2013 03013	D2141 03141	D3007 08003	D3091 08076	D3217 08149
2014 03014	D2142 03142	D3008 08004	D3102 08077	D3218 08150
2016 03016	D2144 03144	D3009 08005	D3103 08078	D3219 08151
2017 03017	D2145 03145	D3010 08006	D3104 08079	D3220 08152
2018 03018	D2147 03147	D3012 08007	D3105 08080	D3221 08153
2020 03020	D2149 03149	D3015 08008	D3106 08081	D3222 08154
2021 03021	D2151 03151	D3016 08009	D3107 08082	D3223 08155
2022 03022	D2152 03152	D3017 08010	D3108 08083	D3224 08156
2025 03025	D2153 03153	D3018 08011	D3109 08084	D3225 08157
2026 03026	D2154 03154	D3019 08012	D3110 08085	D3226 08158
2027 03027	D2155 03155	D3020 08013	D3111 08086	D3227 08159
2029 03029	D2156 03156	D3021 08014	D3112 08087	D3228 08160
2034 03034	D2157 03157	D3022 08015	D3113 08088	D3229 08161
2035 03035	D2158 03158	D3023 08016	D3114 08089	D3230 08162
2037 03037	D2159 03159	D3024 08017	D3115 08090	D3231 08163
2044 03044	D2160 03160	D3025 08018	D3116 08091	D3232 08164
2045 03045	D2161 03161	D3027 08019	D3127 08092	D3233 08165
2047 03047	D2162 03162	D3028 08020	D3128 08093	D3234 08166

D3235 08167	D3310 08240	D3383 08313	D3471 08386	D3573 08458
D3236 08168	D3311 08241	D3384 08314	D3472 08387	D3574 08459
D3237 08169	D3312 08242	D3385 08315	D3503 08388	D3575 08460
D3238 08170	D3313 08243	D3386 08316	D3504 08389	D3576 08461
D3239 08171	D3314 08244	D3387 08317	D3505 08390	D3577 08994
D3240 08172	D3315 08245	D3388 08318	D3506 08391	D3578 08463
D3241 08173	D3316 08246	D3389 08319	D3507 08392	D3579 08464
D3242 08174	D3317 08247	D3390 08320	D3508 08393	D3580 08465
D3243 08175	D3318 08248	D3391 08321	D3509 08394	D3581 08466
D3244 08176	D3319 08249	D3392 08322	D3510 08395	D3582 08467
D3245 08177	D3320 08250	D3393 08323	D3511 08396	D3583 08468
D3246 08178	D3321 08251	D3394 08324	D3512 08397	D3584 08469
D3247 08179	D3322 08252	D3395 08325	D3513 08398	D3585 08470
D3248 08180	D3323 08253	D3396 08326	D3514 08399	D3586 08471
D3249 08181	D3324 08254	D3397 08327	D3515 08400	D3587 08472
D3250 08182	D3325 08255	D3398 08328	D3516 08401	D3588 08473
D3251 08183	D3326 08256	D3399 08329	D3517 08402	D3589 08474
D3252 08184	D3327 08257	D3400 08330	D3518 08403	D3590 08475
D3253 08185	D3328 08258	D3401 08331	D3519 08404	D3591 08476
D3254 08186	D3329 08992	D3402 08332	D3520 08405	D3592 08477
D3256 08187	D3330 08260	D3403 08333	D3521 08406	D3593 08478
D3257 08188	D3331 08261	D3404 08334	D3522 08407	D3594 08479
D3258 08189	D3332 08262	D3405 08335	D3523 08408	D3595 08480
D3259 08190	D3333 08263	D3406 08336	D3524 08409	D3596 08481
D3260 08191	D3334 08264	D3407 08337	D3525 08410	D3597 08482
D3262 08192	D3335 08265	D3408 08338	D3526 08411	D3598 08483
D3263 08193	D3336 08266	D3409 08339	D3527 08412	D3599 08484
D3264 08194	D3337 97801 (08267)	D3410 08340	D3528 08413	D3600 08485
D3265 08195	D3338 08268	D3411 08341	D3529 08414	D3601 08486
D3266 08196	D3339 08269	D3412 08342	D3530 08415	D3602 08487
D3267 08197	D3340 08270	D3413 08343	D3531 08416	D3603 08488
D3268 08198	D3341 08271	D3414 08344	D3532 08417	D3604 08489
D3269 08199	D3342 08272	D3415 08345	D3533 08418	D3605 08490
D3270 08200	D3343 08273	D3416 08346	D3534 08419	D3606 08491
D3271 08201	D3344 08274	D3417 08347	D3535 08420	D3607 08492
D3272 08202	D3345 08275	D3418 08348	D3536 08421	D3608 08493
D3273 08991	D3346 08276	D3419 08349	D3536 09201	D3609 08494
D3274 08204	D3347 08277	D3420 08350	D3537 08422	D3610 08495
D3275 08205	D3348 08278	D3421 08351	D3538 08423	D3611 08496
D3276 08206	D3349 08279	D3422 08352	D3539 08424	D3652 08497
D3277 08207	D3350 08280	D3423 08353	D3540 08425	D3653 08498
D3278 08208	D3351 08281	D3424 08354	D3541 08426	D3654 08499
D3279 08209	D3352 08282	D3425 08355	D3542 08427	D3655 08500
D3280 08210	D3353 08283	D3426 08356	D3543 08428	D3656 08501
D3281 08211	D3354 08284	D3427 08357	D3544 08429	D3657 08502
D3282 08212	D3355 08285	D3428 08358	D3545 08430	D3658 08503
D3283 08213	D3356 08286	D3429 08359	D3546 08431	D3659 08504
D3284 08214	D3357 08287	D3430 08360	D3547 08432	D3660 08505
D3285 08215	D3358 08288	D3431 08361	D3548 08433	D3661 08506
D3286 08216	D3359 08289	D3432 08362	D3549 08434	D3662 08507
D3287 08217	D3360 08290	D3433 08363	D3550 08435	D3663 08508
D3288 08218	D3361 08291	D3434 08364	D3551 08436	D3664 08509
D3289 08219	D3362 08292	D3435 08365	D3552 08437	D3665 09001
D3290 08220	D3363 08293	D3436 08366	D3553 08438	D3666 09002
D3291 08221	D3364 08294	D3437 08367	D3554 08439	D3667 09003
D3292 08222	D3365 08295	D3438 08368	D3555 08440	D3668 09004
D3293 08223	D3366 08296	D3454 08369	D3556 08441	D3669 09005
D3294 08224	D3367 08297	D3455 08370	D3557 08442	D3670 09006
D3295 08225	D3368 08298	D3456 08371	D3558 08443	D3671 09007
D3296 08226	D3369 08299	D3457 08372	D3559 08444	D3672 08510
D3297 08227	D3370 08300	D3458 08373	D3560 08445	D3673 08511
D3298 08228	D3371 08301	D3459 08374	D3561 08446	D3674 08512
D3299 08229	D3372 08302	D3460 08375	D3562 08447	D3675 08513
D3300 08230	D3373 08303	D3461 08376	D3563 08448	D3676 08514
D3301 08231	D3374 08304	D3462 08377	D3564 08449	D3677 08515
D3302 08232	D3375 08305	D3463 08378	D3565 08450	D3678 08516
D3303 08233	D3376 08306	D3464 08379	D3566 08451	D3679 08517
D3304 08234	D3377 08307	D3465 08380	D3567 08452	D3680 08518
D3305 08235	D3378 08308	D3466 08381	D3568 08453	D3681 08519
D3306 08236	D3379 08309	D3467 08382	D3569 08454	D3682 08520
D3307 08237	D3380 08310	D3468 08383	D3570 08455	D3683 08521
D3308 08238	D3381 08311	D3469 08384	D3571 08456	D3684 08522
D3309 08239	D3382 08312	D3470 08385	D3572 08457	D3685 08523

D3686 08524	D3761 08594	D3833 08666	D3905 08737	D3974 08806
D3687 08525	D3762 08595	D3834 08667	D3906 08738	D3975 08807
D3688 08526	D3763 08596	D3835 08668	D3907 08739	D3976 08808
D3689 08527	D3764 08597	D3836 08669	D3908 08740	D3977 08809
D3690 08528	D3765 08598	D3837 08670	D3909 08741	D3978 08810
D3691 08529	D3766 08599	D3838 08671	D3910 08742	D3979 08811
D3692 08530	D3767 08600	D3839 08672	D3911 08743	D3980 08812
D3693 08531	D3768 08601	D3840 08673	D3912 08744	D3981 08813
D3694 08532	D3769 08602	D3841 08674	D3913 08745	D3982 08814
D3695 08533	D3770 08603	D3842 08675	D3914 08746	D3983 08815
D3696 08534	D3771 08604	D3843 08676	D3915 08747	D3984 08816
D3699 08535	D3772 08605	D3844 08677	D3916 08748	D3985 08817
D3700 08536	D3773 08606	D3845 08678	D3917 08749	D3986 08818
D3701 08537	D3774 08607	D3846 08679	D3917 09104	D3987 08819
D3702 08538	D3775 08608	D3847 08680	D3918 08750	D3988 08820
D3703 08539	D3776 08609	D3848 08681	D3919 08751	D3989 08821
D3704 08540	D3777 08610	D3849 08682	D3920 08752	D3990 08822
D3705 08541	D3778 08611	D3850 08683	D3921 08753	D3991 08823
D3706 08542	D3779 08612	D3851 08684	D3922 08754	D3992 08824
D3707 08543	D3780 08613	D3852 08685	D3923 08755	D3993 08825
D3708 08544	D3781 08614	D3853 08686	D3924 08756	D3994 08826
D3709 08545	D3782 08615	D3854 08995	D3925 08757	D3995 08827
D3710 08546	D3783 08616	D3855 08688	D3926 08758	D3996 08828
D3711 08547	D3784 08617	D3856 08689	D3927 08759	D3997 08829
D3712 08548	D3785 08618	D3857 08690	D3927 09106	D3998 08830
D3713 08549	D3786 08619	D3858 08691	D3928 08760	D3999 08831
D3714 08550	D3787 08620	D3859 08692	D3929 08761	D4000 08832
D3715 08551	D3787 09205	D3860 08693	D3930 08762	D4001 08833
D3716 08552	D3788 08621	D3861 08694	D3931 08763	D4002 08834
D3717 08553	D3789 08622	D3862 08695	D3932 08764	D4003 08835
D3718 08554	D3790 08623	D3863 08696	D3933 08765	D4004 08836
D3719 09008	D3791 08624	D3864 08697	D3934 08766	D4005 08837
D3720 09009	D3792 08625	D3865 08698	D3934 09103	D4006 08838
D3721 09010	D3793 08626	D3866 08699	D3935 08767	D4007 08839
D3722 08555	D3794 08627	D3867 08700	D3936 08768	D4008 08840
D3723 08556	D3795 08628	D3868 08701	D3937 08769	D4009 08841
D3724 08557	D3796 08629	D3869 08702	D3938 08770	D4010 08842
D3725 08558	D3797 08630	D3870 08703	D3939 08771	D4011 08843
D3726 08559	D3798 08631	D3871 08704	D3940 08772	D4012 08844
D3727 08560	D3799 08632	D3872 08705	D3941 08773	D4013 08845
D3728 08561	D3800 08633	D3873 08706	D3942 08774	D4014 08846
D3729 08562	D3801 08634	D3874 08707	D3943 08775	D4015 08847
D3730 08563	D3802 08635	D3875 08708	D3944 08776	D4016 08848
D3731 08564	D3803 08636	D3876 08709	D3945 08777	D4017 08849
D3732 08565	D3804 08637	D3877 08710	D3946 08778	D4018 08850
D3733 08566	D3805 08638	D3878 08711	D3947 08779	D4019 08851
D3734 08567	D3806 08639	D3879 08712	D3948 08780	D4020 08852
D3735 08568	D3807 08640	D3880 08713	D3949 08781	D4021 08853
D3736 08569	D3808 08641	D3881 08714	D3949 09203	D4022 08854
D3737 08570	D3809 08642	D3882 08715	D3950 08782	D4023 08855
D3738 08571	D3810 08643	D3883 08716	D3951 08783	D4024 08856
D3739 08572	D3811 08644	D3884 08717	D3952 08784	D4025 08857
D3740 08573	D3812 08645	D3884 09204	D3953 08785	D4026 08858
D3741 08574	D3813 08646	D3886 08718	D3954 08786	D4027 08859
D3742 08575	D3814 08647	D3887 08719	D3955 08787	D4028 08860
D3743 08576	D3815 08648	D3888 08720	D3956 08788	D4029 08861
D3744 08577	D3816 08649	D3889 08721	D3957 08789	D4030 08862
D3745 08578	D3817 08650	D3890 08722	D3958 08790	D4031 08863
D3746 08579	D3818 08651	D3891 08723	D3959 08791	D4032 08864
D3747 08580	D3819 08652	D3892 08724	D3960 08792	D4033 08865
D3748 08581	D3820 08653	D3893 08725	D3961 08793	D4034 08866
D3749 08582	D3821 08654	D3894 08726	D3962 08794	D4035 08867
D3750 08583	D3822 08655	D3895 08727	D3963 08795	D4036 08868
D3751 08584	D3823 08656	D3896 08728	D3964 08796	D4037 08869
D3752 08585	D3824 08657	D3897 08729	D3965 08797	D4038 08870
D3753 08586	D3825 08658	D3898 08730	D3966 08798	D4039 08871
D3754 08587	D3826 08659	D3899 08731	D3967 08799	D4040 08872
D3755 08588	D3827 08660	D3900 08732	D3968 08800	D4041 08873
D3756 08589	D3828 08661	D3900 09202	D3969 08801	D4042 08874
D3757 08590	D3829 08662	D3901 08733	D3970 08802	D4043 08875
D3758 08591	D3830 08663	D3902 08734	D3971 08803	D4044 08876
D3759 08993	D3831 08664	D3903 08735	D3972 08804	D4045 08877
D3760 08593	D3832 08665	D3904 08736	D3973 08805	D4046 08878

D4047 08879	D4182 08952	D5046 24046	D5126 24126	D5203 25053
D4048 08880	D4183 08953	D5047 24047	D5127 24127	D5204 25054
D4095 08881	D4184 08954	D5048 24048	D5128 24128	D5205 25055
D4096 08882	D4185 08955	D5049 24049	D5129 24129	D5206 25056
D4097 08883	D4186 08956	D5050 24050	D5130 24130	D5207 25057
D4098 08884	D4191 08957	D5052 24052	D5132 24132	D5208 25058
D4115 08885	D4192 08958	D5053 24053	D5133 24133	D5209 25059
D4116 08886	D4099 09011	D5054 968008 (24054)	D5134 24134	D5210 25060
D4117 08887	D4100 09012	D5055 24055	D5135 24135	D5211 25061
D4118 08888	D4101 09013	D5056 24056	D5136 24136	D5212 25062
D4119 08889	D4102 09014	D5057 24057	D5137 24137	D5213 25063
D4120 08890	D4103 09015	D5058 24058	D5140 24140	D5214 25064
D4121 08891	D4104 09016	D5059 24059	D5141 24141	D5215 25065
D4122 08892	D4105 09017	D5060 24060	D5142 968009 (24142)	D5216 25066
D4123 08893	D4106 09018	D5061 968007 (24061)	D5143 24143	D5217 25067
D4124 08894	D4107 09019	D5062 24062	D5144 24144	D5218 25068
D4125 08895	D4108 09020	D5063 24063	D5145 24145	D5219 25069
D4126 08896	D4109 09021	D5064 24064	D5146 24146	D5220 25070
D4127 08897	D4110 09022	D5065 24065	D5147 24147	D5221 25071
D4128 08898	D4111 09023	D5066 24066	D5148 24148	D5222 25072
D4129 08899	D4112 09024	D5069 24069	D5150 24150	D5223 25073
D4130 08900	D4113 09025	D5070 24070	D5151 25001	D5224 25074
D4131 08901	D4114 09026	D5071 24071	D5152 25002	D5225 25075
D4132 08902	D4001 09101	D5072 24072	D5153 25003	D5226 25076
D4133 08903	D4000 09102	D5073 24073	D5154 25004	D5227 25077
D4134 08904	D4003 09105	D5074 24074	D5155 25005	D5228 25078
D4135 08905	D4013 09107	D5075 24075	D5156 25006	D5229 25079
D4136 08906	D4501 13001	D5076 24076	D5157 25007	D5230 25080
D4137 08907	D4502 13002	D5077 24077	D5158 25008	D5231 25081
D4138 08908	D4500 13003	D5078 24078	D5159 25009	D5232 25082
D4139 08909	D5000 24005	D5079 24079	D5160 25010	D5233 25083
D4140 08910	D5001 24001	D5080 24080	D5161 25011	D5234 25084
D4141 08911	D5002 24002	D5081 24081	D5162 25012	D5235 25085
D4142 08912	D5003 24003	D5082 24082	D5163 25013	D5236 25086
D4143 08913	D5004 24004	D5083 24083	D5164 25014	D5237 25087
D4144 08914	D5006 24006	D5084 24084	D5165 25015	D5238 25088
D4145 08915	D5007 24007	D5085 24085	D5166 25016	D5239 25089
D4146 08916	D5008 24008	D5086 24086	D5167 25017	D5240 25090
D4147 08917	D5009 24009	D5087 24087	D5168 25018	D5241 25091
D4148 08918	D5010 24010	D5089 24089	D5169 25019	D5242 25092
D4149 08919	D5011 24011	D5090 24090	D5170 25020	D5243 25093
D4150 08920	D5012 24012	D5091 24091	D5171 25021	D5244 25094
D4151 08921	D5013 24013	D5092 24092	D5172 25022	D5245 25095
D4152 08922	D5014 24014	D5094 24094	D5173 25023	D5246 25096
D4153 08923	D5015 24015	D5095 24095	D5174 25024	D5247 25097
D4154 08924	D5016 24016	D5096 24096	D5175 25025	D5248 25098
D4155 08925	D5017 24017	D5097 24097	D5176 25026	D5249 25099
D4156 08926	D5018 24018	D5098 24098	D5177 25027	D5250 25100
D4157 08927	D5019 24019	D5099 24099	D5178 25028	D5251 25101
D4158 08928	D5020 24020	D5100 24100	D5179 25029	D5252 25102
D4159 08929	D5021 24021	D5101 24101	D5180 25030	D5253 25103
D4160 08930	D5022 24022	D5102 24102	D5181 25031	D5254 25104
D4161 08931	D5023 24023	D5103 24103	D5182 25032	D5255 25105
D4162 08932	D5024 24024	D5104 24104	D5183 25033	D5256 25106
D4163 08933	D5025 24025	D5105 24105	D5184 25034	D5257 25107
D4164 08934	D5026 24026	D5106 24106	D5185 25035	D5258 25108
D4165 08935	D5027 24027	D5107 24107	D5186 25036	D5259 25109
D4166 08936	D5029 24029	D5108 24108	D5187 25037	D5260 25110
D4167 08937	D5030 24030	D5109 24109	D5188 25038	D5261 25111
D4168 08938	D5031 24031	D5110 24110	D5189 25039	D5262 25112
D4169 08939	D5032 24032	D5111 24111	D5190 25040	D5263 25113
D4170 08940	D5033 24033	D5112 24112	D5191 25041	D5264 25114
D4171 08941	D5034 24034	D5113 24113	D5192 25042	D5265 25115
D4172 08942	D5035 24035	D5115 24115	D5193 25043	D5266 25116
D4173 08943	D5036 24036	D5116 24116	D5194 25044	D5267 25117
D4174 08944	D5037 24037	D5117 24117	D5195 25045	D5268 25118
D4175 08945	D5038 24038	D5118 24118	D5196 25046	D5269 25119
D4176 08946	D5039 24039	D5119 24119	D5197 25047	D5270 25120
D4177 08947	D5040 24040	D5120 24120	D5198 25048	D5271 25121
D4178 08948	D5041 24041	D5121 24121	D5199 25049	D5272 25122
D4179 08949	D5042 24042	D5123 24123	D5200 25050	D5273 25123
D4180 08950	D5044 24044	D5124 24124	D5201 25051	D5274 25124
D4181 08951	D5045 24045	D5125 24125	D5202 25052	D5275 25125

D5276 25126	D5351 27005	D5508 968016 (31008)	D5581 31163	D5654 31454
D5277 25127	D5352 27006	D5509 31009	D5582 31164	D5655 31229
D5279 25129	D5353 27007	D5510 31010	D5583 31165	D5656 31409
D5280 25130	D5354 27008	D5511 31011	D5584 31166	D5657 31230
D5281 97202 (25131)	D5355 27009	D5512 31012	D5585 31167	D5658 31231
D5282 25132	D5356 27010	D5513 968013 (31013)	D5586 31168	D5659 31232
D5283 25133	D5357 27011	D5514 968015 (31014)	D5587 31457	D5660 31233
D5284 25134	D5358 27012	D5515 31015	D5588 31170	D5661 31234
D5285 25135	D5359 27013	D5516 31016	D5589 31401	D5662 31235
D5286 25136	D5360 27014	D5517 31017	D5590 31171	D5663 31433
D5287 25137	D5361 27015	D5518 31101	D5591 31420	D5664 31237
D5288 25138	D5362 27016	D5519 31019	D5592 31402	D5665 31238
D5289 25139	D5363 27017	D5520 31102	D5593 31173	D5666 31439
D5290 25140	D5364 27018	D5521 31103	D5594 31174	D5667 31240
D5291 25141	D5365 27019	D5522 31418	D5595 31175	D5668 31241
D5292 25142	D5366 27020	D5523 31105	D5596 31403	D5669 31410
D5293 25143	D5367 27021	D5524 31106	D5597 31176	D5670 31242
D5294 25144	D5368 27022	D5525 31107	D5598 31443	D5671 31243
D5295 25145	D5369 27023	D5526 31108	D5599 31178	D5672 31244
D5296 25146	D5370 968028 (27024)	D5527 31109	D5600 31435	D5673 31245
D5297 25147	D5371 27025	D5528 31110	D5601 31180	D5674 31455
D5298 25148	D5372 27026	D5529 31111	D5602 31181	D5675 31247
D5299 25149	D5373 27027	D5530 31112	D5603 31437	D5676 31248
D5300 26007	D5374 27101	D5531 31113	D5604 31183	D5677 31249
D5301 26001	D5375 27028	D5532 31553	D5605 31404	D5678 31250
D5302 26002	D5376 27029	D5533 31466	D5606 31405	D5679 31442
D5303 26003	D5377 27030	D5534 31116	D5607 31184	D5680 31252
D5304 26004	D5378 27031	D5535 31117	D5608 31185	D5681 31531
D5305 26005	D5379 27032	D5536 31118	D5609 31601	D5682 31254
D5306 26006	D5380 27102	D5537 31119	D5610 31187	D5683 31255
D5307 26020	D5381 27033	D5538 31120	D5611 31188	D5684 31459
D5308 26008	D5382 27034	D5539 31121	D5612 31189	D5685 31257
D5309 26009	D5383 27124	D5540 31122	D5613 31190	D5686 31434
D5310 26010	D5384 27035	D5541 31123	D5614 31602	D5687 31259
D5311 26011	D5385 27036	D5542 31124	D5615 31192	D5688 31260
D5312 26012	D5386 27066	D5543 31125	D5616 31406	D5689 31261
D5313 26013	D5387 27104	D5544 31126	D5617 31426	D5690 31262
D5314 26014	D5388 27105	D5545 31127	D5618 31427	D5691 31411
D5315 26015	D5389 27037	D5546 31128	D5619 31195	D5692 31412
D5316 26016	D5390 27038	D5547 31461	D5620 31196	D5693 31263
D5317 26017	D5391 27201	D5548 31130	D5621 31423	D5694 31264
D5318 26018	D5392 27202	D5549 31131	D5622 31198	D5695 31530
D5319 26019	D5393 27203	D5550 31132	D5623 31199	D5696 31460
D5320 26028	D5394 27050	D5551 31450	D5624 31200	D5697 31519
D5321 26021	D5395 27051	D5552 31134	D5625 31201	D5698 31268
D5322 26022	D5396 27052	D5553 31135	D5626 31202	D5699 31429
D5323 26023	D5397 27053	D5554 31136	D5627 31203	D5800 31270
D5324 26024	D5398 27039	D5555 31444	D5628 31440	D5801 31271
D5325 26025	D5399 27054	D5556 31138	D5629 31205	D5802 31272
D5326 26026	D5400 27055	D5557 31538	D5630 31206	D5803 31273
D5327 26027	D5401 27056	D5558 31421	D5631 31207	D5804 31425
D5329 26029	D5402 27040	D5559 31141	D5632 31208	D5805 31275
D5330 26030	D5403 27058	D5560 31142	D5633 31209	D5806 31276
D5331 26031	D5404 968025 (27207)	D5561 31143	D5634 31210	D5807 31569
D5332 26032	D5405 27041	D5562 31144	D5635 31428	D5808 31278
D5333 26033	D5406 27042	D5563 31145	D5636 31212	D5809 31452
D5334 26034	D5407 27208	D5564 31146	D5637 31465	D5810 31280
D5335 26035	D5408 27063	D5565 31147	D5638 31214	D5811 31281
D5336 26036	D5409 27064	D5566 31548	D5639 31215	D5812 31413
D5337 26037	D5410 27059	D5567 31149	D5640 31407	D5813 31282
D5338 26038	D5411 27065	D5568 31150	D5641 31467	D5814 31514
D5339 26039	D5412 27206	D5569 31436	D5642 31217	D5815 31283
D5340 26040	D5413 27047	D5570 31152	D5643 31218	D5816 31284
D5341 26041	D5414 27043	D5571 31432	D5644 31219	D5817 31285
D5342 26042	D5415 27044	D5572 31154	D5645 31541	D5818 31286
D5343 26043	D5500 31018	D5573 31155	D5646 31408	D5819 31287
D5344 26044	D5501 31001	D5574 31156	D5647 31221	D5820 31288
D5345 26045	D5502 968014 (31002)	D5575 31524	D5648 31222	D5821 31289
D5346 26046	D5503 31003	D5576 31158	D5649 31223	D5822 31290
D5347 27001	D5504 31004	D5577 31159	D5650 31224	D5823 31556
D5348 27002	D5505 31005	D5578 31160	D5651 31225	D5824 31415
D5349 27003	D5506 31006	D5579 31400	D5652 31226	D5825 31292
D5350 27004	D5507 31007	D5580 31162	D5653 31227	D5826 31293

D5827 31294	D6538 33118	D6705 37601	D6778 37078	D6851 37667
D5828 31547	D6539 33021	D6706 37798	D6779 37357	D6852 37152
D5829 31296	D6540 33022	D6707 37604	D6780 37080	D6853 37153
D5830 31563	D6541 33023	D6708 37352	D6781 37797	D6854 37154
D5831 97203 (31298)	D6542 33024	D6709 37340	D6782 37602	D6855 37897
D5832 31299	D6543 33025	D6710 37010	D6783 37083	D6856 37156
D5833 31545	D6544 33026	D6711 37011	D6784 37718	D6857 37695
D5834 31301	D6545 33027	D6712 37012	D6785 37711	D6858 37158
D5835 31302	D6546 33028	D6713 37013	D6786 37516	D6859 37372
D5836 31558	D6547 33029	D6714 37709	D6787 37087	D6860 37373
D5837 31304	D6548 33030	D6715 37341	D6788 37088	D6861 37899
D5838 31305	D6549 33031	D6716 37706	D6789 37708	D6862 37162
D5839 31306	D6550 33032	D6717 37503	D6790 37606	D6863 37802
D5840 31549	D6551 33033	D6718 37517	D6791 37358	D6864 37675
D5841 31308	D6552 33034	D6719 37019	D6792 37092	D6865 37165
D5842 31516	D6553 33035	D6720 37702	D6793 37509	D6866 37891
D5843 31309	D6554 33036	D6721 37715	D6794 37716	D6867 37383
D5844 31422	D6555 33037	D6722 37608	D6795 37095	D6868 37890
D5845 31311	D6556 33038	D6723 37023	D6796 37096	D6869 37674
D5846 31312	D6557 33039	D6724 37714	D6797 37097	D6870 97302 (37170)
D5847 31313	D6558 33040	D6725 37025	D6798 37098	D6871 37611
D5848 31314	D6559 33041	D6726 37026	D6799 37099	D6872 37686
D5849 31462	D6560 33042	D6727 37519	D6800 97301 (37100)	D6873 37603
D5850 31546	D6561 33043	D6728 37505	D6801 37345	D6874 37174
D5851 31317	D6562 33044	D6729 37029	D6802 37712	D6875 37175
D5852 31551	D6563 33045	D6730 37701	D6803 37607	D6876 37883
D5853 31319	D6564 33046	D6731 37031	D6804 37104	D6877 37885
D5854 31320	D6565 33047	D6732 37032	D6805 37796	D6878 97303 (37178)
D5855 31468	D6566 33048	D6733 37717	D6806 37106	D6879 37612
D5856 31417	D6567 33049	D6734 37704	D6807 37107	D6880 37886
D5857 31322	D6568 33050	D6735 37035	D6808 37108	D6881 37610
D5858 31323	D6569 33051	D6736 37605	D6809 37109	D6882 37670
D5859 31324	D6570 33052	D6737 37037	D6810 37110	D6883 37884
D5860 31464	D6571 33053	D6738 37038	D6811 37111	D6884 37184
D5861 31970 (31326)	D6572 33054	D6739 37603	D6812 37510	D6885 37185
D5862 31327	D6573 33055	D6740 37040	D6813 37113	D6886 37898
D6500 33001	D6574 33056	D6741 37520	D6814 37114	D6887 37683
D6501 33002	D6575 33057	D6742 37042	D6815 37609	D6888 37188
D6502 33003	D6577 33058	D6743 37354	D6816 37116	D6889 37672
D6503 33003	D6578 33059	D6744 37710	D6817 37521	D6890 37190
D6504 33004	D6579 33060	D6745 37355	D6818 37359	D6891 37191
D6505 33005	D6580 33119	D6746 37046	D6819 37895	D6892 37694
D6506 33006	D6581 33061	D6747 37047	D6820 37887	D6893 37375
D6507 33007	D6582 33062	D6748 37048	D6821 37677	D6894 37194
D6508 33008	D6583 33063	D6749 37343	D6822 37692	D6895 37689
D6509 33009	D6584 33064	D6750 37717	D6823 37679	D6896 37196
D6510 33010	D6585 33065	D6751 37051	D6824 37894	D6897 37197
D6511 33101	D6586 33201	D6752 37713	D6825 37904	D6898 37198
D6512 33011	D6587 33202	D6753 37344	D6826 37676	D6899 37376
D6513 33102	D6588 33203	D6754 37054	D6827 37370	D6900 37377
D6514 33103	D6589 33204	D6755 37055	D6828 37330	D6901 37201
D6515 33012	D6590 33205	D6756 37513	D6829 37669	D6902 37331
D6516 33104	D6591 33206	D6757 37057	D6830 37681	D6903 37203
D6517 33105	D6592 33207	D6758 37058	D6831 37131	D6904 37378
D6518 33013	D6593 33208	D6759 37059	D6832 37673	D6905 37688
D6519 33106	D6594 33209	D6760 37705	D6833 37133	D6906 37906
D6520 33107	D6595 33210	D6761 37799	D6834 37684	D6907 37207
D6521 33108	D6596 33211	D6762 37062	D6835 37888	D6908 37803
D6522 33014	D6597 33212	D6763 37063	D6836 37905	D6909 37209
D6523 33015	D6600 37429	D6764 37515	D6837 37137	D6910 37693
D6524 33016	D6601 37412	D6765 37065	D6838 37138	D6911 37211
D6525 33109	D6602 37416	D6766 37066	D6839 37139	D6912 37212
D6526 33017	D6603 37333	D6767 37703	D6840 37140	D6913 37213
D6527 33110	D6604 37334	D6768 37356	D6841 37141	D6914 37214
D6528 33111	D6605 37407	D6769 37069	D6842 37142	D6915 37215
D6529 33112	D6606 37273 (2)	D6770 37070	D6843 37800	D6916 37216
D6530 33018	D6607 37403	D6771 37071	D6844 37144	D6917 97304 (37217)
D6531 33113	D6608 37308	D6772 37072	D6845 37382	D6918 37218
D6532 33114	D6700 37350	D6773 37073	D6846 37146	D6919 37219
D6533 33115	D6701 37707	D6774 37074	D6847 37371	D6920 37220
D6534 33019	D6702 37351	D6775 37075	D6848 37902	D6921 37221
D6535 33116	D6703 37003	D6776 37518	D6849 37892	D6922 37222
D6536 33117	D6704 37004	D6777 37077	D6850 37901	D6923 37223
D6537 33020				

D6924 37680	D6998 37298	D7571 25221	D7645 25295	D8040 20040
D6925 37225	D6999 37426	D7572 25222	D7646 25906	D8041 20904
D6926 37379	D7500 25150	D7573 25223	D7647 25907	D8042 20312
D6927 37227	D7501 25151	D7574 25224	D7648 25298	D8043 20043
D6928 37696	D7502 25152	D7575 25225	D7649 25299	D8044 20044
D6929 37229	D7503 25153	D7576 25226	D7650 25300	D8045 20045
D6930 37230	D7504 25154	D7577 25227	D7651 25301	D8046 20046
D6931 37896	D7505 25155	D7578 25228	D7652 25302	D8047 20301 (2)
D6932 37232	D7506 25156	D7579 25229	D7653 25303	D8048 20048
D6933 37889	D7507 25157	D7580 25230	D7654 25304	D8049 20049
D6934 37685	D7508 25158	D7581 25231	D7655 97251 (25305)	D8050 20307 (2)
D6935 37235	D7509 25159	D7582 25232	D7656 25306	D8051 20051
D6936 37682	D7510 25160	D7583 25233	D7657 25908	D8052 20052
D6937 37893	D7511 25161	D7584 25234	D7658 25308	D8053 20053
D6938 37238	D7512 25162	D7585 25235	D7659 25909	D8054 20054
D6939 37332	D7513 25163	D7586 25236	D7660 97250 (25310)	D8055 20055
D6940 37240	D7514 25164	D7587 25237	D7661 25311	D8056 20056
D6941 37241	D7515 25165	D7588 25238	D7662 25312	D8057 20057
D6942 37242	D7516 25166	D7589 25239	D7663 25313	D8058 20058
D6943 37697	D7517 25167	D7590 25240	D7664 97252 (25314)	D8059 20059
D6944 37244	D7518 25168	D7591 25241	D7665 25910	D8060 20902
D6945 37245	D7519 25169	D7592 25242	D7666 25911	D8061 20061
D6946 37698	D7520 25170	D7593 25243	D7667 25317	D8062 20062
D6947 37671	D7521 25171	D7594 25244	D7668 25318	D8063 20063
D6948 37248	D7522 25172	D7595 25245	D7669 25319	D8064 20064
D6949 37903	D7523 25173	D7596 25246	D7670 25320	D8065 20065
D6950 37250	D7524 25174	D7597 25247	D7671 25321	D8066 20066
D6951 37251	D7525 25175	D7598 25248	D7672 25912	D8067 20067
D6952 37252	D7526 25176	D7599 25249	D7673 25323	D8068 20068
D6953 37699	D7527 25177	D7600 25250	D7674 25324	D8069 20069
D6954 37254	D7528 25178	D7601 25251	D7675 25325	D8070 20070
D6955 37255	D7529 25179	D7602 25252	D7676 25326	D8071 20071
D6956 37678	D7530 25180	D7603 25253	D7677 25327	D8072 20072
D6957 37668	D7531 25181	D7604 25254	D8000 20050	D8073 20073
D6958 37384	D7532 25182	D7606 25256	D8001 20001	D8074 20074
D6959 37259	D7533 25183	D7607 25257	D8002 20002	D8075 20309
D6960 37260	D7534 25184	D7608 25258	D8003 20003	D8076 20076
D6961 37261	D7535 25185	D7609 25259	D8004 20004	D8077 20077
D6962 37262	D7536 25186	D7610 25260	D8005 20005	D8078 20078
D6963 37263	D7537 25187	D7611 25261	D8006 20006	D8079 20079
D6964 37264	D7538 25188	D7612 25901	D8007 20007	D8080 20080
D6965 37430	D7539 25189	D7613 25263	D8008 20008	D8081 20081
D6966 37422	D7540 25190	D7614 25264	D8009 20009	D8082 20082
D6967 37421	D7541 25191	D7615 25265	D8010 20010	D8083 20903
D6968 37401	D7542 25192	D7616 25266	D8011 20011	D8084 20302 (2)
D6969 37417	D7543 25193	D7617 25267	D8012 20012	D8085 20085
D6970 37409	D7544 25194	D7618 25902	D8013 20013	D8086 20086
D6971 37418	D7545 25195	D7619 25269	D8014 20014	D8087 20087
D6972 37431	D7546 25196	D7620 25270	D8015 20015	D8088 20088
D6973 37410	D7547 25197	D7621 25271	D8016 20016	D8089 20089
D6974 37402	D7548 25198	D7622 25272	D8017 20017	D8090 20090
D6975 37275	D7549 25199	D7623 25273	D8018 20018	D8091 20091
D6976 37413	D7550 25200	D7624 25274	D8019 20019	D8092 20092
D6977 37415	D7551 25201	D7625 25275	D8020 20020	D8093 20093
D6978 37278	D7552 25202	D7626 25903	D8021 20021	D8094 20094
D6979 37424	D7553 25203	D7627 25277	D8022 20022	D8095 20305 (2)
D6980 37280	D7554 25204	D7628 25278	D8023 20023	D8096 20096
D6981 37428	D7555 25205	D7629 25279	D8024 20024	D8097 20097
D6982 37405	D7556 25206	D7630 25280	D8025 20025	D8098 20098
D6984 37381	D7557 25207	D7631 25281	D8026 20026	D8099 20099
D6985 37335	D7558 25208	D7632 25282	D8027 20027	D8100 20100
D6986 37404	D7559 25209	D7633 25904	D8028 20028	D8101 20901
D6987 37414	D7560 25210	D7634 25284	D8029 20029	D8102 20311
D6988 37427	D7561 25211	D7635 25285	D8030 20030	D8103 20103
D6989 37408	D7562 25212	D7636 25905	D8031 20031	D8104 20315
D6990 37411	D7563 25213	D7637 25287	D8032 20032	D8105 20105
D6991 37419	D7564 25214	D7638 25288	D8033 20033	D8106 20106
D6992 37425	D7565 25215	D7639 25289	D8034 20034	D8107 20107
D6993 37293	D7566 25216	D7640 25290	D8035 20035	D8108 20108
D6994 37294	D7567 25217	D7641 25291	D8036 20036	D8109 20109
D6995 37406	D7568 25218	D7642 25292	D8037 20037	D8110 20110
D6996 37423	D7569 25219	D7643 25293	D8038 20038	D8111 20111
D6997 37420	D7570 25220	D7644 25294	D8039 20039	D8112 20112

D8113 20113	D8142 20142	D8171 20171	D8300 20200	D9001 55001
D8114 20114	D8143 20143	D8172 20172	D8301 20201	D9002 55002
D8115 20115	D8144 20144	D8173 20173	D8302 20202	D9003 55003
D8116 20116	D8145 20145	D8174 20174	D8303 20203	D9004 55004
D8117 20314	D8146 20146	D8175 20175	D8304 20204	D9005 55005
D8118 20118	D8147 20147	D8176 20176	D8305 20205	D9006 55006
D8119 20119	D8148 20148	D8177 20177	D8306 20206	D9007 55007
D8120 20304 (2)	D8149 20149	D8178 20178	D8307 20207	D9008 55008
D8121 20121	D8150 20150	D8179 20179	D8308 20208	D9009 55009
D8122 20122	D8151 20151	D8180 20180	D8309 20209	D9010 55010
D8123 20123	D8152 20152	D8181 20181	D8310 20210	D9011 55011
D8124 20124	D8153 20153	D8182 20182	D8311 20211	D9012 55012
D8125 20125	D8154 20154	D8183 20183	D8312 20212	D9013 55013
D8126 20126	D8155 20155	D8184 20184	D8313 20213	D9014 55014
D8127 20303 (2)	D8156 20156	D8185 20185	D8314 20214	D9015 55015
D8128 20228	D8157 20157	D8186 20186	D8315 20215	D9016 55016
D8129 20129	D8158 20158	D8187 20308	D8316 20216	D9017 55017
D8130 20130	D8159 20159	D8188 20188	D8317 20217	D9018 55018
D8131 20306 (2)	D8160 20160	D8189 20189	D8318 20218	D9019 55019
D8132 20132	D8161 20161	D8190 20310	D8319 20906 (3)	D9020 55020
D8133 20133	D8162 20162	D8191 20191	D8320 20220	D9021 55021
D8134 20134	D8163 20163	D8192 20192	D8321 20221	D9524 14901
D8135 20135	D8164 20164	D8193 20193	D8322 20222	E3001 81001
D8136 20136	D8165 20165	D8194 20313	D8323 20223	E3003 81002
D8137 20137	D8166 20166	D8195 20195	D8324 20224	E3004 81003
D8138 20138	D8167 20167	D8196 20196	D8325 20905	E3005 81004
D8139 20139	D8168 20168	D8197 20197	D8326 20226	E3006 81005
D8140 20140	D8169 20169	D8198 20198	D8327 20227	E3007 81006
D8141 20141	D8170 20170	D8199 20199	D9000 55022	E3008 81007

▲ Network Rail has three Class 43 HST power cars for its high-speed infrastructure monitoring train. On 23 February 2019, this has just passed through Lazonby and is seen heading towards Carlisle with 43014 "The Railway Observer" leading and 43062 following on the rear. **Keith Sanders**

E3010 81008	E3067 85104	E3121 86241	E3175 86218	E6011 73105
E3011 81009	E3068 85013	E3122 86612	E3176 86607	E6012 73106
E3012 81010	E3069 85014	E3123 86615	E3177 86217	E6013 73107
E3013 81011	E3070 85015	E3124 86635	E3178 86244	E6014 73108
E3014 81012	E3071 85105	E3125 86209	E3179 86207	E6015 73109
E3015 81013	E3072 85017	E3126 86231	E3180 86608	E6016 73110
E3016 81014	E3073 85018	E3127 86240	E3181 86243	E6017 73111
E3017 81015	E3074 85019	E3128 86613	E3182 86245	E6018 73213
E3018 81016	E3075 85020	E3129 86701	E3183 86251	E6019 73211
E3020 81017	E3076 85106	E3130 86637	E3184 86206	E6020 73114
E3021 81018	E3077 85022	E3131 86222	E3185 86605	E6021 73115
E3022 81019	E3078 85023	E3132 86221	E3186 86425	E6022 73210
E3023 81020	E3079 85107	E3133 86236	E3187 86634	E6023 73117
E3024 83001	E3080 85025	E3134 86224	E3188 86631	E6024 73118
E3025 83002	E3081 85026	E3135 86256	E3189 86250	E6025 73119
E3026 83003	E3082 85027	E3136 86901	E3190 86902	E6026 73209
E3027 83004	E3083 85028	E3137 86259	E3191 86101	E6028 73208
E3028 83005	E3084 85029	E3138 86242	E3192 86247	E6029 73207
E3029 83006	E3085 85030	E3139 86257	E3193 86213	E6030 73206
E3030 83007	E3086 85031	E3140 86258	E3194 86235	E6031 73205
E3031 83008	E3087 85108	E3141 86208	E3195 86426	E6032 73204
E3032 83009	E3088 85033	E3142 86254	E3196 86219	E6033 73126
E3033 83010	E3089 85034	E3143 86103	E3197 86237	E6034 73203
E3034 83011	E3090 85109	E3144 86702	E3198 86633	E6035 73128
E3035 83012	E3091 85110	E3145 86614	E3199 86401	E6036 73129
E3036 84001	E3092 85037	E3146 86417	E3200 86429	E6037 73130
E3037 84002	E3093 85038	E3147 86211	E5000 E5024	E6038 73131
E3038 84003	E3094 85039	E3148 86632	E5001 71001	E6039 73132
E3039 84004	E3095 85040	E3149 86246	E5002 71002	E6040 73133
E3040 84005	E3096 81021	E3150 86102	E5003² 71003	E6041 73134
E3041 84006	E3097 81022	E3151 86212	E5004 71004	E6042 73235
E3042 84007	E3098 83013	E3152 86623	E5005² 71005	E6043 73136
E3043 84008	E3099 83014	E3153 86639	E5006² 71006	E6044 73202
E3044 968021 (84009)	E3100 83015	E3154 86255	E5007 71007	E6045 73138
E3045 84010	E3101 86252	E3155 86234	E5008 71008	E6046 73139
E3047 82001	E3102 86609	E3156 86220	E5009 71009	E6047 73140
E3048 82002	E3103 86604	E3157 86621	E5010 71010	E6048 73141
E3049 82003	E3104 86610	E3158 86223	E5011 71011	E6049 73201
E3050 82004	E3105 86430	E3159 86628	E5012 71012	E6101 74001
E3051 82005	E3106 86214	E3160 86636	E5013 71013	E6102 74002
E3052 82006	E3107 86248	E3161 86249	E5014 71014	E6103 74003
E3053 82007	E3108 86638	E3162 86226	E5018 71003	E6104 74004
E3054 82008	E3109 86416	E3163 86618	E5020 71005	E6105 74005
E3056 85001	E3110 86627	E3164 86225	E5022 71006	E6106 74006
E3057 85002	E3111 86424	E3165 86215	E6001 73001	E6107 74007
E3058 85113	E3112 86606	E3166 86216	E6002 73002	E6108 74008
E3059 85111	E3113 86232	E3167 86228	E6003 73003	E6109 74009
E3060 85005	E3114 86620	E3168 86230	E6004 73004	E6110 74010
E3061 85006	E3115 86603	E3169 86239	E6005 73005	
E3062 85112	E3116 86238	E3170 86602	E6006 73906	PWM650 97650
E3063 85008	E3117 86227	E3171 86611	E6007 73101	PWM651 97651
E3064 85102	E3118 86261	E3172 86233	E6008 73212	PWM652 97652
E3065 85103	E3119 86229	E3173 86204	E6009 73103	PWM653 97653
E3066 85114	E3120 86419	E3174 86622	E6010 73104	PWM654 97654

APPENDIX IV: DEPARTMENTAL NUMBERS

This appendix lists all locomotives that were renumbered for departmental use. It does not include locos that were assigned a departmental number which was not actually carried, or departmental locos that were not given a separate departmental number, such as the Network Rail HSTs (43013, 43014 and 43062). In each case, the departmental number is shown, along with the corresponding locomotive class and the number by which it is listed in this book.

Departmental No.	Class the loco is listed under	Number listed by	Notes
20	Purpose built departmental	97020	
56	Purpose built departmental	56	
82	Purpose built departmental	82	
83	Purpose built departmental	83	
84	Purpose built departmental	84	
85	Purpose built departmental	85	
86	Purpose built departmental	86	
87	Purpose built departmental	87	
88	05	D2612	
89	05	D2615	
100	EB1	26510	
31970	31	31970	Second of two departmental numbers carried by 31326
47971	47	47971	Second of two departmental numbers carried by 47480
47972	47	47972	Second of two departmental numbers carried by 47545
47973	47	47973	Second of two departmental numbers carried by 47561
47974	47	47775	
47975	47	47540	
47976	47	47976	
47981	47	47981	
73951	73/9	73951	
73952	73/9	73952	
86901	86	86901	
86902	86	86902	
97201	24	24061	First of two departmental numbers carried by 24061
97202	25	25131	
97203	31	31298	
97204	31	31970	First of two departmental numbers carried by 31326
97250	25	25310	
97251	25	25305	
97252	25	25314	
97301	37	97301	
97302	37	97302	
97303	37	97303	
97304	37	97304	
97403	46	46035	
97404	46	46045	
97405	40	40060	
97406	40	40135	
97407	40	40012	
97408	40	40118	
97409	45	45022	
97410	45	45029	
97411	45	45034	
97412	45	45040	
97413	45	45066	
97472	47	47472	
97480	47	47971	First of two departmental numbers carried by 47480
97545	47	47972	First of two departmental numbers carried by 47545
97561	47	47973	First of two departmental numbers carried by 47561
97650	Purpose built departmental	97650	
97651	Purpose built departmental	97651	
97652	Purpose built departmental	97652	
97653	Purpose built departmental	97653	
97654	Purpose built departmental	97654	

97800	08	08600	
97801	08	08267	Second of two departmental numbers carried by 08267
97803	05	05001	
97804	06	06003	
97806	09	09017	
ADB966506	08	D3078	
ADB966507	08	D3006	
ADB966508	08	D3035	
ADB966509	08	D3069	
ADB966510	08	D3037	
ADB966511	08	08119	First of two departmental numbers carried by 08119
ADB966512	08	08111	First of two departmental numbers carried by 08111
ADB966513	08	08117	First of three departmental numbers carried by 08117
ADB968000	15	D8243	
ADB968001	15	D8233	
ADB968002	15	D8237	
ADB968003	15	D8203	
ADB968008	24	24054	
ADB968009	24	24142	
ADB968010	08	08117	Third of three departmental numbers carried by 08117
ADB968011	08	08119	Second of two departmental numbers carried by 08119
ADB968012	08	08111	Second of two departmental numbers carried by 08111
ADB968013	08	08117	Second of three departmental numbers carried by 08117
ADB968013[2]	31	31013	
ADB968014	31	31002	
ADB968015	31	31014	
ADB968016	31	31008	
ADB968021	84	84009	
ADB968024	45	45017	
ADB968025	27	27207	
ADB968028	27	27024	
ADB968035	47	47538	
ADB975812	41	41001	
ADB975813	41	41002	
DS1169	Purpose built departmental	DS1169	
ED1	Purpose built departmental	ED1	
ED2	Purpose built departmental	ED2	
ED3	Purpose built departmental	ED3	
ED4	Purpose built departmental	ED4	
ED5	Purpose built departmental	ED5	
ED6	Purpose built departmental	ED6	
ED7	Purpose built departmental	ED7	
PO1	08	08247	
PO1[2]	08	08173	
PWM650	Purpose built departmental	97650	
PWM651	Purpose built departmental	97651	
PWM652	Purpose built departmental	97652	
PWM653	Purpose built departmental	97653	
PWM654	Purpose built departmental	97654	
RDB968007	24	24061	Second of two departmental numbers carried by 24061
RDB968020	08	08267	First of two departmental numbers carried by 08267
S18521	17	D8521	
TDB968006	28	D5705	Formerly carried departmental number S15705
TDB968030	33	33018	

APPENDIX V: LOCOMOTIVE NAMES

This appendix contains a list of all official locomotive names carried during main line service with BR or its successors. Names given during preservation are not included. The name listings are case sensitive as carried on locos and where a locomotive has carried more than one name, they are listed chronologically, in the order they were carried.

Names are listed adjacent to the locomotive number carried in the period when the name was also carried. In the case of subsequently renumbered locomotives, this is not the number under which the locomotive's entry can be found in this book. Please refer to appendices 2 and 3 as necessary to locate where the locomotive's details can be found in this book.

Unofficial names are not included and in cases where it is not clear whether a name is official, names on cast nameplates are included and names painted on to the sides of locomotives have been excluded. Where a crest or plaque is mounted separately, and this also includes text, this is not listed. For example, 31602 had a separate "19B" plaque under the "DRIVER DAVE GREEN" nameplate and only the text on the nameplate is included.

Number	Name/Names
03179	CLIVE
08389	NOEL KIRTON OBE
08442	RICHARD J. WENHAM EASTLEIGH DEPOT DECEMBER 1989 – JULY 1999
08451	M.A. SMITH
	LONGSIGHT TMD
08460	SPIRIT OF THE OAK
08482	DON GATES 1952–2000
08483	DUSTY Driver David Miller
	NEIL/SCOUSEY Neil Morgan 1964–2014 Team Leader O.O.C.
	Bungle
08484	CAPTAIN NATHANIEL DARELL
08495	NOEL KIRTON OBE
08499	REDLIGHT
08502	Lybert Dickinson
08516	RORY
08525	Percy The Pilot
	DUNCAN BEDFORD
08562	The Doncaster Postman
08575	The Doncaster Postman
08578	Lybert Dickinson
08585	Vicky
08598	HERCULES
08604	PHANTOM
08605	G. R. Walker
08611	DOWNHILL C.S.
	M.A. SMITH
	LONGSIGHT TMD
08615	UNCLE DAI
08616	COOKIE
	TYSELEY 100
08617	Steve Purser
08624	Rambo PAUL RAMSEY
08629	BRML WOLVERTON LEVEL 5
	Bradwell
	Wolverton
08630	BOB BROWN
	Celsa Endeavour
08631	EAGLE C.U.R.C.
08633	The Sorter
08644	Laira Diesel Depot 50 Years 1962–2012
08645	Mike Baggott
	St. Piran
08647	CRIMPSALL
08648	Amanda
08649	G.H. Stratton
	Wolverton
	Bradwell
08661	Europa
08663	Jack
	St. Silas

Number	Name/Names
08664	DON GATES 1952–2000
08669	Bob Machin
08682	Lionheart
08690	DAVID THIRKHILL
08691	Terri
08694	PAT BARR
08696	LONGSIGHT TMD
08701	GATESHEAD TMD 1852–1991
	The Sorter
08709	MOLLY'S DAY
08711	EAGLE C.U.R.C.
08714	Cambridge
08721	STARLET
	M.A. Smith
	DOWNHILL C.S.
	LONGSIGHT TMD
08730	The Caley
08735	Geoff Hobbs 42
08738	SILVER FOX
08743	ANGIE
	Bryan Turner
08757	EAGLE C.U.R.C.
08772	CAMULODUNUM
08774	ARTHUR VERNON DAWSON
08780	FRED
	ZIPPY
08782	CASTLETON WORKS
08790	M.A. Smith
	STARLET
	Steve Purser
08799	ANDY BOWER
	FRED
08804	RICHARD J. WENHAM EASTLEIGH DEPOT DECEMBER 1989 – JULY 1999
08805	CONCORDE
	Robin Jones 40 YEARS SERVICE
08810	RICHARD J. WENHAM EASTLEIGH DEPOT DECEMBER 1989 – JULY 1999
08818	MOLLY
08822	John
	Dave Mills
08823	LIBBIE
	KEVLA
08844	CHRIS WREN 1955–2002
08869	THE CANARY
08872	TONY LONG STRATFORD DEPOT 1971–2002
08874	Catherine
08879	Sheffield Childrens Hospital
08888	Postman's Pride
08891	J.R. 1951 – 2005
08896	STEPHEN DENT
08899	Midland Counties Railway 175 1839 – 2014

08903	John W Antill
08905	DANNY DANIELS
08907	MOLLY'S DAY
08908	IVAN STEPHENSON
08911	MATEY
08919	Steep Holm
08950	Neville Hill 1st
	DAVID LIGHTFOOT
08951	FRED
08991	KIDWELLY
08992	GWENDRAETH
08993	ASHBURNHAM
08994	GWENDRAETH
	SPIRIT OF INNOVATION
08995	KIDWELLY
09008	Sheffield Childrens Hospital
09009	Three Bridges C.E.D.
09012	Dick Hardy
09026	William Pearson
	Cedric Wares
20075	Sir William Cooke
20096	Ian Goddard 1938 – 2016
20107	Jocelyn Fielding 1940 – 2020
20118	Saltburn-by-the Sea
20122	Cleveland Potash
20128	Guglielmo Marconi
20131	Almon B. Strowger
20132	Barrow Hill Depot
20137	Murray B. Hofmeyr
20142	SIR JOHN BETJEMAN
20165	Henry Pease
20168	SIR GEORGE EARLE
20187	Sir Charles Wheatstone
20301	FURNESS RAILWAY 150
	Max Joule 1958–1999
20303	Max Joule 1958–1999
20305	Gresty Bridge
20310	Gresty Bridge
20311	Class 20 'Fifty'
20901	NANCY
20902	NANCY
20902	LORNA
20903	ALISON
20904	JANIS
20905	IONA
	Dave Darwin
20906	GEORGINA
	KILMARNOCK 400
25912	TAMWORTH CASTLE
26001	Eastfield
31102	Cricklewood
31105	Bescot TMD
	Bescot TMD Bescot & Saltley Quality Assured
31106	The Blackcountryman
	SPALDING TOWN
31107	John H Carless V.C.
31110	TRACTION magazine
31116	RAIL 1981 – 1991
	RAIL Celebrity
31128	CHARYBDIS
31130	Calder Hall Power Station
31146	Brush Veteran
31147	Floreat Salopia
31165	Stratford Major Depot
31190	GRYPHON
31201	Fina Energy
31233	Phillips Imperial
	Severn Valley Railway
31276	Calder Hall Power Station
31296	Amlwch Freighter/Trên Nwyddau Amlwch
31309	Cricklewood
31327	Phillips Imperial
31405	Mappa Mundi

31410	Granada Telethon
31413	Severn Valley Railway
31421	Wigan Pier
31423	Jerome K. Jerome
31428	North Yorkshire Moors Railway
31430	Sister Dora
31439	North Yorkshire Moors Railway
31444	Keighley and Worth Valley Railway
31452	MINOTAUR
31454	THE HEART OF WESSEX
31455	Our Eli
31459	CERBERUS
31468	The Enginemen's Fund
	HYDRA
31530	Sister Dora
31544	Keighley and Worth Valley Railway
31558	Nene Valley Railway
31568	The Enginemen's Fund
31601	BLETCHLEY PARK 'STATION X'
	THE MAYOR OF CASTERBRIDGE
	GAUGE 'O' GUILD 1956–2006
	Devon Diesel Society
31602	CHIMAERA
	DRIVER DAVE GREEN
33002	Sea King
33008	Eastleigh
33009	Walrus
33012	Lt Jenny Lewis RN
33019	Griffon
33021	Eastleigh
33025	Sultan
	Glen Falloch
33026	Seafire
33027	Earl Mountbatten of Burma
33029	Glen Loy
33035	Spitfire
33046	Merlin
33047	Spitfire
33050	Isle of Grain
33051	Shakespeare Cliff
33052	Ashford
33056	The Burma Star
33057	Seagull
33065	Sealion
33103	SWORDFISH
33108	VAMPIRE
33109	Captain Bill Smith RNR
33112	Templecombe
33114	Sultan
	Ashford 150
33116	Hertfordshire Rail Tours
33202	The Burma Star
	METEOR
33207	Earl Mountbatten of Burma
	Jim Martin
37012	Loch Rannoch
37023	Stratford
	Stratford TMD Quality Approved
37025	Inverness TMD
37026	Loch Awe
	Shapfell
37027	Loch Eli
37037	Gartcosh
37043	Loch Lomond
37049	Imperial
37051	Merehead
37055	RAIL Celebrity
37057	Viking
37059	Port of Tilbury
37062	British Steel Corby
37066	British Steel Workington
37068	Grainflow
37069	Thornaby T.M.D.

Number	Name
37071	British Steel Skinningrove
37073	Fort William An Gearasdan
37077	British Steel Shelton
37078	Teesside Steelmaster
37079	Medite
37081	Loch Long
37087	VULCAN AVRO B1 & B2
	Keighley & Worth Valley Railway 40th Anniversary 1968–2008
37088	Clydesdale
37095	British Steel Teesside
37099	Clydebridge
	MERL EVANS 1947–2016
37108	Lanarkshire Steel
37111	Loch Eil Outward Bound
	Glengarnock
37113	Radio Highland
37114	Dunrobin Castle
	City of Worcester
37116	Sister Dora
37137	Clyde Iron
37152	British Steel Ravenscraig
37154	Johnson Stevens Agencies
37156	British Steel Hunterston
37180	Sir Dyfed County of Dyfed
37185	Lea & Perrins
37188	Jimmy Shand
37190	Dalzell
37191	International Youth Year 1985
37194	British International Freight Association
	NEIL WEBSTER 1957–2001
37196	Tre Pol and Pen
37197	Loch Laidon
37198	CHIEF ENGINEER
37201	Saint Margaret
37207	William Cookworthy
37214	Loch Laidon
37216	Great Eastern
37219	Jonty Jarvis 8-12-1998 to 18-3-2005
37220	Westerleigh
37229	The Cardiff Rod Mill
	Jonty Jarvis 8-12-1998 to 18-3-2005
37232	The Institution of Railway Signal Engineers
37235	The Coal Merchants' Association of Scotland
37239	The Coal Merchants' Association of Scotland
37248	Midland Railway Centre
	Loch Arkaig
37251	The Northern Lights
37254	Cardiff Canton
37260	Radio Highland
37261	Caithness
	Loch Arkaig
37262	Dounreay
37275	Stainless Pioneer
	Oor Wullie
37310	British Steel Ravenscraig
	British Steel Ravenscraig
37311	British Steel Hunterston
37312	Clyde Iron
37314	Dalzell
37320	Shap Fell
37321	Gartcosh
37322	Imperial
37323	Clydesdale
37324	Clydebridge
37325	Lanarkshire Steel
37326	Glengarnock
37332	The Coal Merchants' Association of Scotland
37343	Imperial
37350	NATIONAL RAILWAY MUSEUM
37356	Grainflow
37358	P & O Containers
37379	Ipswich WRD Quality Approved
37401	Mary Queen of Scots
	The Royal Scotsman
	Mary Queen of Scots
37402	Oor Willie
	Bont Y Bermo
	Stephen Middlemore 23.12.1954 – 8.6.2013
37403	Isle of Mull
	Glendarroch
	Ben Cruachan
	Isle of Mull
37404	Ben Cruachan
	Loch Long
37405	Strathclyde Region
37406	The Saltire Society
37407	Loch Long
	Blackpool Tower
	Blackpool Tower
37408	Loch Rannoch
37409	Loch Awe
	Lord Hinton
37410	Aluminium 100
37411	The Institution of Railway Signal Engineers
	Ty Hafan
	The Scottish Railway Preservation Society
	CAERPHILLY CASTLE/CASTELL CAERFFILI
37412	Loch Lomond
	Driver John Elliot
37413	Loch Eil Outward Bound
	The Scottish Railway Preservation Society
37414	Cathays C&W Works 1846 – 1993
37416	Sir Robert McAlpine/Concrete Bob
37417	Highland Region
	RAIL MAGAZINE
	Richard Trevithick
37418	An Comunn Gaidhealach
	Pectinidae
	Gordon Graig
	Pectinidae
	East Lancashire Railway
	An Comuun Gaidhealach
37419	Carl Haviland 1954–2012
	Carl Haviland 1954–2012
37420	The Scottish Hosteller
37421	Strombidae
	Star of The East
	The Kingsman
37422	Robert F. Fairlie Locomotive Engineer 1831–1885
	Cardiff Canton
	Victorious
37423	Sir Murray Morrison 1873–1948 Pioneer of the British Aluminium Industry
	Spirit of the Lakes
37424	Glendarroch
	Isle of Mull
	Avro Vulcan XH558
37425	Sir Robert McAlpine/Concrete Bob
	Pride of the Valleys/Balchder y Cymoedd
	Sir Robert McAlpine/Concrete Bob
37426	Y Lein Fach/Vale of Rheidol
37427	Bont Y Bermo
	Highland Enterprise
37428	David Lloyd George
	The Royal Scotsman
	Loch Long/Loch Awe
37429	Sir Dyfed/County of Dyfed
	Eisteddfod Genedlaethol
37430	Cwmbrân
37431	Sir Powys/County of Powys
	Bullidae
37501	Teesside Steelmaster
37502	British Steel Teesside
37503	British Steel Shelton
37504	British Steel Corby

37505	British Steel Workington
37506	British Steel Skinningrove
37507	Hartlepool Pipe Mill
37510	Orion
37511	Stockton Haulage
37512	Thornaby Demon
37516	Loch Laidon
37517	St Aidan's CE Memorial School Hartlepool Railsafe Trophy Winners 1995
37518	Fort William/An Gearasdan
37521	English China Clays
37601	Class 37-'Fifty'
	Perseus
37608	Andromeda
37610	The MALCOLM Group
	T.S. (Ted) Cassady 14.5.61 – 6.4.08
37611	Pegasus
37667	Wensleydale
	Meldon Quarry Centenary
37668	Leyburn
37670	St. Blazey T&RS Depot
37671	Tre Pol and Pen
37672	Freight Transport Association
37674	Saint Blaise Church 1445 – 1995
37675	William Cookworthy
	Margam TMD
37676	Loch Rannoch
37682	Hartlepool Pipe Mill
37684	Peak National Park
37685	Loch Arkaig
37688	Great Rocks
	Kingmoor TMD
37692	The Lass O' Ballochmyle
	Didcot Depot
37693	Sir William Arrol
37694	The Lass O' Ballochmyle
37698	Coedbach
37702	Taff Merthyr
37706	Conidae
37711	Tremorfa Steel Works
37712	The Cardiff Rod Mill
	Teesside Steelmaster
37713	British Steel Workington
37714	Thornaby TMD
37715	British Steel Teesside
	British Petroleum
37716	British Steel Corby
37717	Stainless Pioneer
	Maltby Lilly Hall Junior School Rotherham Railsafe Trophy Winners 1996
	St Margaret's Church of England Primary School City of Durham Railsafe Trophy Winners 1997
	Berwick Middle School Railsafe Trophy Winners 1998
37718	Hartlepool Pipe Mill
37799	Sir Dyfed/County of Dyfed
37800	Glo Cymru
	Cassiopeia
37801	Aberthaw/Aberddawan
37884	Gartcosh
	Cepheus
37886	Sir Dyfed/County of Dyfed
37887	Castell Caerffili/Caerphilly Castle
37888	Petrolea
37890	The Railway Observer
37892	Ripple Lane
37898	Cwmbargoed D.P.
37899	County of West Glamorgan/Sir Gorllewin Morgannwg
37901	Mirrlees Pioneer
	Mirrlees Pioneer
37902	British Steel Llanwern
37905	Vulcan Enterprise
97304	John Tiley
40010	EMPRESS OF BRITAIN

40011	MAURETANIA
40012	AUREOL
40013	ANDANIA
40014	ANTONIA
40015	AQUITANIA
40016	CAMPANIA
40017	CARINTHIA
40018	CARMANIA
40019	CARONIA
40020	FRANCONIA
40021	IVERNIA
40022	LACONIA
40023	LANCASTRIA
40024	LUCANIA
40025	LUSITANIA
40027	PARTHIA
40028	SAMARIA
40029	SAXONIA
40030	SCYTHIA
40031	SYLVANIA
40032	EMPRESS OF CANADA
40033	EMPRESS OF ENGLAND
40034	ACCRA
40035	APAPA
40145	East Lancashire Railway
43002	Top of the Pops
	TECHNI?UEST
	Sir Kenneth Grange
43003	ISAMBARD KINGDOM BRUNEL
43004	Swan Hunter
	Borough of Swindon
	First for the Future/First ar gyfer y dyfodol
	Caerphilly Castle
43006	Kingdom of Fife
43008	City of Aberdeen
43009	First transforming travel
43010	TSW Today
43011	Reader 125
43012	Exeter Panel Signal Box 21st Anniversary 2009
43013	University of Bristol
	CROSSCOUNTRY VOYAGER
	Mark Carne CBE
43014	The Railway Observer
43016	Gwyl Gerddi Cymru 1992/Garden Festival Wales 1992
	Peninsular Medical School
43017	HTV West
	Hannahs discoverhannahs.org
43018	The Red Cross
43019	Dinas Abertawe/City of Swansea
43020	John Grooms
	MTU Power. Passion. Partnership
43021	David Austin – Cartoonist
43022	The Duke of Edinburgh's Award Diamond Anniversary 1956 – 2016
43023	County of Cornwall
	SQN LDR HAROLD STARR ONE OF THE FEW
43024	Great Western Society 1961 – 2011 Didcot Railway Centre
43025	Exeter
	IRO The Institution of Railway Operators 2000 – 2010 TEN YEARS PROMOTING OPERATIONAL EXCELLENCE
43026	City of Westminster
	Michael Eavis
43027	Westminster Abbey
	Glorious Devon
43030	Christian Lewis Trust
43032	The Royal Regiment of Wales
43033	Driver Brian Cooper 15 June 1947 – 5 October 1999
43034	The Black Horse
	TravelWatch SouthWest
43037	PENYDARREN
43038	National Railway Museum The First Ten Years 1975–1985
43039	The Royal Dragoon Guards

43040	Granite City
	Bristol St. Philip's Marsh
43041	City of Discovery
	Meningitis Trust Support for Life
	St Catherine's Castle
43042	Tregenna Castle
43043	LEICESTERSHIRE COUNTY CRICKET CLUB
43044	Borough of Kettering
43045	The Grammer School Doncaster AD 1350
43046	Royal Philharmonic
43047	Rotherham Enterprise
	Powered by Paxman VP185
43048	T.C.B. Miller MBE
43049	Neville Hill
43051	The Duke and Duchess of York
43052	City of Peterborough
43053	County of Humberside
	Leeds United
	University of Worcester
43055	Sheffield Star
	The Sheffield Star 125 Years
43056	University of Bradford
	The Royal British Legion
43058	MIDLAND PRIDE
43060	County of Leicestershire
	COUNTY OF LEICESTERSHIRE
43061	City of Lincoln
	The Fearless Foxes
43062	John Armitt
43063	Maiden Voyager
	Rio Challenger
43064	City of York
43065	City of Edinburgh
43066	Nottingham Playhouse
43068	The Red Nose
	The Red Arrows
43069	Rio Enterprise
43070	Rio Pathfinder
	The Corps of Royal Electrical and Mechanical Engineers
43071	Forward Birmingham
43072	Derby Etches Park
43073	Neville Hill HST Depot 42 Years
43074	BBC EAST MIDLANDS TODAY
43076	BBC East Midlands Today
	THE MASTER CUTLER 1947–1997
	IN SUPPORT OF HELP for HEROES
43077	County of Nottingham
43078	Shildon County Durham
	Golowan Festival Penzance
43079	Rio Venturer
43081	Midland Valenta
43082	DERBYSHIRE FIRST
	RAILWAY children THE VOICE FOR STREET CHILDREN WORLDWIDE
48084	County of Derbyshire
43085	City of Bradfod
43086	Rio Talisman
43087	Rio Invader
	11 Explosive Ordnance Disposal Regiment Royal Logistic Corps
43088	XIII Commonwealth Games Scotland 1986
43089	Rio Thunderer
	HAYABUSA
43091	Edinburgh Military Tattoo
43092	Highland Chieftain
	Highland Chieftan
	Highland Chieftain
	Institution of Mechanical Engineers 150th Anniversary 1847 – 1997
	Cromwell's Castle
43093	York Festival '88
	Lady in Red
	Old Oak Common HST Depot 1976–2018

43094	St Mawes Castle
43095	Heaton
	Perth
43096	The Queen's Own Hussars
	The Great Racer
	Stirling Castle
43097	The Light Infantry
	Environment Agency
	Castle Drogo
43098	Tyne and Wear Metropolitan County
	railwaychildren
	Walton Castle
43099	Diocese of Newcastle
43100	Craigentinny
43101	Edinburgh International Festival
	The Irish Mail Trên Post Gwyddelig
43102	City of Wakefield
	HST Silver Jubilee
	Diocese of Newcastle
	The Journey Shrinker 148.5 MPH The Worlds Fastest Diesel Train
43103	John Wesley
	Helston Furry Dance
43104	County of Cleveland
	City of Edinburgh
43105	Hartlepool
	City of Inverness
43106	Songs of Praise
	Fountains Abbey
43107	City of Derby
	Tayside
43108	BBC Television Railwatch
	Old Course St Andrews
43109	Yorkshire Evening Press
	Scone Palace
	Leeds International Film Festival
43110	Darlington
	Stirlingshire
43111	Scone Palace
43112	Doncaster
43113	City of Newcastle upon Tyne
	The Highlands
43114	National Garden Festival Gateshead 1990
	East Riding of Yorkshire
43115	Yorkshire Cricket Academy
	Aberdeenshire
43116	City of Kingston upon Hull
	The Black Dyke Band
43117	Bonnie Prince Charlie
43118	Charles Wesley
	City of Kingston upon Hull
43119	Harrogate Spa
43120	National Galleries of Scotland
43121	West Yorkshire Metropolitan County
43122	South Yorkshire Metropolitan County
	Dunster Castle
43123	VALENTA 1972 - 2010
43124	BBC Points West
43125	Merchant Venturer
43126	City of Bristol
43127	Sir Peter Parker 1924–2002 Cotswold Line 150
43130	Sulis Minerva
43131	Sir Felix Pole
43132	Worshipful Company of Carmen
	We Save the Children – Will You?
43134	County of Somerset
43135	Quaker Enterprise
43137	Newton Abbot 150
43139	Driver Stan Martin 25 June 1960–6 November 2004
43140	Landore Diesel Depot 1963 Celebrating 50 Years 2013/ Depo Diesel Glandŵr 1963 Dathlu 50 Mlynedd 2013
43141	Cardiff Panel Signal Box 1966–2016/Blwch Signalau Panel Caerdydd 1966–2016

43142	St Mary's Hospital Paddington
	Reading Panel Signal Box 1965–2010
43143	Stroud 700
43147	Red Cross
	The Red Cross
	Royal Marines Celebrating 350 Years
43149	BBC Wales Today
	University of Plymouth
43150	Bristol Evening Post
43151	Blue Peter II
43152	St. Peter's School York AD 627
43153	University of Durham
	THE ENGLISH RIVIERA TORQUAY PAIGNTON BRIXHAM
	Chun Castle
43154	INTERCITY
	Compton Castle
43155	BBC Look North
	The Red Arrows
	City of Aberdeen
	The Red Arrows 50 Seasons of Excellence
	Rougemont Castle
43156	Dartington International Summer School
43157	Yorkshire Evening Post
	HMS Penzance
43158	Dartmoor The Pony Express
	Kingswear Castle
43159	Rio Warrior
43160	Storm Force
	PORTERBROOK
	Sir Moir Lockhead OBE
43161	Reading Evening Post
	Rio Monach
43162	Borough of Stevenage
	Project Rio
	Exeter Panel Signalbox 21st Anniversary 2009
43163	Exeter Panel Signal Box 21st Anniversary 2009
43165	Prince Michael of Kent
43167	DELTIC 50 1955–2005
43169	THE NATIONAL TRUST
43170	Edward Paxman
	Chepstow Castle
43172	Harry Patch – The last survivor of the trenches
43173	Swansea University
43174	Bristol – Bordeaux
43175	GWR 175th ANNIVERSARY
43177	University of Exeter
43179	Pride of Laira
43180	City of Newcastle upon Tyne
	Rio Glory
43181	Devonport Royal Dockyard 1693–1993
43185	Great Western
43186	Sir Francis Drake
	Taunton Castle
43188	City of Plymouth
	Newport Castle
43189	RAILWAY HERITAGE TRUST
	Launceston Castle
43191	Seahawk
43192	City of Truro
	Trematon Castle
43193	Yorkshire Post
	Plymouth SPIRIT OF DISCOVERY
	Rio Triumph
43194	Royal Signals
	Okehampton Castle
43195	British Red Cross 125th Birthday 1995
	Rio Swift
43196	The Newspaper Society
	The Newspaper Society Founded 1836
	Rio Prince
43197	The RAILWAY MAGAZINE Centenary 1897–1997
	Rio Princess
43198	HMS Penzance

	Rio Victorious
	Oxfordshire 2007
	Driver Stan Martin 25 June 1950 - 6 November 2004 /
	Driver Brian Cooper 15 June 1947 - 5 October 1995
43206	Kingdom of Fife
43208	Lincolnshire Echo
43238	City of Dundee
	National Railway Museum 40 Years 1975–2015
43257	Bounds Green
43274	Spirit of Sunderland
43290	mtu fascination of power
43296	Stirling Castle
43300	Craigentinny
	Blackpool Rock
	Craigentinny
	Craigentinny 100 YEARS 1914–2014
43306	Fountains Abbey
43308	Old Course St Andrews
	HIGHLAND CHIEFTAIN
43309	Leeds International Film Festival
43313	The Highlands
43314	East Riding of Yorkshire
43316	The Black Dyke Band
43318	City of Kingston upon Hull
43320	National Galleries of Scotland
43367	DELTIC 50 1955 – 2005
43423	'VALENTA' 1972 – 2010
43467	British Transport Police Nottingham/Nottinghamshire
	Fire and Rescue Services
43480	West Hampstead PSB
43484	PETER FOX 1942 – 2011 PLATFORM 5
44001	SCAFELL PIKE
44002	HELVELLYN
44003	SKIDDAW
44004	GREAT GABLE
44005	CROSS FELL
44006	WHERNSIDE
44007	INGLEBOROUGH
44008	PENYGHENT
44009	SNOWDON
44010	TRYFAN
45004	ROYAL IRISH FUSILIER
45006	HONOURABLE ARTILLERY COMPANY
45014	THE CHESHIRE REGIMENT
45022	LYTHAM ST ANNES
45023	THE ROYAL PIONEER CORPS
45039	THE MANCHESTER REGIMENT
45040	THE KING'S SHROPSHIRE LIGHT INFANTRY
45041	ROYAL TANK REGIMENT
45043	THE KING'S OWN ROYAL BORDER REGIMENT
45044	ROYAL INNISKILLING FUSILIER
45045	COLDSTREAM GUARDSMAN
45046	ROYAL FUSILIER
45048	THE ROYAL MARINES
45049	THE STAFFORDSHIRE REGIMENT (THE PRINCE OF
	WALES'S)
45055	ROYAL CORPS OF TRANSPORT
45059	ROYAL ENGINEER
45060	SHERWOOD FORESTER
45104	THE ROYAL WARWICKSHIRE FUSILIERS
45111	GRENADIER GUARDSMAN
45112	THE ROYAL ARMY ORDNANCE CORPS
45118	THE ROYAL ARTILLERYMAN
45123	THE LANCASHIRE FUSILIER
45135	3RD CARABINIER
45137	THE BEDFORDSHIRE AND HERTFORDSHIRE
	REGIMENT (TA)
45143	5th ROYAL INNISKILLING DRAGOON GUARDS
	5TH ROYAL INNISKILLING DRAGOON GUARDS 1685–1985
45144	ROYAL SIGNALS
46026	LEICESTERSHIRE AND DERBYSHIRE YEOMANRY
46035	Ixion
47004	Old Oak Common Traction & Rolling Stock Depot

47007	Stratford
47010	Xancidae
47016	The Toleman Group
	ATLAS
47033	The Royal Logisitics Corps
47049	GEFCO
47053	Cory Brothers 1842–1992
	Dollands Moor International
47054	Xancidae
47060	Halewood Silver Jubilee 1988
47076	CITY OF TRURO
47077	NORTH STAR
47078	SIR DANIEL GOOCH
47079	GEORGE JACKSON CHURCHWARD
	G. J. CHURCHWARD
47080	TITAN
47081	ODIN
47082	ATLAS
47083	ORION
47085	MAMMOTH
	Conidae
	REPTA 1893–1993
47086	COLOSSUS
47087	CYCLOPS
47088	SAMSON
47089	AMAZON
	Amazon
47090	VULCAN
47091	THOR
47095	Southampton WRD Quality Approved
47114	Freightlinerbulk
47119	Arcidae
47120	R.A.F. Kinloss
47121	Pochard
47125	Tonnidae
47142	The Sapper
47145	MYRDDIN EMRYS
47146	Loughborough Grammar School
47157	Johnson Stevens Agencies
47158	Henry Ford
47167	County of Essex
47169	Great Eastern
47170	County of Norfolk
47172	County of Hertfordshire
47180	County of Suffolk
47184	County of Cambridgeshire
47186	Catcliffe Demon
47190	Pectinidae
47193	Lucinidae
47194	Bullidae
	Carlisle Currock Quality Approved
47195	Muricidae
47196	Haliotidae
47200	Herbert Austin
	The Fosse Way
47206	The Morris Dancer
47207	Bulmers of Hereford
	The Felixstowe Partnership
47209	Herbert Austin
47210	Blue Circle Cement
47211	Johnson Stevens Agencies
47213	Marchwood Military Port
47214	Tinsley Traction Depot
	Distillers MG
47218	United Transport Europe
47219	Arnold Kunzler
47222	Appleby-Frodingham
	W.A. Camwell
47223	British Petroleum
47224	Arcidae
47228	axial
47231	The Silcock Express
47233	Stombidae

	Strombidae
47236	ROVER GROUP QUALITY ASSURED
47238	Bescot Yard
47241	The Silcock Express
	Halewood Silver Jubilee 1988
47245	The Institute of Export
	V. E. Day 75th Anniversary
47258	Forth Ports Tilbury
47270	Cory Brothers 1842–1992
	SWIFT
47278	Vasidae
47280	Pedigree
47283	Johnnie Walker
47286	Port of Liverpool
47291	The Port of Felixstowe
47293	TRANSFESA
47297	Cobra RAILFREIGHT
47298	Pegasus
47301	Freightliner Birmingham
47303	Freightliner Cleveland
47306	The Sapper
47309	The Halewood Transmission
	European Rail Operator of the Year
47310	Henry Ford
47311	Warrington Yard
47312	Parsec of Europe
47314	Transmark
47315	Templecombe
47316	Cam Peak
47317	Willesden Yard
47319	Norsk Hydro
47323	ROVER GROUP QUALITY ASSURED
47324	Glossidae
47326	Saltley Depot Quality Approved
47330	Amlwch Freighter/Trên Nwyddau Amlwch
47333	Civil Link
47334	P&O Nedlloyd
47337	Herbert Austin
47338	Warrington Yard
47348	St Christopher's Railway Home
47350	British Petroleum
47355	AVOCET
47357	The Permanent Way Institution
47361	Wilton Endeavour
47363	Billingham Enterprise
47365	Diamond Jubilee
47366	The Institution of Civil Engineers
	Capital Radio's Help a London Child
47368	Neritidae
47370	Andrew A Hodgkinson
47374	Petrolea
47375	Tinsley Traction Depot Quality Approved
	TINSLEY TRACTION DEPOT
47376	Freightliner 1995
47379	Total Energy
47380	Immingham
47387	Transmark
47390	Amlwch Freighter/Trên Nwyddau Amlwch
47392	Cory Brothers 1842–1992
47394	Johnson Stevens Agencies
47401	North Eastern
	Star of The East
	North Eastern
47402	Gateshead
47403	The Geordie
47404	Hadrian
47405	Northumbria
47406	Rail Riders
47407	Aycliffe
47408	Finsbury Park
47409	David Lloyd George
47411	The Geordie
47421	The Brontës of Haworth

47424	The Brontës of Haworth
47425	Holbeck
47434	Pride in Huddersfield
47443	North Eastern
47444	University of Nottingham
47448	Gateshead
47452	Aycliffe
47457	Ben Line
47458	County of Cambridgeshire
47461	Charles Rennie Mackintosh
47462	Cambridge Traction & Rolling Stock Depot
47469	Glasgow Chamber of Commerce
47470	University of Edinburgh
47471	Norman Tunna G.C.
47474	Sir Rowland Hill
47475	Restive
47476	Night Mail
47479	Track 29
47484	ISAMBARD KINGDOM BRUNEL
47488	Rail Riders
	DAVIES THE OCEAN
47489	Crewe Diesel Depot
	Crewe Diesel Depot Quality Approved
47490	Bristol Bath Road
	Resonant
47491	Horwich Enterprise
	Resolve
47492	The Enterprising Scot
47500	GREAT WESTERN
47501	Craftsman
	CRAFTSMAN
47503	The Geordie
	Heaton Traincare Depot
47508	Great Britain
	S.S. Great Britain
47509	Albion
47510	Fair Rosamund
47511	Thames
	Grampian Region
47513	Severn
47515	Night Mail
47517	Andrew Carnegie
47520	Thunderbird
47522	Doncaster Enterprise
47524	Res Gestae
47526	Northumbria
47527	Kettering
47528	The Queen's Own Mercian Yeomanry
47531	Respite
47535	University of Leicester
	Saint Aidan
47537	Sir Gwynedd/County of Gwynedd
47538	PYTHON
47539	Rochdale Pioneers
47540	The Institution of Civil Engineers
47541	The Queen Mother
47546	Aviemore Centre
47547	University of Oxford
47549	Royal Mail
47550	University of Dundee
47551	Poste Restante
47555	The Commonwealth Spirit
47558	Mayflower
47559	Sir Joshua Reynolds
47560	Tamar
47562	Sir William Burrell
	Restless
47563	Woman's Guild
47564	COLOSSUS
47565	Responsive
47567	Red Star
	Red Star ISO 9002
47568	Royal Engineers Postal & Courier Services
	Royal Logistic Corps Postal & Courier Services
47569	The Gloucestershire Regiment
47572	Ely Cathedral
47573	THE LONDON STANDARD
47574	LLOYD'S LIST 250TH ANNIVERSARY
	Benjamin Gimbert G.C.
47575	City of Hereford
47576	King's Lynn
47577	Benjamin Gimbert G.C.
47578	The Royal Society of Edinburgh
	Respected
47579	James Nightall G.C.
47580	County of Essex
	Restormel
	County of Essex
47581	Great Eastern
47582	County of Norfolk
47583	County of Hertfordshire
47584	County of Suffolk
	THE LOCOMOTIVE & CARRIAGE INSTITUTION 1911
47585	County of Cambridgeshire
47586	Northamptonshire
47587	Ruskin College Oxford
47588	Carlisle Currock
	Resurgent
47590	Thomas Telford
47592	County of Avon
47593	Galloway Princess
	Galloway Princess
47594	Resourceful
47595	Confederation of British Industry
47596	Aldeburgh Festival
47597	Resilient
47600	Dewi Saint/Saint David
47602	Glorious Devon
47603	County of Somerset
47604	Women's Royal Voluntary Service
47606	ODIN
	Irresistible
47607	Royal Worcester
47609	FIRE FLY
47611	Thames
47612	TITAN
47613	NORTH STAR
47615	Castell Caerffilli/Caerphilly Castle
47616	Y Ddraig Goch/The Red Dragon
47617	University of Stirling
47618	Fair Rosamund
47620	Windsor Castle
47621	Royal County of Berkshire
47622	The Institution of Civil Engineers
47623	VULCAN
47624	CYCLOPS
	Saint Andrew
47625	CITY OF TRURO
	Resplendent
47626	ATLAS
47627	City of Oxford
47628	SIR DANIEL GOOCH
47630	Resounding
47631	Ressalder
47633	ORION
47634	Henry Ford
	Holbeck
47635	Jimmy Milne
	The Lass O' Ballochmyle
47636	Sir John De Graeme
	Restored
47637	Springburn
47638	County of Kent
47639	Industry Year 1986
47640	University of Strathclyde
47641	COLOSSUS

	Fife Region
47642	Strathisla
	Resolute
47644	The Permanent Way Institution
47645	Robert F. Fairlie Locomotive Engineer 1831–1885
47647	THOR
47654	Finsbury Park
47671	Y Ddraig Goch/The Red Dragon
47672	Sir William Burrell
47673	Galloway Princess
	York InterCity Control
47674	Women's Royal Voluntary Service
47675	Confederation of British Industry
47676	Northamptonshire
47677	University of Stirling
47701	Saint Andrew
	Old Oak Common Traction & Rolling Stock Depot
	Waverley
47702	Saint Cuthbert
	County of Suffolk
47703	Saint Mungo
	The Queen Mother
	LEWIS CARROLL
	HERMES
47704	Dunedin
47705	Lothian
	GUY FAWKES
47706	Strathclyde
47707	Holyrood
47708	Waverley
	Templecombe
47709	The Lord Provost
	DIONYSOS
47710	Sir Walter Scott
	Capital Radio's Help a London Child
	LADY GODIVA
	QUASIMODO
47711	Greyfriars Bobby
	County of Hertfordshire
47712	Lady Diana Spencer
	DICK WHITTINGTON
	ARTEMIS
	Pride of Carlisle
47713	Fair Rosamund
	Tayside Region
47714	Thames
	Grampian Region
47715	Haymarket
	POSEIDON
47716	Duke of Edinburgh's Award
47717	Tayside Region
47721	Saint Bede
47722	The Queen Mother
47725	The Railway Mission
	Bristol Barton Hill
47726	Manchester Airport Progress
47727	Duke of Edinburgh's Award
	Castell Caerffilli/Caerphilly Castle
	Rebecca
	Edinburgh Castle / Caisteal Dhun Eide
47733	Eastern Star
47734	Crewe Diesel Depot Quality Approved
47736	Cambridge Traction & Rolling Stock Depot
47737	Resurgent
47738	Bristol Barton Hill
47739	Resourceful
	Robin of Templecombe
47741	Resilient
47742	The Enterprising Scot
47744	Saint Edwin
	The Cornish Experience
	Royal Mail Cheltenham
47745	Royal London Society for the Blind

47746	The Bobby
	Chris Fudge 29.7.70–22.6.10
47747	Res Publica
	Graham Farish
	Florence Nightingale
47749	Atlantic College
	Demelza
	CITY OF TRURO
47750	Royal Mail Cheltenham
	ATLAS
47756	The Permanent Way Institution
	Royal Mail Tyneside
47757	Restitution
	Capabilty Brown
47758	Regency Rail Cruises
47760	Restless
	Ribblehead Viaduct
47764	Resounding
47765	Ressalder
47766	Resolute
47767	Saint Columba
	Mappa Mundi
47768	Resonant
47769	Resolve
47770	Reserved
47771	Heaton Traincare Depot
47772	Carnforth TMD
47773	Reservist
	The Queen Mother
47774	Poste Restante
47775	Respite
47776	Respected
47777	Restored
47778	Irresistible
	Duke of Edinburgh's Award
47781	Isle of Iona
47783	Finsbury Park
	Saint Peter
47784	Condover Hall
47785	The Statesman
	Fiona Castle
47786	Roy Castle OBE
47787	Victim Support
	Windsor Castle
47788	Captain Peter Manisty RN
47789	Lindisfarne
47790	Dewi Saint/Saint David
	Galloway Princess
47791	VENICE SIMPLON ORIENT-EXPRESS
47792	Saint Cuthbert
	Robin Hood
47793	Saint Augustine
	Christopher Wren
47798	FIRE FLY
	Prince William
47799	Windsor Castle
	Prince Henry
47802	Pride of Cumbria
47803	Woman's Guild
47805	Bristol Bath Road
	Pride of Toton
	TALISMAN
	John Scott 12.5.45–22.5.12
	Roger Hosking MA 1925-2013
47808	SAMSON
47809	Finsbury Park
47810	PORTERBROOK
	Captain Sensible
	Peter Bath MBE 1927–2006
	Crewe Diesel Depot
47812	Pride of Eastleigh
47813	S.S. Great Britain
	John Peel

	Solent
	Jack Frost
47814	Totnes Castle
47815	Abertawe Landore
	GREAT WESTERN
	Lost Boys 68 88
47816	Bristol Bath Road Quality Approved
47817	The Institution of Mechanical Engineers
47818	Strathclyde
	Emily
47821	Royal Worcester
47822	Pride of Shrewsbury
47823	SS Great Britain
47824	Glorious Devon
47825	Thomas Telford
47826	Springburn
47828	Severn Valley Railway Kidderminster Bewdley Bridgnorth
	Joe Strummer
47830	BEECHING'S LEGACY
47831	Bolton Wanderer
47832	Tamar
	DRIVER TOM CLARK O.B.E.
	Solway Princess
47833	Captain Peter Manisty RN
47834	FIRE FLY
47835	Windsor Castle
47836	Fair Rosamund
47839	Royal County of Berkshire
	Pride of Saltley
	PEGASUS
47840	NORTH STAR
47841	The Institution of Mechanical Engineers
	Spirit of Chester
	The Institution of Mechanical Engineers
47843	VULCAN
47844	Derby & Derbyshire Chamber of Commerce & Industry
47845	County of Kent
47846	THOR
47847	Railway World Magazine/Brian Morrison
47848	Newton Abbot Festival of Transport
	TITAN STAR
47849	Cadeirlan Bangor Cathedral
47851	Traction Magazine
47853	RAIL EXPRESS
47854	Women's Royal Voluntary Service
	Diamond Jubilee
47971	Robin Hood
47972	The Royal Army Ordnance Corps
47973	Midland Counties Railway 150 1839–1989
	Derby Evening Telegraph
47974	The Permanent Way Institution
47975	The Institution of Civil Engineers
47976	Aviemore Centre
50001	Dreadnought
50002	Superb
50003	Temeraire
50004	St Vincent
50005	Collingwood
50006	Neptune
50007	Hercules
	SIR EDWARD ELGAR
	Hercules
50008	Thunderer
50009	Conqueror
50010	Monarch
50011	Centurion
50012	Benbow
50013	Agincourt
50014	Warspite
50015	Valiant
50016	Barham
50017	Royal Oak

50018	Resolution
50019	Ramillies
50020	Revenge
50021	Rodney
50022	Anson
50023	Howe
50024	Vanguard
50025	Invicible
50026	Indomitable
50027	Lion
50028	Tiger
50029	Renown
50030	Repulse
50031	Hood
50032	Courageous
50033	Glorious
50034	Furious
50035	Ark Royal
50036	Victorious
50037	Illustrious
50038	Formidable
50039	Implacable
50040	Leviathan
	Centurion
50041	Bulwark
50042	Triumph
50043	Eagle
50044	Exeter
	EXETER
	Exeter
50045	Achilles
50046	Ajax
50047	Swiftsure
50048	Dauntless
50049	Defiance
50050	Fearless
55001	ST. PADDY
55002	THE KING'S OWN YORKSHIRE LIGHT INFANTRY
55003	MELD
55004	QUEEN'S OWN HIGHLANDER
55005	THE PRINCE OF WALES'S OWN REGIMENT OF YORKSHIRE
55006	THE FIFE AND FORFAR YEOMANRY
55007	PINZA
55008	THE GREEN HOWARDS
55009	ALYCIDON
55010	THE KING'S OWN SCOTTISH BORDERER
55011	THE ROYAL NORTHUMBERLAND FUSILIERS
55012	CREPELLO
55013	THE BLACK WATCH
55014	THE DUKE OF WELLINGTON'S REGIMENT
55015	TULYAR
55016	GORDON HIGHLANDER
55017	THE DURHAM LIGHT INFANTRY
55018	BALLYMOSS
55019	ROYAL HIGHLAND FUSILIER
55020	NIMBUS
55021	ARGYLL AND SUTHERLAND HIGHLANDER
55022	ROYAL SCOTS GREY
56001	Whatley
56006	Ferrybridge 'C' Power Station
56012	Maltby Colliery
56028	West Burton Power Station
56030	Eggborough Power Station
56031	Merehead
56032	Sir De Morgannwg County of South Glamorgan
56033	Shotton Paper Mill
56034	Castell Ogwr Ogmore Castle
56035	Taff Merthyr
56037	Richard Trevithick
56038	Western Mail
	PATHFINDER TOURS 30 YEARS OF RAILTOURING 1973 – 2003
56039	ABP Port of Hull

56040	Oystermouth
56044	Cardiff Canton
	Cardiff Canton Quality Approved
56045	British Steel Shelton
56049	Robin of Templecombe 1938 – 2013
56050	British Steel Teeside
56051	Isle of Grain
	Survival
56052	The Cardiff Rod Mill
56053	Sir Morgannwg Ganol County of Mid Glamorgan
56054	British Steel Llanwern
56057	British Fuels
56060	The Cardiff Rod Mill
56062	Mountsorrel
56063	Bardon Hill
56069	Thornaby TMD
	Wolverhampton Steel Terminal
56073	Tremorfa Steel Works
56074	Kellingley Colliery
56075	West Yorkshire Enterprise
56076	Blyth Power
	British Steel Trostre
56077	Thorpe Marsh Power Station
56078	Doncaster Enterprise
56080	Selby Coalfied
56086	The Magistrates' Association
56087	ABP Port of Hull
56089	Ferrybridge 'C' Power Station
56091	Castle Donington Power Station
	Stanton
	Driver Wayne Gaskell The Godfather
56093	The Institution of Mining Engineers
56094	Eggborough Power Station
56095	Harworth Colliery
56098	Lost Boys 68 – 88
56099	Fiddlers Ferry Power Station
56101	Mutual Improvement
	Frank Hornby
56102	Scunthorpe Steel Centenary
56103	STORA
56110	Croft
56112	Stainless Pioneer
56114	Maltby Colliery
56115	Bassetlaw
	Barry Needham
56117	Wilton-Coalpower
56122	Wilton-Coalpower
56123	Drax Power Station
56124	Blue Circle Cement
56128	West Burton Power Station
56130	Wardley Opencast
56131	Ellington Colliery
56132	Fina Energy
56133	Crewe Locomotive Works
56134	Blyth Power
56135	Port of Tyne Authority
56302	Wilson Walshe
	PECO The Railway Modeller 2016 40 Years
56312	ARTEMIS
	Jermiah Dixon Son of County Durham Surveyor of the Mason-Dixon Line U.S.A.
57001	Freightliner Pioneer
57002	Freightliner Phoenix
	RAIL EXPRESS
57003	Freightliner Evolution
57004	Freightliner Quality
57005	Freightliner Excellence
57006	Freightliner Reliance
57007	Freightliner Bond
	John Scott 12.5.45-22.5.12
57008	Freightliner Explorer
	Telford International Railfreight Park June 2009
57009	Freightliner Venturer
57010	Freightliner Crusader
57011	Freightliner Challenger
57012	Freightliner Envoy
57301	SCOTT TRACY
	Goliath
57302	VIRGIL TRACY
	Chad Varah
57303	ALAN TRACY
	Pride of Carlisle
57304	GORDON TRACY
	Pride of Cheshire
57305	ALAN TRACY
	JOHN TRACY
	Northern Princess
57306	JEFF TRACY
	Her Majesty's Railway Inspectorate 175
57307	LADY PENELOPE
57308	TIN TIN
	County of Staffordshire
	Jamie Ferguson
57309	BRAINS
	Pride of Crewe
57310	KYRANO
	Pride of Cumbria
57311	PARKER
	Thunderbird
57312	THE HOOD
	Peter Henderson
	Solway Princess
57313	TRACY ISLAND
	Scarborough Castle
57314	FIREFLY
57315	THE MOLE
57316	FAB1
57601	Sheila
	Windsor Castle
57602	Restormel Castle
57603	Tintagel Castle
57604	PENDENNIS CASTLE
57605	Totnes Castle
58002	Daw Mill Colliery
58003	Markham Colliery
58005	Ironbridge Power Station
58007	Drakelow Power Station
58011	Worksop Depot
58014	Didcot Power Station
58017	Eastleigh Depot
58018	High Marnham Power Station
58019	Shirebrook Colliery
58020	Doncaster Works BRE
	Doncaster Works
58021	Hither Green Depot
58023	Peterborough Depot
58032	Thoresby Colliery
58034	Bassetlaw
58037	Worksop Depot
58039	Rugeley Power Station
58040	Cottam Power Station
58041	Ratcliffe Power Station
58042	Ironbridge Power Station
	Petrolea
58043	Knottingley
58044	Oxcroft Opencast
58046	Thoresby Colliery
	Asfordby Mine
58047	Manton Colliery
58048	Coventry Colliery
58049	Littleton Colliery
58050	Toton Traction Depot
59001	YEOMAN ENDEAVOUR
59002	YEOMAN ENTERPRISE
	ALAN J DAY
59003	YEOMAN HIGHLANDER

▲ During the 1960s, several Class 40s were named after ships, including D212 (later 40012) which was named Aureol. This photograph was taken in 2018, before the locomotive was painted into BR Green livery. **Andy Chard**

▼ Each of the Class 50s were named after Royal Navy ships, with some having a crest mounted above or below the nameplate, as demonstrated by 50008 during May 2016. **Andy Chard**

59004	YEOMAN CHALLENGER
	PAUL A HAMMOND
59005	KENNETH J PAINTER
59101	Village of Whatley
59102	Village of Chantry
59103	Village of Mells
59104	Village of Great Elm
59201	Vale of York
59202	Vale of White Horse
	Alan Meddows Taylor MD. Mendip Rail Limited
59203	Vale of Pickering
59204	Vale of Glamorgan
59205	Vale of Evesham
	L. Keith McNair
59206	Pride of Ferrybridge
	John F. Yeoman Rail Pioneer
60001	Steadfast
	The Railway Observer
60002	Capability Brown
	High Peak
	GRAHAM FARISH 50th ANNIVERSARY 1970 - 2020
60003	Christopher Wren
	FREIGHT TRANSPORT ASSOCIATION
60004	Lochnagar
60005	Skiddaw
	BP Gas Avonmouth
60006	Great Gable
	Scunthorpe Ironmaster
60007	Robert Adam
	The Spirit of Tom Kendell
60008	Moel Fammau
	GYPSUM QUEEN II
	Sir William McAlpine
60009	Carnedd Dafydd
60010	Pumlumon Plynlimon
60011	Cader Idris
60012	Glyder Fawr
60013	Robert Boyle
60014	Alexander Fleming
60015	Bow Fell
60016	Langdale Pikes
	RAIL MAGAZINE
60017	Arenig Fawr
	Shotton Works Centenary Year 1996
60018	Moel Siabod
60019	Wild Boar Fell
	PATHFINDER TOURS 30 YEARS OF RAILTOURING
	1973–2003
	Port of Grimsby & Immingham
60020	Great Whernside
	The Willows
60021	Pen-y-Ghent
	Star of the East
	PENYGHENT
60022	Ingleborough
60023	The Cheviot
60024	Elizabeth Fry
	Clitheroe Castle
60025	Joseph Lister
	Caledonian Paper
60026	William Caxton
	HELVELLYN
60027	Joseph Banks
60028	John Flamsteed
60029	Ben Nevis
	Clitheroe Castle
	Ben Nevis
60030	Cir Mhor
60031	Ben Lui
	ABP Connect
60032	William Booth
60033	Anthony Ashley Cooper
	Tees Steel Express
60034	Carnedd Llewelyn
60035	Florence Nightingale
60036	Sgurr Na Ciche
	GEFC
60037	Helvellyn
	Aberddawan Aberthaw
60038	Bidean Nam Bian
	AvestaPolarit
60039	Glastonbury Tor
	Dove Holes
60040	Brecon Beacons
	The Territorial Army Centenary
60041	High Willhays
60042	Dunkery Beacon
	The Hundred of Hoo
60043	Yes Tor
60044	Ailsa Craig
	Dowlow
60045	Josephine Butler
	The Permanent Way Institution
60046	William Wilberforce
	William Wilberforce
60047	Robert Owen
	Faithful
60048	Saddleback
	EASTERN
60049	Scafell
60050	Roseberry Topping
60051	Mary Somerville
60052	Goat Fell
	Glofa Twr The last deep mine in Wales Tower Colliery
60053	John Reith
	NORDIC TERMINAL
60054	Charles Babbage
60055	Thomas Barnardo
	Thomas Barnardo
60056	William Beveridge
60057	Adam Smith
60058	John Howard
60059	Samuel Plimsoll
	Swinden Dalesman
60060	James Watt
60061	Alexander Graham Bell
60062	Samuel Johnson
	Stainless Pioneer
60063	James Murray
60064	Back Tor
60065	Kinder Low
	Spirit of JAGUAR
60066	John Logie Baird
60067	James Clerk-Maxwell
60068	Charles Darwin
60069	Humphry Davy
	Slioch
60070	John Loudon McAdam
60071	Dorothy Garrod
	Ribblehead Viaduct
60072	Cairn Toul
60073	Cairn Gorm
60074	Braeriach
	Teenage Spirit
	Luke
60075	Liathach
60076	Suilven
	Dunbar
60077	Canisp
60078	Stac Pollaidh
60079	Foinaven
60080	Kinder Scout
	Cloudside Junior School, Saniacre EWS Rail Safety
	Competition Winners 2001
	Little Eaton Primary School Little Eaton EWS Railsafe
	Trophy Winners 2002

	Stanley Common C of E Primary School Ilkeston EWS Rail Safety Competition Winners 2003
	Bispham Drive Junior School, Toton EWS Rail Safety Competition Winners 2004
60081	Bleaklow Hill
	ISAMBARD KINGDOM BRUNEL
60082	Mam Tor
	Hillhead '93
	Mam Tor
60083	Shining Tor
	Mountsorrel
60084	Cross Fell
60085	Axe Edge
	MINI Pride of Oxford
	Adept
60086	Schiehallion
60087	Slioch
	Barry Needham
	CLIC Sargent www.clicsargent.co.uk
60088	Buachaille Etive More
	Buachaille Etive Mor
60089	Arcuil
	THE RAILWAY HORSE
60090	Quinag
60091	An Teallach
	Barry Needham
60092	Reginald Munns
60093	Jack Stirk
	Adrian Harrington 1955–2003 Royal Navy/Burges Salmon
60094	Tryfan
	Rugby Flyer
60095	Crib Goch
60096	Ben Macdui
60097	Pillar
	ABP Port of Grimsby & Immingham
60098	Charles Francis Brush
60099	Ben More Assynt
60100	Boar of Badenoch
	Pride of Acton
	Midland Railway - Butterley
60500	RAIL Magazine
66002	Lafarge Buddon Wood
	Lafarge Quorn
66005	Maritime Intermodal One
66022	Lafarge Charnwood
66035	Resourceful
66042	Lafarge Buddon Wood
66047	Maritime Intermodal Two
66048	James the Engine
66050	EWS Energy
66051	Maritime Intermodal Four
66055	Alain Thauvette
66058	Derek Clark
66066	Geoff Spencer
66074	Teesport Express
66077	Benjamin Gimbert G.C.
66079	James Nightall G.C.
66090	Maritime Intermodal Six
66100	Armistice 100 1918 - 2018
66109	Teesport Express
66142	Maritime Intermodal Three
66148	Maritime Intermodal Seven
66152	Derek Holmes Railway Operator
66162	Maritime Intermodal Five
66172	PAUL MELLENEY
66175	Rail Riders Express
66185	DP WORLD London Gateway
66200	RAILWAY HERITAGE COMMITTEE
66250	In Memory of Robert K Romak
66301	Kingmoor TMD
66302	Endeavour
66411	Eddie the Engine

66413	Lest We Forget
66414	James the Engine
66415	You are Never Alone
66418	PATRIOT IN MEMORY OF FALLEN RAILWAY EMPLOYEES
66421	Gresty Bridge TMD
66428	Carlisle Eden Mind
66501	Japan 2001
66502	Basford Hall Centenary 2001
66503	The RAILWAY MAGAZINE
66506	Crewe Regeneration
66526	Driver Steve Dunn (George)
66527	Don Raider
66528	Madge Elliot MBE Borders Railway Opening 2015
66532	P&O Nedlloyd Atlas
66533	Hanjin Express / Senator Express
66534	OOCL Express
66540	Ruby
66552	Maltby Raider
66576	Hamburg Sud Advantage
66581	Sophie
66585	The Drax Flyer
66587	AS ONE, WE CAN
66592	Johnson Stevens Agencies
66593	3MG MERSEY MULTIMODAL GATEWAY
66594	NYK Spirit of Kyoto
66597	Viridor
66601	The Hope Valley
66612	Forth Raider
66614	1916 POPPY 2016
66618	Railways Illustrated Annual Photographic Awards Ian Lothian
	Railways Illustrated Annual Photographic Awards David Gorton
	Railways Illustrated Annual Photographic Awards Alan Barnes
66619	Derek W. Johnson MBE
66623	Bill Bolsover
66701	Railtrack National Logistics
	Whitemoor
66702	Blue Lightning
66703	Doncaster PSB 1981–2002
66704	Colchester Power Signalbox
66705	Golden Jubilee
66706	Nene Valley
66707	Sir Sam Fay GREAT CENTRAL RAILWAY
66708	Jayne
66709	Joseph Arnold Davies
	Sorrento
66710	Phil Packer BRIT
66711	Sence
66712	Peterborough Power Signalbox
66713	Forest City
66714	Cromer Lifeboat
66715	VALOUR IN MEMORY OF ALL RAILWAY EMPLOYEES WHO GAVE THEIR LIVES FOR THEIR COUNTRY
66716	Willesden Traincare Centre
	LOCOMOTIVE & CARRIAGE INSTITUTION CENTENARY 1911–2011
66717	Good Old Boy
66718	Gwyneth Dunwoody
	Sir Peter Hendy CBE
66719	METRO-LAND
66720	Metronet Pathfinder
66721	Harry Beck
66722	Sir Edwards Watkin
66723	Chinook
66724	Drax Power Station
66725	SUNDERLAND
66726	SHEFFIELD WEDNESDAY
66727	Andrew Scott CBE
	Maritime One
66728	Institution of Railway Operators

66729	DERBY COUNTY
66730	Whitemoor
66731	interhubGB
	Capt. Tom Moore A True British Inspiriation
66732	GBRf The First Decade 1999–2009 John Smith – MD
66733	Cambridge PSB
66734	The Eco Express
66735	PETERBOROUGH UNITED
66736	WOLVERHAMPTON WANDERERS
66737	Lesia
66738	HUDDERSFIELD TOWN
66739	Bluebell Railway
66740	Sarah
66741	Swanage Railway
66742	ABP Port of Immingham Centenary 1912–2012
66744	Crossrail
66745	Modern Railways The first 50 Years
66747	Made in Sheffield
66748	West Burton 50
66749	Christopher Hopcroft MBE 60 Years Railway Service
66750	Bristol Panel Signal Box
66751	Inspirational Delivered Hitachi Rail Europe
66752	The Hoosier State
66753	EMD Roberts Road
66754	Northampton Saints
66755	Tony Berkeley OBE
66756	Royal Corps of Signals
66757	West Somerset Railway
66758	The Pavior
66759	Chippy
66760	David Gordon Harris
66761	Wensleydale Railway Association 25 Years 1990 – 2015
66763	Severn Valley Railway
66771	Amanda
66772	Maria
66773	Pride of GB Railfreight
66775	HMS Argyll
	Tony Berkeley OBE RFG Chairman 1997-2018
66776	Joanne
66777	Annette
66778	Darius Cheskin
	Cambois depot 25 Years
66779	EVENING STAR
66780	The Cemex Express
66783	The Flying Dustman
66784	Keighley & Worth Valley Railway 50th Anniversary
	1968-2018
66788	LOCOMOTION 15
66789	British Rail 1948–1997
66791	Neil Bennett
66793	Dave Meehan
66794	Ted Gaffney
66847	Terry Baker
66849	Wylam Dilly
66850	David Maidment OBE www.railwaychildren.org.uk
66857	Stephenson Locomotive Society 1909–2009
67001	Night Mail
67002	Special Delivery
67004	Post Haste
	Cairn Gorm
67005	Queen's Messenger
67006	Royal Sovereign
67010	Unicorn
67012	A Shropshire Lad
67013	Dyfrbont Pontcysyllte
67014	Thomas Telford
67015	David J. Lloyd
67017	Arrow
67018	Rapid
	Keith Heller
67023	Stella
67025	Western Star
67026	Diamond Jubilee

67027	Rising Star
	Charlotte
67029	Royal Diamond
68001	Evolution
68002	Intrepid
68003	Astute
68004	Rapid
68005	Defiant
68006	Daring
68007	Valiant
68008	Avenger
68009	Titan
68010	Oxford Flyer
68016	Fearless
68017	Hornet
68018	Vigilant
68019	Brutus
68020	Reliance
68021	Tireless
68022	Resolution
68023	Achilles
68024	Centaur
68025	Superb
68026	Enterprise
68027	Splendid
68028	Lord President
68029	Courageous
68030	Black Douglas
68031	Felix
68032	Destroyer
70001	PowerHaul
70004	The Coal Industry Society
73003	Sir Herbert Walker
73004	The Bluebell Railway
73005	Mid-Hants WATERCRESS LINE
73100	Brighton Evening Argus
73101	Brighton Evening Argus
	The Royal Alex'
73102	Airtour Suisse
73105	Quadrant
73107	Redhill 1844–1944
	SPITFIRE
	Redhill 1844–1944
	Tracy
73109	Battle of Britain 50th Anniversary
	Force 'O' Weymouth
	Battle of Britain 50th Anniversary
	Battle of Britain 80th Anniversary
73112	University of Kent at Canterbury
73114	County of West Sussex
73114	Stewarts Lane Traction Maintenance Depot
73116	Selhurst
73117	University of Surrey
73118	The Romney, Hythe and Dymchurch Railway
73119	Kentish Mercury
	Borough of Eastleigh
73121	Croydon 1883–1983
73122	County of East Sussex
73123	Gatwick Express
73124	London Chamber of Commerce
73125	Stewarts Lane 1860–1985
73126	Kent & East Sussex Railway
73128	O.V.S. BULLEID C.B.E.
73129	City of Winchester
73130	City of Portsmouth
73131	County of Surrey
73133	The Bluebell Railway
73134	Woking Homes 1885–1985
73136	Kent Youth Music
	Perseverance
	Mhairi
73137	Royal Observer Corps
73138	Post Haste 150 YEARS OF TRAVELLING POST OFFICES

73141	David Gay / Ron Westwood
	Charlotte
73201	Broadlands
73202	Royal Observer Corps
	Dave Berry
	Graham Stenning
73204	Stewarts Lane 1860–1985
	Janice
73205	London Chamber of Commerce
	Jeanette
73206	Gatwick Express
	Lisa
73207	County of East Sussex
73208	Croydon 1883–1983
	Kirsten
73209	Alison
73210	Selhurst
73211	County of West Sussex
73212	Airtour Suisse
	Fiona
73213	University of Kent at Canterbury
	Rhodalyn
73951	Malcolm Brinded
73952	Janis Kong
73961	Alison
73962	Dick Mabbutt
73963	Janice
73964	Jeanette
76038	STENTOR
76039	HECTOR
76046	ARCHIMEDES
76047	DIOMEDES
76049	JASON
76051	MENTOR
76052	NESTOR
76053	PERSEUS
76054	PLUTO
76055	PROMETHEUS
76056	TRITON
76057	ULYSSES
86101	Sir William A Stanier FRS
86102	Robert A Riddles
86103	André Chapelon
86204	City of Carlisle
86205	City of Lancaster
86206	City of Stoke on Trent
86207	City of Lichfield
86208	City of Chester
86209	City of Coventry
86210	City of Edinburgh
	C.I.T. 75th Anniversary
86211	City of Milton Keynes
86212	Preston Guild
	Preston Guild 1328–1992
86213	Lancashire Witch
86214	Sans Pareil
86215	Joseph Chamberlain
	Norwich Cathedral
	Norwich and Norfolk Festival
	The Round Tabler
86216	Meteor
86217	Comet
	Halley's Comet
	City University
86218	Planet
	Harold MacMillan
	YEAR OF OPERA & MUSICAL THEATRE 1997
	NHS 50
86219	Phoenix
86220	Goliath
	The Round Tabler
86221	Vesta
	BBC Look East

86222	Fury
	LLOYD'S LIST 250th ANNIVERSARY
	Clothes Show Live
86223	Hector
	Norwich Union
86224	Caledonian
86225	Hardwicke
86226	Mail
	Royal Mail Midlands
	CHARLES RENNIE MACKINTOSH
86227	Sir Henry Johnson
	Golden Jubilee
86228	Vulcan Heritage
86229	Sir John Betjeman
	Lions Clubs International
86230	The Duke of Wellington
86231	Starlight Express
86232	Harold MacMillan
	Norwich Festival
	Norfolk and Norwich Festival
86233	Laurence Olivier
	ALSTOM Heritage
86234	J B Priestley O.M.
	Suffolk Relax.Refresh.Return
86235	Novelty
	Harold MacMillan
	Crown Point
86236	Josiah Wedgewood MASTER POTTER 1736–1795
86237	Sir Charles Hallé
	University of East Anglia
86238	European Community
86239	L S Lowry
86240	Bishop Eric Treacy
86241	Glenfiddich
86242	James Kennedy G.C.
	Colchester Castle
86243	The Boys' Brigade
86244	The Royal British Legion
86245	Dudley Castle
	Caledonian
86246	Royal Anglian Regiment
86247	Abraham Darby
86248	Sir Clwyd County of Clwyd
86249	County of Merseyside
86250	The Glasgow Herald
	Sheppard 100
86251	The Birmingham Post
86252	The Liverpool Daily Post
	Sheppard 100
86253	The Manchester Guardian
86254	William Webb Ellis
86255	Penrith Beacon
86256	Pebble Mill
86257	Snowdon
86258	Talyllyn The First Preserved Railway
	Talyllyn 50 Years of Railway Preservation 1951–2001
86259	Peter Pan
	GM! Greater MANCHESTER THE LIFE & SOUL OF BRITAIN
	Les Ross
86260	Driver Wallace Oakes G.C.
86261	Driver John Axon G.C.
	THE RAIL CHARTER PARTNERSHIP
86311	Airey Neave
86312	Elizabeth Garrett Anderson
86315	Rotary International
86316	Wigan Pier
86328	Aldaniti
86401	Northampton Town
	Hertfordshire Railtours
	Northampton Town
	Mons Meg
86405	Intercontainer
86407	The Institution of Electrical Engineers

86408	St. John Ambulance
86411	Airey Neave
86412	Elizabeth Garrett Anderson
86413	County of Lancashire
86414	Frank Hornby
86415	Rotary International
86416	Wigan Pier
86417	The Kingsman
86419	Post Haste 150 YEARS OF TRAVELLING POST OFFICES
86421	London School of Economics
86425	Saint Mungo
86426	Pride of the Nation
86427	The Industrial Society
86428	Aldaniti
86429	The Times
86430	Scottish National Orchestra
	Saint Edmund
86432	Brookside
86433	Wulfruna
86434	University of London
86501 (2)	Talyllyn The First Preserved Railway
	Crewe Basford Hall
86502	LLOYD'S LIST 250TH ANNIVERSARY
86503	City of Lancaster
86504	Halley's Comet
86505	Royal Anglian Regiment
86506	Laurence Olivier
86507	L S Lowry
86508	Glenfiddich
86605	Intercontainer
86607	The Institution of Electrical Engineers
86608	St. John Ambulance
86611	Airey Neave
86612	Elizabeth Garrett Anderson
86613	County of Lancashire
86614	Frank Hornby
86615	Rotary International
86620	Philip G Walton
86621	London School of Economics
86627	The Industrial Society
86628	Aldaniti
86632	Brookside
86633	Wulfruna
86634	University of London
86701	Orion
86702	Cassiopeia
86901	CHIEF ENGINEER
86902	RAIL VEHICLE ENGINEERING
87001	STEPHENSON
	Royal Scot
	STEPHENSON
87002	Royal Sovereign
	The AC Locomotive Group
	Royal Sovereign
87003	Patriot
87004	Britannia
87005	City of London
87006	City of Glasgow
	Glasgow Garden Festival
	City of Glasgow
	George Reynolds
87007	City of Manchester
87008	City of Liverpool
	Royal Scot
87009	City of Birmingham
87010	King Arthur
	Driver Tommy Farr
87011	The Black Prince
	City of Wolverhampton
87012	Coeur de Lion
	The Royal Bank of Scotland
	Coeur de Lion
	The Olympian

87013	John O' Gaunt
87014	Knight of the Thistle
87015	Howard of Effingham
87016	Sir Francis Drake
	Willesden Intercity Depot
87017	Iron Duke
87018	Lord Nelson
87019	Sir Winston Churchill
	ACoRP Association of Community Rail Partnerships
87020	North Briton
87021	Robert the Bruce
87022	Cock o' the North
	Lew Adams The Black Prince
	Cock o' the North
87023	Highland Chieftain
	Velocity
	Polmadie
	Velocity
87024	Lord of the Isles
87025	Borderer
	County of Cheshire
87026	Redgauntlet
	Sir Richard Arkwright
87027	Wolf of Badenoch
87028	Lord President
87029	Earl Marischal
87030	Black Douglas
87031	Hal o' the Wynd
	Keith Harper
87032	Kenilworth
	Richard Fearn
87033	Thane of Fife
87034	William Shakespeare
87035	Robert Burns
87101	STEPHENSON
88001	Revolution
88002	Prometheus
88003	Genesis
88004	Pandora
88005	Minerva
88006	Juno
88007	Electra
88008	Ariadne
88009	Diana
88010	Aurora
89001	Avocet
90001	BBC Midlands Today
	Crown Point
	Royal Scot
90002	The Girls' Brigade
	Mission: Impossible
	Eastern Daily Press 1870–2010 SERVING NORFOLK FOR 140 YEARS
	Wolf of Badenoch
90003	THE HERALD
	Rædwald of East Anglia
90004	The D'Oyly Carte Opera Company
	City of Glasgow
	Eastern Daily Press 1870–2010 SERVING NORFOLK FOR 140 YEARS
	City of Chelmsford
90005	Financial Times
	Vice-Admiral Lord Nelson
90006	High Sheriff
	Modern Railways Magazine / Roger Ford
90007	Lord Stamp
	Keith Harper
	Sir John Betjeman
90008	The Birmingham Royal Ballet
	The East Anglian
90009	Royal Show
	The Economist
	Diamond Jubilee

90010	275 Railway Squadron (Volunteers)
	BRESSINGHAM STEAM & GARDENS
90011	The Chartered Institute of Transport
	West Coast Rail 250
	Let's Go East of England
	East Anglian Daily Times Suffolk & Proud
90012	Glasgow 1990 Cultural Capital of Europe
	British Transport Police
	Royal Anglian Regiment
90013	The Law Society
	The Evening Star PRIDE OF IPSWICH 1885–2010 125
	YEARS OF SERVING SUFFOLK
90014	'The Liverpool Phil'
	The Big Dish
	Driver Tom Clark O.B.E.
	Norfolk and Norwich Festival
	Over the Rainbow
90015	BBC North West
	The International Brigades SPAIN 1936–1939
	Colchester Castle
90017	Rail express systems Quality Assured
90018	The Pride of Bellshill
90019	Penny Black
	Multimodal
90020	Colonel Bill Cockburn CBE TD
	Sir Michael Heron
	Collingwood
90022	Freightconnection
90026	Crewe International Electric Maintenance Depot
90027	Allerton T&RS Depot Quality Approved
90028	Vrachtverbinding
	Hertfordshire Rail Tours
	Sir William McAlpine
90029	Frachtverbindungen
	The Institution of Civil Engineers
90030	Fretconnection
	Crewe Locomotive Works
90031	Intercontainer
	The Railway Children Partnership Working For Street
	Children Worldwide
90032	Cerestar
90035	Crewe Basford Hall
90036	Driver Jack Mills
90037	Spirit of Dagenham
	Christine
90040	The Railway Mission
90043	Freightliner Coatbridge
90126	Crewe International Electric Maintenance Depot
90127	Allerton T&RS Depot Quality Approved
90128	Vrachtverbinding
90129	Fratchverbindungen
90130	Fretconnection
90131	Intercontainer
90132	Cerestar
90135	Crewe Basford Hall
90143	Freightliner Coatbridge
90222	Freightconnection
90227	Allerton T&RS Depot Quality Approved
91001	Swallow
91002	Durham Cathedral
91003	THE SCOTSMAN
91004	The Red Arrows
	Grantham
91005	Royal Air Force Regiment
91007	Ian Allan
	SKYFALL
91008	Thomas Cook
91009	Saint Nicholas
	The Samaritans
91010	Northern Rock
91011	Terence Cuneo
91012	County of Cambridgeshire
91013	Michael Faraday
	County of North Yorkshire
91014	Northern Electric
	St. Mungo Cathedral
91015	Holyrood
91017	Commonwealth Institute
	City of Leeds
91018	Robert Louis Stevenson
	Bradford Film Festival
91019	Scottish Enterprise
	County of Tyne & Wear
91021	Royal Armouries
	Archbishop Thomas Cranmer
91022	Robert Adley
	Double Trigger
91024	Reverend W Awdry
91025	BBC Radio One FM
91026	Voice of the North
	York Minster
91027	Great North Run
91028	Guide Dog
91029	Queen Elizabeth II
91030	Palace of Holyroodhouse
91031	Sir Henry Royce
	County of Northumberland
91101	City of London
	FLYING SCOTSMAN
91102	Durham Cathedral
	City of York
91103	County of Lincolnshire
91104	Grantham
91105	County Durham
91106	East Lothian
91107	Newark on Trent
	SKYFALL
91108	City of Leeds
91109	The Samaritans
	Sir Bobby Robson
91110	David Livingstone
	BATTLE OF BRITAIN MEMORIAL FLIGHT
91111	Terence Cuneo
	For the Fallen
91112	County of Cambridgeshire
91113	County of North Yorkshire
91114	St. Mungo Cathedral
	Durham Cathedral
91115	Holyrood
	Blaydon Races
91116	Strathclyde
91117	Cancer Research UK
	WEST RIDING LIMITED
91118	The Fusiliers
	Bradford Film Festival
91119	County of Tyne & Wear
	Bounds Green INTERCITY Depot 1977–2017
91120	Royal Armouries
91121	Archbishop Thomas Cranmer
91122	Double Trigger
	Tam the Gun
91124	Reverend W Awdry
91125	Berwick-upon-Tweed
91126	York Minster
	Darlington Hippodrome
91127	Edinburgh Castle
91128	Peterborough Cathedral
	INTERCITY 50
91129	Queen Elizabeth II
91130	City of Newcastle
	Lord Mayor of Newcastle
91131	County of Northumberland
91132	City of Durham
92001	Victor Hugo
92002	H.G. Wells
92003	Beethoven

92004	Jane Austen	D809	CHAMPION
92005	Mozart	D810	COCKADE
92006	Louis Armand	D811	DARING
92007	Schubert	D812	ROYAL NAVAL RESERVE 1859–1959
92008	Jules Verne	D813	DIADEM
92009	Elgar	D814	DRAGON
	Marco Polo	D815	DRUID
92010	Molière	D816	ECLIPSE
92011	Handel	D817	FOXHOUND
92012	Thomas Hardy	D818	GLORY
92013	Puccini	D819	GOLIATH
92014	Emile Zola	D820	GRENVILLE
92015	D H Lawrence	D821	GREYHOUND
92016	Brahms	D822	HERCULES
92017	Shakespeare	D823	HERMES
	Bart the Engine	D824	HIGHFLYER
92018	Stendhal	D825	INTREPID
92019	Wagner	D826	JUPITER
92020	Milton	D827	KELLY
92021	Purcell	D828	MAGNIFICENT
92022	Charles Dickens	D829	MAGPIE
92023	Ravel	D830	MAJESTIC
92024	J S Bach	D831	MONARCH
92025	Oscar Wilde	D832	ONSLAUGHT
92026	Britten	D866	ZEBRA
92027	George Eliot	D867	ZENITH
92028	Saint Saëns	D868	ZEPHYR
92029	Dante	D869	ZEST
92030	De Falla	D870	ZULU
	Ashford	D833	PANTHER
92031	The Institute of Logistics and Transport	D834	PATHFINDER
92032	César Franck	D835	PEGASUS
	IMechE Railway Division	D836	POWERFUL
92033	Berlioz	D837	RAMILLIES
92034	Kipling	D838	RAPID
92035	Mendelssohn	D839	RELENTLESS
92036	Bertolt Brecht	D840	RESISTANCE
92037	Sullivan	D841	ROEBUCK
92038	Voltaire	D842	ROYAL OAK
92039	Johann Strauss	D843	SHARPSHOOTER
92040	Goethe	D844	SPARTAN
92041	Vaughan Williams	D845	SPRIGHTLY
92042	Honegger	D846	STEADFAST
92043	Debussy	D847	STRONGBOW
92044	Couperin	D848	SULTAN
92045	Chaucer	D849	SUPERB
92046	Sweelinck	D850	SWIFT
97201	Experiment	D851	TEMERAIRE
97250	ETHEL 1	D852	TENACIOUS
97251	ETHEL 2	D853	THRUSTER
97252	ETHEL 3	D854	TIGER
97302	Ffestiniog & Welsh Highland Railways / Rheilffyrdd	D855	TRIUMPH
	Ffestiniog ac Eryri	D856	TROJAN
97304	John Tiley	D857	UNDAUNTED
97403	Ixion	D858	VALOROUS
97407	Aureol	D859	VANQUISHER
97480	Robin Hood	D860	VICTORIOUS
97561	Midland Counties Railway 150 1839 – 1989	D861	VIGILANT
D0226	VULCAN	D862	VIKING
D600	ACTIVE	D863	WARRIOR
D601	ARK ROYAL	D864	ZAMBESI
D602	BULLDOG	D865	ZEALOUS
D603	CONQUEST	D1000	WESTERN ENTERPRISE
D604	COSSACK	D1001	WESTERN PATHFINDER
D800	SIR BRIAN ROBERTSON	D1002	WESTERN EXPLORER
D801	VANGUARD	D1003	WESTERN PIONEER
D802	FORMIDABLE	D1004	WESTERN CRUSADER
D803	ALBION	D1005	WESTERN VENTURER
D804	AVENGER	D1006	WESTERN STALWART
D805	BENBOW	D1007	WESTERN TALISMAN
D806	CAMBRIAN	D1008	WESTERN HARRIER
D807	CARADOC	D1009	WESTERN INVADER
D808	CENTAUR	D1010	WESTERN CAMPAIGNER

D1011	WESTERN THUNDERER
D1012	WESTERN FIREBRAND
D1013	WESTERN RANGER
D1014	WESTSERN LEVIATHAN
D1015	WESTERN CHAMPION
D1016	WESTERN GLADIATOR
D1017	WESTERN WARRIOR
D1018	WESTERN BUCCANEER
D1019	WESTERN CHALLENGER
D1020	WESTERN HERO
D1021	WESTERN CAVALIER
D1022	WESTERN SENTINEL
D1023	WESTERN FUSILIER
D1024	WESTERN HUNTSMAN
D1025	WESTERN GUARDSMAN
D1026	WESTERN CENTURION
D1027	WESTERN LANCER
D1028	WESTERN HUSSAR
D1029	WESTERN LEGIONAIRE
	WESTERN LEGIONNAIRE
D1030	WESTERN MUSKETEER
D1031	WESTERN RIFLEMAN
D1032	WESTERN MARKSMAN
D1033	WESTERN TROOPER
D1034	WESTERN DRAGOON
D1035	WESTERN YEOMAN
D1036	WESTERN EMPEROR
D1037	WESTERN EMPRESS
D1038	WESTERN SOVEREIGN
D1039	WESTERN KING
D1040	WESTERN QUEEN
D1041	WESTERN PRINCE
D1042	WESTERN PRINCESS
D1043	WESTERN DUKE
D1044	WESTERN DUCHESS
D1045	WESTERN VISCOUNT
D1046	WESTERN MARQUIS
D1047	WESTERN LORD

D1048	WESTERN LADY
D1049	WESTERN MONARCH
D1050	WESTERN RULER
D1051	WESTERN AMBASSADOR
D1052	WESTERN VICEROY
D1053	WESTERN PATRIARCH
D1054	WESTERN GOVERNOR
D1055	WESTERN ADVOCATE
D1056	WESTERN SULTAN
D1057	WESTERN CHIEFTAIN
D1058	WESTERN NOBLEMAN
D1059	WESTERN EMPIRE
D1060	WESTERN DOMINION
D1061	WESTERN ENVOY
D1062	WESTERN COURIER
D1063	WESTERN MONITOR
D1064	WESTERN REGENT
D1065	WESTERN CONSORT
D1066	WESTERN PREFECT
D1067	WESTERN DRUID
D1068	WESTERN RELIANCE
D1069	WESTERN VANGUARD
D1070	WESTERN GAUNTLET
D1071	WESTERN RENOWN
D1072	WESTERN GLORY
D1073	WESTERN BULWARK
D1671	THOR
D0260	LION
D0280	FALCON
HS4000	KESTREL
26000	TOMMY
27000	ELECTRA
27001	ARIADNE
27002	AURORA
27003	DIANA
27004	JUNO
27005	MINERVA
27006	PANDORA

▲ Every member of the three "Warship" classes (41, 42 & 43) was named. The bodyside of D832 "ONSLAUGHT" was showing signs of its age in September 2018, but it has since been given a makeover, receiving a coat of BR Blue paint during 2020. **Andy Chard**

▲ Scrapping locomotives is a specialist activity and for the rail enthusiast, it is not pretty. On 6 September 1978, 71005 is part way through the process at the premises of J Cashmore in Newport. 69 of the locomotives listed in this book were disposed of by the firm, including examples of Classes 03, 08, 11, 12, 22, 41, 42, 43, 70, 71, and 74.
Stephen C Marshall

▼ The Bird Group disposed of 45 mainline locomotives at its Long Marston yard, including examples of Classes D2/10, 02, 03, 04, 08, 11, 16, 17, 35, 74, and 84. The former Class 02 D2857 (right) was acquired by the firm in 1971 and used as a yard shunter at Long Marston until it was scrapped there in 1992. It is seen on 22 August 1988, alongside the 1964-built Hibberd four-wheeled shunter 4016.
Gordon Edgar

APPENDIX VI: LOCOMOTIVES WITH UNCONFIRMED SCRAPPING DETAILS

This appendix lists the locomotives for which it has not been possible to confirm some or all of the scrapping details. In many cases the details are thought to be, or are likely to be correct, as stated in the Notes column of the locomotive listings and in this appendix. Any readers with further information about the scrapping of any of these locomotives are invited to contact the author via the publisher's address at the front of this book.

Class	Number	Details (in most cases is the note in main text)
Experimental Shunter	JANUS	Scrapping details not confirmed, but likely to be correct
Experimental Type 1	D9	Scrapping location unknown
Experimental Type 5	HS4000	Scrapping details not confirmed, but may be correct
Departmental	DPM 83	Scrapping details not confirmed, but likely to be correct
Departmental	DPM 84	Scrapping details not confirmed, but likely to be correct
Departmental	DPM 85	Scrapping details not confirmed, but likely to be correct
Departmental	DPM 86	Scrapping details not confirmed, but likely to be correct
Unclassified	1831	Scrapped after 1955, exact date not known
Unclassified	7061	Scrapping details not confirmed, but may be correct
Unclassified	7062	Scrapping details not confirmed, but may be correct
Unclassified	7064	Scrapping details not confirmed, but may be correct
Unclassified	7067	Scrapping details not confirmed, but may be correct
D2/1	D2703	Scrapping details not confirmed, but likely to be correct
D2/1	D2704	Scrapping details not confirmed, but likely to be correct
D2/1	D2705	Scrapping details not confirmed, but likely to be correct
D2/5	D2405	Scrapping details not confirmed, but may be correct
D2/5	D2409	Scrapping details not confirmed, but likely to be correct
D2/10	D2717	Scrapping details not confirmed, but likely to be correct
D2/10	D2720	Scrapping details not confirmed, but likely to be correct
D2/10	D2723	Scrapping details not confirmed, but likely to be correct
D2/10	D2724	Scrapping details not confirmed, but likely to be correct
D2/10	D2734	Scrapping details not confirmed, but likely to be correct
D2/10	D2736	Scrapping details not confirmed, but likely to be correct
D2/10	D2744	Scrapping details not confirmed, but likely to be correct
D2/10	D2745	Scrapping details not confirmed, but likely to be correct
D2/10	D2750	Scrapping details not confirmed, but likely to be correct
D2/10	D2751	Scrapping details not confirmed, but likely to be correct
D2/10	D2768	Scrapping details not confirmed, but likely to be correct
D3/3	D3117	Scrapping details not confirmed, but may be correct
D3/3	D3122	Scrapping details not confirmed, but likely to be correct
D3/5	D3165	Scrapping details not confirmed, but likely to be correct
D3/6	7070	Scrapping details not confirmed, but may be correct
D3/6	7073	Scrapping details not confirmed, but may be correct
D3/6	7075	Scrapping details not confirmed, but may be correct
D3/6	7078	Scrapping details not confirmed, but may be correct
D3/7	12011	Scrapping details not confirmed, but may be correct
D3/7	7105	Scrapping details not confirmed, but may be correct
D3/7	7109	Scrapping details not confirmed, but may be correct
D3/7	12029	Scrapping details not confirmed, but may be correct
D3/7	12030	Scrapping details not confirmed, but may be correct
D3/10	15100	Scrapping details not confirmed, but likely to be correct
D3/11	15106	Scrapping details not confirmed, but likely to be correct
D3/14	15004	Scrapping details not confirmed, but likely to be correct
02	D2850	Scrapping details not confirmed, but likely to be correct
02	D2855	Scrapping details not confirmed, but likely to be correct
02	D2859	Scrapping details not confirmed, but likely to be correct
02	D2861	Scrapping details not confirmed, but likely to be correct
02	D2869	Scrapping details not confirmed, but likely to be correct
03	03010	Locomotive exported and subsequently scrapped. Scrapping details not confirmed
03	03098	Locomotive thought to be exported to Italy and scrapped there, but not confirmed
03	03153	Locomotive exported and subsequently scrapped. Scrapping details not confirmed
03	03169	Scrapping details not confirmed, but likely to be correct
03	D2002	Scrapping details not confirmed, but likely to be correct
03	D2003	Scrapping details not confirmed, but likely to be correct
03	D2019	Was extant in 2002 and current status unknown
03	D2031	Scrapping details not confirmed, but likely to be correct

03	D2032	Was extant in 2002 and current status unknown
03	D2033	Was extant in 2004 and current status unknown
03	D2036	Was extant in 2003 and current status unknown
03	D2042	Scrapping details not confirmed, but likely to be correct
03	D2083	Scrapping details not confirmed, but may be correct
03	D2101	Scrapping details not confirmed, but may be correct
03	D2115	Scrapping details not confirmed, but may be correct
03	D2122	Scrapping details not confirmed, but likely to be correct
03	D2127	Scrapping details not confirmed, but likely to be correct
03	D2136	Scrapping details not confirmed, but may be correct
03	D2183	Scrapping details not confirmed, but likely to be correct
03	D2185	Scrapping details not confirmed, but may be correct
03	D2191	Scrapping details not confirmed, but likely to be correct
03	D2377	Scrapping details not confirmed, but likely to be correct
03	D2379	Scrapping details not confirmed, but likely to be correct
03	D2383	Scrapping details not confirmed, but likely to be correct
03	D2392	Scrapping details not confirmed, but may be correct
03	D2393	Scrapping details not confirmed, but may be correct
04	D2206	Scrapping details not confirmed, but may be correct
04	D2212	Scrapping details not confirmed, but likely to be correct
04	D2232	Locomotive exported and subsequently scrapped. Scrapping details not confirmed, but may be correct.
04	D2251	Scrapping details not confirmed, but likely to be correct
04	D2252	Scrapping details not confirmed, but likely to be correct
04	D2254	Scrapping details not confirmed, but likely to be correct
04	D2256	Scrapping details not confirmed, but likely to be correct
04	D2261	Scrapping details not confirmed, but likely to be correct
04	D2265	Scrapping details not confirmed, but likely to be correct
04	D2266	Scrapping details not confirmed, but likely to be correct
04	D2268	Scrapping details not confirmed, but likely to be correct
04	D2277	Scrapping details not confirmed, but likely to be correct
04	D2278	Scrapping details not confirmed, but likely to be correct
04	D2283	Scrapping details not confirmed, but likely to be correct
04	D2285	Scrapping details not confirmed, but likely to be correct
04	D2295	Locomotive exported and subsequently scrapped. Scrapping details not confirmed, but may be correct.
04	D2296	Scrapping details not confirmed, but likely to be correct
04	D2297	Scrapping details not confirmed, but likely to be correct
04	D2309	Scrapping details not confirmed, but likely to be correct
04	D2312	Scrapping details not confirmed, but may be correct
04	D2318	Scrapping details not confirmed, but may be correct
04	D2320	Scrapping details not confirmed, but may be correct
04	D2323	Scrapping details not confirmed, but likely to be correct
04	D2330	Scrapping details not confirmed, but likely to be correct
04	D2331	Scrapping details not confirmed, but may be correct
04	D2338	Scrapping details not confirmed, but may be correct
04	D2339	Scrapping details not confirmed, but may be correct
04	D2341	Scrapping details not confirmed, but likely to be correct
05	D2550	Scrapping details not confirmed, but likely to be correct
05	D2560	Scrapping details not confirmed, but likely to be correct
05	D2571	Scrapping details not confirmed, but may be correct
05	D2573	Scrapping details not confirmed, but likely to be correct
05	D2576	Scrapping details not confirmed, but likely to be correct
05	D2577	Scrapping details not confirmed, but likely to be correct
05	D2579	Scrapping details not confirmed, but likely to be correct
05	D2582	Scrapping details not confirmed, but likely to be correct
05	D2583	Scrapping details not confirmed, but likely to be correct
05	D2585	Scrapping details not confirmed, but likely to be correct
05	D2592	Scrapping details not confirmed, but likely to be correct
05	D2593	Scrapping details not confirmed, but may be correct
05	D2602	Scrapping details not confirmed, but likely to be correct
05	D2612	Scrapping details not confirmed, but likely to be correct
05	D2617	Scrapping details not confirmed, but may be correct
06	D2410	Scrapping details not confirmed, but likely to be correct
06	D2411	Scrapping details not confirmed, but likely to be correct
06	D2412	Scrapping details not confirmed, but likely to be correct
06	D2418	Scrapping details not confirmed, but likely to be correct
06	D2419	Scrapping details not confirmed, but likely to be correct
06	D2427	Scrapping details not confirmed, but likely to be correct
06	D2429	Scrapping details not confirmed, but likely to be correct
06	D2430	Scrapping details not confirmed, but likely to be correct
06	D2432	Locomotive exported and subsequently scrapped. Scrapping details not confirmed, but may be correct.
06	D2434	Scrapping details not confirmed, but likely to be correct
06	D2435	Scrapping details not confirmed, but may be correct
06	D2438	Scrapping details not confirmed, but may be correct

06	D2442	Scrapping details not confirmed, but may be correct
07	07009	Locomotive exported and subsequently scrapped. Scrapping details not confirmed, but may be correct.
08	D3020	Scrapping details not confirmed, but may be correct
08	D3034	Scrapping details not confirmed, but may be correct
08	D3051	Scrapping details not confirmed, but may be correct
08	D3093	Scrapping details not confirmed
08	D3096	Scrapping details not confirmed, but likely to be correct
08	D3172	Scrapping details not confirmed, but likely to be correct
08	D3183	Scrapping details not confirmed, but likely to be correct
08	D3193	Scrapping details not confirmed, but likely to be correct
10	D3137	Scrapping details not confirmed, but likely to be correct
10	D3140	Scrapping details not confirmed, but likely to be correct
10	D3141	Scrapping details not confirmed, but likely to be correct
10	D3142	Scrapping details not confirmed, but likely to be correct
10	D3143	Scrapping details not confirmed, but likely to be correct
10	D3144	Scrapping details not confirmed, but likely to be correct
10	D3146	Scrapping details not confirmed, but likely to be correct
10	D3150	Scrapping details not confirmed, but likely to be correct
10	D3151	Scrapping details not confirmed, but likely to be correct
10	D3440	Scrapping details not confirmed, but likely to be correct
10	D3443	Scrapping details not confirmed, but likely to be correct
10	D3445	Scrapping details not confirmed, but likely to be correct
10	D3446	Scrapping details not confirmed, but likely to be correct
10	D3448	Scrapping details not confirmed, but likely to be correct
10	D3453	Scrapping details not confirmed, but likely to be correct
10	D3474	Scrapping details not confirmed, but likely to be correct
10	D3479	Scrapping details not confirmed, but likely to be correct
10	D3483	Scrapping details not confirmed, but likely to be correct
10	D3484	Scrapping details not confirmed, but likely to be correct
10	D3485	Scrapping details not confirmed, but likely to be correct
10	D3487	Scrapping details not confirmed, but likely to be correct
10	D3492	Scrapping details not confirmed, but likely to be correct
10	D3617	Scrapping details not confirmed, but likely to be correct
10	D3621	Scrapping details not confirmed, but may be correct
10	D3629	Scrapping details not confirmed, but likely to be correct
10	D3630	Scrapping details not confirmed, but likely to be correct
10	D3631	Scrapping details not confirmed, but likely to be correct
10	D3633	Scrapping details not confirmed, but likely to be correct
10	D3634	Scrapping details not confirmed, but likely to be correct
10	D3640	Scrapping details not confirmed, but likely to be correct
10	D3643	Scrapping details not confirmed, but likely to be correct
10	D3644	Scrapping details not confirmed, but likely to be correct
10	D3646	Scrapping details not confirmed, but likely to be correct
10	D3647	Scrapping details not confirmed, but likely to be correct
10	D3650	Scrapping details not confirmed, but likely to be correct
10	D3651	Scrapping details not confirmed, but likely to be correct
10	D4049	Scrapping details not confirmed, but likely to be correct
10	D4051	Scrapping details not confirmed, but likely to be correct
10	D4054	Scrapping details not confirmed, but likely to be correct
10	D4058	Scrapping details not confirmed, but likely to be correct
10	D4059	Scrapping details not confirmed, but likely to be correct
10	D4060	Scrapping details not confirmed, but likely to be correct
10	D4064	Scrapping details not confirmed, but likely to be correct
10	D4081	Scrapping details not confirmed, but likely to be correct
10	D4082	Scrapping details not confirmed, but likely to be correct
10	D4084	Scrapping details not confirmed, but may be correct
10	D4085	Scrapping details not confirmed, but may be correct
10	D4086	Scrapping details not confirmed, but likely to be correct
10	D4091	Scrapping details not confirmed, but likely to be correct
11	12034	Scrapping details not confirmed, but likely to be correct
11	12035	Scrapping details not confirmed, but likely to be correct
11	12046	Scrapping details not confirmed, but likely to be correct
11	12053	Scrapping details not confirmed, but likely to be correct
11	12055	Scrapping details not confirmed, but likely to be correct
11	12062	Scrapping details not confirmed, but may be correct
11	12065	Scrapping details not confirmed, but likely to be correct
11	12069	Scrapping details not confirmed, but likely to be correct
11	12071	Scrapping details not confirmed, but likely to be correct
11	12079	Scrapping details not confirmed, but likely to be correct
11	12089	Scrapping details not confirmed, but may be correct
11	12091	Scrapping details not confirmed, but may be correct
11	12112	Scrapping details not confirmed, but likely to be correct
11	12116	Scrapping details not confirmed, but likely to be correct

11	12117	Scrapping details not confirmed, but likely to be correct
11	12121	Scrapping details not confirmed, but likely to be correct
11	12125	Scrapping details not confirmed, but likely to be correct
11	12135	Scrapping details not confirmed, but likely to be correct
12	15213	Scrapping details not confirmed, but likely to be correct
12	15216	Scrapping details not confirmed, but likely to be correct
12	15217	Scrapping details not confirmed, but likely to be correct
14	D9501	Scrapping details not confirmed, but likely to be correct
14	D9534	Locomotive exported and subsequently scrapped. Scrapping details not confirmed but may be correct.
14	D9548	Locomotive exported and subsequently scrapped. Scrapping details not confirmed but may be correct.
17	D8547	Scrapping details not confirmed, but likely to be correct
17	D8554	Scrapping details not confirmed, but likely to be correct
17	D8576	Scrapping details not confirmed, but likely to be correct
17	D8578	Scrapping details not confirmed, but likely to be correct
17	D8589	Scrapping details not confirmed, but likely to be correct
17	D8591	Scrapping details not confirmed, but likely to be correct
17	D8609	Scrapping details not confirmed, but likely to be correct
17	D8611	Scrapping details not confirmed, but likely to be correct
21	D6104	Scrapping details not confirmed, but likely to be correct
21	D6105	Scrapping details not confirmed, but likely to be correct
21	D6111	Scrapping details not confirmed, but likely to be correct
21	D6117	Scrapping details not confirmed, but likely to be correct
21	D6121	D6121 and D6122 are believed to have swapped identities in 1964. D6121, the former D6122, was re-engined in 1966 with a Paxman Ventura engine and reclassified as Class 29
21	D6122	D6121 and D6122 are believed to have swapped identities in 1964. D6121, the former D6122, was re-engined in 1966 with a Paxman Ventura engine and reclassified as Class 29
21	D6125	Scrapping details not confirmed, but likely to be correct
21	D6127	Scrapping details not confirmed, but likely to be correct
21	D6134	Scrapping details not confirmed, but likely to be correct
21	D6136	Scrapping details not confirmed, but likely to be correct
21	D6143	Scrapping details not confirmed, but likely to be correct
21	D6152	Scrapping details not confirmed, but likely to be correct
24	D5383	Scrapping details not confirmed, but likely to be correct
56	56015	Scrapping details not confirmed, but likely to be correct
76	26000	Scrapping details not confirmed, but likely to be correct
76	26017	Scrapping details not confirmed, but likely to be correct
76	26035	Scrapping details not confirmed, but likely to be correct
76	26042	Scrapping details not confirmed, but likely to be correct
80	E2001	Scrapping details not confirmed, but likely to be correct
82	E3055	Scrapping details not confirmed, but likely to be correct

▲ On 30 March 1970, Baguley diesel-mechanical shunter 3355 heads a line-up of Class 03s at the Bird Group's Long Marston scrapyard. From left to right these are D2123, D2194, D2190, D2177 and D2183, not all of which ended up being scrapped at this location. **Gordon Edgar**